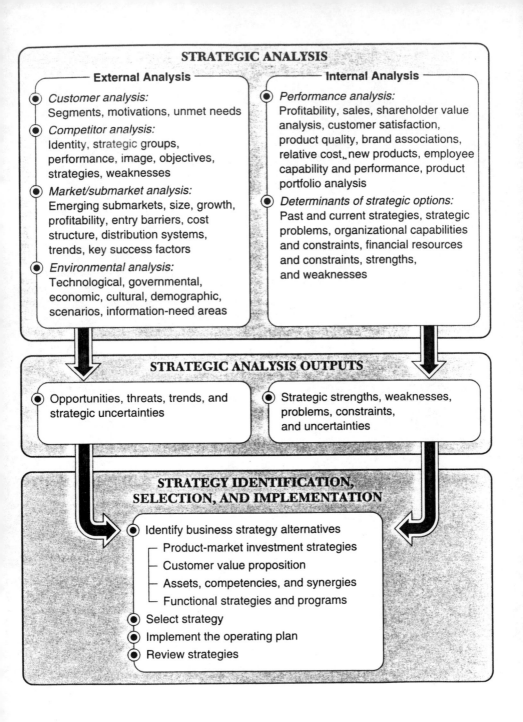

STRATEGIC ANALYSIS

External Analysis

- *Customer analysis:* Segments, motivations, unmet needs
- *Competitor analysis:* Identity, strategic groups, performance, image, objectives, strategies, weaknesses
- *Market/submarket analysis:* Emerging submarkets, size, growth, profitability, entry barriers, cost structure, distribution systems, trends, key success factors
- *Environmental analysis:* Technological, governmental, economic, cultural, demographic, scenarios, information-need areas

Internal Analysis

- *Performance analysis:* Profitability, sales, shareholder value analysis, customer satisfaction, product quality, brand associations, relative cost, new products, employee capability and performance, product portfolio analysis
- *Determinants of strategic options:* Past and current strategies, strategic problems, organizational capabilities and constraints, financial resources and constraints, strengths, and weaknesses

STRATEGIC ANALYSIS OUTPUTS

- Opportunities, threats, trends, and strategic uncertainties
- Strategic strengths, weaknesses, problems, constraints, and uncertainties

STRATEGY IDENTIFICATION, SELECTION, AND IMPLEMENTATION

- Identify business strategy alternatives
  - Product-market investment strategies
  - Customer value proposition
  - Assets, competencies, and synergies
  - Functional strategies and programs
- Select strategy
- Implement the operating plan
- Review strategies

STRATEGIC
MARKET
MANAGEMENT

SEVENTH EDITION

STRATEGIC
MARKET
MANAGEMENT

David A. Aaker
Vice-Chairman, Prophet
Professor Emeritus, University of California, at Berkeley

WILEY

John Wiley & Sons, Inc.

There is a tide in the affairs of men,
Which, taken at the flood, leads on to fortune;
Omitted, all the voyage of their life
Is bound in shallows and in miseries.
On such a full sea are we now afloat,
And we must take the current when it serves,
Or lose our ventures.
—*William Shakespeare, from Julius Caesar*

Publisher	*Susan Elbe*
Associate Publisher	*Judith R. Joseph*
Project Editor	*Cindy Rhoads*
Marketing Manager	*David Woodbury*
Program Assistant	*Jessica Bartelt*
Production Manager	*Pam Kennedy*
Associate Production Manager	*Kelly Tavares*
Production Editor	*Sarah Wolfman-Robichaud*
Managing Editor	*Kevin Dodds*
Illustration Editor	*Benjamin Reece*
Cover Design	*Benjamin Reece*

This book was set in New Caledonia by Leyh Publishing LLC, and printed and bound by Courier Westford, Inc. The cover was printed by Lehigh Press, Inc.

This book is printed on acid-free paper. ⊚

ISBN 0-471-48426-1

WIE ISBN 0-471-65903-7

Printed in the United States of America

10 9 8 7 6 5 4 3 2 1

The development, evaluation, and implementation of business strategies are essential to successful management. The key is a management system that will help managers:

- Monitor and understand a dynamic environment
- Generate visionary and creative strategic options that will be responsive to changes facing a business
- Develop strategies based on sustainable competitive advantages
- Provide vision to their businesses

FIVE THRUSTS

This book has five thrusts. The first is external analysis, a structure and methodology for analyzing the external environment. Strategic planning that represents an automatic extension of what was done last year and that is dominated by financial objectives and spreadsheets will be inadequate and may even inhibit or prevent strategy change and innovation. Rather, strategy development should look outside the business to sense changes, trends, threats, and opportunities and then create strategies that are responsive. This book describes and illustrates a structured approach to external analysis that business managers will find helpful in generating strategic options. This approach is supported by a summary flow diagram, a set of agendas to help start the process, and a set of planning forms.

The second thrust is toward sustainable competitive advantages (SCAs). Having SCAs is crucial to long-term success. Without them a business will eventually be treading water if it survives at all. SCAs need to be based on organizational assets and competencies. Thus, this book presents methods and concepts that will help readers to select relevant assets and competencies and our understanding of the strengths, weaknesses, and strategic problems of the organization. Thus, this book presents methods and concepts that will help readers to conduct an internal analysis to select relevant assets and competencies.

The third thrust is to create customer-oriented business strategies, each with a value proposition that is relevant, meaningful, and sustainable. A business strategy whose primary focus is inside of the firm, rather than on its customers, will eventually be vulnerable and lose its relevance. A customer orientation implies not only that customers are understood in some depth but that competitors are monitored, that markets are tracked, and that the firm may have to invest in anticipation of emerging submarkets.

The fourth thrust involves the investment decision. The need is to select investment or disinvestment levels for existing product-market business areas and to chart growth directions. Among the alternative growth directions are market penetration, product expansion, market expansion, diversification, and vertical integration. By using a variety of concepts and methods, such as strategic uncertainties, portfolio models, and scenario analysis, this book will help managers identify and evaluate numerous strategic investment alternatives.

The fifth thrust is implementation. It is important to understand how an organization's structure, systems, people, and culture contribute to strategic success. In addition, how can an organization create dynamic strategies that are responsive to changing conditions? How can alliances be used to gain strategic advantage? What are the implementation issues when markets are hostile or declining or when competition is global in scope?

THE SEVENTH EDITION

One notable change in this seventh edition from the previous one is in the definition of a business strategy. It now includes a value proposition, reflecting the fact that a business strategy should be customer-oriented in order to stay relevant. A second is the introduction of strategic options (rather than strategic thrusts) as the organizational force for Chapters 9, 10, and 11. This change provides a better link to business strategies and allows the concept of the value proposition to be expressed strategically. So the "low cost" and "the preemptive move" thrusts discussed in the previous edition have been replaced with the value and innovation options.

This seventh edition also provides vehicles for readers to apply and practice the concepts of the book. A "For Discussion" section with questions and exercises has been added at the end of each chapter. In addition, there are seven case challenges that appear at the end of Parts II, III, IV, and V.

A popular feature of this book has been its compactness, and the seventh edition retains that quality. Although about one-fourth of the book is new, the length and structure are similar. There are new illustrative examples throughout the book. Further, there are a host of new or revised sections on such topics as:

- Emerging submarkets and the relevance challenge
- The distinction between fads and trends
- Maintaining relevance
- Disruptive versus sustaining innovation
- Country selection in global management
- Global management styles (including four that are dysfunctional)
- Creating thinking approaches
- Super-premium offerings
- Challenges of decentralization

OBJECTIVES OF THE BOOK

This book has a number of objectives that influence its approach and style. The book attempts to:

- Introduce a long-term perspective that may help a business avoid weaknesses or problems caused by the dominance of short-term goals or operational problems: The focus on assets and competencies and away from short-term financials provides one approach.

- Provide methods and structures to create entrepreneurial thrusts: In many organizations the key problem is how to support both efficiency and an entrepreneurial spirit.

- Emphasize a global perspective: Increasingly, effective strategies must consider—and be responsive to—international competitors and markets.

- Present a proactive approach to strategic market management in which, rather than merely detecting and reacting to change, a business anticipates or even creates it: In this approach, the strategy development process is driven by a dynamic analysis of the market and the environment. The inclusion of the term *market* into the phrase "strategic market management" emphasizes the external orientation and the proactive approach.

- Encourage on-line strategy development, which involves gathering information, analyzing the strategic context, precipitating strategic decisions, and developing strategic implementation plans outside the annual planning cycle.

- Draw on multiple disciplines: During the past decade many disciplines have made relevant and important contributions to strategic market management. An effort has been made to draw on and integrate developments in marketing, economics, organizational behavior, finance, accounting, management science, and the field of strategy itself.

- Incorporate several important empirical research streams that have helped strategic market management become more professional and scientific.

- Introduce concepts, models, and methods that are or have promise of being useful to the strategy development process: Among the concepts covered are business strategies, value proposition, and strategic groups; exit, entry, and mobility barriers; industry structure; segmentation; unmet needs; positioning; strategic problems; strategic uncertainties; strengths; weaknesses; strategic assets and competencies; brand equity; flexibility; sustainable competitive advantage; synergy; relevance challenges, business strategy options; strategic alliances; key success factors; corporate culture; organizational structure; the virtual corporation; strategic types; strategic vision; strategic opportunism; strategic intent; and global strategies. The models and methods covered include researching lead customers, scenario analysis, impact analysis, total quality control, reengineering, the competitor strength grid, technological forecasting, the experience curve, value chain analysis, portfolio models, customer-based competitor identification, and shareholder value analysis.

AN OVERVIEW

This book is divided into five parts. The first part, Chapters 1 and 2, defines a business strategy and provides an overview of the book. The second part, Chapters 3 to 7, covers strategic analysis that includes external analysis (the analysis of the customer, competitors, market, and environment) and internal analysis (which includes performance analysis, the analysis of strategically important organizational characteristics, and portfolio analysis). The third part, Chapters 8 to 12, focuses on the development of successful strategies. It discusses the role of synergy, the tension between vision and opportunism, strategic options (such as quality, value, innovation, focus, and being global), and strategic positioning. The fourth part, Chapters 13 to 15, covers growth strategies, including competing in mature and hostile markets. The fifth part, Chapter 16, contains material on how organizational components interact with strategy. Seven case challenges are positioned at the end of Parts II, III, IV, and V. An appendix includes a set of sample planning forms.

THE AUDIENCE

This book is suitable for any management or business school course that focuses on the management of strategies. It is especially appropriate for:

- Marketing strategy courses, such as strategic market management, strategic market planning, strategic marketing, or marketing strategy
- Policy or entrepreneurship courses, such as strategic management, strategic planning, business policy, entrepreneurship, or policy administration

The book is also designed to be used by managers who need to develop strategies—especially those who have recently moved into a general management position or who run a small business and want to improve their strategy development and planning processes. Another intended audience consists of those general managers, top executives, and planning specialists who would like an overview of recent issues and methods in strategic market management.

A WORD TO INSTRUCTORS

The seventh edition contains an extensive on-line instructor's resource guide authored by Jim Prost located on the text companion Web site at **www.wiley.com /college/aaker.** The resource guide has several course outlines, a list of cases to consider, test questions, additional resources, a PowerPoint presentation organized by chapter, a set of lecture suggestions for each chapter, and discussion notes for each chapter's For Discussion section.

ACKNOWLEDGMENTS

This book could not have been created without help from my friends and colleagues. This edition benefited from the helpful comments of many students who attended my course in strategic market management and the work of some able research assistants: Satoshi Akutsu, Nicholas Lurie, Heather Honea, and Andrew Schwarz and several insightful MBA students: Amy Luna Capelle, Iris M. Cardenas, Robert B. Spears, Kevin Stonelake, Leslie Trigg, Pablo Valencia, Kevin A. Yen, T. Jason Young, and José Rizo-Patron. Among the people who read large portions of earlier editions were Norm Smothers, Gregory Gundlach, Robert Headen, Chauncey Burke, Tom Gilpatrick, Frank Acito, George Jackson, Sid Dudley, R. Vishwanathan, Andrew Forman, Patricia Hopkins, Bruce McNab, John B. Lord, Yama Yelkur, Gene Laczniak, Don Leemon, Baruch Lev, Ray Miles, Steve Penman, Charles O'Reilly, and David Teece. I owe a large debt to all of these people.

I owe a special debt to some Nestlé people who helped with the pet food example used in the planning forms. Leah Porter helped to develop the case study and updated it through several editions, and John Carmichael contributed to this edition. My colleagues at Prophet, especially Trevor Wade, have been a source of ideas and support. My daughter, Jennifer, helps keep me rigorous in my thinking. Andy Smith and Brian Krug provided useful suggestions.

I give special thanks to my friend and colleague Jim Prost, a strategy teacher extraordinaire who made numerous suggestions about the book and has created a world-class teacher's resource manual.

I am pleased to be associated with the publisher, John Wiley, a class organization, and its superb editors—Rich Esposito (who helped give birth to the first edition), John Woods, Tim Kent, Ellen Ford, Jeff Marshall, and Judith Joseph (who guided this edition). Thanks also to Cindy Rhoads and Kevin Dodds, who kept everything on schedule. It is a pleasure to be supported by competent, supportive professionals who are fun to be around. Chris Kelly, a superb copy editor, helped make this edition more readable as he has on so many of my books.

This book is dedicated to my parents, Ida and Oscar, who lived a life full of energy and love, and to Samantha, Maile, Devon, and Cooper, who live a life of energy and promise.

David A. Aaker
January, 2004

CONTENTS

PART ONE

INTRODUCTION AND OVERVIEW

CHAPTER ONE

Business Strategy: The Concept and Trends in Its Management

Plans are nothing, planning is everything.
—Dwight D. Eisenhower

Even if you are on the right track, you'll get run over if you just sit there.
—Will Rodgers

Where absolute superiority is not attainable, you must produce a relative one at the decisive point by making skillful use of what you have.
—Karl von Clausewitz, On War, 1832

*I*n the 1930s, Sears and Montgomery Ward were approximately equal in sales, profits, capability, and potential. Two decades later, Sears was roughly three times bigger than a stagnant Wards. One reason that Wards failed to keep pace can be traced to the belief of its chairman, Sewell Avery, that depressions inevitably follow wars. Based on that belief, he failed to open a single new store from 1941 to 1957. Another reason was that in 1946, recognizing the automobile's growing role in shopping, Sears decided to begin an aggressive and costly move into suburban shopping centers. But both stores had trouble adjusting their strategy to compete with the discounters from below and the specialty stores from above. Wards ultimately went out of business whereas Sears has survived, in part by leveraging its strong brands (such as Kenmore appliances and Craftsman tools) and becoming more of a series of specialty stores focused on clothes, automobile service, the home, and appliances.

Kmart, Wal-Mart, and Target all started around 1962 and have pursued broadly similar strategies. But while Target has prospered and Wal-Mart has grown to become the largest U.S. firm, Kmart has declared bankruptcy. Target defined itself as the upscale discount store, with name designers such as the Michael Graves houseware products and a successful wedding registry, and Wal-Mart became synonymous with value. Kmart, however, struggled to find a value proposition; further, it failed to develop the operational competencies needed in that competitive space.

Clearly, the fortunes of Sears, Kmart, Wal-Mart, and others in the future will depend in large measure on their ability to analyze their competitive context, make sound strategic choices, and support those choices with needed strategic initiatives. The fact is that nearly every organization is affected by strategic decisions or, sometimes, nondecisions.

This book is concerned with helping managers identify, select, and implement strategies. The intent is to provide decision makers with concepts, methods, and procedures by which they can improve the quality of their strategic decision making.

This and the following chapter have several functions. First, they identify the approach toward strategy and its management that is taken in this book. Second, they introduce and position most of the concepts and methods that are covered in the book. Third, they position and structure the other parts and chapters. Fourth, they provide a general overview and summary. Thus, the reader can productively reread these two chapters as a way to review.

This chapter begins by defining the concept of a business strategy. It then describes strategic options, the building blocks of a business strategy, provides a historical perspective to strategy, and, finally, presents some characteristics, trends, and rationales of strategic market management.

WHAT IS A BUSINESS STRATEGY?

Before discussing the process of developing sound business strategies, it is fair to address two questions: What is a business? What is a business strategy? Having groups of managers provide answers to these questions can be particularly interesting and useful. What you quickly learn from such an exercise is that the issues are complex, and there is no consensus answer.

A Business Is . . .

A business is generally an organizational unit that has a distinct business strategy and a manager with sales and profit responsibility. An organization will thus have many business units that relate to each other horizontally and vertically. For example, HP needs to set strategic directions for the many product markets in which it competes, and each product market will typically have its own business strategy. Thus, there may be a business strategy for the LaserJet product group, but within that line, there may also be separate business strategies for products such as the LaserJet printer supplies business, for segments such as large companies in the United States, for geographies such as South America.

Organizationally and strategically, there are trade-offs in deciding how many businesses should be operated. On one hand, it can be compelling to have many businesses, because then each can develop a strategy that is optimal for its market.

Thus, a strategy for each country or each region or each major segment may have some benefits. Having too many business units, on the other hand, can result in inefficiency through programs that lack scale economies and fail to leverage the strategic skills of the best managers. These considerations create pressure to combine businesses into larger entities.

Business units can be aggregated to create a critical mass, to coordinate strategies, and leverage similarities in markets and strategies. Businesses that are too small to justify a strategy will need to be aggregated so that the management structure, even if small, can be supportable. Larger business units afford staff and programs that enhance changes of success. Of course, two business units can share some elements of operations, such as a sales force or a facility, to gain economies without merging.

Another benefit of larger business units is to achieve synergy with closer strategic interaction among the subunits. For example, P&G aggregates brands such as Head & Shoulders, Pert, and Pantene into a hair care category in part to create promotions more easily, to optimize the application of product innovations, and to provide shelf space guidance of retailers. Similarly, HP might aggregate some of its LaserJet printers designed for the business market to take advantage of cost reduction opportunities afforded by overlapping product components and customers. Mobil groups countries into regions, and others merge regions into global business units. In fact, the choice between country, regional, or global aggregation is a crucial decision facing many firms.

A final incentive toward aggregation is leveraging the knowledge of similar markets and strategies. Thus, in Eastern Europe, Coca-Cola might consider aggregating its Coke and Diet Coke business units, but not Fanta and Sprite. HP might aggregate its LaserJet and InkJet printers in some countries, as they face very similar market contexts and will have overlapping strategies.

A Business Strategy Is . . .

Four dimensions define a business strategy: the product-market investment strategy, the customer value proposition, assets and competencies, and functional strategies and programs. The first specifies where to compete, and the remaining three indicate how to compete to win (see Figure 1.1).

The Product-Market Investment Strategy—Where to Compete

The scope of the business, and the dynamics within that scope, represent a very basic strategy dimension. Which sectors are receiving investments in resources and management attention?

The scope of a business is defined by the products it offers and chooses not to offer, by the markets it does and does not seek to serve, by the competitors it chooses to compete with or to avoid, and by its level of vertical integration. Sometimes the most important business scope decision is what products or segments to avoid, because such a decision (if followed with discipline) can conserve resources needed to compete successfully elsewhere. Such judgments can sometimes involve painful decisions to divest or liquidate a business.

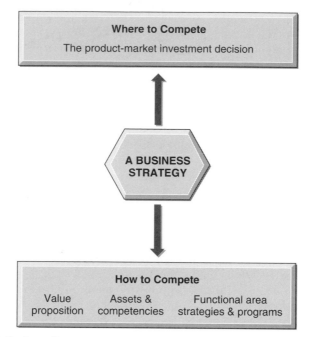

Figure 1.1   A Business Strategy

Many organizations have demonstrated the advantages of having a well-defined business scope. Williams-Sonoma offers products for the home and kitchen. IBM turned itself around under the direction of Lou Gerstner in part by dialing up its service component. Dell offers computer-associated products. P&G provides a broad spectrum of packaged consumer goods. Wal-Mart and Amazon have a wide scope offering both scale economies and a one-stop shopping value proposition.

More important than the scope itself are its dynamics. What product markets will be entered or exited in coming years? Which will be dialed up or down? Financial resources, generated either internally or externally, plus non-financial resources such as plant, equipment, and people, all need to be allocated based on these decisions. Which business sectors will receive investment resources because of their increased importance in the future? Even for a small organization, the allocation decision is key to strategy.

The investment pattern will determine the future direction of the firm. Although there are obvious variations and refinements, the broad conceptual choices are as follows:

- Invest to grow (or enter the product market)
- Invest only to maintain the existing position
- Milk the business by minimizing investment
- Recover as many of the assets as possible by liquidating or divesting the business

P&G had lost half its stock value in the six months before A. G. Lafley took over as CEO in the middle of 2000, in part because the firm invested considerable resources behind new business initiatives such as Olay Cosmetics and Fit Wash that disappointed or failed.[1] Two years later it had recovered most of that decline, even as the overall stock market dropped more than a third of its value during that time. A key to the turnaround was a strategy of focusing on twelve billion-dollar brands such as Tide, Arial (in Europe), Always/Whisper, Crest, Folgers, Iams, Pampers, Charmin, Bounty, Pantene, Downy/Lenor, and Pringles. For example, with resources no longer diverted elsewhere, the hair care group could focus on revitalizing Pantene. Lesser brands received less attention, and some that lacked a strategic fit (such as Jif and Crisco) were jettisoned.

The Customer Value Proposition

A customer value proposition is the perceived functional, emotional, social, or self-expressive benefit that is provided by the organization's offering. One or more value propositions need to be relevant and meaningful to the customer and reflected in the positioning of the product or service. To support a successful strategy, the propositions should be sustainable over time and differentiate the offering from its competitors. The customer value proposition can involve elements such as providing:

- A good value (Wal Mart)
- Excellence on an important product or service attribute (for Tide, getting clothes clean)
- The best overall quality (Lexus)
- Product line breadth (Amazon)
- Innovative offerings (3M)
- A shared passion for an activity or a product (Harley-Davidson)
- Global connections and prestige (Citigroup)

In 2003, IBM's new CEO, Sam Palmisano, had to follow the remarkable success of his predecessor, Lou Gerstner, who had achieved a dramatic turnaround during the 1990s in part by making the synergy and technology of the IBM organization work for the customer.[2] Palmisano's strategy for IBM was based on a new value proposition, called "on-demand." The core idea was that computer resources (in particular, unused computer capacity) and computer-driven information sources should be available to those who need them *when* they are needed. The on-demand concept ultimately implies that computer systems and networks be simplified so that software and hardware seamlessly connect with each other through a software-managed network grid.

Assets and Competencies

The strategic assets or competencies that underlie the strategy provide the sustainable competitive advantage (SCA). A *strategic competency* is what a business unit does exceptionally well, such as manufacturing or promotion, which has strategic importance to the business. It is usually based on knowledge or a process. A *strategic asset* is a resource, such as a brand name or installed customer base that is strong relative to that of competitors. Strategy formulation must consider the cost and feasibility of generating or maintaining assets or competencies that will provide the basis for a sustainable competitive advantage.

Assets and competencies can involve a wide spectrum, from buildings and locations to R&D expertise or a metaphoric symbol, such as the Michelin Man. Though a strong asset or competency is often difficult to build, it can result in an advantage that is significant and enduring.

An important asset and SCA source can be the synergies obtained from operating a business that spans product markets. Synergy occurs, for example, when two businesses can reduce costs by sharing a sales force or logistics system. Gillette created synergy after buying Duracell by leveraging the fact that both products are sold in the same distribution channel. Businesses also may be able to offer retailers and/or customers a combination of coordinated products (such as athletic shoes and apparel), thereby creating a value that would not exist if the two businesses were distinct. Organizational synergy-based SCAs tend to be sustainable because they are defined with respect to an organization, its product-market scope, and its business strategy, which are not easily duplicated. Synergies and the concept of a sustainable competitive advantage are both discussed in more depth in Chapter 8.

The ability of an organization's assets and competencies to support a strategy will in part depend on their power relative to those of competitors. To what extent are the assets and competencies strong and in place? To what extent are they ownable because of a symbol trademark or long-standing investment in a capability? To what extent are they based on synergy within a unique organization that others cannot duplicate?

Functional Strategies and Programs

A target value proposition or a set of assets and competencies should mandate some strategy imperatives, in the form of a supportive set of functional strategies or programs. These strategies and programs, in turn, will be implemented with a host of short-term tactics.

Some of the functional strategies or programs that could drive the business strategy include the following:

- Manufacturing strategy
- Distribution strategy
- Brand-building strategy
- Communication strategy
- Information technology strategy
- Global strategy
- Segmentation strategy
- Quality program
- Customer relationship program

The need for functional strategies and programs can be determined by asking a few questions. What must happen for the firm to be able to deliver on the value proposition? Are the assets and competencies needed in place? Do they need to be created, strengthened, or supported? How?

IBM's on-demand value proposition led to a cross-company R&D effort that pushed all parts of the firm to develop on-demand products and services, and an internal initiative to make IBM itself an on-demand company. The server software group, for instance, developed products to support access to computer hardware whenever it was needed. To successfully define the new on-demand business area and to link it to IBM, the strategy could not be merely a tagline or empty rhetoric; programs had to be created to put substance behind the vision.

STRATEGIC OPTIONS

A business strategy will involve a host of elements organized by these four dimensions (the product-market investment strategy, the customer value proposition, assets and competencies, and functional strategies and programs). The complexity and apparent number of alternative strategies can become overwhelming. Usually, however, a business strategy will be based on a limited number of strategic options. A strategic option is a particular value proposition for a specific product market with supporting assets and competencies and functional strategies and programs. Conceptualizing and labeling strategic options help crystallize and describe alternative business strategies. It also provides a way to describe the selected business strategy to employees, partners, investors, and customers.

A strategy can involve more than one strategic option; in fact, most successful strategies do. Virgin Atlantic Airways, for example, has a value strategy coupled with an innovation and customer intimacy strategy. To fulfill these strategies, Virgin continually stretches its service boundaries. So strategic options can be viewed as the building blocks of a business strategy. Analogously, a business strategy can be perceived as a set of integrated strategic options.

Several of the most common and important strategic options—such as quality, value, innovation, focus and being global—are explored in some detail in Chapters 9, 10, and 11. Chapter 9 also discusses strategic options driven by a product attribute, product design, product line breadth, corporate social responsibility, brand familiarity, and customer intimacy. These discussions provide an overview of strategic options that are widely used, are often successful, and for which a body of knowledge exists. The list of possible options discussed is not complete, but those that are described can provide insights into others.

STRATEGIC MARKET MANAGEMENT: A HISTORICAL PERSPECTIVE

The process of developing and implementing strategies has been described over the years by various terms, including budgeting, long-range planning, strategic planning, and strategic market management. All these terms have similar meanings and are often used interchangeably. However, when they are placed in a historical perspective, some useful distinctions emerge.[3]

Budgeting

The development of budgeting management systems can be roughly associated with the early 1900s. The emphasis is on controlling deviations and managing complexity. An annual budget is set for various departments, and deviations from that budget are carefully scrutinized to find explanations and determine whether remedial action is appropriate. The basic assumption is that the past will repeat itself. Figure 1.2 summarizes this approach.

Long-Range Planning

The second management system shown in Figure 1.2 is long-range planning, the development of which Igor Ansoff, long a leading strategy theorist, has associated with the 1950s and 1960s. Its focus is on anticipating growth and managing complexity. The basic assumption is that past trends will continue into the future. The planning process typically involves projecting sales, costs, technology, and so on into the future using data and experience from the past. The planning task is then to develop human resources and facilities to accommodate the anticipated growth or contraction. The time frame is not necessarily as limited as in the budgeting system and can anticipate two, five, or ten years, depending on the context.

Included under long-range planning is gap analysis. A gap occurs if the projected sales and profits do not meet the organizational goals. Changes in operations, such as increasing the sales force and/or plant capacity, are then considered to remove the gap.

Strategic Planning

Strategic planning, the emergence of which is associated with the 1960s, 1970s, and 1980s is concerned with changing strategic options and capabilities. The basic assumption is that past extrapolations are inadequate and that discontinuities from past projections and new trends will require strategic adjustments. An adjustment in strategic options or direction could involve moving into a new product market. The enhancement of research and development competence could represent an adjustment in strategic capability.

Strategic planning focuses on the market environment facing the firm. Thus, the emphasis is not only on projections, but also on an in-depth understanding of the market environment, particularly the competitors and customers. The hope is not only to gain insight into current conditions, but also to be able to anticipate changes that have strategic implications.

One characteristic that strategic planning shares with budgeting and long-range planning is that it is largely based on a periodic planning system, usually an annual system. Typically, an organization will develop a strategic plan in the spring and summer and then, during the fall, will use that plan as a base for developing the annual operating plans and budgets for the next year. The periodic planning

	Budgeting	Long-Range Planning	Strategic Planning	Strategic Market Management
Management Emphasis	Control deviations and manage complexity	Anticipate growth and manage complexity	Change strategic thrust and capability	Cope with strategic surprises and fast-developing threats/opportunities
Assumption	The past repeats	Past trends will continue	New trends and discontinuities are predictable	Planning cycles are inadequate to deal with rapid changes
Process	←————————————— Periodic —————————————→			Real time
Time Period Associated with System	From 1900s	From 1950s	From 1970s	From 1990s

Figure 1.2 Evolution of Management Systems

11

cycle does provide a time in which managers must address strategic questions. Without such a device, artificial though it may be, even managers who realize the importance of strategic thinking might find their time absorbed by day-to-day operations and crises.

The difficulty with the periodic planning process is that the need for strategic analysis and decision making does not always occur on an annual basis. The environment and technology may change so rapidly and environmental shocks may occur so unexpectedly that being tied to a planning cycle can be disadvantageous or even disastrous. If the planning process is allowed to suppress strategic response outside the planning cycle, performance can suffer, particularly in dynamic industries.

A study of managers making strategy decisions in a simulated business focused on the impact of planning. The study found that when the environment was made more turbulent (by reducing product life cycles and increasing product change), those businesses that were asked to plan formally (by projecting performance using planning forms) had performances inferior to those that did not plan.[4] Planning enhanced those in a less turbulent environment, however.

Strategic Market Management

Strategic market management, or simply, strategic management, is motivated by the assumption that the planning cycle is inadequate to deal with the rapid rate of change that can occur in a firm's external environment. To cope with strategic surprises and fast-developing threats and opportunities, strategic decisions need to be precipitated and made outside the planning cycle.

Recognition of the demands of a rapidly changing environment has stimulated the development or increased use of methods, systems, and options that are responsive. In particular, it suggests a need for continuous, real-time information systems rather than, or in addition to, periodic analysis. More sensitive environmental scanning, the identification and continuous monitoring of information-need areas, efforts to develop strategic flexibility, and the enhancement of the entrepreneurial thrust of the organization may be helpful. An information-need area is an area of uncertainty that will affect strategy, such as an emerging consumer-interest area. Strategic flexibility involves strategic options that allow quick and appropriate responses to sudden changes in the environment.

Strategic market management is proactive and future oriented. Rather than simply accepting the environment as given, with the strategic role confined to adaptation and reaction, strategy may be proactive, affecting environmental change. Thus, governmental policies, customer needs, and technological developments can be influenced—and perhaps even controlled—with creative, active strategies.

Gary Hamel and C. K. Prahalad argue that managers should have a clear and shared understanding of how their industry may be different in ten years and a strategy for competing in that world.[5] They challenge managers to evaluate the extent to which:

- Management has a distinctive and farsighted view, rather than a conventional and reactive view, about the future.

- Senior management focuses on regenerating core strategies rather than on reengineering core processes.
- Competitors view the company as a rule maker rather than a rule follower.
- The company's strength is in innovation and growth rather than in operational efficiency.
- The company is mostly out in front rather than catching up.

The evolving systems shown in Figure 1.2 build on, rather than replace, earlier systems. In that spirit, strategic market management actually includes all four management systems: the budgeting system, the projection-based approach of long-range planning, the elements of strategic planning, and the refinements needed to adapt strategic decision making to real time. In strategic market management, a periodic planning process is normally supplemented by techniques that allow the organization to be strategically responsive outside the planning process.

The inclusion of the term *market* in the phrase "strategic management" emphasizes that strategy development needs to be driven by the market and its environment rather than by an internal orientation. It also points out that the process should be proactive rather than reactive and that the task should be to try to influence the environment as well as respond to it.

STRATEGIC MARKET MANAGEMENT: CHARACTERISTICS AND TRENDS

Several distinct characteristics and trends have emerged in the strategy field, some of which have already been mentioned. A review of these thrusts or trends will provide additional insight into strategic market management and into the perspective and orientation of the balance of the book.

External Market Orientation

As already noted, organizations need to be oriented externally—toward customers, competitors, the market, and the market's environment. In sharp contrast to the projection-based, internally oriented, long-range planning systems, the goal is to develop market-driven strategies that are sensitive to the customer.

Proactive Strategies

A proactive strategy attempts to influence events in the environment rather than simply react to environmental forces as they occur. A proactive strategy is important for at least two reasons. First, one way to be sure of detecting and quickly reacting to major environmental changes is to participate in their creation. Second, because environmental changes can be significant, it may be important to be able to influence them. For example, it may be beneficial for an insurance firm to be involved in tort reform strategy.

Importance of the Information System

An external orientation puts demands on the supporting information system. The determination of what information is needed, how it can be obtained efficiently and effectively, and how it should best be analyzed, processed, and stored can be key to an effective strategy development process.

Knowledge Management

Knowledge management is becoming critical because the key issue for companies increasingly is knowledge, whether it be knowledge of technology, marketing, processes, or other ingredient of success. Because knowledge resides in the minds of individuals, the challenge is to capture that knowledge in a form that can be retained and nurtured over time and can be shared by a wide group of people.

On-Line Analysis and Decision Making

Organizations are moving away from relying only on the annual planning cycle and toward a more continuous, on-line system of information gathering, analysis, and strategic decision making. The design of such a system is demanding and requires new methods and concepts. The system must be structured enough to provide assistance in an inherently complex decision context, sensitive enough to detect the need to precipitate a strategic choice, and flexible enough to be applied in a variety of situations.

Entrepreneurial Thrust

The importance of developing and maintaining an entrepreneurial thrust is increasingly being recognized. There is a need for the development of organizational forms and strategic market management support systems that allow the firm to be responsive to opportunities. The entrepreneurial skill is particularly important to large, diversified firms and to firms involved in extremely fast-moving industries, such as high-tech firms or industries that produce "hit" products such as video games, CDs, or movies. The strategy in such contexts must include providing an environment in which entrepreneurs can flourish.

Implementation

Implementation of strategy is critical. There needs to be a concern about whether the strategy fits the organization—its structure, systems, people, and culture—or whether the organization can be adapted to the strategy. The strategy needs to be linked to the functional area policies and the operating plan. Chapter 16 is devoted to implementation issues.

Global Realities

Increasingly, the global dimension is affecting strategy. Global markets are extremely relevant to many businesses, from Boeing to McDonald's, and it is a rare firm that is not affected by competitors either based in or with operations in other countries. The global element represents both direct and indirect opportunities and threats. The financial difficulty of a major country or a worldwide shortage of some raw material may have a dramatic impact on an organization's strategy. Chapter 11 focuses on global strategies.

Longer Time Horizon

A longer time horizon is needed for most businesses in order to create and implement strategic initiatives needed to develop assets and competences. This requires the ability to balance discipline and patience with the need for real time analysis and the pressures for short-term results. It also requires methods and measures that reflect a long-term perspective.

Empirical Research

Historically, the field of strategy has been dominated by conceptual contributions based on personal experience and insights, as the writings of Alfred Sloan, the architect of General Motors, and Peter Drucker, the author of the classic book, *The Practice of Management*, illustrate.[6] More recently, an empirical research tradition has begun. The qualitative case-study approach provides useful hypotheses and insights. In addition, a host of quantitative research streams compare and study the performance and characteristics of samples of business units over time. These research streams can now be found in most of the basic disciplines and in the field of strategy itself. They are an important indication that the field is finally reaching a maturity in which theories can be, and are being, subjected to scientific testing.

Interdisciplinary Developments

One purpose of this book is to draw on and integrate a variety of disciplines that are making important conceptual and methodological contributions to strategic market management. Among these disciplines, which have been remarkably isolated from strategic market management and each other, are the following.

Marketing

Marketing is by its very nature concerned with the interaction between the firm and the marketplace. During the last decade, strategic decisions have received increasing attention. Tools and concepts such as brand equity, customer satisfaction, positioning, product life cycle, global brand management, category management, and customer-need analysis all have the potential to improve strategy decision making.

Organizational Behavior

Organizational behavior theorists have made considerable contributions on the relationship between strategy and organizational structure, culture, and systems. They have shown how a lack of fit can impact success. They have also provided a host of theories and constructs that provide guidance to the implementation of strategies.

Finance and Accounting

One major contribution of these disciplines to strategy is shareholder value analysis (covered in Chapter 7)—the concept that strategists should be concerned with the impact of strategy on the value of the firm. Another is a rich research tradition relating to diversification efforts, acquisitions, and mergers. Finance has also contributed to an understanding of the concept of risk and its management.

Economics

The industrial organization theory subarea of economics has been applied to strategy using concepts and methods such as industry structure, exit barriers, entry barriers, and strategic groups. Furthermore, the concept of transaction costs has been developed and applied to the issue of vertical integration. Finally, economists have contributed to the experience curve concept, which has considerable strategic implications.

Strategy

The discipline of strategy is not only increasingly overlapping with other disciplines, but is itself maturing. One sign of this maturity is the emergence of quantitative research streams; another is the maturity of some of its tools and techniques. In addition, the premier strategy journal, *Strategic Management Journal,* has given exposure for more than two decades to the top academic efforts that provide theoretical and empirical insights into strategy.

WHY STRATEGIC MARKET MANAGEMENT?

Strategic market management is often frustrating because the environment is so difficult to understand and predict. The communication and choices required within the organization can create strain and internal resistance. The most valuable organizational resource, management time, is absorbed. The alternative of simply waiting for and reacting to exceptional opportunities often seems efficient and adequate.

Despite these costs and problems, however, strategic market management has the potential to:

- *Precipitate the consideration of strategic choices.* What is happening externally that is creating opportunities and threats to which a timely and appropriate reaction should be generated? What strategic issues face the firm? What strategic options should be considered? The alternative to strategic market management is usually to drift strategically, becoming absorbed in day-to-day problems. Nothing is more tragic than an organization that fails because a strategic decision was not addressed until it was too late.

- *Force a long-range view.* The pressures to manage with a short-term focus are strong and frequently lead to strategic errors.

- *Make visible the resource allocation decision.* Allowing allocation of resources to be dictated by the accounting system, political strengths, or inertia (the same as last year) is too easy. One result of this approach is that the small but promising business with "no problems" or the unborn business may suffer from a lack of resources, whereas the larger business areas with "problems" may absorb an excessive amount.

- *Aid strategic analysis and decision making.* Concepts, models, and methodologies are available to help a business collect and analyze information and address difficult strategic decisions.

- *Provide a strategic management and control system.* The focus on assets and competencies and the development of objectives and programs associated with strategic thrusts provide the basis for managing a business strategically.

- *Provide both horizontal and vertical communication and coordination systems.* Strategic market management provides a way to communicate problems and proposed strategies within an organization; in particular, its vocabulary adds precision.

- *Help a business cope with change.* If a particular environment is extremely stable and the sales patterns are satisfactory, there may be little need for meaningful strategic change—either in direction or intensity. In that case, strategic market management is much less crucial. However, most organizations now exist in rapidly changing and increasingly unpredictable environments and therefore need approaches for coping strategically.

KEY LEARNINGS

- A business strategy includes the determination of the product-market scope and its dynamics (as reflected in the intensity of the business investment), the customer value proposition, assets and competencies, and functional strategies and programs.

- Available strategy options include quality, value, focus, innovation, global, product attribute, product design, product line breadth, corporate social responsibility, brand familiarity, and customer intimacy. A business strategy involves the selection and integration of a set of strategic options.

- Strategic market management has evolved from and encompasses budgeting, long-range planning, and strategy planning.

- Strategic market management is externally oriented, proactive, timely, entrepreneurial, and globally supported by information systems and knowledge management programs.

FOR DISCUSSION

1. What is a business strategy? Do you agree with the definition proposed in this chapter? Illustrate your answer with examples.

2. Consider one of the firms in the list below. Read the description in the text, then go to the firm's Web site and use it to gain an understanding of the business strategy. Look at elements such as the products and services offered, the history of the firm, and its values. What is the business strategy? What product markets does the firm serve? What value propositions does it use? How are the value propositions delivered? What are the firm's assets and competencies? What strategic options has it pursued?

   a. Dell

   b. Charles Schwab

   c. Pampers

   d. A firm of your choice

NOTES

1. Katrina Booker, "The Un-CEO," *Fortune*, September 16, 2002, pp. 68–78.

2. Spenser E. Ante, "The New Blue," *Business Week*, March 17, 2003, pp. 79–88.

3. This section and Figure 1.2 draw on the work of H. Igor Ansoff. Typical examples are his articles "Strategic Issue Management," *Strategic Management Journal*, April-June 1980, pp. 131–148, and "The State of Practice in Planning Systems," *Sloan Management Review*, Winter 1977, pp. 61–69.

4. Rashi Glazer and Alan Weiss, "Planning in a Turbulent Environment," *Journal of Marketing Research*, November 1993, pp. 509–521.

5. Gary Hamel and C. K. Prahalad, "Competing for the Future," *Harvard Business Review*, July-August 1994, pp. 122–128.

6. Alfred P. Sloan, Jr., *My Years with General Motors*, New York: Doubleday, 1963; and Peter F. Drucker, *The Practice of Management*, New York: Harper & Row, 1954.

CHAPTER TWO

Strategic Market Management: An Overview

Chance favors the prepared mind.
—*Louis Pasteur*

Far better an approximate answer to the right question, which is often vague, than an exact answer to the wrong question, which can always be made precise.
—*John Tukey, statistician*

If you don't know where you're going, you might end up somewhere else.
Casey Stengel

Strategic market management is a system designed to help management both precipitate and make strategic decisions, as well as create strategic visions. A strategic decision involves the creation, change, or retention of a strategy. In contrast to a tactical decision, a strategic decision is usually costly in terms of the resources and time required to reverse or change it. The cost of altering a wrong decision may be so high as to threaten the very existence of an organization. Normally, a strategic decision has a time frame greater than one year; sometimes decades are involved.

A strategic vision is a vision of a future strategy or sets of strategies. The realization of an optimal strategy for a firm may involve a delay because the firm is not ready or the emerging conditions are not yet in place. A vision will provide direction and purpose for interim strategies and strategic activities.

An important role of the system is to precipitate as well as make strategic decisions. The identification of the need for a strategic response is frequently a critical step. Many strategic blunders occur because a strategic decision process was never activated, not because an incorrect decision was made. Furthermore, the role of strategic market management is not limited to selecting from among decision alternatives, but it

19

includes the identification of alternatives as well. Much of the analysis is therefore concerned with identifying alternatives.

Figure 2.1 shows an overview of the external analysis and internal analysis that provide the input to strategy development and the set of strategic decisions that is the ultimate output. It provides a structure for strategic market management and for this book. A brief overview of its three principal elements and an introduction to the key concepts will be provided in this chapter.

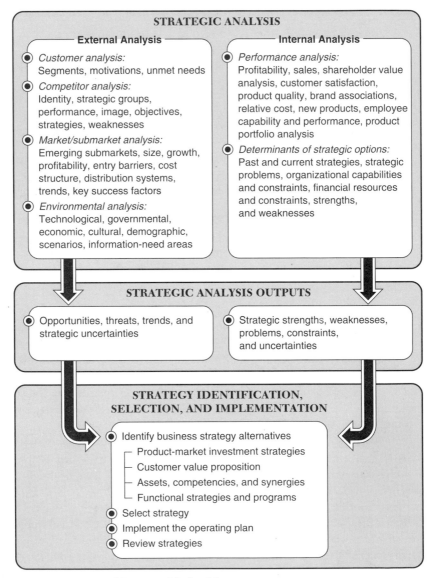

Figure 2.1 Overview of Strategic Market Management

EXTERNAL ANALYSIS

External analysis involves an examination of the relevant elements external to an organization. The analysis should be purposeful, focusing on the identification of opportunities, threats, trends, strategic uncertainties, and strategic choices. There is a danger in being excessively descriptive. Because there is literally no limit to the scope of a descriptive study, the result can be a considerable expenditure of resources with little impact on strategy.

One output of external analysis is an identification and understanding of opportunities and threats, both present and potential, facing the organization. An opportunity is a trend or event that could lead to a significant upward change in sales and profit patterns—given the appropriate strategic response. A threat is a trend or event that will result, in the absence of a strategic response, in a significant downward departure from current sales and profit patterns. For example, consumers' concern with calories and cholesterol represents a threat to the dairy industry.

Another output is the identification of strategic uncertainties regarding a business or its environment that have the potential to affect strategy. If the uncertainty is important and urgent, an in-depth analysis leading to a strategy decision may be needed; otherwise, an information-gathering effort is usually appropriate.

The frame of reference for an external analysis is typically a defined business, but it is useful to conduct the analysis at several levels. External analyses of submarkets provide insight sometimes critical to developing strategy. Thus, an external analysis of the mature beer industry might contain analyses of the import and nonalcoholic beer submarkets, which are growing and have important differences. It is also possible to conduct external analyses for groups of businesses, such as divisions, that have characteristics in common, such as segments served, competition, and environmental trends.

External analysis, discussed at the outset of Chapter 3, is divided into four sections or components: customer analysis, competitor analysis, market analysis, and environmental analysis.

Customer Analysis

Customer analysis, the first step of external analysis and a focus of Chapter 3, involves identifying the organization's customer segments and each segment's motivations and unmet needs. Segment identification defines alternative product markets and thus structures the strategic investment decision (what investment levels to assign to each market). The analysis of customer motivations provides information needed to decide which customer value proposition to pursue. An unmet need (a need not currently being met by existing products) can be strategically important because it may represent a way to dislodge entrenched competitors.

For example, consider the luxury hotel industry. One segmentation scheme distinguishes between tourists, convention attendees, and business travelers. Each type of traveler has a very different set of motivations. The tourist is concerned with price, the conventioneer with convention facilities, and the business traveler with comfort and Internet access. The tourist segment might have an unmet need for tickets for events such as plays or concerts.

Frozen-novelty industry products include individually packaged, single servings of a frozen snack or dessert, such as chocolate-covered ice cream, Popsicles, juice bars, pudding bars, and ice cream-cookie combinations. One way to segment this industry is to distinguish between retail and food service. Food service includes schools, hospitals, and recreational facilities, which may be attracted by the ease of storing and serving the product. The market might also be segmented by motivation. Groups can be identified according to whether they are primarily concerned with calories, fat, taste, refreshment, price, or convenience. An unmet need for a nutritious snack in this industry provided an opening for the frozen fruit bar.

Competitor Analysis

Competitor analysis, covered in Chapter 4, starts with the identification of competitors, current and potential. Some competitors compete more intensely than others.

PowerBar makes an energy bar that competes most intensely with other energy snacks (for example, Balance). However, it also competes with energy drinks and other snacks such as candy. Although intense competitors should be examined most closely, all competitors are usually relevant to strategy development.

Especially when there are many competitors, it is helpful to combine those with similar characteristics (e.g., size and resources), strengths (e.g., brand name, distribution), and strategies (e.g., high quality) into strategic groups. The luxury hotel industry might be divided into hotels that offer business-oriented amenities and hotels that are ultraplush and prestigious. These two groups might be further divided into those that are members of chains with central reservation systems and those that are autonomous. Regional dairies with strong ice cream brands are one strategic group in the frozen-novelty industry, a group that is declining in the face of competitors with national advertising and promotion support.

To develop a strategy, it is important to understand the competitor's:

- *Performance.* What do this competitor's sales, sales growth, and profitability indicate about its health?
- *Image and personality.* How is the competitor positioned and perceived?
- *Objectives.* Is this competitor committed to the business? Does this competitor aim for high growth?
- *Current and past strategy.* What are the implications for future strategic moves?
- *Culture.* What is most important to the organization—cost control, entrepreneurship, or the customer?
- *Cost structure.* Does the competitor have a cost advantage?
- *Strengths and weaknesses.* Is the brand name, distribution, or R&D a strength or a weakness?

Of special interest are the competitor's strengths and weaknesses. Strategy development often focuses on exploiting a competitor's weakness or neutralizing or bypassing a competitor's strength.

Market/Submarket Analysis

Market analysis, the subject of Chapter 5, has two primary objectives. The first is to determine the attractiveness of the market and submarkets. On average, will competitors earn attractive profits or will they lose money? If the market is so difficult that everyone is losing money, it is not a place in which to invest. The second objective is to understand the dynamics of the market so that threats and opportunities can be detected and strategies adapted. The analysis should include an examination of the market size, growth, profitability, cost structure, channels, trends, and key success factors.

Emerging Submarkets

The evolution of submarkets is a key market dynamic. Even a strong business can become irrelevant if it is not attached to the emerging submarkets. The automobile market, for instance, has seen the emergence of two-seat sports cars, minivans, SUVs, gas-electric hybrids, and other submarkets. A carmaker needs to be aware of these dynamics and have a responsive strategy— even if the ultimate strategy is to avoid the submarket.

Size

A basic characteristic of a market (or a submarket) is its size. In addition to current sales, the analysis should consider the market's potential, that is, the additional sales that could be obtained if new users were attracted, new uses were found, or existing buyers were enticed to use the product or service more frequently.

Growth Prospects

The analysis needs to assess the growth trend and product life-cycle stage for the industry and its submarkets. An investment in a declining industry is not always unwise, but it would be if the strategist held the erroneous impression that it was a growth situation. Conversely, it is important to recognize growth contexts even though they will not always be attractive investments for a given firm.

Market Profitability

The profitability of the market depends on five factors—the number and vigor of existing competitors, the threat of new competitors, the threat of substitute products, the profit impact of powerful suppliers, and the power of customers to force price concessions. For example, a luxury hotel could be faced with convention organizers who have the power to negotiate low rates and thus affect the profitability of the market. Important structural components are the barriers to entry that must be overcome by potential competitors entering the industry. A barrier to entry for the luxury hotel business in Chicago is the availability of desirable sites.

Cost Structures

One issue is what value-added stage represents the most important cost component. In the parcel delivery system, there is local pickup and delivery versus sorting and combining versus between-city transportation versus customer service. Achieving a cost advantage in an important value-added stage can be crucial. Another cost issue is whether the industry is appropriate for a low-cost strategy based on the experience curve model, discussed in Chapter 10.

Distribution Channels

An understanding of the alternative distribution channels and trends can be of strategic value. Growth in the importance of self-service retail gasoline stations and companion growth in the convenience store industry have strategic significance to oil companies such as Shell and ARCO as well as to food retailing firms, as the ARCO chain of AM/PM stores illustrates.

A significant factor in the frozen-novelty business is the distribution squeeze caused by product proliferation. There is space for only 100 of the more than 2,000 products in the frozen-food section of a grocery store. The products without substantial backing and the ability to generate sales will be in trouble. In this case, being a comfortable number three in the category is risky.

Market Trends

Trends within the market can affect current or future strategies and assessments of market profitability. For example, an important trend in luxury hotels is business suites that include a host of amenities, such as a living room/den with a library of books and VCR movies, Internet access, a well-stocked refrigerator, and elegant furnishings. Several chains are aggressively building and promoting all-suite hotels. Such hotels, particularly popular among businesswomen, have an occupancy rate of 70 percent, about 6 percent higher than that of all hotels.

Trends in the frozen-novelty industry include the demand for "healthy" snacks, the exploitation of strong brand names such as Dole, the consolidation of competitors, product proliferation, and increased promotion and advertising.

Key Success Factors

A key success factor is any competitive asset or competence that is needed to win in the marketplace, whether it is an SCA (actually representing a sustainable point of advantage) or merely a point of parity with the company's competitors. In the luxury hotel business, key success factors might be characteristics that contribute to image, such as ambience or quality of service.

In the e-commerce arena, three key success factors are emerging that impact the emerging ability to track individual buying habits and motivations, to tailor the product offering and its presentation to specific customers, and to interact with customers. The firms that gain position in the short run and become contenders for winning in the long-run will address those key success factors.

Environmental Analysis

Important forces outside an organization's immediate markets and competitors will shape its operation and thrust. Environmental analysis, the subject of Chapter 6, is the process of identifying and understanding emerging opportunities and threats created by these forces. It is important to limit environmental analysis to what is manageable and relevant, because it can easily get bogged down by excessive scope and volume. It is helpful to divide environmental analysis into five components: technological, governmental, cultural, economic, and demographic.

A technological development can dramatically change an industry and create difficult decisions for those who are committed to profitable, old technologies. For example, the microprocessor, the Internet, and wireless communication have changed a host of industries. Information technology has created a significant advantage for those hotels able to develop and exploit systems that allow them to service customers more efficiently and with a personalized touch.

The governmental environment can be especially important to multinational corporations that operate in politically sensitive countries. A luxury hotel chain may be interested in building codes and restrictions that might affect new hotels it is planning.

Strategic judgments in many contexts are affected by the cultural environment. For example, the key success factor for many clothing industries is the capability to be in tune with current fashion, and understanding the reasons behind the public's interest in nutrition and health is important to strategists in the frozen-novelty business.

Knowledge of the economic environment facing a country or an industry helps in projecting that industry's sales over time and in identifying special risks or threats. The hotel industry, for example, can see a link between the overall health of the economy and its primary customer segments. When the economy is down, travel, especially business travel, also turns down.

Demographic trends are important to many firms. Age patterns are crucial to those whose customers are in certain age groups, such as infants, students, baby boomers, or retirees. The frozen-novelty industry was fighting a losing demographic battle until it developed products that appealed to adults as well as children. Geographic patterns can affect the investment decisions of such service firms as hotels.

A strategic uncertainty stimulated by any external analysis component can generate an information-need area, a strategically important area for which there is likely to be a continuing need for information. Special studies and ongoing information gathering might be justified.

A strategic uncertainty can also be used to create two or three future scenarios, relatively comprehensive views of the future environment. One scenario might be optimistic, another pessimistic, and a third in between. For example, a pessimistic scenario for the frozen-novelty business in five years might depict a high level of competition in terms of the number and intensity of competitors. Each scenario should have strategic implications.

INTERNAL ANALYSIS

Internal analysis, presented in Chapter 7 and summarized in Figure 2.1, aims to provide a detailed understanding of strategically important aspects of the organization. In particular, it covers performance analysis and an examination of the key determinants of strategy, such as strengths, weaknesses, and strategic problems. Internal analysis, like external analysis, usually has a business unit as a frame of reference but can also be productive at the level of aggregations of businesses, such as divisions or firms.

Performance Analysis

Profitability and sales provide an evaluation of past strategies and an indication of the current market viability of a product line. Return on assets (ROA), the most commonly used measure of profitability, needs to be compared to the cost of capital in order to determine if the business is adding value for the shareholder. ROA can be distorted by the limitations of accounting measures—in particular, it ignores intangible assets, such as brand equity. Sales is another performance measure that can reflect changes in the customer base that have long-term implications.

Shareholder value analysis is based on generating a discounted present value of the cash flow associated with a strategy. It is theoretically sound and appropriately forward-looking (as opposed to current financials that measure the results of past strategies). However, it focuses attention on financial measures rather than on other indicators of strategic performance. Developing the needed estimates is difficult and subject to a variety of biases.

Other, nonfinancial performance measures often provide better measures of long-term business health:

- *Customer satisfaction/brand loyalty:* How are we doing relative to our competitors at attracting customers and building loyalty?
- *Product/service quality:* Is our product delivering value to the customer and is it performing as intended?
- *Brand/firm associations:* What do our customers associate with our business in terms of perceived quality, innovativeness, product class expertise, customer orientation, and so on?
- *Relative cost:* Are we at a cost disadvantage with respect to materials, assembly, product design, or wages?
- *New product activity:* Do we have a stream of new products or product improvements that have made an impact?
- *Manager/employee capability and performance:* Have we created the type, quantity, and depth of personnel needed to support projected strategies?

Product Portfolio Analysis

This analysis considers the performance/strength of each business area, together with the attractiveness of the business area in which it competes. One goal is to generate a business mix with an appropriate balance between new and mature products. An organization that lacks a flow of new products faces stagnation or decline. A balance must also exist between products that generate cash and those that use cash.

Determinants of Strategic Options

Internal analysis should also review characteristics of the business that will influence strategic options. Five areas are noted in Figure 2.1: past and current strategy, strategic problems, organizational capabilities and constraints, financial resources and constraints, and strengths and weaknesses.

Strategy Review

The past and current strategy provides an important reference point and should be understood. Has the strategy been one of milking, maintenance, or growth? What has been the value proposition? What are its target segments: What are the assets and competencies that would be the basis for a sustainable competitive advantage?

Strategic Problems

A strategic problem is one that, if uncorrected, could have damaging strategic implications. An airline faces a strategic problem if it needs to finance new equipment. An instrument firm may have a quality problem. A weakness is more a characteristic, such as a bad location, that the organization may have to endure. In general, problems are corrected, and weaknesses are neutralized by a strategy or overcome by strengths.

Organizational Capabilities and Constraints

Internal analysis includes an examination of the internal organization, its structure, systems, people, and culture. The internal organization can be important strategically when it is a source of:

- **A strength**—The culture in some firms can be so strong and positive as to provide the basis for a sustainable competitive advantage.
- **A weakness**—A firm may lack the marketing personnel to compete in a business in which a key success factor is marketing.
- **A constraint**—A proposed strategy must fit the internal organization. A realistic appraisal of an organization may preclude some strategies.

Financial Resources and Constraints

An analysis of the financial resources available for investment, either from planned cash flow or from debt financing, helps determine how much net investment should be considered. One result could be a financial constraint, such as having only $20 million per year available for investment during the next few years.

Strengths and Weaknesses

Future strategies are often developed by building on strengths and neutralizing weaknesses. Strengths and weaknesses are based on assets, such as a brand name, or competencies, such as advertising or manufacturing.

GALLO: A CASE STUDY

At one time, the E. & J. Gallo Winery produced roughly one out of every four bottles of wine sold in the United States, primarily in the form of cheap wines sold under the Gallo name. Sales of higher-end varietal wines grew at double-digit rates through most of the 1990s, however, sales of "jug" wines like Gallo were shrinking.

To adapt to this change in the market, Gallo entered the premium wine business with a series of better wines. The firm used the Gallo family heritage to build a franchise with such brands as Ernest & Julio Gallo Coastal Vineyards, Ernest & Julio Gallo Sonoma, Ernest & Julio Gallo Sycamore Canyon, and Turning Leaf from Ernest and Julio Gallo. Several of these brands were sold to restaurants in order to achieve credibility. There was even a reverse snobbery effect, as some wine connoisseurs prided themselves as recognizing fine wine "despite" the Gallo name on the label. As part of the strategy, the Gallo brand name was withdrawn from the low end of the market, which was instead serviced by Gallo brands such as Carlo Rossi, Peter Vella boxed wine, and Wild Vines.

The firm enjoyed several potential sustainable competitive advantages in addition to the Gallo family tradition (which, of course, was a mixed blessing in the U.S. because of its jug wine associations). The grapes available to Gallo from Sonoma country in Northern California—whose climate, some say, is superior to the famous Napa region—coupled with the company's willingness and ability to make great wine, have resulted in a product that has won some major international wine competitions. In addition, the brand gained synergies from Gallo's substantial distribution clout and operational scale efficiencies.

CREATING A VISION FOR THE BUSINESS

A business vision can play several roles for many decades. First, it can guide strategy, suggesting strategic paths for the business. Second, it can help perpetuate the core of the business and ensure that its core competencies are preserved. Third, and perhaps most important, it can inspire those in the organization by providing a purpose that is worthwhile and ennobling and that gets beyond maximizing shareholder wealth.

James Collins and Jerry Porras, in an insightful study of visionary companies, suggested that a business vision should include the following three components, as shown in Figure 2.2: core values, a core purpose, and one or more BHAGs, or "Big, Hairy, Audacious Goals."[1]

Core values, usually three to five in number, are the timeless, passionately held guiding principles of an organization. At Procter & Gamble, the core values are delivering consumer value, breakthrough innovation, and building strong brands. The core values for the Walt Disney Company might be imagination and wholesomeness, while at Nordstrom they could be service to the customer, trust, and products with style. Core values come from within the organization; they represent what the organization is at its very essence, as opposed to what it might like to be.

The **core purpose,** which should last for at least a hundred years, is the organization's reason for being that goes beyond current products and services. For 3M

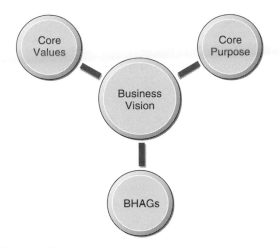

Figure 2.2   The Business Vision

the core purpose is "to solve unsolved problems innovatively." For Hewlett-Packard it is "to make technical contributions for the advancement and welfare of humanity." For McKinsey & Company it is "to help leading corporations and governments to be more successful." For Merck it is "to preserve and improve human life." And for the Walt Disney Company it is "to make people happy." One approach to finding a core purpose is to ask five whys. Start with a description of the business and ask, "Why is that important?" five times; after a few whys you get to the very essence of the business.

BHAGs (big, hairy, audacious goals) provide a clear and compelling aspiration and challenge. They can take several forms, such as focusing on a:

- *Sales goal.* Throughout its history, Wal-Mart has set extremely specific ambitious sales goals.
- *Common enemy.* The Adidas organization has been focused on and been energized by the goal of competing with a common enemy, Nike.
- *Role model.* Watkins-Johns has wanted to be as respected as Hewlett-Packard.
- *Internal transformation.* Rockwell aspired to transform the company into the best-diversified high-technology company in the world.

One challenge is to distinguish between BHAGs that are simply bravado or wishful thinking and those that are genuinely effective. James Collins identified eleven companies (which he termed "good to great" companies) that achieved a return three times that of the stock market over fifteen years.[2] One conclusion he reached is that in comparison to reference companies, the good-to-great firms had BHAGs which satisfied three criteria:

- *The BHAG leveraged something in which the organization excelled.* For Wells Fargo, it was running a bank in the western United States, as opposed to a global financial services business. For Abbott Laboratories, it was creating hospital nutritional products and diagnostic devices, rather than being a pharmaceutical company.

- *The BHAG resulted in economic value by moving the needle with respect to key economic metrics.* For Wells Fargo and Abbott Labs, the key metric was profit-per-employee (as opposed to profit-per-loan, or profit-per-precut line).

- *The BHAG was something the organization was deeply passionate about.* It went beyond short-term financials into something that made employees feel worthwhile and provided a customer value proposition which mattered.

STRATEGY IDENTIFICATION AND SELECTION

The purpose of external analysis and internal analysis is twofold: to help generate strategic alternatives and to provide criteria for selecting from among them.

Figure 2.3 highlights the four dimensions of a business strategy. The first is selecting the product markets in which the firm will operate and deciding how much investment should be allocated to each; the second is determining the customer value proposition; the third is identifying the assets and competencies leading to sustainable competitive advantages; and the fourth is to develop functional area strategies.

GENERIC CUSTOMER NEED

In his classic article, "Marketing Myopia," Theodore Levitt suggested that firms that myopically define their business in product terms can stagnate even though the basic customer need that they are serving is enjoying healthy growth.[3] Because of a myopic product focus, others gain the benefits of growth. Thus, if firms regard themselves as being in the transportation rather than the railroad business, the energy instead of the petroleum business, or the communication rather than the telephone business, they are more likely to exploit opportunities.

The concept is simple. Define the business in terms of the basic customer need rather than the product. Xerox changed its focus from copiers when it became the "document" company. Visa has defined itself as being in the business of enabling a customer to exchange value—to exchange any asset including cash on deposit, the cash value of life insurance, the equity in a home—for virtually anything anywhere in the world. As the business is redefined, both the set of competitors and the range of opportunities are often radically expanded. After redefining its business, Visa estimated that it had reached only 5 percent of its potential given the new definition.

Defining a business in terms of generic need can be extremely useful for fostering creativity, in generating strategic options, and avoiding an internally oriented product/production focus.

IDENTIFICATION OF STRATEGIC ALTERNATIVES

- Product-market investment strategies
  - Product-market scope
  - Growth directions
  - Investment strategies
- Customer value proposition
- Bases of competitive advantage – assets, competencies, synergies
- Functional area strategies

CRITERIA FOR STRATEGY SELECTION

- Consider scenarios suggested by strategic uncertainties and environmental opportunities/threats
- Generate an attractive ROI
- Pursue a sustainable competitive advantage
  - Exploit organizational strengths or competitor weaknesses
  - Neutralize organizational weaknesses or competitor strengths
- Be consistent with organizational vision/objectives
  - Achieve a long-term return on investment
  - Be compatible with vision/objectives
- Be feasible
  - Resources are available
  - Be compatible with the internal organization
- Consider the relationship to other strategies within the firm
  - Foster product portfolio balance
  - Consider flexibility
  - Exploit synergy

Figure 2.3   Selecting Strategic Alternatives

Product-Market Investment Strategies

Product Definition

As a practical matter, many strategic decisions involve products—which product lines to continue, which to add, and which to delete. Mother's Cookies, for instance, is in the cookie business, but not in the cracker or bakery business. Nike got back on track when it decided it was in the sports and fitness business, rather than the business of making casual sportswear.

Market Definition

Businesses need to select markets in which they will have a competitive advantage. A small California savings and loan firm defined its business as serving individual savers who lived near its office. A brokerage firm has focused on individual investors and moved away from mortgage banking. Gerber Products used age, defining its market as infants and young children. ServiceMaster has defined its business as servicing the maintenance needs of hospitals and other health-care facilities. Such statements of focus can drive the operations of a firm.

Vertical Integration

A strategic option not covered by product-market scope is vertical integration. Some publishing companies have integrated backward into paper and wood products. General Motors makes batteries, spark plugs, and a host of other components. Other firms, such as Nike and Levi Strauss, have the option of integrating forward into retailing. The question is, at what vertical levels should the business operate? The trade-offs between increased control and potential return from vertical integration on the one hand, and increased risk and loss of flexibility caused by the associated investment on the other, are discussed in detail in Chapter 13.

Growth Directions

It is crucial in strategy development to have a focus that is dynamic rather than static. The concept of a product-market matrix shown in Figure 2.4 is helpful for identifying options and encouraging a dynamic perspective.

In the product-market matrix, five growth options are shown. The first is to penetrate the existing product market. A firm may attempt to attract customers from competitors or increase usage by existing customers. A second option involves product expansion while remaining in the current market. Thus, a firm offering cleaning services to health-care facilities might expand into supervision of other health-care functions, such as purchasing and building maintenance. A third option is to apply the same products in new markets. The cleaning firm could expand its cleaning services into other industries. These first three growth options are explored in more detail in Chapter 12. The fourth growth option, to diversify into new product markets, is discussed in detail in Chapter 13. Figure 2.4 also adds another dimension to the product-market matrix representing a fifth growth option: vertical integration.

Investment Strategies

For each product market, four investment options are possible. The firm could invest to enter or grow, invest to hold the existing position, milk the business by avoiding any

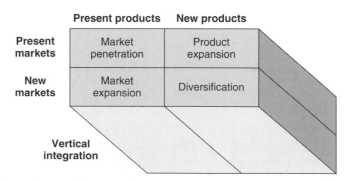

Figure 2.4   Product-Market Growth Directions

investment, or exit. The exit option might arise if prospects become extremely unattractive or if the business area becomes incompatible with the overall thrust of the firm.

Strategic Options

Even given a specification of a product-market investment plan, a business strategy will still involve choices. An organization cannot be good at all things, nor create an infinite number of assets and competencies. Value propositions and programs that are too broad and ambitious will lack credibility with customers and may end up demoralizing employees. There are an unlimited number of such choices that involve specifying the value proposition, functional area strategies, and assets and competencies that will be the bases for a sustainable competitive advantage.

These choices can be conceptualized in the form of one or more strategic options, as introduced in the last chapter and elaborated in Chapters 9, 10, and 11. These options include, but are not limited to: quality, value, focus, innovation, globalness, product attributes, product design, product-line breadth, corporate social responsibility, brand familiarity, and customer intimacy. Of course, each of these options has many variants, depending on the industry and firm context.

The strategic options will specify the following:

- *Value propositions*—what the offering provides to the buyer and user of the product or service. The value proposition is not limited to functional benefits but can include social, emotional, and self-expressive benefits.

- *Assets and competencies*—the bases for a sustainable competitive advantage. Assets and competencies usually require time, resources, and talent to create, and they are sustainable because they are often hard to replicate. Approaches to identifying candidate assets and competencies are presented in Chapter 4.

- *Functional strategies and programs*—to support the value proposition and the development and enhancement of the assets and competencies. These strategies and programs can involve such functional areas as manufacturing, distribution, information technology, quality, customer relationships, brand building, and communications.

Strategic positioning, the subject of Chapter 12, specifies how the business is to be perceived relative to its competitors and market by its customers and employees/partners. As such, it often represents the essence of a business strategy. Neiman-Marcus is positioned as a retailer with flair for fashion-conscious upscale buyers, while Harley-Davidson is the serious, powerful motorcycle for bikers who treasure the freedom of the road.

SELECTING AMONG STRATEGIC ALTERNATIVES

Figure 2.3 provides a list of some of the criteria useful for selecting alternatives, grouped into five general areas.

- **Consider scenarios.** A future scenario can be stimulated by strategic uncertainties or environmental opportunities or threats. Thus, the strategic uncertainty, "Will a breakthrough in storage batteries make a general-use electric automobile feasible?" could lead to both yes and no scenarios. The threat of severe pollution controls could also generate scenarios relevant to the strategies of automobile and energy firms. It is useful and prudent to evaluate strategic options in the context of any major scenarios identified.

- **Generate an attractive ROI.** Creating a value proposition that is appealing to customers may not be worthwhile if the investment or operating cost is excessive. Starbucks opened in Japan in 1996 in the Ginza district and grew to over 400 units, many of which were in the highest-rent areas. The result was a trendy brand, but one that was vulnerable to competitors who matched or exceeded Starbucks' product offerings and were not handicapped with such high overhead (because they developed less costly sites).

- **Pursue a sustainable competitive advantage.** A useful operational criterion is whether a sustainable competitive advantage exists as part of the strategy. Unless the business unit has or can develop a real competitive advantage that is sustainable over time in the face of competitor reaction, an attractive long-term return will be unlikely. To achieve a sustainable competitive advantage, a strategy should exploit organizational assets and competencies and neutralize weaknesses.

- **Be consistent with organizational vision and objectives.** A primary purpose of an organization's vision—what a future strategy should be—and objectives is to help make strategic decisions. Thus, it is appropriate to look toward them for guidance. They can be changed, of course, if circumstances warrant. An explicit decision to change a strategy is very different from ignoring it in the face of a tempting alternative.

- **Be feasible.** A practical criterion is that the strategy be feasible. It should be within the resources of the organization. It also should be internally consistent with other organizational characteristics, such as structure, systems, people, and culture. These organizational considerations will be covered in Chapter 16.

- **Consider the relationship to other firm strategies.** A strategy can relate to other business units by:

  - *Balancing the sources and uses of cash flow.* Some business units should generate cash and others should provide attractive places to invest that cash. Chapter 7 and 15 elaborate.

  - *Enhancing flexibility.* Flexibility is generally reduced when heavy commitments are made in the form of fixed investment, long-term contracts, and vertical integration.

  - *Exploiting synergy.* A firm that does not exploit potential synergy may be missing an opportunity.

Implementation

The implementation stage involves converting strategic alternatives into an operating plan. If a new product market is to be entered, then a systematic program is required to develop or acquire products as an entry vehicle. If a strong R&D group is to be assembled, a program to hire people, organize them, and obtain facilities will be needed. The operating plan may span more than one year. It might be useful to provide a detailed plan for the upcoming year that contains specific short-term objectives.

Strategy Review

One of the key questions in a strategic market management system is to determine when a strategy requires review and change. It is usually necessary to monitor a limited number of key measures of strategy performance and the environment. Thus, sales, market share, margins, profit, and ROA may be regularly reported and analyzed. Externally, the process is more difficult, requiring an effective information-scanning system. The heart of such a system will be an identified set of strategic uncertainties or issues that need to be continuously considered.

THE PROCESS

Figure 2.1 implies a logical, sequential process. After external and internal analyses are completed, the strategic options are then detailed and the optimal ones selected. Finally, the operating plan and strategy review program are implemented. Later, perhaps in the next annual planning cycle, the process is repeated and the plan updated.

Although Figure 2.1 provides a useful structure, the process should be more iterative and circular than sequential. The identification and selection of strategies should occur during external and internal analysis. Furthermore, the process of evaluating strategies often suggests the need for additional external analysis, making it necessary to cycle through the process several times. As suggested earlier, strategies and indicators of the need to change them should be continually monitored to avoid being tied to an annual planning cycle. The process supporting the development of business strategies is covered in Chapter 16.

KEY LEARNINGS

- External analysis includes analyses of customers, competitors, markets, and the environment. The role of these analyses is to identify existing or emerging opportunities, threats, trends, strategic uncertainties, and strategic options.
- Internal analysis includes a performance appraisal and an examination of organizational strengths, weaknesses, problems, constraints, and strategic options.

- Business vision should specify the core values (timeless guiding principles), core purpose (reason for being), and BHAGs (big, hairy, audacious goals).

- A business strategy specification includes the product-market scope and the selection of a set of strategic options that include the value proposition, assets and competencies, and strategies for functional areas.

- Strategy selection should consider scenarios, ROI prospects, SCAs, the organization vision, strategy feasibility, and other firm strategies.

FOR DISCUSSION

1. Consider the Gallo strategic decision. Evaluate or describe how you would go about evaluating that decision with respect to the criteria in Figure 2.3. Create a hypothetical BHAG for Gallo and evaluate it with respect to the three criteria for good BHAGs.

2. What is the difference between key success factors and sustainable competitive advantages? Illustrate your understanding by discussing several constructs such as the cola market or the luxury car market.

3. Which quote from the beginning of either Chapter 1 or Chapter 2 do you find the most insightful? Why?

NOTES

1. For a discussion of the business vision see James C. Collins and Jerry I. Porras, "Building Your Company's Vision," *Harvard Business Review*, September–October 1996, pp. 65–77. The authors also include a fourth element: a "vivid description" of the envisioned future. For a description of the study of visionary companies see the authors' excellent book *Built to Last: Successful Habits of Visionary Companies*, HarperBusiness, New York, 1994.

2. Jim Collins, *Good to Great*, New York: Harper Business, 2003, p. 95.

3. Theodore Levitt, "Marketing Myopia," *Harvard Business Review*, July–August 1960, pp. 45–56.

PART TWO

STRATEGIC ANALYSIS

CHAPTER THREE

External and
Customer Analysis

To be prepared is half the victory.
—*Miguel Cervantes*

The purpose of an enterprise is to create and keep a customer.
—*Theodore Levitt*

Consumers are statistics. Customers are people.
—*Stanley Marcus*

Strategy development or review logically starts with external analysis, an analysis of the factors external to a business that can affect strategy. The first four chapters of Part Two present concepts and methods useful in conducting an external analysis. The final chapter of Part Two turns to internal analysis: the analysis of the firm's strengths, weaknesses, problems, constraints, and options.

EXTERNAL ANALYSIS

A successful external analysis needs to be directed and purposeful. There is always the danger that it will become an endless process resulting in an excessively descriptive report. In any business there is no end to the material that appears potentially relevant. Without discipline and direction, volumes of useless descriptive material can easily be generated.

Affecting Strategic Decisions

The external analysis process should not be an end in itself. Rather, it should be motivated throughout by a desire to affect strategy, to generate or evaluate strategic options. As Figure 3.1 shows, it can impact strategy directly by suggesting strategic decision alternatives or influencing a choice among them. More specifically, it should contribute to the investment decision and the development of a strategic option that includes the value proposition, assets and competencies, and functional strategies and programs.

The investment decision—where to compete—involves questions like:

- Should existing business areas be liquidated, milked, maintained, or a target for investment?
- What growth directions should receive investment?
- Should there be market penetration, product expansion, or market expansion?
- Should new business areas be entered?

The selection of strategic options—that is, how to compete—suggests questions like the following:

- What are the value propositions?
- What are the key success factors?
- What assets and competencies should be created, enhanced, or maintained?
- What strategies and programs should be implemented in functional areas?
- What should be the positioning strategy, segmentation strategy, distribution strategy, brand-building strategy, manufacturing strategy, and so on?

Additional Analysis Objectives

Figure 3.1 also suggests that an external analysis can contribute to strategy indirectly by identifying:

- Significant trends and future events.
- Threats and opportunities.
- Strategic uncertainties that could affect strategy outcomes.

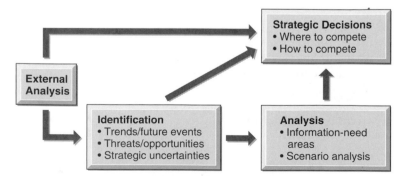

Figure 3.1   The Role of External Analysis

A significant trend or event, such as concern about saturated fat or the emergence of a new competitor, can dramatically affect the evaluation of strategy options. A new technology can represent both a threat to an established firm and an opportunity to a prospective competitor.

Strategic Uncertainties

Strategic uncertainty is a particularly useful concept in conducting an external analysis. If you could know the answer to one question prior to making a strategic commitment, what would that question be? If the Buick car division of General Motors were to consider whether to add a gas-electric hybrid to its line, important strategy uncertainties might include the following:

- What will the automotive sales profile of hybrids be in upcoming years? How many will be sold in what categories?
- What will be the hybrid strategies of Buick's direct competitors?
- What new technologies might emerge that will affect the demand for hybrids?

Strategic uncertainties focus on specific unknown elements that will affect the outcome of strategic decisions. "Should Buick extend its line to hybrids?" is a strategic decision, whereas "What is the future demand for hybrids?" is a strategic uncertainty. Most strategic decisions will be driven by a set of these uncertainties.

Below are some examples of strategic uncertainties and the strategic decisions to which they might relate. A strategic uncertainty can often lead to additional sources of strategic uncertainty. One common strategic uncertainty, as portrayed in the figure on the top of page 42, is what the future demand for a product (such as ultrasound diagnostic equipment) will be. Asking, "On what does that depend?" will usually generate additional strategic uncertainties. One uncertainty might address technological improvements, whereas another might consider the technological development and cost/benefit levels achieved by competitive technologies. Still another might look into the financial capacity of the healthcare industry to continue capital improvements. Each of these strategic uncertainties can, in turn, generate still another level of strategic uncertainties.

Strategic Uncertainties	Strategic Decisions
• Will a major firm enter?	• Investment in a product market
• Will a tofu-based dessert product be accepted?	• Investment in a tofu-based product
• Will a technology be replaced?	• Investment in a technology
• Will the dollar strengthen against an offshore currency?	• Commitment to offshore manufacturing
• Will computer-based operations be feasible with current technology?	• Investment in a new system
• How sensitive is the market to price?	• A strategy of maintaining price parity

Strategic Uncertainties	Second-Level Strategic Uncertainties
	• Performance improvements?
• What will be the future demand?	• Competitive technological developments?
	• Financial capacity of health care industry?

Analysis

There are three ways of handling uncertainty, as suggested by Figure 3.1. First, a strategic decision can be precipitated because the logic for a decision is compelling and/or because a delay would be costly or risky. Second, it may be worthwhile to attempt to reduce the uncertainty by information acquisition and analysis of an information-need area. The effort could range from a high-priority task force to a low-key monitoring effort. The level of resources expended will depend on the potential impact on strategy and its immediacy. Third, the uncertainty could be modeled by a scenario analysis.

A scenario is an alternative view of the future environment that is usually prompted by an alternative possible answer to a strategic uncertainty or by a prospective future event or trend. Is the current popularity of fresh juice bars a fad or does it indicate a solid growth area? Such a question could be the basis for a positive and a negative scenario. Each could be associated with very different environmental profiles and strategy recommendations. In Chapter 6, information-need areas and scenario analysis will be covered in more detail.

A host of concepts and methods are introduced in this and the following three chapters. It would, of course, be unusual to employ all of them in any given context, and the strategist should resist any compulsion to do so. Rather, those that are most relevant to the situation at hand should be selected. Furthermore, some areas of analysis will be more fruitful than others and will merit more effort.

External Analysis as a Creative Exercise

In part, external analysis is an exercise in creative thinking. In fact, there is often too little effort devoted to developing new strategic options and too much effort directed to solving operational problems of the day. The essence of creative thinking is considering different perspectives, and that is exactly what an external analysis does. The strategist is challenged to look at strategy from the perspectives of customer, competitor, market, and environment as well as from an internal perspective. Within each there are several subdimensions. In Figure 2.1 more than two dozen are identified. The hope is that by examining strategy from different viewpoints, options will be generated that would otherwise be missed.

The Level of Analysis–Defining the Market

An external analysis of what? To conduct an external analysis, the market or submarket boundaries need to be specified. The scope of external analysis can involve an industry such as:

- Sporting goods
- Ski clothing and equipment
- Skis and snowboards
- Downhill skis
- High-performance skis

envergure de marché

The level of analysis will depend on the organizational unit and strategic decisions involved. A sporting goods company, such as Wilson, will be making resource decisions across sports and thus needs to be concerned with the whole industry. A ski equipment manufacturer may only be concerned with elements of sporting goods relating to skis, boots, and clothing. The maker of high-performance skis might be interested in only a subsegment of the ski industry. One approach to defining the market is to specify the business scope. The scope can be identified in terms of the product market and in terms of the competitors. Relevant, of course, are the future product market and competitors as well as the present.

There is always a trade-off to be made. A narrow scope specification will inhibit a business from identifying trends and opportunities that could lead to some attractive options and directions. Thus, a maker of downhill skis may want to include snowboards and cross-country skis because they represent business options or because they will impact the ski equipment business. On the other hand, depth of analysis might be sacrificed when the scope is excessively broad. A more focused analysis may generate more insight.

The analysis usually needs to be conducted at several levels. The downhill ski and snowboard industry might be the major focus of the analysis. However, an analysis of sporting goods might suggest and shed light on some substitute product pressures and market trends. Also, an analysis may be needed at the segment level (e.g., high-performance skis) because entry, investment, and strategy decisions are often made at that level. Furthermore, the key success factors could differ for different product markets within a market or industry. One approach is a layered analysis, with the primary level receiving the most depth of analysis. Another approach could be multiple analyses, perhaps consecutively conducted. The first analysis might stimulate an opportunity that would justify a second analysis.

When Should an External Analysis Be Conducted?

There is often a tendency to relegate the external analysis to an annual exercise. Each year, of course, it may not require the same depth as the initial effort. It may be more productive to focus on a part of the analysis in the years immediately following a major effort.

The annual planning cycle can provide a healthy stimulus to review and change strategies. However, a substantial risk exists in maintaining external analysis as an annual event. The need for strategic review and change is often continuous. Information sensing and analysis therefore also need to be continuous. The framework and concepts of external analysis can still play a key role in providing structure even when the analysis is continuous and addresses only a portion of the whole.

External analysis deliberately commences with customer and competitor analyses because they can help define the relevant industry or industries. An industry can be defined in terms of the needs of a specific group of customers—those buying fresh cookies on the West Coast, for instance. Such an industry definition then forms the basis for the identification of competitors and the balance of external analysis. An industry such as the cookie industry can also be defined in terms of all its competitors.

Because customers have such a direct relationship to a firm's operation, they are usually a rich source of relevant operational opportunities, threats, and uncertainties.

THE SCOPE OF CUSTOMER ANALYSIS

In most strategic market-planning contexts, the first logical step is to analyze the customers. Customer analysis can be usefully partitioned into an understanding of how the market segments, an analysis of customer motivations, and an exploration of unmet needs. Figure 3.2 presents a basic set of questions for each area of inquiry.

SEGMENTATION

Segmentation is often the key to developing a sustainable competitive advantage. In a strategic context, *segmentation* means the identification of customer groups that respond differently from other groups to competitive offerings. A segmentation strategy couples the identified segments with a program to deliver an offering to those

---

SEGMENTATION

- Who are the biggest customers? The most profitable? The most attractive potential customers? Do the customers fall into any logical groups based on needs, motivations, or characteristics?
- How could the market be segmented into groups that would require a unique business strategy?

CUSTOMER MOTIVATIONS

- What elements of the product/service do customers value most?
- What are the customers' objectives? What are they really buying?
- How do segments differ in their motivation priorities?
- What changes are occurring in customer motivation? In customer priorities?

UNMET NEEDS

- Why are some customers dissatisfied? Why are some changing brands or suppliers?
- What are the severity and incidence of consumer problems?
- What are unmet needs that customers can identify? Are there some of which consumers are unaware?
- Do these unmet needs represent leverage points for competitors?

Figure 3.2   Customer Analysis

segments. Thus, the development of a successful segmentation strategy requires the conceptualization, development, and evaluation of a targeted competitive offering.

A segmentation strategy should be judged on three dimensions. First, can a competitive offering be developed and implemented that will be appealing to the target segment? Second, can the appeal of the offering and the subsequent relationship with the target segment be maintained over time despite competitive responses? Third, is the resulting business from the target segment worthwhile, given the investment required to develop and market an offering tailored to it? The concept behind a successful segmentation strategy is that within a reduced market space, it is possible to create a dominant position that competitors will be unwilling or unable to attack successfully.

How Should Segments Be Defined?

The task of identifying segments is difficult, in part, because in any given context there are literally hundreds of ways to divide up the market. Typically, the analysis will consider five, ten, or more segmentation variables. To avoid missing a useful way of defining segments, it is important to consider a wide range of variables. These variables need to be evaluated on the basis of their ability to identify segments for which different strategies are (or should be) pursued.

The most useful segment-defining variables for an offering are rarely obvious. Among the variables frequently used are those shown in Figure 3.3.

The first set of variables describes segments in terms of general characteristics unrelated to the product involved. Thus, a bakery might be concerned with geographically defined segments related to communities or even neighborhoods. A consulting company may specialize in the hospitality industry. A fast food firm in the United States may target Hispanics because this segment is projected to grow to 44 million people in 2010.

Demographics are particularly powerful for defining segments, in part because a person's life stage affects his or her activities, interests, and brand loyalties. Another reason is that demographic trends are predictable. The U.S. population over 65 is expected to grow to 50 million in 2020, when more than 5 million people will be 85 or older. Gold Violin, recognizing this trend, has established itself as a source of products designed for the active elderly. Specialized items such as a talking watch, a bed-vibrating alarm clock, a doorknob turner, and a lighted hands-free magnifier (all with tasteful, attractive designs) are just some of the Gold Violin products that appeal to this long-ignored demographic segment.

Another demographic play is represented by the Toyota Scion, a small car with a funky design (tall, angular, and boxy) aimed at Generation Y, the so-called echo boomers. The average age of a Toyota buyer is 48, the company's inexpensive entries are considered boring, and Scion is an effort to become relevant and interesting to a key target segment. To create a buzz around Scion so that it appeals to the next generation of drivers, Toyota is aiming at the 15% of the echo-boomer target market who are seen as "leaders and influencers"—those who encourage their peers to gravitate to a new style, whether it be in music, sports, or cars. If a product can get acceptance in that group, the argument is that other buyers will follow.[1]

CUSTOMER CHARACTERISTICS

- Geographic
- Small Southern communities as markets for discount stores
- Type of organization
- Computer needs of restaurants versus manufacturing firms versus banks versus retailers
- Size of firm
- Large hospital versus medium versus small
- Lifestyle
- Jaguar buyers tend to be more adventurous, less conservative than buyers of Mercedes-Benz and BMW
- Sex
- Mothers of young children
- Age
- Cereals for children versus adults
- Occupation
- The paper copier needs of lawyers versus bankers versus dentists

PRODUCT-RELATED APPROACHES

- User type
- Appliance buyer—home builder, remodeler, home owner
- Usage
- Concert—season ticket holders, occasional patrons, nonusers
- Benefits sought
- Dessert eaters—those who are calorie-conscious versus those who are more concerned with convenience
- Price sensitivity
- Price-sensitive Honda Civic buyer versus the luxury Mercedes-Benz buyer
- Competitor
- Users of competing products
- Application
- Professional users of chain saws versus home owners
- Brand loyalty
- Those committed to Heinz ketchup versus price buyers

Figure 3.3 Examples of Approaches to Defining Segments

The second category of segment variables includes those that are related to the product. One of the most frequently employed is usage. A bakery may follow a very different strategy in serving restaurants that rely heavily on bakery products than in serving those that use fewer such products. A manufacturer of lawn equipment may design a special line for a large customer such as Wal-Mart, but sell through distributors using another brand name for other outlets. Four other useful segment variables are benefits, price sensitivity, loyalty, and applications.

Benefits

If there is a most useful segmentation variable, it would be benefits sought from a product, because the selection of benefits can determine a total business strategy. In gourmet frozen dinners/entrées, for example, the market can be divided into buyers who are calorie-conscious, those who focus on nutrition and health, those interested in taste, and the price-conscious buyers. Each segment implies a very different strategy.

Price Sensitivity

The benefit dimension representing the trade-off between low price and high quality is both useful and pervasive; hence it is appropriate to consider it separately. In many product classes, there is a well-defined breakdown between those customers concerned first about price and others who are willing to pay extra for higher quality and features. General merchandise stores, for example, form a well-defined hierarchy from the discounters to the prestige department stores. Automobiles span the spectrum from the Honda Civic to the Lexus to the Rolls Royce. Airline service is partitioned into first class, business class, and economy class. In each case the segment dictates the strategy.

Loyalty

Brand loyalty, an important consideration in allocating resources, can be structured using a loyalty matrix as shown in Figure 3.4.[2] Each cell represents a very different strategic priority and can justify a very different program. Generally it is too easy to take the loyal customer for granted. However, a perspective of total profits over the life of a customer makes the value of an increase in loyalty more vivid. A study by Bain shows that a 5 percent increase in loyalty can nearly double the lifetime profits generated by customers in several industries, including banking, insurance, automobile service, publishing, and credit cards.[3] The key is often to reward the loyal customer by living up to expectations consistently, providing an ongoing relationship, and offering extras that surprise and delight.

The loyalty matrix suggests that the brand fence-sitters, including those of competitors, should also have high priority. Using the matrix involves estimating the size of each of the six cells, identifying the customers in each group, and designing programs that will influence their brand choice and loyalty level.

Applications

Some products and services, particularly industrial products, can best be segmented by use or application. A portable computer may be needed by some for use while traveling, whereas others may need a computer at the office that can be conveniently stored when not in use. One segment may use a computer for word processing and another may be more interested in data processing. Some might use a four-wheel drive for light industrial hauling and others may be buying primarily for recreation.

	Low Loyalty	Moderate Loyalty	Loyal
Customer	Medium	High	Highest
Noncustomer	Low to Medium	High	Zero

Figure 3.4 The Loyalty Matrix: Priorities

The athletic shoe industry segments into the serious athletes (small in number but influential), the weekend warriors, and the casual wearers using athletic shoes for street wear. Recognizing that the casual wearer segment is 80 percent of the market and does not really need performance, several shoe firms have employed a style-focused strategy as an alternative to the performance strategy adopted by such firms as Nike.

Multiple Segments versus a Focus Strategy

Two distinct segmentation strategies are possible. The first focuses on a single segment, which can be much smaller than the market as a whole. Wal-Mart, now the largest U.S. retailer, started by concentrating on cities with populations under 25,000 in eleven south central states, a segment totally neglected by its competition, the large discount chains. This rural geographic focus strategy was directly responsible for several significant SCAs, including an efficient and responsive warehouse supply system, a low-cost, motivated workforce, relatively inexpensive retail space, and a lean and mean, hands-on management style. Union Bank, California's eighth largest bank, makes no effort to serve individuals and thus provides a service operation tailored to business accounts that is more committed and comprehensive than those of its competitors.

An alternative to a focusing strategy is to involve multiple segments. General Motors provides the classic example. In the 1920s the firm positioned the Chevrolet for price-conscious buyers, the Cadillac for the high end, and the Oldsmobile, Pontiac, and Buick for well-defined segments in between. A granulated potato company has developed different strategies for reaching fast-food chains, hospitals and nursing homes, and schools and colleges.

In many industries aggressive firms are moving toward multiple-segment strategies. Campbell Soup, for example, makes its nacho cheese soup spicier for customers in Texas and California and offers a Creole soup for southern markets and a red-bean soup for Hispanic markets. In New York, Campbell uses promotions linking Swanson frozen dinners with the New York Giants football team, and in the Sierra Nevada mountains, skiers are treated to hot soup samples. Developing multiple strategies is costly and often must be justified by an enhanced aggregate impact.

There can be important synergies between segment offerings. For example, in the alpine ski industry, the image developed by high-performance skis is important to sales at the recreational-ski end of the business. Thus, a manufacturer that is weak at the high end will have difficulty at the low end. Conversely, a successful high-end firm will want to exploit that success by having entries in the other segments. A key success factor in the general aviation industry is a broad product line, ranging from fixed-gear, single-engine piston aircraft to turboprop planes, because customers tend to trade up and will switch to a different firm if the product line has major gaps.

CUSTOMER MOTIVATIONS

After identifying customer segments, the next step is to consider their motivations: What lies behind their purchase decisions? And how does that differ by segment? It is helpful to list the segments and the motivation priorities of each, as shown in Figure 3.5 for air travelers.

Internet retailers have learned that there are distinct shopper segments, and each has a very different set of driving motivations.[4]

- ***Newbie shoppers***—need a simple interface, as well as a lot of hand-holding and reassurance.

- ***Reluctant shoppers***—need information, reassurance, and access to live customer support.

- ***Frugal shoppers***—need to be convinced that the price is good and they don't have to search elsewhere.

- ***Strategic shoppers***—need access to the opinions of peers or experts, and choices in configuring the products they buy.

- ***Enthusiastic shoppers***—need community tools to share their experiences, as well as engaging tools to view the merchandise and personalized recommendations.

- ***Convenience shoppers***—(the largest group) wants efficient navigation, a lot of information from customers and experts, and superior customer service.

Some motivations will help to define strategy. A truck, for example, might be designed and positioned with respect to power. Before making such a strategic commitment, it is crucial to know where power fits in the motivation set. Other motivations may not define a strategy or differentiate a business, but represent a dimension for which adequate performance must be obtained or the battle will be lost. If the prime motivation for buyers of gourmet frozen-food dinners is taste, a viable firm must be able to deliver at least acceptable taste.

Determining Motivations

As Figure 3.6 suggests, consumer motivation analysis starts with the task of identifying motivations for a given segment. Although a group of managers can identify motivations, a more valid list is usually obtained by getting customers to discuss the product or service in a systematic way. Why is it being used? What is the objective? What is associated with a good or bad use experience? For a motivation such as car safety, respondents might be asked why safety is important. Such probes might result in the identification of more basic motives, such as the desire to feel calm and secure rather than anxious.

Segment	Motivation
Business	Reliable service, convenient schedules, easy-to-use airports, frequent-flyer programs, and comfortable service
Vacationers	Price, feasible schedules

Figure 3.5   Customer Motivation Grid: Air Travelers

Figure 3.6   Customer Motivation Analysis

Customers can be accessed with group or individual interviews. Griffin and Hauser of the MIT Quality Function Deployment (QFD) program compared the two approaches in a study of food-carrying devices.[5] They found that individual interviews were more cost-effective and that the group processes did not generate enough extra information to warrant the added expense. They also explored the number of interviews needed to gain a complete list of motivations and concluded that twenty to thirty will cover 90 to 95 percent of the motivations.

The number of motivations can be in the hundreds, so the next task is to cluster them into groups and subgroups. Affinity charts developed by a managerial team are commonly used. Each team member is given a set of motives on cards. One member puts a motive on the table or pins it to a wall, and the others add similar

BUYER HOT BUTTONS

Motivations can be categorized as important or unimportant, yet the dynamics of the market may be better captured by identifying current buyer hot buttons. Hot buttons are motivations whose salience and impact on markets are significant and growing. What are buyers talking about? What are stimulating changes in buying decisions and use patterns?

In consumer retail food products, for example, hot buttons include:

- Freshness and naturalness. Grocery stores have responded with salad bars, packaged precut vegetables, and efforts to upgrade the quality and selection of their fresh produce.
- Healthy eating. Low fat is a prime driver, but concern about sodium, sugar, and processed foods is also growing and affecting product offerings in most food categories.
- Ethnic eating. A growing interest in ethnic flavors and cooking such as Asian, Mediterranean, and Caribbean cuisines, has led to an explosion of new offerings. Brands usually start in ethnic neighborhoods, move into natural-food and gourmet stores, and finally reach the mainstream markets.
- Gourmet eating. The success of Williams-Sonoma and similar retailers reflects the growth of gourmet cooking and has led to the introduction of a broader array of interesting cooking aids and devices.
- Meal solutions. The desire for meal solutions has led to groups of products being bundled together as a meal and to a host of carryout prepared foods offered by both grocery stores and restaurants.
- Low-carb foods. The influence of low-carb diets has created a demand for reduced carb food variants in both grocery stores and restaurants.

cards to the pile, discussing the decision to do so. The process continues until there is a consensus that the piles represent reasonable groupings. Each pile is then structured into a hierarchy with the more general and strategic motives at the top and the more specific and tactical at the bottom.

An alternative is to use customers or groups of customers to sort the motives into piles. The customers are then asked to select one card from each pile that best represents their motives. When a set of customers or groups go through the exercise, the judgments can be combined using cluster analysis statistical programs. Although managers gain buy-in and learning by going through the process themselves, Griffin and Hauser report that in the twenty applications at one firm, the managers considered customer-based approaches better representations than their own.

Another task of customer motivation analysis is to determine the relative importance of the motivations. Again, the management team can address this issue. Alternatively, customers can be asked to assess the importance of the motivations directly or perhaps through trade-off questions. If an engineer had to sacrifice response time or accuracy in an oscilloscope, which would it be? Or, how would an airline passenger trade off convenient departure time with price? The trade-off question asks customers to make difficult judgments about attributes. Another approach is to see which judgments are associated with actual purchase decisions. Such an approach revealed that mothers often selected snack food based on what "the child likes" and what was "juicy" instead of qualities they had said were important (nourishing and easy-to-eat).

A fourth task is to identify the motivations that will play a role in defining the strategy of the business. The selection of motivations central to strategy will depend not only on customer motivations, but on other factors as well, such as competitors' strategies that emerge in the competitor analysis. Another factor is how feasible and practical the resulting strategy is for the business. Internal analysis will be involved in making that determination, as will an analysis of the strategy's implementation.

Qualitative Research

Qualitative research is a powerful tool in understanding customer motivation. It can involve focus-group sessions, in-depth interviews, customer case studies, or on-site customer visits. The concept is to search for the real motivations that do not emerge from structured lists. For instance, buyers of sports utility vehicles might really be expressing their youth or a youthful attitude. The perception that a product is too expensive might really reflect a financing gap. Getting inside the customer can provide strategic insights that do not emerge any other way.

Modeling the customer experience from beginning to end, then analyzing each step, can result in detailed insights that can generate real change. Canadian Pacific (CP) Hotels was proficient with conventions and group travel, for example, but was weak among business travelers.[6] Customer research indicated that these customers were not motivated as much by a rewards program as they were by getting over-the-top responsiveness to problems, recognition of their individual needs, and lots of flexibility with respect to arrival and departure times. Modeling the experience of these travelers from parking to checkout provided direction as to what standards were needed with respect to processes, staffing, and interaction patterns. As a result of improving its standards, CP Hotels enjoyed a 16% jump in its share of the Canadian business travel market.

Although a representative cross section of customers is usually sought, special attention to some is often merited. Very loyal customers are often best able to articulate the bonds that the firm is capable of establishing. Lost customers (those who have defected) are often particularly good at graphically communicating problems with the product or service. New customers or customers who have recently increased their usage may suggest new applications. Those using multiple vendors may have a good perspective of the firm relative to the competition.

Changing Customer Priorities

It is particularly critical to gain insight into changes in customers' priorities.[7] In the high-tech area, customer priorities often evolve from needing help in selecting and installing the right equipment to wanting performance to looking for low cost. In the coffee business, customer tastes and habits have evolved from buying coffee at grocery stores to drinking coffee at gourmet cafés to buying their own whole-bean gourmet coffees. Assuming that customer priorities are not changing can be risky. It is essential to ask whether a significant and growing segment has developed priorities that are different from the basic business model.

The Customer as Active Partner

Customers are increasingly becoming active partners in the buying process, rather than passive targets of product development and advertising. The trend is illustrated by Cisco's customers helping design products, patients taking control of medical issues, the control of media shifting as audiences move from the VCR to TiVo (a device that can preprogram shows by name and even genres), and the power-enhancing access to information and fellow customers provided by the Internet. To harness this change, managers should:[8]

- *Encourage active dialogue.* Contact with customers must now be considered a dialogue of equals. The interaction of Schwab with its customers (both on-line and offline) shows how active dialogues can create a strong relationship.

- *Mobilize customer communities.* The Internet facilitates stronger and more widespread online customer communities. The challenge is to organize and create the context for the communities so that they become an extension of the brand experience and a source of customer input into the product and its use.

- *Manage customer diversity.* Particularly in technology products there will be a wide range of sophistication among customers, and the challenge will be to deal with multiple levels. The more sophisticated group will be the most active partners.

- *Cocreating personalized experiences.* An on-line florist might let customers design the type and arrangement of flowers and vases, rather than merely providing a menu of choices. Cocreating experiences go beyond customization in tailoring the offering to the needs of individuals.

UNMET NEEDS

An unmet need is a customer need that is not being met by the existing product offerings. For example, ski areas have a need for snowmaking equipment that can access steep, advanced trails. A major extension of the temporary-services industry has been created by firms responding to an unmet need for temporary lawyers, high-tech specialists, and doctors. Executive Jet Aviation was formed to sell one-eighth interests in small jets to firms that needed their own jet transportation but could not justify buying and maintaining their own fleet.

Unmet needs are strategically important because they represent opportunities for firms to increase their market share, break into a market, or create and own new markets. They can also represent threats to established firms in that they can be a lever that enables competitors to disrupt an established position. Ariat, for example, broke into the market for equestrian footwear by providing high-performance athletic footwear to riders who were not well served by traditional riding boots. Driven by the belief that riders are athletes, Ariat developed a brand and product line that was responsive to an unmet need.

Sometimes customers may not be aware of their unmet needs because they are so accustomed to the implicit limitations of existing equipment. The farmer of the 1890s would have longed for a horse that worked harder and ate less, but would not have mentioned a tractor in his or her wish list. Unmet needs that are not obvious may be more difficult to identify, but they can also represent a greater opportunity for an aggressive business because there will be little pressure on established firms to be responsive. The key is to stretch the technology or apply new technologies in order to expose unmet needs.

Using Customers to Identify Unmet Needs

Customers are a prime source of unmet needs. The trick is to access them, to get customers to detect and communicate unmet needs. The first step is to conduct market research using individual or group interviews. The research usually starts with a discussion of an actual product-use experience. What problems have emerged? What is frustrating about it? How does it compare with other product experiences? With expectations? Are there problems with the total-use system in which the product is embedded? How can the product be improved? This kind of research helped Dow come up with Spiffits, a line of premoistened, disposable cleaning towels that addressed the need for a towel that was already moistened with a cleaning compound.

A panel of customers can provide more in-depth insights. Black & Decker developed its line of Quantum midpriced tools by forming a panel of fifty do-it-yourselfers

USER-DEVELOPED PRODUCTS

For an internal application, IBM designed and built the first printed circuit card insertion machine of a particular type to be used in commercial production.[9] After building and testing the design in-house, IBM sent engineering drawings of its design to a local machine builder, along with an order for eight units. The machine builder completed this and subsequent orders and applied to IBM for permission to build essentially the same machine for sale on the open market. IBM agreed, and as a result the machine builder became a major force in the component insertion equipment business.

In the early 1970s, store owners and sales personnel in southern California began to notice that youngsters were fixing up their bicycles to look like motorcycles complete with imitation tailpipes and chopper-type handlebars. Sporting crash helmets and Honda motorcycle T-shirts, the youngsters raced fancy 20-inchers on dirt tracks. Obviously onto a good thing, the manufacturers came out with a whole new line of motorcross models. California users refined this concept into the mountain bike. Manufacturers were guided by the California customers to develop new refinements including the 21-speed gear shift that doesn't require removing one's hands from the bars. Mountain bike firms are enjoying booming growth and are still watching their West Coast customers.

(DIYs) who owned more than six power tools.[10] Executives of Black & Decker hung out with panelists in their homes and saw firsthand how the tools were used and the problems and frustrations that arose. One of the problems observed was that cordless drills ran out of power before the job was done. The solution was a drill with a detachable battery pack that recharged in an hour. Sawdust problems prompted a saw and sander with a bag that acted as a minivacuum. To address safety issues, an automatic braking system (ABS) was built into the saws.

Customer surveys can play an important role, as can the monitoring of customer complaints. USAA, the successful Texas financial services company, mails 500,000 questionnaires to customers every year and includes some open-ended questions about problems and new product ideas. As a result, the firm has launched several mutual funds. At Hewlett-Packard each customer complaint is assigned to an employee who becomes its owner and not only makes sure that the customer receives a response but determines if a new product or service is suggested by the problem.

A structured approach, termed *problem research*, develops a list of potential problems with the product.[11] The problems are then prioritized by asking a group of 100 to 200 respondents to rate each problem as to whether (1) the problem is important, (2) the problem occurs frequently, and (3) a problem solution exists. A problem score is obtained by combining these ratings. A dog-food problem research study found that buyers felt dog food smelled bad, cost too much, and was not available in different sizes for different dogs. Subsequently, products responsive to these criticisms emerged. Another study led an airline to modify its cabins to provide more legroom.

Eric von Hippel, a researcher at MIT who studies customers as sources of service innovations, suggests that lead users provide a particularly fertile ground for discovering unmet needs and new product concepts. Lead users are users who:[12]

- Face needs that will be general in the marketplace, but face them months or years before the bulk of the marketplace. A person who is very into health foods and nutrition would be a lead user with respect to health foods, if we assume that there is a trend toward health foods.
- Are positioned to benefit significantly by obtaining a solution to those needs. Lead users of office automation would be firms that today would benefit significantly from technological advancement.

The Ideal Experience

The conceptualization of an ideal experience can also help to identify unmet needs. A major publisher of directories polled its customers, asking each to describe its ideal experience with the firm. The publisher found that its very large customers (the top 4% that were generating 45% of its business) wanted a single contact point to resolve problems, customized products, consultation on using the service, and help in tracking results. In contrast, smaller customers wanted a simple ordering process and to be left alone. These responses provided insights into improving service while cutting costs.[13]

Use Creative Thinking

Thinking out of the box (or just throwing away the box) is a key challenge in discovering new offerings that are responsive to unmet needs. Thinking differently can generate a new offering that creates or changes a category, making the existing competitors less relevant as the new offering becomes the frame of reference and the standard. What could be better?

For example, for years the travel-guide industry was rather mature, with little energy. Then a company called Rough Guides hit on the simple idea that a lot of 30- to 40-year-olds might be interested getting off the beaten track. So it created guides more specific not only to their interests but also to their destinations, so they did not have to buy thick guide books whose material was 90 percent useless. The Rough Guides website offers guides to over 14,000 destinations and a host of related references and news items around travel, plus a travel insurance offering.[14]

Creative thinking is a route to big ideas that lead to significant growth opportunities. It can be the difference between fine-tuning the Folger's Coffee package and promotion set and creating the Starbucks chain. The creative thinking process is based on three principles that, with discipline, any organizational unit can follow. First, separate ideation from evaluation. Rather than killing ideas prematurely—by burying them in negatives, give seemingly bad ideas enough breathing room to perhaps lead you to good ones. Second, approach the problem from different mental and physical perspectives—a sailboat in the ocean, a camping site in Maine, the mind of a Barbie doll character, whatever. Finally, have a mechanism to take the most promising ideas and improve them until they turn into potential winners worth trying. Some further creative thinking guidelines are presented in Chapter 13.

KEY LEARNINGS

- External analysis should influence strategy by identifying opportunities, threats, trends, and strategic uncertainties. The ultimate goal is to improve strategic choices—decisions as to where and how to compete.

- Segmentation (identifying customer groups that can support different competitive strategies) can be based on a variety of customer characteristics, such as benefits sought, customer loyalty, and applications.

- Customer motivation analysis can provide insights into what assets and competencies are needed to compete, as well as indicate possible SCAs.

- Unmet needs that represent opportunities (or threats) can be identified by projecting technologies, by accessing lead users, and by systematic creative thinking.

FOR DISCUSSION

1. Why do a strategic analysis? What are the objectives? What, in your view, are the three keys to making a strategic analysis helpful and important? Is there a downside to conducting a full-blown strategic analysis?

2. Consider the buyer "hot buttons" described in the insert. What are the implications for Betty Crocker? What new business areas might be considered, given each hot button? Answer the same questions for a grocery store chain such as Safeway.

3. What is a customer buying at Nordstrom? At Gap? At Old Navy?

4. Pick a company or brand/business on which to focus. What are the major segments? What are the customer motivations by segments? What are the unmet needs?

NOTES

1. Andrew Tilim, "Will the Kids Buy It?", *Business 2.0,* May 2003, pp. 95–99.
2. International Data Group, "How to Target: A Profit-Based Segmentation of the PC Industry," November 1993.
3. Patricia Sellers, "Keeping the Buyers You Already Have," *Fortune,* Autumn/Winter 1993, pp. 56–58.
4. Melinda Cuthbert, "All Buyers Not Alike," *Business 2.0,* December 26, 2000.

5. Abbie Griffin and John R. Hauser, "The Voice of the Customer," *Marketing Science*, Winter 1993, pp. 1–27.

6. George S. Day, "Creating a Superior Customer-Relating Capability," *Sloan Management Review*, Spring 2003, pp. 82–83.

7. For a fuller discussion of customer priorities see Adrian J. Slywotzky, *Value Migration*, Harvard Business School Press, Boston, 1996.

8. C.K. Prahalad and Venkatram Ramaswamy, "Co-opting Customer Competence," *Harvard Business Review*, January-February, 2000, pp. 79–87.

9. Eric von Hippel, "Lead Users: A Source of Novel Product Concepts," *Management Science*, July 1986, p. 802.

10. Susan Caminti, "A Star Is Born," *Fortune*, Autumn/Winter 1993, pp. 45–47.

11. E. E. Norris, "Seek Out the Consumer's Problem," *Advertising Age*, March 17, 1975, pp. 43–44.

12. Eric von Hippel, "Lead Users."

13. George S. Day, op. cit., p. 81.

14. Michael Lynton, Comment, *Fast Company*, January, 1999, p. 78.

CHAPTER FOUR

Competitor Analysis

Induce your competitors not to invest in those products, markets and services where you expect to invest the most ... that is the fundamental rule of strategy.
—*Bruce Henderson, founder of BCG*

There is nothing more exhilarating than to be shot at without result.
—*Winston Churchill*

The best and fastest way to learn a sport is to watch and imitate a champion.
—*Jean-Claude Killy, skier*

*T*here are numerous well-documented reasons why the Japanese automobile firms were able to penetrate the U.S. market successfully, especially during the 1970s. One important reason, however, is that they were much better than U.S. firms at doing competitor analysis.[1]

David Halberstam, in his account of the automobile industry, graphically described the Japanese efforts at competitor analysis in the 1960s. "They came in groups.... They measured, they photographed, they sketched, and they tape-recorded everything they could. Their questions were precise. They were surprised how open the Americans were."[2] The Japanese similarly studied European manufacturers, especially their design approaches. In contrast, according to Halberstam, the Americans were late in even recognizing the competitive threat from Japan and never did well at analyzing Japanese firms or understanding the new strategic imperatives created by the revised competitive environment.

Competitor analysis is the second phase of external analysis. Again, the goal should be insights that will influence the product-market investment decision or the effort to obtain or maintain an SCA. The analysis should focus on the identification of threats, opportunities, or strategic uncertainties created by emerging or potential competitor moves, weaknesses, or strengths.

Competitor analysis starts with identifying current and potential competitors. There are two very different ways of identifying current competitors. The first examines the perspective of the customer who must make choices among competitors. This approach groups competitors according to the degree they compete for a buyer's choice. The second approach attempts to place competitors in strategic groups on the basis of their competitive strategy.

After competitors are identified, the focus shifts to attempting to understand them and their strategies. Of particular interest is an analysis of the strengths and weaknesses of each competitor or strategic group of competitors. Figure 4.1 summarizes a set of questions that can provide a structure for competitor analysis.

IDENTIFYING COMPETITORS— CUSTOMER-BASED APPROACHES

In most instances, primary competitors are quite visible and easily identified. Thus, Coke competes with Pepsi, other cola brands and private labels, such as President's Choice. CitiBank competes with Chase, BofA, and other major banks. NBC competes with ABC, CBS, and Fox. And Folgers competes with Maxwell House. The competitor analysis for this group should be done with depth and insight. However, the businesses that compete most directly will often use the same business model and the same assumptions about customers. Winning within this common competitive framework requires doing similar things better and focusing on price. The result can be an erosion of profitability.

WHO ARE THE COMPETITORS?

- Against whom do we usually compete? Who are our most intense competitors? Less intense but still serious competitors? Makers of substitute products?
- Can these competitors be grouped into strategic groups on the basis of their assets, competencies and/or strategies?
- Who are the potential competitive entrants? What are their barriers to entry? Is there anything that can be done to discourage them?

EVALUATING THE COMPETITORS

- What are their objectives and strategies? Their level of commitment? Their exit barriers?
- What is their cost structure? Do they have a cost advantage or disadvantage?
- What is their image and positioning strategy?
- Which are the most successful/unsuccessful competitors over time? Why?
- What are the strengths and weaknesses of each competitor or strategic group?
- What leverage points (our strategic weaknesses or customer problems or unmet needs) could competitors exploit to enter the market or become more serious competitors?
- Evaluate the competitors with respect to their assets and competencies. Generate a competitor strength grid.

Figure 4.1 Questions to Structure Competitor Analysis

In many markets the basic business model is eroding because customer priorities are changing, and indirect competitors are strategically relevant. Colas are no longer as dominant in beverages. Television viewers have options outside network programming. Banks are no longer the only transaction game in town. Coffee is bought and consumed differently. Because some of the new competitors are small or appear to be very different, they may not appear on the radar screen. Expanding the radar screen's sensitivity can allow these key industry dynamics to surface:[3]

- Coke focused on Pepsi and ignored for many years the emerging submarkets in water, iced tea, and fruit-based drinks. The result was a missed opportunity and the eventual need to pursue an expensive and difficult catch-up strategy.

- While the major television networks struggle against each other, independent networks are emerging; strong cable networks, such as ESPN and CNN, have flourished; and home shopping, pay-per-view, and even Nintendo, the Internet, and Blockbuster Video are competing for the leisure time of viewers.

- While banks focus on competing banks, their markets have been eroded by mutual funds, insurers, brokers (including discount brokers, such as Charles Schwab), and even software companies, such as Microsoft.

- While Folgers, Maxwell House, and others compete for supermarket business using coupon promotions, other firms, such as Starbucks, are succeeding in selling a very different kind of coffee in different ways.

The competitive analysis in nearly all cases will benefit from extending the perspective beyond the obvious direct competitors. By explicitly considering indirect competitors, the strategic horizon is expanded, and the analysis more realistically mirrors what the customer sees. In the real world, the customer is never restricted to a firm's direct competitors, but instead is always poised to consider other options.

The energy bar category, established in the mid-1980s by PowerBar, includes direct competitors such as Clif, Balance, and dozens of small, local niche firms. There are also a host of indirect competitors, many with very similar products: candy bars (Snickers was called "the energy bar" for many years), breakfast bars, diet bars, granola bars, and the more recent cereal bar category. Understanding the positioning and new product strategies of these indirect competitors will be strategically important to businesses in the energy bar category.

Both direct and indirect competitors can be further categorized in terms of how relevant they are, as determined by similar positioning. Thus, candy bars will be more relevant to Balance than to PowerBar because of where the former has positioned itself (Balance Gold is even marketed as being "like a candy bar"). For the same reason, Clif will a closer competitor to PowerBar than to Balance.

A key issue with respect to strategic analysis in general, and competitor analysis in particular, is the level at which the analysis is conducted. Is it at the level of a business unit, the firm, or some other aggregation of businesses? Because an analysis will be needed at all levels at which strategies are developed, multiple analyses might ultimately be necessary. For example, when Clif developed Luna, an energy bar designed for women, PowerBar countered with Pria. The manager of the Luna business may need a competitive analysis of energy bars for women, in which case the other energy bars might be considered indirect competitors.

Customer Choices

One approach to identifying competitor sets is to look at competitors from the perspective of customers—what choices are customers making? A Cisco buyer could be asked what brand would have been purchased had Cisco not made the required item. A buyer for a nursing home meal service could be asked what would be substituted for granulated potato buds if they increased in price. A sample of sports car buyers could be asked what other cars they considered and perhaps what other showrooms they actually visited.

Product-Use Associations

Another approach that provides insights is the association of products with specific-use contexts or applications.[4] Perhaps twenty or thirty product users could be asked to identify a list of use situations or applications. For each use context they would then name all the products that are appropriate. Then for each product they would identify appropriate use contexts so that the list of use contexts would be more complete. Another group of respondents would then be asked to make judgments about how appropriate each product is for each use context. Then products would be clustered based on the similarity of their appropriate use contexts. Thus, if Pepsi was regarded as appropriate for snack occasions, it would compete primarily with products similarly perceived. The same approach will work with an industrial product that might be used in several distinct applications.

Both the customer-choice and product-use approaches suggest a conceptual basis for identifying competitors that can be employed by managers even when marketing research is not available. The concept of alternatives from which customers choose and the concept of appropriateness to a use context can be powerful tools in helping to understand the competitive environment.

IDENTIFYING COMPETITORS—STRATEGIC GROUPS

The concept of a strategic group provides a very different approach toward understanding the competitive structure of an industry. A strategic group is a group of firms that:

- Over time pursue similar competitive strategies (for example, the use of the same distribution channel, the same type of communication strategies, or the same price/quality position)
- Have similar characteristics (e.g., size, aggressiveness)
- Have similar assets and competencies (such as brand associations, logistics capability, global presence, or research and development)

For example, there have historically been three strategic groups in the pet food industry, which is the subject of an illustrative industry analysis in the appendix to this book. One strategic group consists of very large diversified, branded consumer and food product companies. All distribute through mass merchandisers and supermarkets, have strong established brands, use advertising and promotions effectively, and enjoy economies of scale. The major players include Nestlé Ralston Petcare, Del Monte, and Mars.

A second strategic group of highly focused ultra-premium, specially producers, such as Hill's Petfood (Science Diet and Prescription Diet) and the Iams Company sells product through veterinary offices and specialty pet stores. They have historically used referral networks to reach pet owners concerned with health. When P&G acquired Iams and introduced it into mass merchandiser and supermarkets, the distinction between the two strategic groups blurred and new competitive dynamics were introduced. Iams became a threat to established brands in this space and the Hill's brands found their competitive context very different.

The third strategic group, private-label producers, is led by Doanne Products, who supplies Wal-Mart and other major retailers.

Each strategic group has mobility barriers that inhibit or prevent businesses from moving from one strategic group to another. For example, each of the pet food strategic groups is protected from entry by barriers. The ultrapremium group has the brand reputation, product, and manufacturing knowledge needed for the health segment, access to the influential veterinarians and retailers, and a local customer base. The private-label manufacturers have low-cost production, low overhead, and close relationships with customers. It is possible to bypass or overcome the barriers, of course. A private label manufacturer could create a branded entry, especially if markets are selected to minimize conflicts with existing customers. The barriers are real, however, and a firm competing across strategic groups is usually at a disadvantage.

A member of a strategic group can have exit as well as entry barriers. For example, assets such as plant investment or a specialized labor force can represent a meaningful exit barrier, as can the need to protect a brand's reputation.

The mobility barrier concept is crucial because one way to develop a sustainable competitive advantage is to pursue a strategy that is protected from competition by assets and competencies that represent barriers to competitors. Consider the PC and server market. Dell, Gateway, and a few others have marketed computers direct to consumers—first by catalogues and telephone, and then by the Internet. They developed a host of assets and competencies to support their direct channels, including an impressive product support system. Competitors such as IBM and HP—which have used indirect channels involving retailers and systems firms—have found it very difficult to shift strategies. Not only is the development of assets and competencies costly and difficult, their links with their existing channels create significant barriers.

Using the Strategic Group Concept

The conceptualization of strategic groups can make the process of competitor analysis more manageable. Numerous industries contain many more competitors than can be analyzed individually. Often it is simply not feasible to consider thirty competitors, to say nothing of hundreds. Reducing this set to a small number of strategic groups makes the analysis compact, feasible, and more usable. For example, in the wine industry, competitor analysis by a firm like Robert Mondavi might examine three strategic groups: jug wines, premium wines ($6 to $20), and super-premium wines (over $20). Little strategic content and insight will be lost in most cases, because firms in a strategic group will be affected by and react to industry developments in similar ways. Thus, in projecting future strategies of competitors, the concept of strategic groups can be helpful.

Strategic groupings can refine the strategic investment decision. Instead of determining in which industries to invest, the decision can focus on what strategic group warrants investment. Thus, it will be necessary to determine the current profitability and future potential profitability of each strategic group. One strategic objective is to invest in attractive strategic groups in which assets and competencies can be employed to create strategic advantage.

Ultimately, the selection of a strategy and its supporting assets and competencies will often mean selecting or creating a strategic group. Thus, a knowledge of the strategic group structure can be extremely useful.

Projecting Strategic Groups

The concept of strategic groups can also be helpful in projecting competitive strategies into the future. A classic McKinsey study of the effects of deregulation on five deregulated industries (summarized in Figure 4.2) forecasts with remarkable accuracy that successful firms will move toward one of three strategic groups.[5]

The evolution of the first group involves three phases. During the first phase, the medium and small firms attempt— usually unsuccessfully—to gain enough market

Group	Industry	Examples
1. National distribution company with full line of differentiated products and emphasis on attractive service/price trade-offs	Brokerage Airlines Trucking Railroads Business terminals	Merrill Lynch Delta Consolidated Freightways Burlington Northern Lucent Technologies
2. Low-cost producer—often a new entrant following deregulation	Brokerage Airlines Trucking Railroads Business terminals	Charles Schwab Southwest Airlines Overnite Transportation Oki
3. Specialty firm with strong customer loyalty and specialized service targeted toward an attractive customer group	Brokerage Airlines Trucking Railroads Business terminals	Goldman Sachs Air Wisconsin Ryder Systems Santa Fe Northern Telecom

Figure 4.2   Strategic Groups Emerging from Deregulation

share by merging to compete with the large firms. In the second phase, strong firms make acquisitions to fill in product lines or market gaps. During this phase, which occurs about three to five years following deregulation, the major firms try to develop broad product lines and distribution coverage. In the third phase, interindustry mergers occur. Strong firms merge with others outside their industry.

The second strategic group consists of low-cost producers entering the industry after deregulation by providing simple product lines with minimal service to the price-sensitive segment. The third group includes those pursuing a focus strategy, with a specialized service targeted toward a specific customer group.

POTENTIAL COMPETITORS

In addition to current competitors, it is important to consider potential market entrants, such as firms that might engage in:

1. **Market expansion.** Perhaps the most obvious source of potential competitors is firms operating in other geographic regions or in other countries. A cookie company may want to keep a close eye on a competing firm in an adjacent state, for example.

2. **Product expansion.** The leading ski firm, Rossignol, has expanded into ski clothing, thus exploiting a common market, and has moved to tennis equipment, which takes advantage of technological and distribution overlap.

3. **Backward integration.** Customers are another potential source of competition. General Motors bought dozens of manufacturers of components during its formative years. Major can users, such as Campbell Soup, have integrated backward, making their own containers.

4. **Forward integration.** Suppliers attracted by margins are also potential competitors. Apple Computer, for example, opened a chain of retail stores. Suppliers, believing they have the critical ingredients to succeed in a market, may be attracted by the margins and control that come with integrating forward.

5. **The export of assets or competencies.** A current small competitor with critical strategic weaknesses can turn into a major entrant if it is purchased by a firm that can reduce or eliminate those weaknesses. Predicting such moves can be difficult, but sometimes an analysis of competitor strengths and weaknesses will suggest some possible synergistic mergers. A competitor in an above-average growth industry that does not have the financial or managerial resources for the long haul might be a particularly attractive candidate for merger.

6. **Retaliatory or defensive strategies.** Firms that are threatened by a potential or actual move into their market might retaliate. Thus, Microsoft has made several moves (including into the Internet space) in part to protect its dominant software position.

COMPETITOR ANALYSIS— UNDERSTANDING COMPETITORS

Understanding competitors and their activities can provide several benefits. First, an understanding of the current strategy strengths and weaknesses of a competitor can suggest opportunities and threats that will merit a response. Second, insights into future competitor strategies may allow the prediction of emerging threats and opportunities. Third, a decision about strategic alternatives might easily hinge on the ability to forecast the likely reaction of key competitors. Finally, competitor analysis may result in the identification of some strategic uncertainties that will be worth monitoring closely over time. A strategic uncertainty might be, for example, "Will Competitor A decide to move into the western U.S. market?"

As Figure 4.3 indicates, competitor actions are influenced by eight elements. The first of these reflects financial performance, as measured by size, growth, and profitability.

Size, Growth, and Profitability

The level and growth of sales and market share provide indicators of the vitality of a business strategy. The maintenance of a strong market position or the achievement of rapid growth usually reflects a strong competitor (or strategic group) and a successful strategy. In contrast, a deteriorating market position can signal financial or organizational strains that might affect the interest and ability of the business to pursue certain strategies. To provide a crude sales estimate for businesses that are buried in

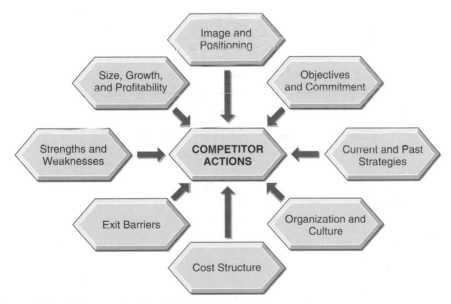

Figure 4.3 Understanding the Competitors

a large company, take the number of employees and multiply it by the average sales per employee in the industry. For many businesses, this method is very feasible and remarkably accurate.

After size and growth comes profitability. A profitable business will generally have access to capital for investment unless it has been designated by the parent to be milked. A business that has lost money over an extended time period or has experienced a recent sharp decrease in profitability may find it difficult to gain access to capital either externally or internally.

Image and Positioning Strategy

A cornerstone of a business strategy can be an association, such as being the strongest truck, the most durable car, the smallest consumer electronics equipment, or the most effective cleaner. More often, it is useful to move beyond class-related product attributes to intangibles that span product class, such as quality, innovation, sensitivity to the environment, or brand personality. Chapter 12 on strategic positioning elaborates.

In order to develop positioning alternatives, it is helpful to determine the image and brand personality of the major competitors. Weaknesses of competitors on relevant attributes or personality traits can represent an opportunity to differentiate and develop advantage. Strengths of competitors on important dimensions may represent challenges to exceed them or to outflank them. In any case it is important to know the competitive profiles.

Competitor image and positioning information can be deduced in part by studying a firm's products, advertising, Web site, and actions, but often customer research is helpful to ensure that an accurate current portrayal is obtained. The conventional approach is to start with qualitative customer research to find out what a business and its brands mean to customers. What are the associations? If the business were a person, what kind of person would it be? What visual imagery, books, animals, trees, or activities are associated with the business? What is its essence?

Competitor Objectives and Commitment

A knowledge of competitor objectives provides the potential to predict whether or not a competitor's present performance is satisfactory or strategic changes are likely. The financial objectives of the business unit can indicate the competitor's willingness to invest in that business even if the payout is relatively long term. In particular, what are the competitor's objectives with respect to market share, sales growth, and profitability? Nonfinancial objectives are also helpful. Does the competitor want to be a technological leader? Or to develop a service organization? Or to expand distribution? Such objectives provide a good indication of the competitor's possible future strategy.

The objectives of the competitor's parent company (if one exists) are also relevant. What are the current performance levels and financial objectives of the parent? If the business unit is not performing as well as the parent, pressure might be exerted to improve or the investment might be withdrawn. Of critical importance is the role attached to the business unit. Is it central to the parent's long-term plans, or is it peripheral? Is it seen as a growth area, or is it expected to supply cash to fund other areas? Does the business create synergy with other operations? Does the parent have an emotional attachment to the business unit for any reason? Deep pockets can sometimes be accompanied by short arms; just because resources exist does not mean they are available.

Current and Past Strategies of Competitors

The competitor's current and past strategies should be reviewed. In particular, past strategies that have failed should be noted, because such experiences can inhibit the competitor from trying similar strategies again. Also, a knowledge of a competitor's pattern of new product or new market moves can help anticipate its future growth directions. Is the strategy based on product-line breadth, product quality, service, distribution type, or brand identification? If a low-cost strategy is employed, is it based on economies of scale, the experience curve, manufacturing facilities and equipment, or access to raw material? What is its cost structure? If a focus strategy is evident, describe the business scope.

Competitor Organization and Culture

Knowledge about the background and experience of the competitor's top management can provide insight into future actions. Are the managers drawn from marketing, engineering, or manufacturing? Are they largely from another industry or company? Clorox, for example, has a very heavy Procter & Gamble influence in its management, lingering from the years that Procter & Gamble operated Clorox before the courts ordered divestiture.

An organization's culture, supported by its structure, systems, and people, often has a pervasive influence on strategy. A cost-oriented, highly structured organization that relies on tight controls to achieve objectives and motivate employees may have difficulty innovating or shifting into an aggressive, marketing-oriented strategy. A loose, flat organization that emphasizes innovation and risk taking may similarly have difficulty pursuing a disciplined product-refinement and cost-reduction program. In general, as Chapter 16 will make clearer, organizational elements such as culture, structure, systems, and people limit the range of strategies that should be considered.

Cost Structure

Knowledge of a competitor's cost structure, especially when the competitor is relying on a low-cost strategy, can provide an indication of its likely future pricing strategy and its staying power. The goal should be to obtain a feel for both direct costs and fixed costs, which will determine breakeven levels. The following information can usually be obtained and can provide insights into cost structures:

- The number of employees and a rough breakdown of direct labor (variable labor cost) and overhead (which will be part of fixed cost)

- The relative costs of raw materials and purchased components
- The investment in inventory, plant, and equipment (also fixed cost)
- Sales levels and number of plants (on which the allocation of fixed costs is based)

Exit Barriers

Exit barriers can be crucial to a firm's ability to withdraw from a business area, and thus are indicators of commitment. They include:[6]

- Specialized assets—plant, equipment, or other assets that are costly to transform to another application and therefore have little salvage value
- Fixed costs, such as labor agreements, leases, and a need to maintain parts for existing equipment
- Relationships to other business units in the firm resulting from the firm's image or from shared facilities, distribution channels, or sales force
- Government and social barriers—for example, governments may regulate whether a railroad can exit from a passenger service responsibility, or firms may feel a sense of loyalty to workers, thereby inhibiting strategic moves
- Managerial pride or an emotional attachment to a business or its employees that affects economic decisions

Assessing Strengths and Weaknesses

Knowledge of a competitor's strengths and weaknesses provides insight that is key to a firm's ability to pursue various strategies. It also offers important input into the process of identifying and selecting strategic alternatives. One approach is to attempt to exploit a competitor's weakness in an area where the firm has an existing or developing strength. The desired pattern is to develop a strategy that will pit "our" strength against a competitor's weakness. Conversely, a knowledge of "their" strength is important so it can be bypassed or neutralized.

One firm that developed a strategy to neutralize a competitor's strength was a small software firm that lacked a retail distribution capability or the resources to engage in retail advertising. It targeted value-added software systems firms, which sell total software and sometimes hardware systems to organizations such as investment firms or hospitals. These value-added systems firms could understand and exploit the power of the product, integrate it into their systems, and use it in quantity. The competitor's superior access to a distribution channel or resources to support an advertising effort was thus neutralized.

The assessment of a competitor's strengths and weaknesses starts with an identification of relevant assets and competencies for the industry and then evaluates the competitor on the basis of those assets and competencies. We now turn to these topics.

COMPETITOR STRENGTHS AND WEAKNESSES

What Are the Relevant Assets and Competencies?

Competitor strengths and weaknesses are based on the existence or absence of assets or competencies. Thus, an asset such as a well-known name or a prime location could represent a strength, as could a competency such as the ability to develop a strong promotional program. Conversely, the absence of an asset or competency can represent a weakness.

To analyze competitor strengths and weaknesses, it is thus necessary to identify the assets and competencies that are relevant to the industry. As Figure 4.4 summarizes, five sets of questions can be helpful.

1. *What businesses have been successful over time? What assets or competencies have contributed to their success? What businesses have had chronically low performance? Why? What assets or competencies do they lack?*

   By definition, assets and competencies that provide SCAs should affect performance over time. Thus, businesses that differ with respect to performance over time should also differ with respect to their assets and competencies. Analysis of the causes of the performance usually suggests sets of relevant competencies and assets. Typically, the superior performers have developed and maintained key assets and competencies that have been the basis for their performance. Conversely, weakness in several assets and competencies relevant to the industry and its strategy should visibly contribute to the inferior performance of the weak competitors over time.

   For example, in the CT scanner industry the best performer, General Electric, has superior product technology and R&D, an established systems capability, a strong sales and service organization owing, in part, to its X-ray product line, and an installed base.

2. *What are the key customer motivations? What is really important to the customer?*

   Customer motivations usually drive buying decisions and thus can dictate what assets or competencies potentially create meaningful advantages. In

---

1. Why are successful businesses successful? Why are unsuccessful businesses unsuccessful?
2. What are the key customer motivations?
3. What are the large cost components?
4. What are the industry mobility barriers?
5. Which components of the value chain can create competitive advantage?

Figure 4.4   Identifying Relevant Assets and Competencies

the heavy-equipment industry, customers value service and parts backup. Caterpillar's promise of "24-hour parts service anywhere in the world" has been a key asset because it is important to customers. Apple has focused on the motivation of designers for user-friendly design platforms.

An analysis of customer motivations can also identify assets and competencies that a business will need to deliver unless a strategy can be devised that will make them unimportant. If the prime buying criterion for a snack is freshness, a brand will have to develop the skills to deliver that attribute. A business that lacks competence in an area important to the customer segment can experience problems even if it has other substantial SCAs.

3. **What are the large value-added parts of the product or service? What are the large cost components?**

   An analysis of the cost structure of an industry can reveal which value-added stage represents the largest percentage of total cost. Obtaining a cost advantage in a key value-added stage can represent a significant SCA whether that advantage is used to support a low price or another strategy. Cost advantages in lower value-added stages have less leverage. In the metal can business, transportation costs are relatively high; thus a competitor that can locate plants near customers or on a customer's premises will have a significant cost advantage.

4. **Consider the components of the value chain. Do any provide the potential to generate competitive advantage?**

   One tool to identify significant value-added components is the value chain, a conceptual model developed by Michael Porter.[7] A business's value chain (see Figure 4.5) consists of two types of value-creating activities and should be considered in assessing a competitor. The components of the value chain are defined as follows:

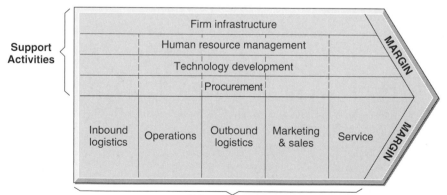

Figure 4.5   The Value Chain

Primary Value Activities

- **Inbound logistics**—material handling and warehousing
- **Operations**—transforming inputs into the final product
- **Outbound logistics**—order processing and distribution
- **Marketing and sales**—communication, pricing, and channel management
- **Service**—installation, repair, and parts

Secondary Value Activities

- **Procurement**—procedures and information systems
- **Technology development**—improving the product and processes/systems
- **Human resource management**—hiring, training, and compensation
- **Firm infrastructure**—general management, finance, accounting, government relations, and quality management

The linear flow suggested by the value chain may not always be the most useful representation of a competitor, especially in the Internet space. Another perspective is to simply address the question—what are the significant added-value components for a competitor, components that yield either customer benefits or reduced cost.[8] For eBay, for example, these components might be found in operations, customer support, and auction services. There will also be some network alliances that add value, such as those with AOL and iEscrow.

A Checklist of Strengths and Weaknesses

Figure 4.6 provides an overview checklist of the areas in which a competitor can have strengths and weaknesses. The first category is innovation. One of the strengths of Kao Corporation is its ability to develop innovative products in soaps, detergents, skin care, and even floppy disks. Its new products usually have a distinct technological advantage. In a highly technical industry the percentage spent on R&D and the emphasis along the basic/applied continuum can be indicators of the cumulative ability to innovate. The outputs of the process in terms of product characteristics and performance capabilities, new products, product modifications, and patents provide more definitive measures of the company's ability to innovate.

The second area of competitor strengths and weaknesses is manufacturing. Perhaps the major area of strength of Texas Instruments' semiconductor and related businesses has been manufacturing. One of the key potential strength areas in manufacturing involves sources of sustainable cost advantages. Is there anything about the nature of the plant or equipment, the raw material access, the level of vertical integration, or the type of workforce that would support a sustainable cost advantage? Excess

INNOVATION

- Technical product or service superiority
- New product capability
- R&D
- Technologies
- Patents

MANUFACTURING

- Cost structure
- Flexible production operations
- Equipment
- Access to raw materials
- Vertical integration
- Workforce attitude and motivation
- Capacity

FINANCE—ACCESS TO CAPITAL

- From operations
- From net short-term assets
- Ability to use debt and equity financing
- Parent's willingness to finance

MANAGEMENT

- Quality of top and middle management
- Knowledge of business
- Culture
- Strategic goals and plans
- Entrepreneurial thrust
- Planning/operation system
- Loyalty—turnover
- Quality of strategic decision making

MARKETING

- Product quality reputation
- Product characteristics/differentiation
- Brand name recognition
- Breadth of the product line—systems capability
- Customer orientation
- Segmentation/focus
- Distribution
- Retailer relationship
- Advertising/promotion skills
- Sales force
- Customer service/product support

CUSTOMER BASE

- Size and loyalty
- Market share
- Growth of segments served

Figure 4.6   Analysis of Strengths and Weaknesses

capacity can increase fixed costs, but it can also be a source of strength if the market is volatile or growing.

The third area is finance, the ability to generate or acquire funds in the short as well as the long run. Companies with deep pockets (financial resources) have a decisive advantage because they can pursue strategies not available to smaller firms. Compare General Motors with Chrysler, for example, or Miller and Budweiser with some of the smaller regional breweries. Operations provide one major source of funds. What is the nature of cash flow that is being generated and will be generated given the known uses for funds? Cash or other liquid assets provide other sources, as does a parent firm. The key is the ability of the business to justify the use of debt or equity and the will to access this source.

Management is the fourth area. Controlling and motivating a set of highly disparate business operations are strengths for GE, Sony, Disney, and other firms that have successfully diversified. The quality, depth, and loyalty (as measured by turnover) of top and middle management provide an important asset for others. Another aspect to analyze is the culture. The values and norms that permeate an organization can energize some strategies and inhibit others. In particular, some organizations, such as 3M, possess both an entrepreneurial culture that allows them to initiate new directions and the organizational skill to nurture them. The ability to set strategic goals and plans can represent significant competencies. To what extent does the business have a vision and the will and competence to pursue it?

The fifth area is marketing. Often the most important marketing strength, particularly in the high-tech field, involves the product line: its quality reputation, breadth, and the features that differentiate it from other products. Brand image and distribution have been key assets for businesses as diverse as Gatorade, Dell, and Bank of America. The ability to develop a true customer orientation can be an important strength. Another strength can be based on the ability and willingness to advertise effectively. The success of Perdue chickens was due in part to Perdue's ability to generate superior advertising. Other elements of the marketing mix, such as the sales force and service operation, can also be sources of sustainable competitive advantage. One of Caterpillar's strengths is the quality of its dealer network. Still another possible strength, particularly in the high-tech field, is a competitor's ability to stay close to its customers.

The final area of interest is the customer base. How substantial is the customer base and how loyal is it? How are the competitor's offerings evaluated by its customers? What are the costs that customers will have to absorb if they switch to another supplier? Extremely loyal and happy customers are going to be difficult to dislodge. What are the size and growth potentials of the segments served?

The Competitive Strength Grid

With the relevant assets and competencies identified, the next step is to scale your own firm and the major competitors or strategic groups of competitors on those assets and competencies. The result is termed a competitive strength grid and serves to summarize the position of the competitors with respect to assets and competencies.

A sustainable competitive advantage is almost always based on having a position superior to that of the target competitors in one or more asset or competence area that is relevant both to the industry and to the strategy employed. Thus, information about each competitor's position with respect to relevant assets and competencies is central to strategy development and evaluation.

If a superior position does not exist with respect to assets and competencies important to the strategy, it probably will have to be created or the strategy may have to be modified or abandoned. Sometimes there simply is no point of difference with respect to the firms regarded as competitors. A competency that all competitors have will not be the basis for an SCA. For example, flight safety is important among airline passengers, but if airlines are perceived to be equal with respect to pilot quality and plane maintenance, it cannot be the basis for an SCA. Of course, if some airlines can convince passengers that they are superior with respect to antiterrorist security, then an SCA could indeed emerge.

The Luxury Car Market

A competitor strength grid is illustrated in Figure 4.7 for the luxury car market. The relevant assets and competencies are listed on the left, grouped as to whether they are considered keys to success or are of secondary importance. The principal competitors are shown as column headings across the top. Each cell is coded as to whether the brand is strong, above average, average, below average, or weak in that asset or competence category.

The resulting figure provides a summary of the profile of the strengths and weaknesses of ten brands. Two can be compared, such as Ford and Lexus or BMW and Audi. BMW and Lexus have enviable positions.

Analyzing Submarkets

It is often desirable to conduct an analysis for submarkets or strategic groups and perhaps for different products. A firm may not compete with all other firms in the industry but only with those engaged in similar strategies and markets. For example, a competitive strength grid may look very different for the safety submarket, with Volvo having more strength. Similarly, the handling submarket may also involve a competitive grid that will look different, with BMW having more strength.

The Analysis Process

The process of developing a competitive strength grid can be extremely informative and useful. One approach is to have several managers create their own grids independently. The differences can usually illuminate different assumptions and information bases. A reconciliation stage can disseminate relevant information and identify and structure strategic uncertainties. For example, different opinions about the quality reputation of a competitor may stimulate a strategic uncertainty that justifies marketing research. Another approach is to develop the grid in a group setting, perhaps supported by preliminary staff work. When possible, objective information based on laboratory tests or customer perception studies should be used. The need for such information becomes clear when disagreements arise about where competitors should be scaled on the various dimensions.

OBTAINING INFORMATION ON COMPETITORS

A competitor's Web site is usually a rich source of information and the first place to look. The strategic vision (along with a statement about values and culture) is often posted, and the portfolio of businesses are usually laid out. The way that the latter are organized can provide clues as to business priorities and strategies. When IBM emphasizes its e-servers, for example, that says something about their direction in the server business. The Web site also can provide information about such business assets as plants, global access, and brand symbols. Research on the competitor's site can be

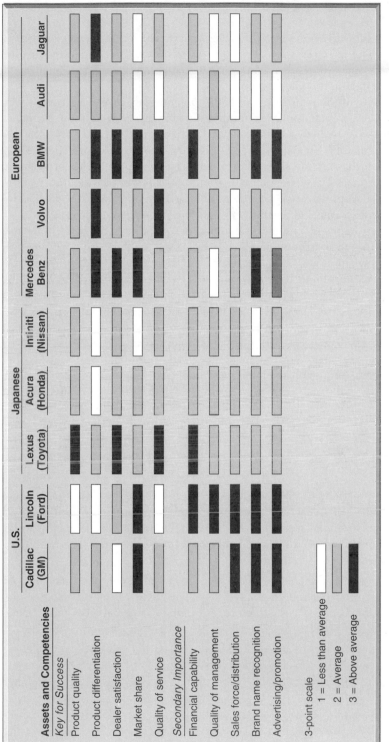

Figure 4.7 Illustrative Example of a Competitive Strength Grid for the U.S. Luxury Car Market

supplemented with search-engines, access to articles and financial reports about the business. General-information sites (such as business.com), and Web sites for trade shows, trade magazines, channel members (such as retailers), and financial analysts can also provide useful information.

Detailed information on competitors is generally available from a variety of sources. Competitors usually communicate extensively with their suppliers, customers, and distributors; security analysts and stockholders; and government legislators and regulators. Contact with any of these can provide information. Monitoring of trade magazines, trade shows, advertising, speeches, annual reports, and the like can be informative. Technical meetings and journals can provide information about technical developments and activities. Thousands of databases accessible by computer now make available detailed information on most companies.

Detailed information about a competitor's standing with its customers can be obtained through market research. For example, regular telephone surveys could provide information about the successes and vulnerabilities of competitors' strategies. Respondents could be asked questions such as the following: Which store is closest to your home? Which do you shop at most often? Are you satisfied? Which has the lowest prices? Best specials? Best customer service? Cleanest stores? Best-quality meat? Best-quality produce? And so on. Those chains that were well positioned on value, on service, or on product quality could be identified, and tracking would show whether they were gaining or losing position. The loyalty of their customer base (and thus their vulnerability) could be indicated in part by satisfaction scores and the willingness of customers to patronize stores even when they were not the most convenient or the least expensive.

KEY LEARNINGS

- Competitors can be identified by customer choice (the set from which customers select) or by clustering them into strategic groups, (firms that pursue similar strategies and have similar assets, competencies, and other characteristics). In either case, competitors will vary in terms of how intensely they compete.

- Competitors should be analyzed along several dimensions, including their size, growth and profitability, image, objectives, business strategies, organizational culture, cost structure, exit barriers, and strengths and weaknesses.

- Potential strengths and weaknesses can be identified by considering the characteristics of successful and unsuccessful businesses, key customer motivation, and value-added components.

- The competitive strength grid, which arrays competitors or strategic groups on each of the relevant assets and competencies, provides a compact summary of key strategic information.

FOR DISCUSSION

1. Consider the television industry. Identify the competitors to NBC and organize them in terms of their intensity of competition. Also organize them in terms of strategic groups. Are there differences in the two methods of organization?

2. Evaluate Figure 4.7. What surprises are there in the figure? What are the implications for Cadillac? For Audi?

3. Pick a company or brand/business on which to focus. What business is it in? Who are its direct and indirect competitors? Which in each category are the most relevant competitors?

4. Consider the automobile industry. Identify competitors to Ford and organize them in terms of their intensity of competition. Also organize them into strategic groups. What are the KSFs for the strategic groups? Do you think that will change in the next five years?

NOTES

1. David Halberstam, *The Reckoning*, New York: William Morrow, 1986, p. 310.
2. Ibid.
3. For a fuller discussion of expanding the radar screen see Adrian J. Slywotzky, *Value Migration*, Harvard Business School Press, Boston, 1996.
4. George S. Day, Allan D. Shocker, and Rajendra K. Srivastava, "Customer-Oriented Approaches to Identifying Product Markets," *Journal of Marketing* 43, Fall 1979, pp. 8–19.
5. Donald C. Waite III, "Deregulation and the Banking Industry," *Bankers Magazine* 163, January–February 1982, pp. 76–85.
6. Michael E. Porter, *Competitive Strategy*, New York: The Free Press, 1980, pp. 20–21. The concept of exit barriers will be discussed again in Chapter 13.
7. Michael E. Porter, *Competitive Advantage*, New York: The Free Press, 1985, Chapter 2.
8. Shawn D. Cartwright and Richard W. Oliver, "Untangling the Value Web," *Journal of Business*, January–February, 2000, pp. 22–27.

CHAPTER FIVE

Market/Submarket Analysis

As the economy, led by the automobile industry, rose to a new high level in the twenties, a complex of new elements came into existence to transform the market: installment selling, the used-car trade-in, the closed body, and the annual model. (I would add improved roads if I were to take into account the environment of the automobile.)
—*Alfred P. Sloan, Jr., General Motors*

Before you build a better mousetrap, it helps to know if there are any mice out there.
—*Mortimer B. Zuckerman*

The most effective way to cope with change is to help create it.
—*I. W. Lynett*

Market analysis builds on customer and competitor analyses to make some strategic judgments about a market (and submarket) and its dynamics. One of the primary objectives of a market analysis is to determine the attractiveness of a market (or submarket) to current and potential participants. Market attractiveness, the market's profit potential as measured by the long-term return on investment achieved by its participants, will provide important input into the product-market investment decision. The frame of reference is all participants. Of course, participating in an attractive market will not guarantee success for all competitors. Whether a market is appropriate for a particular firm is a related but very different question, depending not only on the market attractiveness, but also on how the firm's strengths and weaknesses match up against those of its competitors.

A second objective of market analysis is to understand the dynamics of the market. The need is to identify emerging submarkets, key success factors, trends, threats, opportunities, and strategic uncertainties that can guide information gathering and analysis. A key success factor is an asset or competency that is needed to play the game. If a firm has a strategic weakness in a key success factor that isn't neutralized by a well-conceived strategy, its ability to compete will be limited. The market trends can include those identified in customer or competitor analysis, but the perspective here is broader and others will usually emerge as well.

DIMENSIONS OF A MARKET ANALYSIS

The nature and content of an analysis of a market and its relevant product markets will depend on context, but will often include the following dimensions:

- Emerging submarkets
- Actual and potential market and submarket size
- Market and submarket growth
- Market and submarket profitability
- Distribution systems
- Trends and developments
- Key success factors

Figure 5.1 provides a set of questions structured around these dimensions that can serve to stimulate a discussion identifying opportunities, threats, and strategic uncertainties. Each dimension will be addressed in turn, starting with assessment of market size. The chapter concludes with a discussion of the risks of growth markets.

Emerging Submarkets

The management of a firm in any dynamic market requires addressing the challenge and opportunity of relevance, as described in the boxed insert (page 81). In essence, the challenge is to detect and understand emerging submarkets, identify those that are attractive to the firm given its assets and competencies, and then adjust offerings and brand portfolios in order to increase their relevance to the chosen submarkets. The opportunity is to influence these emerging submarkets so that competitors become less relevant. A review of some of the many forces and events behind the rise or fall of submarkets will be helpful in the difficult task of detecting and understanding them.

First, the product or service can be augmented or expanded to include a new dimension. Saturn and Lexus, for example, changed the way customers interacted with car dealers and, for some, created a submarket that made some of the other brands less relevant. Banquet Homestyle Bakes successfully entered the shelf-stable meal market where Betty Crocker's Hamburger Helper resides with a meat-included meal package, thereby creating a new submarket.

Second, the market can be broken into niches. The energy bar market created by PowerBar ultimately fragmented into a variety of submarkets, including one designed for women (Luna), high protein (Balance), low calories (Pria), and candy bar taste (Balance Gold). Each of these niches represents an arena for which the original PowerBar was not relevant.

Third, the application scope can be expanded from components to systems or turnkey solutions; in essence there is an aggregation into submarkets, the inverse of

SUBMARKETS

Are forces such as augmented products, the emerging of niches, a trend toward systems, new applications, repositioned product classes, customer trends, or new technologies creating worthwhile submarkets? How should they be defined?

SIZE AND GROWTH

What are the important and potentially important submarkets? What are their size and growth characteristics? What submarkets are declining or will soon decline? How fast? What are the driving forces behind sales trends?

PROFITABILITY

For each major submarket consider the following: Is this a business area in which the average firm will make money? How intense is the competition among existing firms? Evaluate the threats from potential entrants and substitute products. What is the bargaining power of suppliers and customers? How attractive/profitable are the market and its submarkets both now and in the future?

COST STRUCTURE

What are the major cost and value-added components for various types of competitors?

DISTRIBUTION SYSTEMS

What are the alternative channels of distribution? How are they changing?

MARKET TRENDS

What are the trends in the market?

KEY SUCCESS FACTORS

What are the key success factors, assets, and competencies needed to compete successfully? How will these change in the future? How can the assets and competencies of competitors be neutralized by strategies?

Figure 5.1 Questions to Help Structure a Market Analysis

breaking the category up into submarkets. In the late 1990s, Siebel took the lead in creating Internet-based customer relationship management (CRM) solutions by pulling together a host of application areas, including customer loyalty programs, customer acquisition, call centers, customer service, customer contact, and sales force automation.

Fourth, the emergence of a new and distinct application can define relevant brand options. Bayer helped define a new subcategory—taking baby aspirin regularly to ward off heart attacks, with its Bayer 81 mg. It attempted to further define the subcategory by introducing its Enteric Safety Coating to reassure those who might be concerned about the effects of regular aspirin use on the stomach.

Fifth, a product class can be repositioned. In the United Kingdom, Ford Galaxy introduced itself as being roomy and comfortable, like first-class air travel, and therefore suitable for busy executives. In doing so, Ford repositioned the minivan experience (and thus a portion of the product class) as something far different than that

RELEVANCE

All too frequently, despite retaining high levels of awareness, attitude, and even loyalty, a brand loses market share because it is not perceived to be relevant to emerging submarkets. If a group of customers want hybrid cars, it simply does not matter how good they think your firm's SUV is. They might love it and recommend it to others, but if they are interested in an hybrid because of their changing needs and desires, then your brand is irrelevant to them. This may be true even if your firm also makes hybrids under the same brand. The hybrid submarket is different than SUVs and has a different set of relevant brands.

Relevance for a brand occurs when two conditions are met. First, there must be a perceived need or desire by customers for a submarket defined by some combination of an attribute set, an application, a user group, or other distinguishing characteristic. Second, the brand needs to be among the set considered to be relevant for that submarket by the prospective customers.

Winning among brands within a submarket, however, is not enough. There are two additional relevance challenges. One is to make sure that the submarket associated with the brand is relevant. The problem may not be that the customer picks the wrong brand, but rather that the wrong submarket (and brand set) is picked. The second challenge is to make sure that the brand is considered by customers to be an option with respect to a submarket. This implies that a brand needs to be positioned against the submarket in addition to whatever other positioning strategies may be pursued. It must also be visible and be perceived to meet minimal performance levels.

Nearly every marketplace is undergoing change—often dramatic, rapid change—that creates relevance issues. Examples appear in nearly every industry, from computers, consulting, airlines, power generators, and financial services to snack food, beverages, pet food, and toys. Hardware, paint and flooring stores struggle with the reality of Home Depot. Xerox and Kodak face a relevance challenge as a variety of other firms (including HP, Microsoft, and Canon) are carving up the digital imaging world. Merrill Lynch faces threats to its basic value proposition from several sides. Relevance is an issue as well for brands attempting to open up new business arenas, such as Toyota's hybrid cars or TiVo's personal video recorder.

The key to managing such change is twofold. First, a business must detect and understand emerging submarkets, projecting how they are evolving. Second, it must maintain relevance in the face of these emerging submarkets. Businesses that perform these tasks successfully have organizational skills at detecting change, the organizational vitality to respond, and a well-conceived brand strategy.

There is also the option of creating or influencing the emergence of submarkets that will serve to make competitors less relevant. IBM did this with e-business, and again with its on-demand concept. Gillette did it with the Sensor and Mach III brands. Charles Schwab did it with Schwab OneSource. Creating and owning subcategories can only occur when the right firm, armed with the right idea and offering, is ready to act at the right time. (Recall that Apple's Newton, the first PDA, was premature, while Palm got the timing right.) But when it happens, it can be a strategic home run.[1]

associated with a soccer mom or family-outing vehicle. Starbucks similarly repositioned the retail coffee market.

Sixth, a customer trend can be a driver of a submarket. The dual trends toward wellness and the use of herbs and natural supplements have supported a new category, healthy-refreshment beverages (HRB). This arena now contains a host of subcategories, such as enhanced teas, fruit drinks, soy-based drinks, and waters. The pioneer and submarket leader is SoBe, which started in 1996 (with SoBe Black Tea 3G, containing ginseng, ginkgo, and guarana) and now has an extensive line of teas, juices, and energy drinks.

Seventh, a new technology—such as disposable razors, notebook computers, a new fabric, or hybrid cars—can drive the perception of a submarket. By creating a subcategory of dry beer, Asahi Super Dry Beer made Kirin, the leading lager beer brand, irrelevant for a significant and growing segment in Japan. A minor player with under 8% of the market in 1986, Asahi grew to gain market share leadership in the late 1990s, in large part by taking share from Kirin.

Finally, a whole market can simply be invented. eBay created an online auction category that has spawned many imitators, who have had difficulty matching both the operational performance and the critical mass of users established by eBay.

ACTUAL AND POTENTIAL MARKET SIZE

A basic starting point for the analysis of a market or submarket is the total sales level. If it is reasonable to believe that a successful strategy can be developed to gain a 15 percent share, it is important to know the total market size. Among the sources that can be helpful are published financial analyses of the firm, customers, government data, and trade magazines and associations. The ultimate source is often a survey of product users in which the usage levels are projected to the population.

Potential Market—The User Gap

In addition to the size of the current, relevant market, it is often useful to consider the potential market. A new use, new user group, or more frequent usage could dramatically change the size and prospects for the market.

There is unrealized potential for the cereal market in Europe and among institutional customers in the United States—restaurants and schools/day-care facilities.[2] All these segments have room for dramatic growth. In particular, Europeans buy only about 25 percent as much cereal as their U.S. counterparts. If technology allowed cereals to be used more conveniently away from home by providing shelf-stable milk products, usage could be further expanded. Of course, the key is not only to recognize the potential, but also to have the vision and program in place to exploit it. A host of strategists have dismissed investment opportunities in industries because they lacked the insight to see the available potential and take advantage of it.

Ghost Potential

Sometimes an area becomes so topical and the need so apparent that potential growth seems assured. As a Lewis Carroll character observed, "What I tell you three times is true." However, this potential can have a ghostlike quality caused by factors inhibiting or preventing its realization. For example, the demand for computers exists in many underdeveloped countries, but a lack of funds inhibit buying and government regulations make productive, efficient operations difficult if not impossible. Many dot-com concepts were the beneficiaries of considerable hype, but failed because the growth of their application never materialized.

Small Can Be Beautiful

Some firms have investment criteria that prohibit them from investing in small markets. Mobil, Marriott, Frito-Lay, and Procter & Gamble, for example, have historically looked to new products that would generate large sales levels within a few years. Yet in an era of micromarketing, much of the action is in smaller niche segments. If a firm avoids them, it can lock itself out of much of the vitality and profitability of a business area. Furthermore, most substantial business areas were small at the outset, sometimes for many years. Avoiding the small market can thus mean that a firm must later overcome the first-mover advantage of others.

MARKET AND SUBMARKET GROWTH

After the size of the market and its important submarkets have been estimated, the focus turns to growth rate. What will be the size of the markets submarkets in the future? If all else remains constant, growth means more sales and profits even without increasing market share. It can also mean less price pressure when demand increases faster than supply and firms are not engaged in experience curve pricing, anticipating future lower costs. Conversely, declining sales can mean reduced sales and often increased price pressure as firms struggle to hold their shares of a diminishing pie.

It may seem that the strategy of choice would thus be to identify and avoid or disinvest in declining situations and to identify and invest in growth contexts. Of course, the reality is not that simple. In particular, declining product markets can represent a real opportunity for a firm, in part because competitors may be exiting and disinvesting, instead of entering and investing for growth. The firm may attempt to become a profitable survivor by encouraging others to exit and by becoming dominant in the most viable segments. The pursuit of this strategy is considered in detail in Chapter 15.

The other half of the conventional wisdom, that growth contexts are always attractive, can also fail to hold true. Growth situations can involve substantial risks. Because of the importance of correctly assessing growth contexts, a discussion of these risks is presented at the end of this chapter.

Identifying Driving Forces

In many contexts, the most important strategic uncertainty involves the prediction of market sales. A key strategic decision, often an investment decision, can hinge on not only being correct but also understanding the driving forces behind market dynamics.

Addressing most key strategic uncertainties starts with asking on what the answer depends. In the case of projecting sales of a major market, the need is to determine what forces will drive those sales. For example, the sales of a new consumer electronics device may be driven by machine costs, the evolution of an industry standard, or the emergence of alternative technologies. Each of these three drivers will provide the basis for key second-level uncertainties.

In the wine market, the impact of anti-alcohol movements (such as MADD), the tax policy, the relationship of wine to health, and the future demand for premium reds might be driving forces. One second-level strategic uncertainty might then focus on the likely strength of the anti-alcohol movements.

Forecasting Growth

Historical data can provide a useful perspective and help to separate hope from reality, but they need to be used with care. Apparent trends in data such as those shown in Figure 5.2 can be caused by random fluctuations or by short-term economic conditions, and the urge to extrapolate should be resisted. Furthermore, the strategic interest is not on projections of history but rather on the prediction of turning points, times when the rate and perhaps direction of growth change.

Sometimes leading indicators of market sales may help in forecasting and predicting turning points. Examples of leading indicators include:

- **Demographic data.** The number of births is a leading indicator of the demand for education, and the number of people reaching age 65 is a leading indicator of the demand for retirement facilities.
- **Sales of related equipment.** Personal computer and printer sales provide a leading indicator of the demand for supplies and service needs.

Market sales forecasts, especially of new markets, can be based on the experience of analogous industries. The trick is to identify a prior market with similar characteristics. Sales of color televisions might be expected to have a pattern similar to sales of black-and-white televisions, for example. Sales of a new type of snack might look to the history of other previously introduced snack categories or other consumer

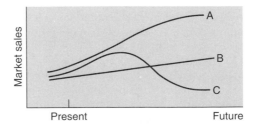

Present   Future

Figure 5.2   Sales Patterns

products such as some of the energy bars or granola bars. The most value will be obtained if several analogous product classes can be examined and the differences in the product class experiences related to their characteristics.

Methods now exist to provide remarkably accurate forecasts of sales patterns for durable products such as appliances, cameras, and VCRs. They are based, in part, on decomposing sales into first purchases and replacement sales.

Detecting Maturity and Decline

One particularly important set of turning points in market sales occurs when the growth phase of the product-life cycle changes to a flat maturity phase and when the maturity phase changes into a decline phase. These transitions are important indicators of the health and nature of the market. Often they are accompanied by changes in key success factors. Historical sales and profit patterns of a market can help to identify the onset of maturity or decline, but the following often are more sensitive indicators:

- *Price pressure caused by overcapacity and the lack of product differentiation.* When growth slows or even reverses, capacity developed under a more optimistic scenario becomes excessive. Furthermore, the product evolution process often results in most competitors matching product improvements. Thus, it becomes more difficult to maintain meaningful differentiation.

- *Buyer sophistication and knowledge.* Buyers tend to become more familiar and knowledgeable as a product matures, and thus they become less willing to pay a premium price to obtain the security of an established name. Computer buyers over the years have gained confidence in their ability to select computers—as a result, the value of big names such as IBM has receded.

- *Substitute products or technologies.* The sales of personal TV services like TiVo provide an indicator of the decline of VCRs.

- *Saturation.* When the number of potential first-time buyers declines, market sales should mature or decline.

- *No growth sources.* The market is fully penetrated and there are no visible sources of growth from new uses or users.

- *Customer disinterest.* The interest of customers in applications, new product announcements, and so on falls off.

MARKET AND SUBMARKET PROFITABILITY ANALYSIS

Economists have long studied why some industries or markets are profitable and others are not. Harvard economist and business strategy guru Michael Porter applied his theories and findings to the business strategy problem of evaluating the investment value of an industry or market.[3] The problem is to estimate how profitable the average firm will be. It is hoped, of course, that a firm will develop a strategy that will bring above-average profits. If the average profit level is low, however, the task of succeeding financially will be much more difficult than if the average profitability were high.

Porter's approach can be applied to any industry, but it also can be applied to a market or submarket within an industry. The basic idea is that the attractiveness of an industry or market as measured by the long-term return on investment of the average firm depends largely on five factors that influence profitability, shown in Figure 5.3:

- The intensity of competition among existing competitors.
- The existence of potential competitors who will enter if profits are high.
- Substitute products that will attract customers if prices become high.
- The bargaining power of customers.
- The bargaining power of suppliers.

Each factor plays a role in explaining why some industries are historically more profitable than others. An understanding of this structure can also suggest which key success factors are necessary to cope with the competitive forces.

Figure 5.3   Porter's Five-Factor Model of Market Profitability

Source: The concept of five factors is due to Michael E. Porter. See his book *Competitive Advantage,* New York: The Free Press, 1985, Chapter 1.

Existing Competitors

The intensity of competition from existing competitors will depend on several factors, including:

- The number of competitors, their size, and their commitment.
- Whether their product offerings and strategies are similar.
- The existence of high fixed costs.
- The size of exit barriers.

The first question to ask is, how many competitors are already in the market or making plans to enter soon? The more competitors that exist, the more competition intensifies. Are they large firms with staying power and commitment, or small and vulnerable ones? The second consideration is the amount of differentiation. Are the competitors similar, or are some (or all) insulated by points of uniqueness valued by customers? The third factor is the level of fixed costs. A high fixed-cost industry like telecommunication or airlines experiences debilitating price pressures when overcapacity gets large. Finally, one should assess the presence of exit barriers such as specialized assets, long-term contract commitments to customers and distributors, and relationship to other parts of a firm.

One major factor in the shakeout of both e-commerce and content Internet firms was the excessive number of competitors. Because the barriers to entry were low and the offered products so similar, margins were insufficient (and often nonexistent), especially given the significant investment in infrastructure and brand building that was needed. Given the hysterical market growth and the low barriers to entry, the results should have been anticipated; at one time there were a host of pet-supply and drugstore e-commerce offerings competing for a still-embryonic market.

Potential Competitors

Chapter 4 discusses identifying potential competitors that might have an interest in entering an industry or market. Whether potential competitors, identified or not, actually do enter depends in large part on the size and nature of barriers to entry. Thus, an analysis of barriers to entry is important in projecting likely competitive intensity and profitability levels in the future.

Various barriers to entry include required capital investment (the infrastructure in cable television and telecommunication), economies of scale (the success of Internet portals like Yahoo! or AOL is largely based on scale economies), distribution channels (Frito-Lay and IBM have access to customers that is not easily duplicated), and product differentiation (Apple and Harley-Davidson have highly differentiated products that protect them from new entrants).

Substitute Products

Substitute products compete with less intensity than do the primary competitors. They are still relevant, however. They can influence the profitability of the market and can be a major threat or problem. Thus, plastics, glass, and fiber-foil products exert pressure on the metal can market. Electronic alarm systems are substitutes for the security guard market. E-mail provides a threat to some portion of the express-delivery market of FedEx and UPS. Substitutes that show a steady improvement in relative price/performance and for which the customer's cost of switching is minimal are of particular interest.

Customer Power

When customers have relatively more power than sellers, they can force prices down or demand more services, thereby affecting profitability. A customer's power will be greater when its purchase size is a large proportion of the seller's business, when alternative suppliers are available, and when the customer can integrate backward and make all or part of the product. Thus, tire manufacturers face powerful customers in the automobile firms. The customers of metal can manufacturers are large packaged-goods manufacturers who have over time demanded price and service concessions and who have engaged in backward integration. Cereal firms face a super-market industry that has become strong and assertive in part because of its developing strengths in information technology. Soft-drink firms sell to fast-food restaurant chains and athletic teams that have strong bargaining power.

Supplier Power

When the supplier industry is concentrated and sells to a variety of customers in diverse markets, it will have relative power that can be used to influence prices. Power will also be enhanced when the costs to customers of switching suppliers are high. Thus, the highly concentrated oil industry is often powerful enough to influence profits in customer industries that find it expensive to convert from oil. However, the potential for regeneration whereby industries can create their own energy supplies, perhaps by recycling waste, may have changed the balance of power in some contexts.

COST STRUCTURE

An understanding of the cost structure of a market can provide insights into present and future key success factors. The first step is to conduct an analysis of the value chain presented in Figure 5.4 to determine where value is added to the product (or service). As suggested in Figure 5.4, the proportion of value added attributed to one value chain stage can become so important that a key success factor is associated with that stage. It may be possible to develop control over a resource or technology, as did the OPEC oil cartel. More likely, competitors will aim to be the lowest-cost competitor in a high value-added stage of the value chain. Advantages in lower value-added stages will simply have less leverage. Thus, in the metal can business, transportation costs are relatively high and a competitor that can locate plants near customers will have a significant cost advantage.

It may not be possible to gain an advantage at high value-added stages. For example, a raw material, such as flour for bakery firms, may represent a high value

Production Stage	Markets that Have Key Success Factors Associated with the Production Stage
• Raw material procurement	• Gold mining, wine making
• Raw material processing	• Steel, paper
• Production fabricating	• Integrated circuits, tires
• Assembly	• Apparel, instrumentation
• Physical distribution	• Bottled water, metal cans
• Marketing	• Branded cosmetics, liquor
• Service backup	• Software, automobiles
• Technology development	• Razors, medical systems

Figure 5.4   Value Added and Key Success Factors

added, but because the raw material is widely available at commodity prices, it will not be a key success factor. Nevertheless, it is often useful to look first at the highest value-added stages, especially if changes are occurring. For example, the cement market was very regional when it was restricted to rail or truck transportation. With the development of specialized ships, however, waterborne transportation costs dropped dramatically. Key success factors changed from local ground transportation to production scale and access to the specialized ships.

DISTRIBUTION SYSTEMS

An analysis of distribution systems should include three types of questions:

- What are the alternative distribution channels?
- What are the trends? What channels are growing in importance? What new channels have emerged or are likely to emerge?
- Who has the power in the channel, and how is that likely to shift?

Sometimes the creation of a new channel of distribution can lead to a sustainable competitive advantage. A dramatic example is the success that L'eggs hosiery achieved by its ability to market hosiery in supermarkets. L'eggs supported the idea of using supermarkets with a comprehensive program that addressed a host of issues. The L'eggs program involved selling on consignment, packaging the hosiery in a container that made it relatively difficult to shoplift, using a space-efficient vertical display, providing a high-quality, low-priced product supported by national advertising, and performing in-store functions, such as ordering and stocking. Thus, it is useful to consider not only existing channels but potential ones.

An analysis of likely or emerging changes within distribution channels can be important in understanding a market and its key success factors. The increased sale of wine in supermarkets made it much more important for wine makers to focus on packaging and advertising. The emergence of e-commerce, the growth of convenience stores in gas stations, the success of category-dominating chains like Best Buy and Home Depot, and the growth of specialty—catalogue retailing illustrate trends that have strategic importance to firms affected by these channels.

MARKET TRENDS

Often one of the most useful elements of external analysis comes from addressing the question, what are the market trends? The question has two important attributes: it focuses on change, and it tends to identify what is important. Strategically useful insights almost always result. A discussion of market trends can serve as a useful summary of customer, competitor, and market analyses. It is thus helpful to identify trends near the end of market analysis.

In the wine market, a distinct trend is the growth of premium wines—those priced above $15 a bottle. During the 1990s, their sales ballooned from under $400 million to more than $6 billion, whereas popular-priced wines (from $4 to $15 per bottle) enjoyed only a three-fold increase, and sales of jug wines declined. While the soft-drink market stagnated in the United States, noncarbonated beverages grew sharply, and sales of herb- and vitamin-fortified beverages exploded. Not surprisingly, the major soft-drink companies sought to obtain a position in these trendy categories.

Trends versus Fads

It is crucial to distinguish between trends that will drive growth and reward those who develop differentiated strategies, and fads that will only last long enough to attract investment (which is subsequently underemployed or lost forever). Schwinn, the classic name in bicycles, proclaimed mountain biking a fad in 1985, with disastrous results to its market position and, ultimately, its corporate health.[4] The mistaken belief that certain e-commerce markets, such as those for cosmetics and pet supplies, were solid trends caused strategists to undertake initial share-building strategies that eventually led to the ventures' demise.

One firm, the Zandl Group, suggests that three questions can help detect a real trend, as opposed to a fad.[5]

1. **What is driving it?** A trend will have a solid foundation with legs. Trends are more likely to be driven by demographics (rather than pop culture), values (rather than fashion), lifestyle (rather than a trendy crowd), or technology (rather than media).

2. **How accessible is it in the mainstream?** Will it be constrained to a niche market for the foreseeable future? Will it require a major change in ingrained habits? Is the required investment in time or resources a barrier (perhaps because the product is priced too high or is too hard to use)?

3. **Is it broadly based?** Does it find expression across categories or industries? Eastern influences, for example, are apparent in health care, food, fitness, and design—a sign of a trend.

Faith Popcorn observes that fads are about products, while trends are about what drives consumers to buy products. She also suggests that trends (which are big and broad, lasting an average of ten years) cannot be created or changed, only observed.[6]

Still another perspective on fads comes from Peter Drucker, who opined that a change is something that people do, whereas a fad is something people talk about. The implication is that a trend demands substance and action supported by data, rather than simply an idea that captures the imagination. Drucker also suggests that the leaders of today need to move beyond innovation to be change agents—the real payoff comes not from simply detecting and reacting to trends, even when they are real, but from creating and driving them.[7]

KEY SUCCESS FACTORS

An important output of market analysis is the identification of key success factors for strategic groups in the market. These are assets and competencies that provide the basis for competing successfully. There are two types. Strategic necessities do not necessarily provide an advantage, because others have them, but their absence will create a substantial weakness. The second type, strategic strengths, are those at which a firm excels, the assets or competencies that are superior to those of competitors and provide a base of advantage. The set of assets and competencies developed in competitor analysis provides a base set from which key success factors can be identified. The points to consider are which are the most critical assets and competencies now and, more important, which will be most critical in the future.

It is important not only to identify KSFs, but also to project them into the future and, in particular, to identify emerging KSFs. Many firms have faltered when KSFs changed and the competencies and assets on which they were relying became less relevant. For example, for industrial firms, technology and innovation tend to be most important during the introduction and growth phases, whereas the roles of systems capability, marketing, and service backup become more dominant as the market matures. In consumer products, marketing and distribution skills are crucial during the introduction and growth phases, but operations and manufacturing become more crucial as the product settles into the maturity and decline phases.

RISKS IN HIGH-GROWTH MARKETS

The conventional wisdom that the strategist should seek out growth areas often overlooks a substantial set of associated risks. As shown in Figure 5.5, there are the risks that:

- The number and commitment of competitors may be greater than the market can support.
- A competitor may enter with a superior product or low-cost advantage.
- Key success factors might change and the organization may be unable to adapt.
- Technology might change.

Figure 5.5   Risks of High-Growth Markets

- The market growth may fail to meet expectations.
- Price instability may result from overcapacity or from retailers' practice of pricing hot products low to attract customers.
- Resources might be inadequate to maintain a high growth rate.
- Adequate distribution may not be available.

Competitive Overcrowding

Perhaps the most serious risk is that too many competitors will be attracted by a growth situation and enter with unrealistic market share expectations. The reality may be that sales volume is insufficient to support all competitors. Overcrowding has been observed in virtually all hyped markets, from railroads to airplanes, radio stations and equipment, televisions sets, and personal computers.

Overcrowding was never more vividly apparent (in retrospect, at least) than in the dot-com frenzy. At one point there were at least 150 online brokerages, 1,000 travel-related sites, and thirty health and beauty sites that were competing for attention. Dot-com business-to-business (B2B) exchanges were created for the buying and selling of goods and services, information exchanges, logistics services, sourcing industry data and forecasts, and a host of other services. The number of B2B companies grew from under 250 to over 1,500 during the year 2000, then fell to under 250 again in 2003. At the peak, there were estimated to be more than 140 such exchanges in the industrial supplies industry alone.[8]

The following conditions are found in markets in which a surplus of competitors is likely to be attracted and a subsequent shakeout is highly probable. These factors were all present in the B2B dot-com experience:

1. The market and its growth rate have high visibility. As a result, strategists in related firms are encouraged to consider the market seriously and may even fear the consequences of turning their backs on an obvious growth direction.

2. Very high forecast and actual growth in the early stages are seen as evidence confirming high market growth as a proven phenomenon.

3. Threats to the growth rate are not considered or are discounted, and little exists to dampen the enthusiasm surrounding the market. The enthusiasm may be contagious when venture capitalists and stock analysts become advocates.

4. Few initial barriers exist to prevent firms from entering the market. There may be barriers to eventual success (such as limited retail space), however, that may not be evident at the outset.

5. Some potential entrants have low visibility, and their intentions are unknown or uncertain. As a result, the quantity and commitment of the competitors are likely to be underestimated.

Superior Competitive Entry

The ultimate risk is that a position will be established in a healthy growth market and a competitor will enter late with a product that is demonstrably superior or that has an inherent cost advantage.

Thus, the Apple Newton was first to market with a handheld computing device, but it failed in part because it was priced too high, badly designed, and too complex to use. The cheaper, better, and simpler PalmPilot won the market, even though it came later. The success of late-entry, low-cost products from the Far East has occurred in countless industries, from automobiles to TVs to VCRs.

Changing Key Success Factors

A firm may successfully establish a strong position during the early stages of market development, only to lose ground later when key success factors change. One forecast is that the surviving personal computer makers will be those able to achieve low-cost production through vertical integration or exploitation of the experience curve, those able to obtain efficient, low-cost distribution, and those able to provide software for their customers—capabilities not necessarily critical during the early stages of market evolution. Many product markets have experienced a shift over time from a focus on product technology to a focus on process technology. A firm that might be capable of achieving product-technology-based advantages may not have the resources, competencies, and orientation/culture needed to develop the process-technology-based advantages that the evolving market demands.

Changing Technology

Developing first-generation technology can involve a commitment to a product line and production facilities that may become obsolete and to a technology that may not survive. A safe strategy is to wait until it is clear which technology will dominate and then attempt to improve it with a compatible entry. When the principal competitors have committed themselves, the most promising avenues for the development of a sustainable competitive advantage become more visible. In contrast, the early entry has to navigate with a great deal of uncertainty.

Disappointing Market Growth

Many shakeouts and price wars occur when market growth falls below expectations. Sometimes the market was an illusion to begin with. B2B exchanges did not provide value to firms that already had systems built with relationships that were, on balance, superior to the B2B exchanges. There was an absence of a compelling value proposition to overcome marketplace inertia. In other cases, the demand may be healthy, but the market is still hostile because competitors have built capacity to match over-optimistic expectations. Or the demand might simply take longer to materialize because the technology is not ready, or because customers are slow to change. Demand for electronic banking, for example, took many years longer than expected to materialize.

Forecasting demand is difficult, especially when the market is new, dynamic, and glamorized. This difficulty is graphically illustrated by an analysis of more than ninety forecasts of significant new products, markets, and technologies that appeared in *Business Week, Fortune,* and the *Wall Street Journal* from 1960 to 1979.[9] Forecast growth failed to materialize in about 55 percent of the cases cited. Among the reasons were overvaluation of technologies (e.g., three-dimensional color TV and tooth-decay vaccines), consumer demand (e.g., two-way cable TV, quadraphonic stereo, and dehydrated foods), a failure to consider the cost barrier (e.g., the SST and moving sidewalks), or political problems (e.g., marine mining). The forecasts for roll-your-own cigarettes, small cigars, Scotch whiskey, and CB radios suffered from shifts in consumer needs and preferences.

Price Instability

When the creation of excess capacity results in price pressures, industry profitability may be short-lived, especially in an industry, such as airlines or steel, in which fixed costs are high and economies of scale are crucial. However, it is also possible that some will use a hot product as a loss leader just to attract customer flow.

CDs, a hot growth area in the late 1980s, fueled the overexpansion of retailers from 5,500 in 1987 to over 7,000 in 1992.[10] The retailers were very profitable when they sold CDs for about $15. However, when Best Buy, a home-electronics chain, decided to sell CDs for under $10 to attract customers to their off-mall locations, and when Circuit City followed suit, the result was a dramatic erosion in margins and volume and the ultimate bankruptcy of a substantial number of the major CD retailers. A hot growth area had spawned a disaster, not by a self-inflicted price cut, but by price instability from a firm that chose to treat the retailing of CDs as nothing more than a permanent loss leader.

Resource Constraints

The substantial financing requirements associated with a rapidly growing business are a major constraint for small firms. Royal Crown's Diet-Rite cola lost its leadership position to Coca-Cola's Tab and Diet Pepsi in the mid-1960s when it could not match the advertising and distribution clout of its larger rivals. Furthermore, financing requirements frequently are increased by higher than expected product development and market entry costs and by price erosion caused by aggressive or desperate competitors.

The organizational pressures and problems created by growth can be even more difficult to predict and deal with than financial strains. Many firms have failed to survive the rapid-growth phase because they were unable to obtain and train people to handle the expanded business or to adjust their systems and structures.

Distribution Constraints

Most distribution channels can support only a small number of brands. For example, few retailers are willing to provide shelf space for more than four or five brands of a houseware appliance. As a consequence, some competitors, even those with attractive products and marketing programs, will not gain adequate distribution, and their marketing programs will become less effective.

Distribution limitations fueled the shakeout that began in the software business in the mid-1980s. More than 120 firms were making financial spreadsheet programs, whereas the market and distribution channels could not support more than a handful.

A corollary of the scarcity and selectivity of distributors as market growth begins to slow is a marked increase in distributor power. Their willingness to use this power to extract price and promotion concessions from manufacturers or to drop suppliers is often heightened by their own problems in maintaining margins in the face of extreme competition for their customers. Many of the same factors that drew in an overabundance of manufacturers also contribute to overcrowding in subsequent stages of a distribution channel. The eventual shakeout at this level can have equally serious repercussions for suppliers.

KEY LEARNINGS

- The emergence of submarkets can signal a relevance problem.
- Market analysis should assess the attractiveness of a market, as well as its structure and dynamics.
- A usage gap can cause the market size to be understated.
- Market growth can be forecast by looking at driving forces, leading indicators, and analogous industries.
- Market profitability will depend on five factors—existing competitors, supplier power, customer power, substitute products, and potential entrants.
- Cost structure can be analyzed by looking at the value added at each production stage.
- Distribution channels and trends will often affect who wins.

- Market trends will affect both the profitability of strategies and key success factors.

- Key success factors are the skills and competencies needed to compete in a market.

- Growth-market challenges involve the threat of competitors, market changes, and firm limitations.

FOR DISCUSSION

1. What are the emerging submarkets in the fast food industry? What are the alternative responses available to McDonald's, assuming that it wants to stay relevant to customers interested in healthier eating?

2. Identify markets in which actual sales and growth was less than expected. Why was that the case? What would you say was the most important reason that the bottom fell out of the dot-com boom? Why did all the B2B sites emerge, and why did they collapse so suddenly?

3. Why were some brands (like Gatorade) able to fight off competitors in high-growth markets and other (like Palm) were not?

4. Pick a company or brand/business on which to focus. What are the emerging submarkets? What are the trends? What are the strategic implications of the submarkets and trends for the major players?

NOTES

1. For more details in the relevance concept see David A. Aaker, "The Brand Relevance Challenge," *Strategy & Business*, Spring 2004, and David A. Aaker, *Brand Portfolio Strategy*, Chapter 3, New York: The Free Press, 2004.

2. Greg Stanger, Clark Newby, Todd Andrews, Rob Wamer, Presley Stokes, and Lisen Stromberg. "The Ready to Eat Cereal Market," unpublished paper, 1991.

3. This section draws on Michael E. Porter, *Competitive Advantage*, New York: The Free Press, 1985, chapter 1.

4. Scott Davis of Prophet Brand Strategy suggested the Schwinn case.

5. Irma Zandl, "How to Separate Trends from Fads," *Brandweek*, October 23, 2000, pp. 30–35.

6. Faith Popcorn and Lys Marigold, *Clicking*, HarperCollins, 1997, pp. 11–12.

7. James Daly, "Sage Advice—Interview with Peter Drucker," *Business 2.0*, August 22, 2000, pp. 134–144.

8. George S. Day, Adam J. Fein, Gregg Ruppersberger, "Shakeouts in Digital Markets: Lessons for GB2B Exchanges," *California Management Review*, Winter 2003, p. 131–133.

9. Steven P. Schnaars, "Growth Market Forecasting Revisited: A Look Back at a Look Forward," *California Management Review* 28(4), Summer 1986.

10. Tim Carvell, "These Prices Really Are Insane," *Fortune*, August 4, 1997, pp. 109–114.

CHAPTER SIX

Environmental Analysis and Strategic Uncertainty

We are watching the dinosaurs die, but we don't know what will take their place.
—*Lester Thurow, MIT economist*

There is something in the wind.
—*William Shakespeare, The Comedy of Errors*

A poorly observed fact is more treacherous than a faulty train of reasoning
 Paul Valéry, French philosopher

*I*n this chapter, the focus changes from the market to the environment surrounding the market. The interest is in environmental trends and events that have the potential to affect strategy, either directly or indirectly. Environmental analysis should identify such trends and events and estimate their likelihood and impact.

Although environmental analysis is one step removed from the market or industry, it is only one step. When conducting environmental analysis, it is very easy to get bogged down in an extensive, broad survey of trends. However, it is necessary to restrict the analysis to those areas relevant enough to have a significant impact on strategy.

Environmental analysis can be divided usefully, as shown in Figure 6.1, into five areas: technological, governmental, economic, cultural, and demographic. Each area is discussed and illustrated. Then, methods of forecasting trends and events are presented.

After describing environmental analysis, the last of the four dimensions of external analysis, the chapter will turn to the task of dealing with strategic uncertainty, a key output of external analysis. Impact analysis and scenario analysis are tools that help to evolve that uncertainty into strategy. Impact analysis—the assessment of the relative

TECHNOLOGY
- To what extent are existing technologies maturing?
- What technological developments or trends are affecting or could affect the industry?

GOVERNMENT
- What changes in regulation are possible? What will their impact be?
- What tax or other incentives are being developed that might affect strategy?
- What are the political risks of operating in a governmental jurisdiction?

ECONOMICS
- What are the economic prospects and inflation outlets for the countries in which the firm operates? How will they affect strategy?

CULTURE
- What are the current or emerging trends in lifestyles, fashions, and other components of culture? Why? What are their implications?

DEMOGRAPHICS
- What demographic trends will affect the market size of the industry or its submarkets? What demographic trends represent opportunities or threats?

GENERAL EXTERNAL ANALYSIS QUESTIONS
- What are the significant trends and future events?
- What threats and opportunities do you see?
- What are the key areas of uncertainty as to trends or events that have the potential to impact strategy? Evaluate these strategic uncertainties in terms of their impact.

SCENARIOS
- What strategic uncertainties are worth being the basis of a scenario analysis?

Figure 6.1   Environmental Analysis

importance of strategic uncertainties—is addressed first. Scenario analysis—ways of creating and using future scenarios to help generate and evaluate strategies—follows.

DIMENSIONS OF ENVIRONMENTAL ANALYSIS

Technology

One dimension of environmental analysis is technological trends or technological events occurring outside the market or industry that have the potential to impact strategies. They can represent opportunities and threats to those in a position to capitalize. For example, the cable TV industry, with its massive investment in the wiring of homes, should be concerned with the technology related to satellite alternatives. Express delivery services such as FedEx have been affected by new forms of communication. While e-mail can replace the use of overnight delivery, Internet-based e-commerce has provided a major source of new business for FedEx.

Forecasting Technologies

It is often easy to compile a list of technologies in the wings; the hard part is sorting out the winners from the losers. The experience of the retail sector may provide some guidance. Among the big winners were the 1936 invention of the shopping cart (which allowed customers to buy more and do so more easily) and the UPC scanner (which improved checkout and provided a rich information source). Among the losers were Videotex in 1983 and interactive television in 1993, two premature forerunners to e-commerce. To those we can add Ted Turner's Checkout Channel (color monitors positioned by the checkout counters in grocery stores) and the VideOcart (screens attached to shopping carts that could highlight specials and guide shoppers).

Ray Burke, a retail expert from Indiana University, drew upon a variety of research sources to develop a set of guidelines for separating winners from losers. Although his context is retailing, any organization exploring new technologies can benefit from considering each of the guidelines:[1]

- Use technology to create an immediate, tangible benefit for the consumer. The benefit, in short, needs to be perceived as such. The Checkout Channel was designed to help entertain, but consumers saw it as an intrusive annoyance.

- Make the technology easy to use. Consumers resist wasting time and becoming frustrated, and too often new technologies are perceived as doing exactly these things. Research shows that it takes customers an average of 20 to 30 minutes just to learn how to shop in most text-based Internet grocery shopping systems. AOL beat its main rival Compuserve in part because it was easier to use.

- Execution matters: prototype, test, and refine. One in-store kiosk had no way to inform frustrated customers that it had run out of paper. A bank found customers more receptive to an interactive videoconferencing system when the screens were placed in inviting locations.

- Recognize that customer response to technology varies. One bank found that ATM customers rejected video conferencing options because they actually did not want to interact with humans. Some retailers use loyalty cards to provide receipts and promotions tailored to individual customers.

Disruptive and Sustaining Technologies

Clayton Christensen, a Harvard Business School professor, developed a theory about disruptive versus sustaining innovations that explains the dynamics of many industries.[2] Sustaining innovations are those that help incumbent companies sell better products for more money to their best customers. Both simple, incremental improvements and breakthrough leaps in technology can be sustaining as long as the focus is on improving margins for the best existing customers. Successful organizations develop structures, staff, incentives, and skills designed to generate and implement a continuous flow of sustaining innovations—the pursuit of which is considered a reliable route to profitable growth, and the absence of which risks loss of position.

Incumbent organizations are not always the first to market with a sustaining innovation, but they usually win because of their resources and motivation.

Disruptive innovations, in contrast, appeal to customers who are unattractive to incumbents, usually because they are not in the high-volume, high-margin "sweet spot" of the market. Instead, these innovations take one of two routes into the marketplace.[3] First, they look toward potential customers who are not currently buying the product because it is too complex or expensive. Examples of this would include how Apple's Macintosh attracted new users into the computer market, online retail stockbrokers enabled day traders to thrive, and the PalmPilot appealed to people wanting a simple organizer as opposed to a handheld computer. These products did not appeal to the best customers of incumbent firms.

A second route for disruptive technologies is to enter the market at the low end, focusing on customers who are "overserved." As sustainable innovation drives performance upward, there will be a segment that simply does not need the extra capabilities and would be satisfied with (indeed, would prefer) a simpler, cheaper product with satisfactory performance. Japanese car companies entered the U.S. car market in the 1960s and the copier market in the 1970s with a disruptive innovation strategy. Wal-Mart, Southwest Airlines, and Dell Computers all used this route as well.

Disruptive innovations are often the basis for attractive growth, but incumbent firms—especially successful ones—rarely participate. When an organization is doing well, there is pressure to enhance short-term growth and margins, which can best be achieved through sustaining innovations. When the business turns downward (perhaps because of a competitor's disruptive technology), there are no resources available to support an initiative to catch up to the disruptive innovation.

To participate in disruptive innovations, a firm needs to recognize that its existing organization is likely to be a liability. Thus, a separate organization may be required, or at least a group within the current organization that has very different people, processes, and culture. Further, it is important to explore disruptive innovations before performance turns bad, resources are less available, and others have achieved a first-mover advantage. Finally, top management should participate in the decision to develop a disruptive innovation; without a high-level commitment, the pursuit may become an endless exercise in observation and fact-finding.

Impact of New Technologies

Certainly it can be important, even critical, to manage the transition to a new technology. The appearance of a new technology, however, even a successful one, does not necessarily mean that businesses based on the prior technology will suddenly become unhealthy.

A group of researchers at Purdue studied fifteen companies in five industries in which a dramatic new technology had emerged:[4]

- Diesel-electric locomotives versus steam
- Transistors versus vacuum tubes

- Ballpoint pens versus fountain pens
- Nuclear power versus boilers for fossil-fuel plants
- Electric razors versus safety razors

Two interesting conclusions emerged that should give pause to anyone attempting to predict the impact of a dramatic new technology. First, the sales of the old technology continued for a substantial period, in part because the firms involved continued to improve it. Safety-razor sales have actually increased 800 percent since the advent of the electric razor. Thus, a new technology may not signal the end of the growth phase of an existing technology. In all cases, firms involved with the old technology had a substantial amount of time to react to the new technology.

Second, it is relatively difficult to predict the outcome of a new technology. The new technologies studied tended to be expensive and crude at first. Furthermore, they started by invading submarkets. Transistors, for example, were first used in hearing aids and pocket radios. In addition, new technologies tended to create new markets instead of simply encroaching on existing ones. Throwaway ballpoint pens and many of the transistor applications opened up completely new market areas.

Government

The addition or removal of legislative or regulatory constraints can pose major strategic threats and opportunities. For example, the ban of some ingredients in food products or cosmetics has dramatically affected the strategies of numerous firms. The impact of governmental efforts to reduce piracy in industries such as software (more than one-fourth of all software used is copied), CDs, DVDs, and movie videos is of crucial import to those affected. Deregulation in banking, energy, and other industries is having enormous implications for the firms involved. The automobile industry is affected by fuel-economy standards and by the luxury tax on automobiles. The relaxation of regulatory constraints in India and China can have enormous implications for global firms.

In an increasingly global economy with interdependencies in markets and in the sourcing of products and services, possible political hot spots need to be understood and tracked. In a classic study of environmental trends and events that were forecast in *Fortune* magazine during the 1930s and 1940s, predictions were found to be remarkably good in many areas such as synthetic vitamins, genetic breakthroughs, the decline of railroads, and the advent of TVs, house-trailers, and super-highways. However, forecasting was extremely poor when international events were involved.[5] Thus, a mid-1930s article did not consider the possibility of U.S. involvement in a European war. A 1945 article incorrectly forecast a huge growth in trade with the Soviet Union, not anticipating the advent of the cold war. A Middle East scenario failed to forecast the emergence of Israel. International political developments, which can be critical to multinational firms, are still extremely difficult to forecast. A prudent strategy is one that is both diversified and flexible, so that a political surprise will not be devastating.

Economics

The evaluation of some strategies will be affected by judgments made about the economy, particularly about inflation and general economic health as measured by unemployment and economic growth. Heavy investment in a capital-intensive industry might need to be timed to coincide with a strong economy to avoid a damaging period of losses. Usually it is necessary to look beyond the general economy to the health of individual industries. In the early 2000s, for example, high tech was weaker and the housing industry stronger than the economy as a whole.

A forecast of the relative valuations of currencies can be relevant for industries with multinational competitors. Thus, an analysis of the balance of payments and other factors affecting currency valuations might be needed. For example, in most developed countries, the automobile industry is extremely sensitive to changes in currency valuation.

Culture

Cultural trends can present both threats and opportunities for a wide variety of firms, as the following examples illustrate.

A dress designer conducted a study that projected women's lifestyles. It predicted that a more varied lifestyle would prevail, that more time would be spent outside the home, and that those who worked would be more career oriented. These predictions had several implications relevant to the dress designer's product line and pricing strategies. For example, a growing number and variety of activities would lead to a broader range of styles and larger wardrobes, with

IBM AND THE INTERNET

In 1993, an IBM engineer wrote a research paper entitled "Get Connected" which outlined six principles of Internet-based communication that led to a total refocus of IBM toward the Internet years before Microsoft and others got the message. It has to be one of the most influential environmental analyses of our time. The principles were—that e-mail would become pervasive; e-mail directory assistance would be needed; e-mail would allow vertical communication within an organization; e-mail addresses would be on all communication; companies would create Web sites with information repositories; and e-commerce would explode. These insights seem obvious in retrospect, but they were visionary at the time.

In 1994, the then-new CEO, Lou Gerstner, bought into the idea. He "got it"—during the first e-commerce demo, Gerstner was reported to ask, "Where is the Buy button?" A flurry of initiatives followed, turning IBM from a sick firm on the brink of collapse to a leader of the new economy. Among the more visible strategic moves were the purchase of Lotus Notes, the creation of NetCommerce, (an outgrowth of the IBM support for the 1996 Olympics), a general e-business positioning, and the renaming of the server line to "e-servers."[6]

INFORMATION TECHNOLOGY

In nearly every industry it is useful to ask what potential impact new information technology based on new databases will have on strategies. How will it create SCAs and key success factors? Apparel manufacturers such as Levi Strauss, drug wholesalers such as McKesson, and retailers such as the Limited all have developed systems of inventory control, ordering, and shipping that represent substantial SCAs. FedEx has stayed ahead of competitors by investing heavily in information technology. It was the first express delivery service to have the ability to track packages throughout its systems and the first to link its systems with customers computers. Merrill Lynch's Cash Management Account provided substantial customer benefits.

In supermarket retailing, "smart cards," cards that customers present during checkout to pay for purchases, provide a record of all purchases that allow:

- Stores to build loyalty by rewarding cumulative purchase volume.
- Promotions to target individual customers based on their brand preferences and household characteristics.
- The use of cents-off coupons without the customer or store having to handle pieces of paper; the purchase of a promoted product can be discounted automatically.
- The store to identify buyers of slow-moving items and predict the impact on the store's choice of dropping an item.
- Decisions as to shelf-space allocation, special displays, and store layout to be refined based on detailed information about customer shopping.

perhaps somewhat less spent on each garment. Furthermore, consumers' increased financial and social independence would probably reduce the number of follow-the-leader fashions and the perception that certain outfits were required for certain occasions.

There is a trend toward tribing, the affinity toward a social unit that is centered around an interest or activity and is not bound by conventional social links.[7] Harley-Davidson events such as the annual rally in Sturgis, South Dakota, can attract hundreds of thousands of participants. The Macintosh users group has been a strong part of Apple's survival in a PC world. The Internet has generated a host of communities and chat groups; Environmental Defense, for example, has well over 100,000 members and plays an influential role through information exchange and political action. Tribing has significance for brand-building and communication programs, both positively and negatively.

Faith Popcorn has uncovered and studied cultural trends that, in her judgment, will shape the future. Her efforts provide a provocative view of the future environment of many organizations. Consider, for example, the following trends:[8]

- ***Cocooning.*** Consumers are retreating into safe, cozy "homelike" environments to shield themselves from the harsh realities of the outside world. This trend supports on-line and catalogue shopping, home security systems, gardening, and smart homes.

- *Fantasy adventure.* Consumers crave low-risk excitement and stimulation to escape from stress and boredom. Responsive firms offer theme restaurants, exotic cosmetics, adventure travel, fantasy clothes that suggest role-playing, fantasy-based entertainment, and fantasy cars.

- *Pleasure revenge.* Consumers are rebelling against rules to cut loose and savor forbidden fruits (for example, indulgent ice creams, cigars, martinis, tanning salons, and furs).

- *Small indulgences.* Busy, stressed-out people are rewarding themselves with affordable luxuries that will provide quick gratification: fresh-squeezed orange juice, chocolate-dipped Tuscan biscotti, crusty bread, and upscale-fountain pens. For the financially well off, the range of possibilities might include Porsche flatware, a mahogany Cris-Craft canoe, or Range Rover night-vision binoculars.

- *Down-aging.* Consumers seek symbols of youth, renewal, and rejuvenation to counterbalance the intensity of their adult lives. The over-55 crowd going to school and participating in active sports (including ironman competitions and outdoor adventures) reflect this trend, but it really extends to a wide age group who favor products, apparel, activities, and entertainment that capture the nostalgia of youth.

- *Being alive.* Consumers focus on the quality of life and the importance of wellness, taking charge of their personal health rather than delegating it to the health care industry. Examples of this include the use of holistic medical approaches, vegetarian products and restaurants, organic products, water filters, and health clubs.

- *99 lives.* Consumers are forced to assume multiple roles to cope with their increasingly busy lives. Retailers serving multiple needs, ever-faster ways to get prepared food, a service that manages your second home and prepares it for visits, noise neutralizers, e-commerce, and yoga are all responsive to this trend.

Demographics

Demographic trends can be a powerful underlying force in a market and it can be predictable. Among the influential demographic variables are age, income, education, and geographic location.

The older demographic group is of particular interest, because it is growing rapidly and is blessed with not only resources but the time to use them. The over-65 population in the United States will grow from 33 million in 2000 to 49 million in 2020. The over-85 group will grow from 3.6 million to over 6.5 million in the same time period, and its members will be much more likely to live independently (perhaps in one of roughly 50,000 assisted-living units). Women tend to outlive men, so their portion of the population increases sharply over age groups; within the 85-year-old group there are only 41 men per 100 women. Research suggests that elderly women are dissatisfied at having to choose from products generally geared to younger segments.

Teens are back as the baby boomers age. The 13-to-19-year-old population in the United States will peak at 31 million in the year 2010.[9] Teens mirror the age in which they live. They take for granted the consumer electronics spectrum, deal with adult issues such as AIDS and abortion, and have been called the MTV generation because of the MTV-influenced culture to which they have been exposed. Reaching them can be profitable, as retailers such as Old Navy and Express and brands such as Clearasil and Diesel Jeans have found.

Ethnic populations are rising rapidly and support whole firms and industries, as well as affect the strategies of mainline companies. Hispanic populations, for example, are growing about five times faster than are non-Hispanic populations and are gaining in income as well. Hispanics will soon be the largest minority group. The Asian-American population, currently numbering over 6 million in the United States, is increasing rapidly.

The nuclear family was once the model of American life. No more! The proportion of U.S. households defined as traditional families (that is, a husband, a wife, and kids under 18) was at 45% in 1960, 30.2% in 1980, and 23.5% in 2000.[10] One of six traditional families has the dad staying home and the mom going to work. One implication is this demographic evolution is an increased demand for handyman services, household cleaning, and meal preparation.

The movement of businesses and populations into different areas of the country has implications for many service organizations, such as brokerage houses, real estate ventures, and insurance companies. Furthermore, the revival of downtown urban areas has had considerable implications for retailers and real estate developers, just as the earlier development of suburbia had.

DEALING WITH STRATEGIC UNCERTAINTY

Strategic uncertainty, uncertainty that has strategic implications, is a key construct in external analysis. A typical external analysis will emerge with dozens of strategic uncertainties. To be manageable, they need to be grouped into logical clusters or themes. It is then useful to assess the importance of each cluster in order to set priorities with respect to information gathering and analysis. Impact analysis, described in the next section, is designed to accomplish that assessment.

Sometimes the strategic uncertainty is represented by a future trend or event that has inherent unpredictability. Information gathering and additional analysis will not be able to reduce the uncertainty. In that case, scenario analysis can be employed. Scenario analysis basically accepts the uncertainty as given and uses it to drive a description of two or more future scenarios. Strategies are then developed for each. One outcome could be a decision to create organizational and strategic flexibility so that as the business context changes the strategy will adapt. Scenario analysis will be detailed in the final section of this chapter.

"YES, BUT…"

Some trends are real, but have obvious implications that need to be qualified. For example:

Yes, the number of women in the workforce has been increasing, *but*…
>The increase is slow and long-term, with the total proportion rising from 42% in 1980 to 45% in 1990 and 47% in 2000. Further, only a small percentage of these women fit the image of the young MBA.

Yes, Internet access and usage are growing rapidly, *but*…
>A significant proportion of the population still sees no need for the Internet. In fact, the Forrester research firm estimated in 2000 that 47 percent of the U.S. population could be termed technology pessimists—people who are ambivalent or outright hostile toward technology. This percentage is much higher among those older than 65, only 13 percent of whom were connected in 2000.

Yes, people can and will price shop on the Internet, *but*…
>A study by NFO in 2000 showed that only about half of those who made an on-line purchase in the prior six months knew about the price-comparison services, and less than 15 percent used them even occasionally. Another study showed that 90 percent of CD buyers and 80 percent of book buyers were loyal to a single site.

Yes, there is a strong trend to healthy eating and exercise, *but*…
>Two of the fastest-growing and most successful retail concepts are Krispy Kreme, the makers of famously indulgent doughnuts, and In-and-Out Burgers, a chain serving a limited menu of high-fat burgers and fries.

IMPACT ANALYSIS—ASSESSING THE IMPACT OF STRATEGIC UNCERTAINTIES

An important objective of external analysis is to rank the strategic uncertainties and decide how they are to be managed over time. Which uncertainties merit intensive investment in information gathering and in-depth analysis, and which merit only a low-key monitoring effort?

The problem is that dozens of strategic uncertainties and many second-level strategic uncertainties are often generated. These strategic uncertainties can lead to an endless process of information gathering and analysis that can absorb resources indefinitely. A publishing company may be concerned about cable TV, lifestyle patterns, educational trends, geographic population shifts, and printing technology. Any one of these issues involves a host of subfields and could easily spur limitless research. For example, cable TV might involve a variety of pay-TV concepts, suppliers, technologies, and viewer reactions. Unless distinct priorities are established, external analysis can become descriptive, ill-focused, and inefficient.

The extent to which a strategic uncertainty should be monitored and analyzed depends on its impact and immediacy.

1. The impact of a strategic uncertainty is related to:
   - The extent to which it involves trends or events that will impact existing or potential businesses
   - The importance of the involved businesses
   - The number of involved businesses

2. The immediacy of a strategic uncertainty is related to:
   - The probability that the involved trends or events will occur
   - The time frame of the trends or events
   - The reaction time likely to be available, compared with the time required to develop and implement appropriate strategy

Impact of a Strategic Uncertainty

Each strategic uncertainty involves potential trends or events that could have an impact on present, proposed, and even potential businesses. For example, a strategic uncertainty for a beer firm could be based on the future prospects of the microbrewery market. If the beer firm has both a proposed microbrewery entry and an imported beer positioned in the same area, trends in the microbrewery beer market could have a high impact on the firm. The trend toward natural foods may present opportunities for a sparkling water product line for the same firm and be the basis of a strategic uncertainty.

The impact of a strategic uncertainty will depend on the importance of the impacted business to a firm. Some businesses are more important than others. The importance of established businesses may be indicated by their associated sales, profits, or costs. However, such measures might need to be supplemented for proposed or growth businesses for which present sales, profits, or costs may not reflect the true value to a firm. Finally, because an information-need area may affect several businesses, the number of involved businesses can also be relevant to a strategic uncertainty's impact.

Immediacy of Strategic Uncertainties

Events or trends associated with strategic uncertainties may have a high impact but such a low probability of occurrence that it is not worth actively expending resources to gather or analyze information. Similarly, if occurrence is far in the future relative to the strategic-decision horizon, then it may be of little concern. Thus, the harnessing of tide energy may be so unlikely or may occur so far in the future that it is of no concern to a utility.

Finally, there is the reaction time available to a firm, compared with the reaction time likely to be needed. After a trend or event crystallizes, a firm needs to develop a reaction strategy. If the available reaction time is inadequate, it becomes important to anticipate emerging trends and events better so that future reaction strategies can be initiated sooner.

Managing Strategic Uncertainties

Figure 6.2 suggests a categorization of strategic uncertainties for a given business. If both the immediacy and impact are low, then a low level of monitoring may suffice. If the impact is thought to be low but the immediacy is high, the area may merit monitoring and analysis. If the immediacy is low and the impact high, then the area may require monitoring and analysis in more depth, and contingent strategies may be considered but not necessarily developed and implemented. When both the immediacy and potential impact of the underlying trends and events are high, then an in-depth analysis will be appropriate, as will be the development of reaction plans or strategies. An active task force may provide initiative.

SCENARIO ANALYSIS

Scenario analysis can help deal with uncertainly. It provides an alternative to investing in information to reduce uncertainty that is often an expensive and futile process. By creating a small number of marketplace or market context scenarios and assessing their likelihood and impact, scenario analysis can be a powerful way to deal with complex environments.

There are two types of scenario analyses. In the first type, strategy-developing scenarios, the object is to provide insights into future competitive contexts, then use these insights to evaluate existing business strategies and stimulate the creation of new ones. Such analyses can help create contingency plans to guard against disasters—an airline adjusting to a terror incident, for example, or a pharmaceutical

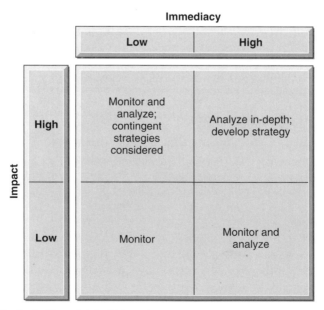

Figure 6.2   Strategic Uncertainty Categories

company reacting to a product safety problem. They can also suggest investment strategies that enable the organization to capitalize on future opportunities caused by customer trends or technological breakthroughs.

In the second type of analyses, decision-driven scenarios, a strategy is proposed and tested against several scenarios that are developed.[11] The goal is to challenge the strategies, thereby helping to make the go/no-go decision and suggesting ways to make the strategy more robust in withstanding competitive forces. If the decision is to enter a market with a technology strategy, alternate scenarios could be built around variables such as marketplace acceptance of the technology, competitor response, and the stimulation of customer applications.

In either case, a scenario analysis will involve three general steps: the creation of scenarios, relating those scenarios to existing or potential strategies, and assessing the probability of the scenarios (see Figure 6.3).

Identify Scenarios

Strategic uncertainties can drive scenario development. The impact analysis will identify the strategic uncertainty with the highest priority for a firm. A manufacturer of a medical imagery device may want to know whether a technological advance will allow its machine to be made at a substantially lower cost. A farm equipment manufacturer or ski area operator may believe that the weather—whether a drought will continue, for example—is the most important area of uncertainty. A server firm may want to know whether a single software standard will emerge or multiple standards will coexist. The chosen uncertainty could then stimulate two or more scenarios.

A competitor scenario analysis can be driven by the uncertainty surrounding a competitor's strategy. For example, could the competitor aggressively extend its brand? Or might it divest a product line or make a major acquisition? Perhaps the competitor could change its value proposition, or become more aggressive in its pricing.[12]

When a set of scenarios is based largely on a single strategic uncertainty, the scenarios themselves can usually be enriched by related events and circumstances. Thus, an inflation-stimulated recession scenario would be expected to generate a host of conditions for the appliance industry, such as price increases and retail failures. Similarly, a competitor scenario can be comprehensive, specifying such strategy dimensions as product-market investment, acquisition or joint ventures, pricing, positioning, product, and promotions.

It is sometimes useful to generate scenarios based on probable outcomes: optimistic, pessimistic, and most likely. The consideration of a pessimistic scenario is

Figure 6.3   Scenario Analysis

THE NEW CYBERLIFE—A FUTURE SCENARIO

Steve Barnett of Scenario Planning at OgilvyOne looked at the world of 2020 and projected a pervasive "Internet 2" allowing anything to be instantly retrieved, tracked, customized, and experienced.[13] Television sets, PCs, and smart appliances will be seamlessly linked, using voice activation more than keyboards. Remote forms of education, medical care, shopping, and visiting will be routine.

These changes will affect both work and lifestyle. Working at home will become commonplace, with companies moving toward fluid work groups joined around specific tasks. Rich, sustained, and often profound on-line experiences allowing self-expression and personal growth will be available. Brands will be redefined as enablers of customer power (which will evolve from buyers and sellers sharing the same information). Consumer behavior will be modeled not by segments but by individuals or transient groupings. The aging and handicapped will create new, interactive cyberskills to compensate for physical limitations. Online "tribes" will emerge as people create virtual communities that become a part of the social fabric.

often useful in testing existing assumptions and plans. The aura of optimism that often surrounds a strategic plan may include implicit assumptions that competitors will not aggressively respond, the market will not fade or collapse, or technological problems will not surface. Scenario analysis provides a nonthreatening way to consider the possibility of clouds or even rain on the picnic.

Often, of course, several variables are relevant to the future period of interest. The combination can define a relatively large number of scenarios. For example, a large greeting-card firm might consider three variables important: the success of small boutique card companies, the life of a certain card type, and the nature of future distribution channels. The combination can result in many possible scenarios. Experience has shown that two or three scenarios are the ideal number with which to work; any more, and the process becomes unwieldy and any value is largely lost. Thus, it is important to reduce the number of scenarios by identifying a small set that ideally includes those that are plausible/credible and those that represent departures from the present that are substantial enough to affect strategy development.

Relate Scenarios to Strategies

After scenarios have been identified, the next step is to relate them to strategy—both existing strategies and new options. If an existing strategy is in place, it can be tested with respect to each scenario. Which scenario will be the best one? How bad will the strategy be if the wrong scenario emerges? What will its prospects be with respect to customer acceptance, competitor reactions, and sales and profits? Could it be modified to enhance its prospects?

Even if the scenario analysis is not motivated by a desire to generate new strategy options, it is always useful to consider what strategies would be optimal for each scenario. A scenario by its nature will provide a perspective that is different from the status quo. Any strategy that is optimal for a given scenario should become a viable option. Even if it is not considered superior or even feasible, some elements of it might be captured.

Estimate Scenario Probabilities

To evaluate alternative strategies it is useful to determine the scenario probabilities. The task is actually one of environmental forecasting, except that the total scenario may be a rich combination of several variables. Experts could be asked to assess probabilities directly. A deeper understanding will often emerge, however, if causal factors underlying each scenario can be determined. For example, the construction equipment industry might develop scenarios based on three alternative levels of construction activity. These levels would have several contributing causes. One would be the interest rate. Another could be the availability of funds to the homebuilding sector, which in turn would depend on the emerging structure of financial institutions and markets. A third cause might be the level of government spending on roads, energy, and other areas.

KEY LEARNINGS

- Environmental analysis of changes in technology, demographics, culture, the economy, and governmental actions should detect and analyze current and potential trends and events that will create opportunities or threats to an organization.
- Impact analysis involves assessing systematically the impact and immediacy of the trends and events that underlie each strategy uncertainty.
- Scenario analysis, a vehicle to explore different assumptions about the future, involves the creation of two to three plausible scenarios, the development of strategies appropriate to each, the assessment of scenario probabilities, and the evaluation of the resulting strategies across the scenarios.

FOR DISCUSSION

1. What did the fax machine replace, if anything? What will replace (or has replaced) the fax machine? When will the fax machine disappear?

2. Develop a scenario based on the proposition that hybrid cars will continue to improve and take 30 percent of the automotive market in a few years. Analyze it from the point of view of an energy company like Shell, or a car company like Mercedes. What are the top three or four dimensions to consider?

3. A recent important technology development is Wi-Fi, the wireless Internet access concept. Supported by Intel's Centrino chip (which

frees computers from hard-wired connections), the development has raised expectations throughout the computer industry.

    a. Will this change the use of computers? How many people will actually use computers connected to the Internet in coffeehouses and airports? Think of some other similarly hyped phenomena, from railroads to airplanes to television to VCRs. What happened in those cases?

    b. What are the action alternatives for organizations such as Starbuck's and McDonald's?

4. Pick a company or brand/business on which to focus. What are the major trends that come out of an environmental analysis? What are the major areas of uncertainty? How would a major company in the industry handle those best?

5. Focusing on the airline industry, develop a list of strategic uncertainties and possible strategic actions.

NOTES

1. Raymond Burke, "Confronting the Challenges That Face Bricks- and-Mortar Stores," *Harvard Business Review,* July–August 1999, pp. 160–167.

2. Clayton M. Christensen, Mark W. Johnson, and Darrell K. Rigby, "Foundations for Growth," *MIT Sloan Management Review,* Spring 2002, pp. 22–31.

3. Ibid.

4. Arnold Cooper, Edward Demuzilo, Kenneth Hatten, Elijah Hicks, and Donald Tock, "Strategic Responses to Technological Threats," *Academy of Management Proceedings,* 1976, pp. 54–60.

5. Richard N. Farmer, "Looking Back at Looking Forward," *Business Horizons,* February, 1973, pp. 21–28.

6. IBM, *Red Herring,* November, 1999, pp. 120–128.

7. Sam Hill, *60 Trends in 60 Minutes,* New York: John Wiley & Sons, 2003, p. 96.

8. Faith Popcorn and Lys Marigold, *Clicking,* HarperCollins, 1997, p. 11–12.

9. Laura Zinn, "Teens," *Business Week,* April 11, 1994, pp. 76–84.

10. Sam Hill, op. cit., p. 93.

11. Hugh Courtney, "Decision-Driven Scenarios for Assessing Four Levels of Uncertainty," *Strategy & Leadership,* Vol. 31, No. 1, 2003, pp. 14–16.

12. Liam Fahey, "Competitor Scenarios," *Strategy & Leadership,* Vol. 31, No. 1, 2003, pp. 32–44.

13. Steve Barnett, "The New Cyberlife," *American Demographics,* December, 1999, pp. 7–9.

CHAPTER SEVEN

Internal Analysis

We have met the enemy and he is us.
—*Pogo*

Self-conceit may lead to self-destruction.
—*Aesop, "The Frog and the Ox"*

The fish is last to know if it swims in water.
—*Chinese proverb*

*I*n addition to external threats and opportunities, strategy development must be based on the objectives, strengths, and capabilities of a business. For example, Grand Met (which at one time was involved with hotels, dairies, betting, child care, pubs, and dozens of other businesses) decided to restructure its firm to leverage its strengths in marketing branded food and drink products and managing worldwide operations. Amazon leveraged its strengths in operations related to e-commerce.

Understanding a business in depth is the goal of internal analysis. A business internal analysis is similar to a competitor analysis, but it has a greater focus on performance assessment and is much richer and deeper. It is more detailed because of its importance to strategy and because much more information is available. The analysis is based on specific, current information on sales, profits, costs, organizational structure, management style, and other factors.

Just as strategy can be developed at the level of a business, a group of businesses, or the firm, internal analysis can also be conducted at each of these levels. Of course, analyses at different levels will differ from each other in emphasis and content, but their structure and thrust will be the same. The common goal is to identify organizational strengths, weaknesses, constraints, and, ultimately, to develop responsive strategies, either exploiting strengths or correcting or compensating for weaknesses.

Internal analysis begins by examining the financial performance of a business, its profitability and sales. Indications of unsatisfactory or deteriorating performance might stimulate strategy change. In contrast, the conclusion that current or future performance is acceptable can suggest the old adage, "If it ain't broke, don't fix it." Of course, something that is not broken may still need some maintenance, refurbishing, or vitalization. Performance analysis is especially relevant to the strategic decision of how much to invest in or disinvest from a business.

The first section of this chapter considers financial performance, as measured by sales, return on assets, and the shareholder value concept. The next section covers other performance dimensions linked to future profitability, such as customer satisfaction, product quality, brand associations, relative cost, new products, and employee capability.

Another perspective on internal analysis considers those business characteristics that limit or drive strategy choice. The third section of this chapter examines five issues: past and current strategy, strategic problems, organizational capabilities and constraints, financial resources and constraints, and organizational strengths and weaknesses. The final section discusses business portfolio analysis, which evaluates each business by assessing its performance and the attractiveness of the market in which it competes.

FINANCIAL PERFORMANCE— SALES AND PROFITABILITY

Internal analysis often starts with an analysis of current financials, measures of sales and profitability. Changes in either can signal a change in the market viability of a product line and the ability to produce competitively. Furthermore, they provide an indicator of the success of past strategies and thus can often help in evaluating whether strategic changes are needed. In addition, sales and profitability at least appear to be specific and easily measured. As a result, it is not surprising that they are so widely used as performance evaluation tools.

Sales and Market Share

A sensitive measure of how customers regard a product or service can be sales or market share. After all, if the relative value to a customer changes, sales and share should be affected, although there may be an occasional delay caused by market and customer inertia.

Sales levels can be strategically important. Increased sales can mean that the customer base has grown. An enlarged customer base, if we assume that new customers will develop loyalty, will mean future sales and profits. Increased share can provide the potential to gain SCAs in the form of economies of scale and experience curve effects. Conversely, decreased sales can mean decreases in customer bases and a loss of scale economies.

A problem with using sales as a measure is that it can be affected by short-term actions, such as promotions by a brand and its competitors. Thus, it is necessary to separate changes in sales that are caused by tactical actions from those that represent fundamental changes in the value delivered to the customer, and it is important to couple an analysis of sales or share with an analysis of customer satisfaction, which will be discussed shortly.

Profitability

The ultimate measure of a firm's ability to prosper and survive is its profitability. Although both growth and profitability are desirable, establishing a priority between the two can help guide strategic decision making.

A host of measures and ratios reflect profitability, includings margins, costs, and profits. Building on the assets employed leads to the return on assets (ROA) measure, which can be decomposed with a formula developed by General Motors and DuPont in the 1920s.

$$\text{ROA} = \frac{\text{profits}}{\text{sales}} \times \frac{\text{sales}}{\text{assets}}$$

Thus, return on assets can be considered as having two causal factors. The first is the profit margin, which depends on the selling price and cost structure. The second is the asset turnover, which depends on inventory control and asset utilization.

The determination of both the numerator and denominator of the ROA terms is not as straightforward as might be assumed. Substantial issues surround each, such as the distortions caused by depreciation and the fact that book assets do not reflect intangible assets, such as brand equity, or the market value of tangible assets.

Measuring Performance: Shareholder Value Analysis

The concept of shareholder value, an enormously influential concept during the past two decades, provides an answer to this question. Each business should earn an ROA (based on a flow of profits emanating from an investment), that meets or exceeds the costs of capital, which is the weighted average of the cost of equity and cost of debt. Thus, if the cost of equity is 16 percent and the cost of debt is 8 percent, the cost of capital would be 12 percent if the amount of debt was equal to the amount of equity; if there were only one-fourth as much debt as equity, then the cost of capital would be 14 percent. If the return is greater, the cost of capital shareholder value will increase, and if it is less shareholder value will decrease.

Some of the routes to increasing shareholder value are as follows:

- Earn more profit by reducing costs or increasing revenue without using more capital.
- Invest in high-return products (this, of course, is what strategy is all about).
- Reduce the cost of capital by increasing the debt to equity ratio or by buying back stock to reduce the cost of equity.

- Use less capital. Under shareholder value analysis, the assets employed are no longer a free good, so there is an incentive to reduce it. If improved just-in-time operations can reduce the inventory, it directly affects shareholder value.

The concept of shareholder value is theoretically valid.[1] If a profit stream can be estimated accurately from a strategic move, the analysis will be sound. The problem is that short-term profits (known to affect stock return and thus shareholder wealth) are easier to estimate and manipulate than long-term profits. Investors who assume that short-term profits predict longer-term profits pay undue attention to the former, as does the top management of a company with numerical targets to meet. The discipline to invest in a strategy that will sacrifice short-term financial performance for long-term prospects is not easy to come by, especially if some of the future prospects are in the form of options. For example, the investment in Saturn by General Motors gave it an option to expand that nameplate into other sectors. Similarly, when Black & Decker bought the small-appliance division of GE, it bought an option to take the business into related areas.

The impact of reducing investment is also not without risks. When, for example, Coca-Cola sold off its bottlers to reduce investment and improve shareholder value, its control of the quality of its product may have been reduced. In general, investment reduction often means outsourcing, with its balancing act between flexibility and loss of control over operations. A broadband company that outsources its installations loses a chance to interact with its customers.

One danger of shareholder value analysis is that it reduces the priority given to other stakeholders such as employees, suppliers, and customers, each of whom represents assets that can form the basis for long-term success. The radical downsizing of some firms has resulted in going beyond trimming fat to reducing future prospects. Even GE has reduced its expenditures on R&D (as a percentage of sales) in part to enhance shareholder value, a move that may yet prove harmful. General Motors aggressive move to reduce supplier costs damaged some relationships that were generating technological advances and cost savings. An effort to reduce costs can too easily cut into customer service and thus customer loyalty.

In fact, shareholder value management has met with very mixed results. However, one study of the experience of 125 firms found similarities among those that had applied shareholder value concepts successfully.[2] These companies:

- Gave priority to shareholder value over other goals, particularly growth goals.
- Provided intensive training throughout the organization regarding shareholder value and made it a practical tool for business managers at all levels. The philosophy was not restricted to the executive suite.
- Were disciplined in identifying the drivers of shareholder value. For example, for a call center, drivers could be the length of time to answer calls and the quality of responses.
- Reduced overhead by adapting the current accounting system and integrating shareholder value analysis with strategic planning.

These firms found a variety of benefits. First, the concept led to value-creating divestments that otherwise would not have occurred. Second, firms were able to transfer corporate planning and decision making to decentralized business units because all units tended to use the same logic, metrics, and mindset. Third, the business investment horizon tended to be longer, with projects with multi-year time frames getting approved. Fourth, the new recognition that capital had a cost tended to generate better strategic decisions.

PERFORMANCE MEASUREMENT— BEYOND PROFITABILITY

One of the difficulties in strategic market management is developing performance indicators that convincingly represent long-term prospects. The temptation is to focus on short-term profitability measures and to reduce investment in new products and brand images that have long-term payoffs.

The concept of net present value represents a long-term profit stream, but it is not always operational. It often provides neither a criterion for decision making nor a useful performance measure. It is somewhat analogous to preferring $6 million to $4 million. The real question involves determining which strategic alternative will generate $6 million and which will generate $4 million.

It is necessary to develop performance measures that will reflect long-term viability and health. The focus should be on the assets and competencies that underlie the current and future strategies and their SCAs. What are the key assets and competencies for a business during the planning horizon? What strategic dimensions are most crucial: to become more competitive with respect to product offerings, to develop new products, or to become more productive? These types of questions can help identify performance areas that a business should examine. Answers will vary depending on the situation, but, as suggested by Figure 7.1, they will often include customer satisfaction/brand loyalty, product/service quality,

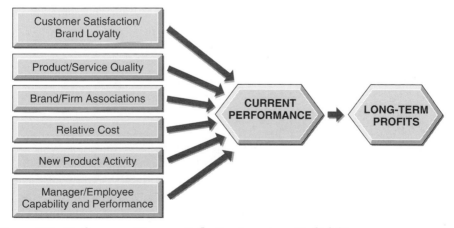

Figure 7.1   Performance Measures Reflecting Long-term Profitability

brand/firm associations, relative cost, new product activity, and manager/employee capability and performance.

Customer Satisfaction/Brand Loyalty

Perhaps the most important asset of many firms is the loyalty of the customer base. Measures of sales and market share are useful but potentially inaccurate indicators of how customers really feel about a firm. Such measures can reflect market inertia and are noisy, in part, because of competitor actions and market fluctuations. Measures of customer satisfaction and brand loyalty are much more sensitive and provide diagnostic value as well.

Guidelines for Measuring Satisfaction and Loyalty

First, problems and causes of dissatisfaction that may motivate customers to change brands or firms should be identified. Second, often the most sensitive and insightful information comes from those who have decided to leave a brand or firm. Thus, exit interviews for customers who have abandoned a brand can be productive. Third, there is a big difference between a brand or firm being liked and the absence of dissatisfaction. The size and intensity of the customer group that truly likes a brand or firm should be known. Fourth, measures should be tracked over time and compared with those of competitors. Relative comparisons and changes are most important.

Product and Service Quality

A product (or service) and its components should be critically and objectively compared both with the competition and with customer expectations and needs. How good a value is it? Can it really deliver superior performance? How does it compare with competitor offerings? How will it compare with competitor offerings in the future given competitive innovations? One common failing of firms is to avoid tough comparisons with a realistic assessment of competitors' current and potential offerings.

Product and service quality are usually based on several critical dimensions that can be identified and measured over time. For example, an automobile manufacturer can measure defects, ability to perform to specifications, durability, repairability, and features. A bank might be concerned with waiting time, accuracy of transactions, and the quality of the customer experience. A computer manufacturer can examine relative performance specifications and product reliability as reflected by repair data. A business that requires better marketing of a good product line is very different from one that has basic product deficiencies.

Brand/Firm Associations

An often overlooked asset of a brand or firm is what customers think of it. What are its associations? What is its perceived quality? Perceived quality, sometimes very different from actual quality, can be based on experience with past products or services and on quality cues, such as retailer types, pricing strategies, packaging, advertising, and typical customers. Is a brand or firm regarded as expert in a product or technology area (such as designing and making sailboats)? Innovative? Expensive? For the country club set? Is it associated with a country, a user type, or an application area (such as racing)? Such associations can be key strategic assets for a brand or firm.

Associations can be monitored by regularly asking customers in focus groups to describe their use experiences and to tell what a brand or firm means to them. The identification of changes in important associations will likely emerge from such efforts. Structured surveys using a representative sample of customers can provide even more precise tracking information.

Relative Cost

A careful cost analysis of a product (or service) and its components, which can be critical when a strategy is dependent on achieving a cost advantage or cost parity, involves tearing down competitors' products and analyzing their systems in detail. The Japanese consultant Ohmae suggested that such an analysis, when coupled with performance analysis, can lead to one of the four situations shown in Figure 7.2.[3]

If a component such as a car's braking system or a bank's teller operation is both more expensive than and inferior to that of the competition, a strategic problem requiring change may exist. An analysis could show, however, that the component is such a small item both in terms of cost and customer impact that it should be ignored. If the component is competitively superior, however, a cost-reduction program may not be the only appropriate strategy. A value analysis, in which the component's value to the customer is quantified, may suggest that the point of superiority could support a price increase or promotion campaign. If, on the other hand, a component is less expensive than that of the competition, but inferior, a

Figure 7.2   Relative Cost vs. Relative Performance—Strategic Implications

value analysis might suggest that it be de-emphasized. Thus, for a car with a cost advantage but handling disadvantage, a company might de-emphasize its driving performance and position it as an economy car. An alternative is to upgrade this component. Conversely, if a component is both less expensive and superior, a value analysis may suggest that the component be emphasized, perhaps playing a key role in positioning and promotion strategies.

Sources of Cost Advantage

The many routes to cost advantage will be discussed in Chapter 10. They include economies of scale, the experience curve, product design innovations, and the use of a no-frills product offering. Each provides a different perspective to the concept of competing on the basis of a cost advantage.

Average Costing

In average costing, some elements of fixed or semivariable costs are not carefully allocated but instead are averaged over total production. Thus, a plant may contain new machines and older machines that differ in the amount of support required for their operation. If support expenses are averaged over all output, the new machines will appear less profitable than they are and some inappropriate decisions could be precipitated.

Average costing can provide an opening for competitors to enter an otherwise secure market. For example, the J. B. Kunz Company, a maker of passbooks for banks, created a situation in which large-order customers were subsidizing small-order customers because of average costing.[4] The cost system inflated the costs of processing very large orders and thus provided an opportunity for competitors to underbid Kunz on the very profitable large orders. A product line that is subsidizing other lines is vulnerable, representing an opportunity to competitors and thus a potential threat to a business.

New Product Activity

Does the R&D operation generate a stream of new product concepts? Is the process from product concept to new product introduction well managed? Is there a track record of successful new products that have affected the product performance profile and market position?

One measure of new product innovation is the number of patents awarded. IBM was awarded more U.S. patents than any other organization in any industry through most of the 1990s, significantly ahead of Canon and other R&D-intensive firms. In addition, IBM has a good track record of getting its inventions into the marketplace. Time-to-market, a key point of competition in the car industry with regard to new models, is another measure of successful innovations.[5]

Manager/Employee Capability and Performance

Also key to a firm's long-term prospects are the people who must implement strategies. Are the human resources in place to support current and future strategies? Do those who are added to the organization match its needs in terms of types and quality or are there gaps that are not being filled? Tandem Computers sustained rapid growth by deliberately staffing and organizing for the next growth phase. In contrast, a host of firms that enjoyed explosive growth could not develop the systems, people, and structure to cope with expansion and subsequently failed.

An organization should be evaluated not only on how well it obtains human resources but also on how well it nurtures them. A healthy organization will consist of individuals who are motivated, challenged, fulfilled, and growing in their professions. Each of these dimensions can be observed and measured by employee surveys and group discussions. Certainly the attitude of production workers was a key factor in the quality and cost advantage that Japanese automobile firms enjoyed throughout the past three decades. In service industries such as banking and fast foods, the ability to sustain positive employee performance and attitude is usually a key success factor.

DETERMINANTS OF STRATEGIC OPTIONS

Another approach to internal analysis is to consider the determinants of strategic options. What characteristics of a business make some options unfeasible without a major organizational change? What characteristic will be pivotal in choosing among strategic options? Again, the answers to these questions will depend on the situation, but as noted in Figure 7.3, five areas warrant close scrutiny.

Past and Current Strategies

To understand the bases of past performance and attempt to sort out new options, it is important to be able to make an accurate profile of past and current strategies. Sometimes a strategy has evolved into something very different from what was assumed. For example, a firm positioned itself as an innovator and spent heavily on R&D to repeat its early breakthrough innovation. However, an honest analysis of its operations over the previous two decades indicated that its success was based on manufacturing strengths and scale economies. Other companies had introduced

BENCHMARKING

Comparing the performance of a business component with others is called benchmarking. The goal is to generate specific ideas for improvement, and also to define standards at which to aim. One target may be competitors: what cost and performance levels are they achieving, and how? Knowing your deficits with respect to the competition is the first step to developing programs to eliminate them. Another target is best-practice companies. Thus, many benchmark against Disney in terms of delivering consistent service, or Dell as the standard for Internet e-commerce operations and customer support. Looking outside one's own industry is often a way to break away from the status quo and thereby create a real advantage.

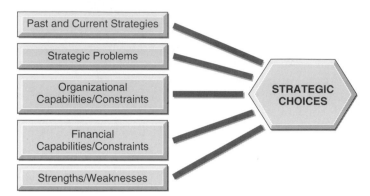

Figure 7.3   Determinants of Strategic Options and Choices

almost all the meaningful innovations in the industry during that period. A recognition that the R&D effort had been successful in improving product features, reliability, and cost, but not in developing any technological breakthroughs, was helpful in structuring strategic options.

Strategic Problems

Another relevant and helpful construct is the strategic problem—that is, a problem with strategic implications. For example, the exposure of Ford and its Explorer brand to the issue of Firestone tires disintegrating created a need for programs and for the active management of the involved brands. An automobile brand that finds it has a fit-and-finish deficit with respect to competitors requires some strategic moves involving product design and production.

A strategic problem differs from a weakness or liability, which is the absence of an asset (such as good location) or competence (for example, new-product introduction skills). A business copes over time with a weakness or liability by adjusting strategies. Strategic problems, in contrast, need to be addressed aggressively and corrected even if the fix is difficult and expensive.

Organizational Capabilities/Constraints

The internal organization of a company—its structure, systems, people, and culture—can be an important source of both strengths and weaknesses. The flexible, entrepreneurial organizational structure of 3M, in which new business teams and divisions are continually spun off, is a key to its growth. The systems of McDonald's and some other fast-food chains are important strengths. The background of Texas Instruments' management, largely in engineering and manufacturing, has been a source of strength in its semiconductor businesses, but it has been a weakness in its consumer products efforts. The productive, low-cost culture at Dana and White has allowed it to pursue a low-cost strategy.

Internal organization can affect the cost and even the feasibility of some strategies. There must be a fit between a strategy and the elements of an organization. If the strategy does not fit well, making it work might be expensive or even impossible. For example, an established centralized organization with a background oriented to one industry may have difficulty implementing a diversification strategy requiring a decentralized organization and an entrepreneurial thrust. Internal organization is considered in more detail in Chapter 16, which discusses strategy implementation and the concept of fit.

Financial Resources and Constraints

Ultimately, judgments need to be made about whether or not to invest in a business or withdraw cash from it. A similar decision needs to be made about the aggregate of businesses. Should a firm increase its net investment or decrease it by holding liquid assets or returning cash to shareholders or debt holders? A basic consideration is the firm's ability to supply investment resources.

A financial analysis to determine probable, actual, and potential sources and uses of funds can help provide an estimate of this ability. A cash flow analysis projects the cash that will be available from operations and depreciation and other assets. In particular, a growth strategy, even if it simply involves greater penetration of the existing product market, usually requires working capital and other assets, which may exceed the funds available from operations. The appendix to this chapter provides a discussion of how to conduct a cash flow analysis.

In addition, funds may be obtained either by debt or equity financing. To determine the desirability and feasibility of either option, an analysis of the balance sheet may be needed. In particular, the current debt structure and a firm's ability to support it will be relevant. The appendix also reviews some financial ratios that are helpful in this regard.

A division or subsidiary may need to consider how much support and involvement it can expect from a parent organization, particularly in regard to its investment proposals. The scenario of multiple businesses all planning investments that, in the aggregate, are far beyond a firm's willingness and ability to support, is all too common. A realistic appraisal of a firm's resources can make strategy development more effective.

Organizational Strengths and Weaknesses

A key step in internal analysis is to identify the strengths and weaknesses of an organization that are based on its assets and competencies. In fact, much of internal analysis is motivated by the need to detect strengths and weaknesses. There are, of course, many possible sources of strengths and weaknesses. In Chapter 4, methods to identify such sources are presented; in Chapter 8, we discuss how assets and competencies become the bases of sustainable competitive advantages.

FROM ANALYSIS TO STRATEGY

In internal analysis, organizational strengths and weaknesses need to be not only identified, but also related to competitors and the market. Strategic market management, as noted in Chapter 1, has four interrelated elements. The first is to determine areas in which to invest or disinvest. Investment could go to growth areas, such as new product markets or programs designed to create new strength areas, or to existing ones. The second is the value proposition offered to customers. The third is the development of assets and competencies to provide the bases of competitive advantage. The fourth is the specification and implementation of functional area strategies and programs such as product policy, manufacturing strategy, distribution choices, and so on.

In making strategic decisions, inputs from a variety of assessments are relevant, as the last several chapters have already made clear. However, the core of any strategic decision should be based on three types of assessments. The first concerns organizational strengths and weaknesses. The second evaluates competitor strengths, weaknesses, and strategies, because an organization's strength is of less value if it is neutralized by a competitor's strength or strategy. The third assesses the competitive context, the customers and their needs, the market, and the market environment. These assessments focus on determining how attractive the selected market will be, given the strategy selected.

The goal is to develop a strategy that exploits business strengths and competitor weaknesses and neutralizes business weaknesses and competitor strengths. The ideal is to compete in a healthy, growing industry with a strategy based on strengths that are unlikely to be acquired or neutralized by competitors. Figure 7.4 summarizes how these three assessments combine to influence strategy.

Figure 7.4 Structuring Strategic Decisions

GE's decision to sell its small-appliance division illustrates these strategic principles.[6] Small appliances were a part of GE's legacy and linked to its lamp and major-appliance product lines in the minds of retailers and customers. The small-appliance industry was not profitable, however, in part because of overcapacity and the power of the retailer. Also, cost pressures contributed to a reduction in product performance and reliability. Further, GE's strengths, such as its technological superiority and financial resources, were not leveraged in the small-appliance business, as any innovation could be copied. Thus, GE decided that a strategic fit did not exist, and it sold the small-appliance business to Black & Decker.

BUSINESS PORTFOLIO ANALYSIS

Business portfolio analysis provides a structured way to evaluate business units on two key dimensions: the attractiveness of the market involved and the strength of the firm's position in that market. The result is a graphical portrayal of the various business units on these key dimensions. The analysis and representation naturally lead to a resource allocation decision. Which businesses merit investment and which should be spun off? These are very basic strategic investment issues.

The resource allocation question is usually very difficult organizationally. In a decentralized organization, it is natural for the managers of cash-generating businesses to control the available cash that funds investment opportunities and for each business to be required or encouraged to fund its own growth. As a result, however, a fast-growing business with enormous potential but low profit or even losses will often be starved of needed cash. The irony is that businesses involving mature products may have inferior investment alternatives, but because cash flow is plentiful, their investments will still be funded. The net effect is that available cash is channeled to areas of low potential and withheld from the most attractive areas. A business portfolio analysis helps force the issue of which businesses should receive the available cash.

The Market Attractiveness–Business Position Matrix

Figure 7.5 shows the market attractiveness–business position matrix into which each business unit is to be positioned. The concept is credited to strategy efforts of General Electric planners and the consulting firm McKinsey & Company.

Consider first market attractiveness, the horizontal axis. The basic question is, how attractive is the market for a competitor in terms of the cash flow that it will generate? Scaling a market should start with the Porter five-factor model of industry attractiveness (Chapter 5). However, the other elements of the market analysis as well as the analyses of customers, competitors, and the environment of the business should also contribute. A set of nine factors are set forth in the figure as a point of departure. The actual factors will depend on what is relevant for the context.

Consider next the business-position assessment, as shown on the vertical axis. The business position should be based on the internal analysis of the business and, in particular, on an evaluation of its assets and competencies relative to those of its

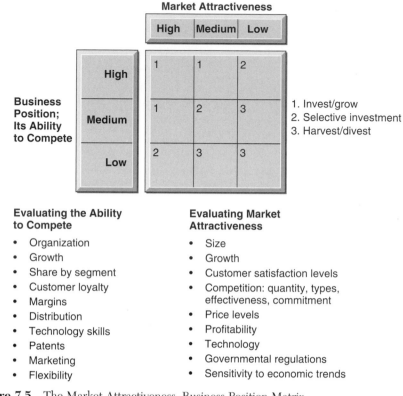

Figure 7.5   The Market Attractiveness–Business Position Matrix

competitors. Eleven dimensions are suggested in the figure, but an appropriate set will need to be generated for each particular context.

Applying the Matrix

The market attractiveness–business position matrix is a formal, structured way to match a firm's strengths with market opportunities. One implication is that when both firm position and market attractiveness are positive, as in the boxes marked 1 in Figure 7.5, a firm should probably invest and attempt to grow. When the assessment is more negative, as in the boxes marked 3, however, the recommendation would be either harvest or divest. For the three boxes marked 2, a selective decision to invest would be made only when there was a specific reason to believe the investment would be profitable.

A useful exercise is to attempt to predict whether either your position or the attractiveness of the market will change if it is assumed the current strategy is followed. A predicted movement to another cell can signal the need to consider a change in strategy.

THE BCG GROWTH-SHARE MATRIX

Portfolio analysis started in the mid-1960s with the BCG growth-share matrix which was pioneered and used extensively by the BCG consulting group. The concept was to position each business within a firm on the two-dimensional matrix shown in Figure 7.6. The market-share dimension (actually the ratio of share to that of the largest competitor) was regarded as pivotal because it reflected cost advantages resulting from scale economies and manufacturing experience. The growth dimension was considered the best single indicator of market strength.

The BCG growth-share matrix is associated with a colorful cast of characters representing strategy recommendations. The stars (the high-share, high-growth quadrant) are important to the current businesses and should receive resources if needed. Cash cows (the high-share, low-growth quadrant) should be the source of substantial amounts of cash that can be channeled to other business areas. Dogs (low-growth, low-share quadrant) are potential cash traps because they perpetually absorb cash. Problem children (low-share, high-growth quadrant) are assumed to have heavy cash needs before they can convert into stars and eventually cash cows.

The BCG growth-share model was very influential in its day. It made visible the issue of allocation across business units, that some businesses should generate cash that supports others. It also introduced the experience curve into strategy and showed that, under some conditions, market share could lead to experience-curve-based advantage. The experience curve is discussed in more detail in Chapter 10.

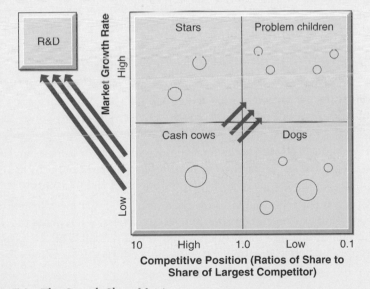

Figure 7.6 The Growth-Share Matrix

In structuring strategies, the following are among the logical alternatives:

- **Invest to hold.** Attempt to stop erosion in position by investing enough to compensate for environmental and competitive forces.
- **Invest to penetrate.** Aggressively attempt to move the position up, even at the sacrifice of earnings.
- **Invest to rebuild.** Attempt to regain a previously held position that was lost by a milking strategy that, for whatever reason, is no longer appropriate.
- **Selective investment.** Attempt to strengthen position in some segments and let position weaken in other segments.
- **Low investment.** Attempt to harvest the business, drawing cash out and cutting investment to a minimum.
- **Divestiture.** Sell or liquidate the business.

KEY LEARNINGS

- Sales and profitability analysis provide an evaluation of past strategies and an indication of the current market viability of a product line.
- Shareholder value holds that the flow of profits emanating from an investment should exceed the cost of capital (which is the weighted average of the cost of equity and cost of debt). Routes to achieving shareholder value—such as downsizing, reducing assets employed, and outsourcing—can be risky when they undercut assets and competences.
- Performance assessment should go beyond financials to include such dimensions as customer satisfaction/brand loyalty, product/service quality, brand/firm associations, relative cost, new product activity, and manager/employee capability and performance.
- Five business characteristics limit or drive strategic choice: past and current strategy, strategic problems, organizational capabilities and constraints, financial resources and constraints, and strengths and weaknesses.
- Business portfolio analysis provides a structured way to evaluate businesses on two key dimensions: the attractiveness of the market involved, and the strength of the firm's position in that market. The analysis and representation lead naturally to a resource allocation decision.

FOR DISCUSSION

1. Explain shareholder value analysis. Why might it help firms? Why might it result in bad decisions?
2. Explain the market attractiveness–business position matrix. What role should it have in strategy development? Choose an industry (such as

automobiles or snacks) and attempt to identify brands that are high or low on each dimension.

3. Look at the quotations that begin Chapters 3 through 7. Which one do you find the most insightful? Why? Under what circumstances would its implications not hold?

4. In implementing a market attractiveness-business position matrix, what metrics are likely to be applied in any industry context? Pick an industry and determine if specialized metrics would be needed.

NOTES

1. For an excellent review of the risks of shareholder value see Allan A. Kennedy, *The End of Shareholder Value,* Cambridge, MA: Perseus Publishing, 2000.
2. Philippe Haspeslagh, Tomo Noda, and Fares Boulos, "It's Not Just About the Numbers," *Harvard Business Review,* July–August 2001, pp. 65–73.
3. Kenichi Ohmae, *The Mind of the Strategist,* New York: Penguin Books, 1982, p. 26.
4. J.B. Kunz Company A, Case 9-577-115, Boston: Intercollegiate Case Clearing House, 1977.
5. IBM, *Red Herring,* November, 1999, pp. 120–128.
6. Robert Slater, *The New GE,* Homewood, IL: Irwin, 1993, p. 101.

APPENDIX: PROJECTING CASH FLOW—SOURCES AND USES OF FUNDS

A projection of cash flow during the strategy horizon is essential to determine what base of cash resources is available and what cash needs will be required. At the outset, a reasonable baseline assumption might be that current strategies and trends will extend into the near future. It can be helpful also to project the flow of funds given both optimistic and pessimistic scenarios. The impact of changes in strategies and the introduction of new strategies can then be determined.

Figure 7A.1 shows a simplified balance sheet and the major categories of sources and uses of funds. It will provide a context in which to discuss the principal elements of a cash flow analysis. As the sources and uses of funds are presented, some useful balance-sheet ratios will be introduced. They provide measures of the financial health of a firm in terms of its assets and debt structure. As such, they are helpful in making judgments concerning the desirability and feasibility of raising money through debt or equity financing.

The first item under the sources and uses of funds in Figure 7A.1 is changes in net working capital. Working capital is defined as current assets less current liabilities (generally liabilities under one year). The current ratio is one way of measuring the adequacy of working capital:

$$\text{current ratio} = \frac{\text{current assets}}{\text{current liabilities}}$$

Balance Sheet, December 31 (Millions)

Current Assets		6.0	Current Liabilities		3.0
• Cash, receivables, investments	3.5		• Accounts payable	2.0	
• Inventory	2.5		• Other	1.0	
			Long-term Liabilities		2.0
Fixed Assets		6.0			
• Property, plant, and equipment	10.0		Equity		7.0
			• Capital stock	4.0	
• Less accumulated depreciations	4.0		• Retained earnings and other	3.0	
Total Assets		12.0	Total Liabilities and Equity		12.0

Projected Sources and Uses of Funds

Sources of Funds		Uses of Funds	
• Decrease in net working capital	0.0	• Increase in net working capital	1.0
• Sale of fixed assets	0.0	• Purchase of fixed assets	2.5
• Issue long-term liabilities	2.0	• Retire long-term liabilities	0.0
• Sell capital stock	0.0	• Buy back capital stock	0.0
• Operations: net income	1.0	• Operations: net losses	0.0
• Depreciation	0.5	• Dividends	0.0
Total Sources of Funds	3.5	Total Uses of Funds	3.5

Figure 7A.1   Balance Sheet and Sources and Uses of Funds Statement

The most desirable ratio will depend, of course, on the nature of a business. In particular, firms with large amounts of assets in inventories may require a higher ratio. Another ratio that deletes inventories is called the quick or acid-test ratio:

$$\text{quick ratio} = \frac{\text{current assets less inventory}}{\text{current liabilities}}$$

As sales grow, of course, working capital will have to grow also so that it will continue to be adequate for supporting operations.

The second item concerning the sources and uses of funds in Figure 7A.1 is the sale or purchase of fixed assets. The acquisition of fixed assets might be divided into those necessary for maintaining current operation levels and those needed for more discretionary expenditures to generate growth.

Again, the analysis of the sources and uses of funds should reflect the implications of any proposed growth strategy.

The third category is the issue or retirement of long-term debt. In determining the appropriate debt level, useful ratios are:

$$\text{debt-to-equity ratio} = \frac{\text{long-term liabilities}}{\text{equity}}$$

$$\text{total debt-to-equity ratio} = \frac{\text{total liabilities}}{\text{equity}}$$

Of course, the higher these ratios are, the larger the interest burden in a downturn and the lower the ability to obtain new debt in an emergency. The optimal level will depend on the ability of the earnings to carry added interest expense, the policy of a firm toward debt and its associated risk, the return expected on future investment, and the debt-to-equity ratio of competing firms. The use of funds obtained from debt financing will be relevant for determining how much debt to undertake. If the funds are to be used to buy a firm, the structure of the resulting combined balance sheet and funds flow must be considered.

The fourth category shown in Figure 7A.1 is changes in capital stock. To what extent is it feasible and desirable to raise capital through the sale of stock? Conversely, it may be beneficial to use funds to buy stock if the stock is undervalued compared with alternative investments.

Finally, there are the sources of funds from operations, which provide the base from which investment planning will begin. Depreciation expense is added to, and dividends to be paid are subtracted from, net income. Depreciation is an expense item that does not involve cash outflow. Thus, depreciation is actually a source of funds. Obviously, the net income from operations will interact with other sources. For example, increasing debt will increase interest expense, which will reduce the funds available for future operations. And, the ability to raise stock may depend on dividend policy. Furthermore, investment or disinvestment in assets will affect depreciation in future years.

In evaluating the balance sheet, considerable judgment and reservation may be appropriate. There may be bad debts among the reported receivables, the depreciation may not reflect plant deterioration, and assets and liabilities may have market values that differ substantially from their reported book value. Inflation effects contribute to the interpretation difficulties. Thus, it might be appropriate to interpret or adjust the ratios and cash flow projection accordingly.

A NEW, DYNAMIC INDUSTRY: THE ENERGY BAR INDUSTRY

In 1986, PowerBar single-handedly created the energy bar category. Positioned as an athletic energy food, it was distributed at bike shops and events that usually involved running or biking. The target segment was the athlete who needed an efficient, effective energy source.

Six years later, seeking to provide an alternative to the sticky, dry nature of the PowerBar, a competitor developed an energy bar with superior taste and texture and branded it the Clif bar. About the same time, another competitor introduced the Balance bar, which offered a blend of protein, fat, and carbohydrates based on the nutrition formula associated with the "Zone diet." Faced with these challengers, PowerBar responded with Harvest (a bar with a much more accessible taste and texture) and ProteinPlus (an entry into the high-protein subcategory closely related to that defined by Balance).

The makers of the Clif bar observed that many women were athletes and many more were involved in fitness. They further observed that this half of the population had unique needs in terms of vitamins and supplements, and that the energy bar industry had yet to recognize or fill them—a classic case of unmet needs. As a result, they introduced Luna as the first nutritional (not energy) bar for women, using media and promotions targeting active females. The bar had a light crunchy texture, came in flavors like "lemon zest" and chai tea, and contained nearly two dozen vitamins, minerals, and nutrients. The target market consisted of time-strapped women who wanted both taste and nutrition and would appreciate a bar tailored to their needs.

Both in reaction to Luna's success and to expand the segments for which the category was relevant, PowerBar studied why women did not buy its products, which the firm considered to be nutritious, convenient, tasty, and able to provide a quick pick-me-up in mid-morning or mid-afternoon. One answer was that the calorie hit from any member of the PowerBar family was simply too great. In response, the firm created the almost-indulgent, PowerBar-endorsed Pria. With only 110 calories, Pria was designed to respond to Luna while attracting new users into the category.

The Balance strategy was to introduce a series of products, all of which stuck to the original bar's 40/30/30 nutritional formula but had different taste and textures. These spinoffs included Balance Plus, Balance Outdoor (with no chocolate coating to melt), Balance Gold, Balance Satisfaction, and the Balance-endorsed Oasis, a bar designed for women. The big success was Balance Gold, which was positioned close to the candy bar category (indeed, its tagline was "like a candy bar") by containing ingredients like nuts and caramel. Such a bar probably risked some of Balance's perceived authenticity as being an energy bar. However, because Balance entered the category from the diet perspective anyway and probably was never considered in the center of the energy bar world, the risk may have been acceptable.

In addition to the major brands, challengers from a variety of small and large firms advanced subcategories by positioning themselves around such factors as age (bars for seniors and kids) and health (products to fit dairy-free, diabetic, and heart-conscious diets), to say nothing of numerous textures, flavors, sizes, and coatings. For example, the popularity of low-carbohydrate diets has prompted a host of entries, including Atkins Advantage, developed by the Atkins organization. Other participating brands include ZonePerfect, Met-Rx, GeniSoy, EAS, CarboLite, Carb Solutions, and Gatorade energy bars. Masterfoods' Snickers Marathon—a candy bar with a blend of vitamins, minerals, and protein—has blurred the division between candy and energy bars by seeking to gain share in the latter market. One concern of the energy bar industry is the skepticism among some quarters as to how qualitatively different its products are from candy bars in the first place.

The motivation for using an energy bar is primarily to provide a convenient energy boost. The original heritage of being a product to enhance the performance of top athletes engaged in demanding physical activities (like Lance Armstrong, a PowerBar endorser) created credibility and self expressive benefits in the category's early years. Because household penetration was still under 20 percent, however, the major firms worked to generalize "performance" to be relevant to anyone who needs to perform well during the day. In fact, the industry dream is to get people to label the category "performance nutrition" and think of it as enhancing one's ability to complete any task.

New products in the category are going in several directions. A trend toward indulgent icings, coatings, and coverings has led some to morph toward candy bars. Others go the opposite way, using whole-grain ingredients for products somewhat like the original Clif bar and Quaker's Oatmeal Squares for women. The makers of the Clif bar also have introduced a Mojo line of salty snack bars to provide alternatives to sweet-tasting bars. There are positioning options involving natural, sugar-free, and organic bars, as well as those containing no preservatives and no genetically altered ingredients.

The energy bar category has gone mainstream, moving from the bike shops to the grocery stores and exploding from just over $100 million in revenue in 1996 to an estimated $1 billion or more in 2003, with expected future growth exceeding 20 percent per year. Along the way, it became large enough to attract the attention of major packaged-goods firms. In 2000, Nestlé purchased PowerBar, which has remained the leading player, with the Clif bar (which has remained independent) emerging as its most formidable competitor. The Balance line of products was bought by Kraft, also in 2000.

Energy bars can be considered a part of a larger food bar category whose size was estimated to be well over $3 billion in 2002, nearly double that of 1998. The market is divided fairly equally between granola bars (positioned as a snack food that is healthier than candy bars), breakfast/cereal/snack bars (used as a meal replacement), and energy bars. Energy bars have a far lower household penetration than the other food bar forms. The top marketers of food bars are Kellogg's (Nutri-grain), Quaker Oats, General Mills, and Slim-Fast. Of course, any sales estimates in this arena are difficult to generate because of definitional issues, and because Wal-Mart does not cooperate with sales measuring services.

FOR DISCUSSION

1. Conduct a thorough analysis of this category's customers, competitors, market, and environment from the perspective of PowerBar. What are the key strategic questions? What additional information would you like to obtain? How would you obtain it? What are the threats and opportunities? In particular, address the following issues:

   a. How is the market segmented? What are the key customer motivations and unmet needs? What are the similarities and differences among the segments? How might a company link customer motivations to value propositions?

   b. Identify the competitors. Who are the most direct competitors? The indirect competitors? Substitute products? What are the strategic groups?

   c. What are the market trends? The growth submarkets? The key success factors?

   d. What are the environmental trends that will affect the industry? Generate two or three viable future scenarios.

2. How would you go about evaluating emerging submarkets? What criteria would you use to enter each?

3. What innovation would support a new entry? How should entries be branded? Can brands such as Harvest, Luna, Balance Gold, Balance Satisfaction, and others be leveraged?

4. Will the energy bar category morph into food bars, with elements like diet, tasting like candy, and breakfast replacement dominating as the energy definition recedes? How can Nestlé's PowerBar keep that from happening and still maintain its mainstream/supermarket posture?

5. At what stage is the energy bar market relative to the product-life cycle? What strategies can be used to extend the life cycle? Do you see a consolidation on the horizon?

6. Relative to the concept of the "big idea," do you think there is an opportunity to develop a product that can deliver the same nutritional elements in a different form (for example, a small pill)?

7. Develop a positioning map and note if there are any obvious customer needs that are currently not being met.

Source: Adapted with the permission of the Free Press, a division of Simon & Schuster Adult Publishing Group from *Brand Portfolio Strategy: Creating Relevance, Differentiation, Energy, Leverage, and Clarity,* by David A. Aaker. Copyright © 2004 by David A. Aaker. All rights reserved.

COMPETING AGAINST THE INDUSTRY GIANT: COMPETING AGAINST WAL-MART

Wal-Mart is the most successful retailer ever. In 2002, at $218 billion in sales, it was by far the world's largest retail company, three times the size of the runner-up, France's Carrefour. Measures of Wal-Mart's success are mind-blowing. Its share of the U.S. grocery business was 19 percent in 2003 and could grow to 35 percent if its five-year planned growth materializes. It was the third largest pharmacy with a 16 percent share. It sold 32 percent of the disposable diapers in the United States, 30 percent of all hair care products, 26 percent of toothpaste, 20 percent of pet food, and 13 percent of home textiles. In 2003, *Fortune* named Wal-Mart the most admired company in America.

Wal-Mart was founded in Arkansas by Sam Walton in 1962. Six years later it expanded into neighboring states, and in the 1970s it ventured beyond the South. Over time it added products such as jewelry and food, as well as pharmacy and automotive departments. By 2002, there were some 1,650 Wal-Marts and over 1,000 Wal-Mart Supercenters in the United States. In 1983, Wal-Mart went into the wholesale club business under the Sam's Club brand name; this concept grew to 500 stores within two decades. In 1991, it began its international quest by opening a store in Mexico. In 2002, Wal-Mart had nearly 1,200 stores outside the United States and was the leading retailer in both Mexico and Canada.

For its first thirty years, Sam Walton was the heart and soul of Wal-Mart. An inspirational and visionary influence, he created strategies, policies, and cultural values that fueled the firm's success. He would spend much of his time visiting stores and meeting customers and "associates" (employees). The visits would always result in customer and merchandising insights, pats on the back for workers, and suggestions for improvement. He would summon managers back to the headquarters in Bentonville, Arkansas, for Saturday morning meetings that kept the firm focused and provided a pervasive work ethic. He also enjoyed celebrating successes, once keeping a promise to do the hula on Wall Street if the company achieved an 8 percent pretax profit. For employees and customers alike, Sam Walton *was* Wal-Mart.

In 1962, Walton started his firm with three basic beliefs—respect for the individual employee, exceptional customer service, and a striving for excellence. He developed a host of rules for associates. He challenged them to engage in "aggressive hospitality," to be ready with a smile and assistance to all customers. The "ten-foot rule" decreed that whenever an associate was within ten feet of a customer, the associate was to look that customer in the eye and ask if he or she needed help. His "sundown rule" meant that any task that could be done today would be not put off until tomorrow—especially if the task involved customer service. Exemplifying his belief in empowerment, Walton instituted the Volume Producing Item (VPI) program, in which an associate would pick an item, design a merchandising effort for it, and monitor and communicate the results.

In his 1992 book *Made in America*—a title that reflects Wal-Mart's positioning strategies in the early 1980s, as well as a comment on the founder's career—Sam Walton listed ten key factors that he felt were key to his success. One was to appreciate your associates and their contribution; a second item was to share your profits with them. A third factor was to talk to the customer and listen to what that customer is saying. Another item was to exceed your customer's expectations ("satisfaction guaranteed" really meant something to Sam Walton). Still another factor was to control your expenses better than your competition, as Walton prided himself on having a number-one ranking in the ratio of expenses to sales.

Sam Walton offered strategies as well as charisma. One basic early strategy was to bring discount stores to cities of roughly 50,000 people. While the large discount stores of the day were fighting for prime spots in large cities, Wal-Mart had the smaller metropolitan areas to itself. Second, because of the location of its early stores and its headquarters site, Wal-Mart had an employee cost advantage from top to bottom. Third, by setting up distribution centers, Wal-Mart from the outset gained operational and logistic efficiencies. Over time Wal-Mart relentlessly innovated in warehousing, logistics, information technology, and operations to create more and more savings. In part, this innovation was done in partnership with suppliers like P&G.

Wal-Mart continued to prosper after 1992 when Sam Walton passed away. Although his strategic flair and connection with employees and customers was missed, many of his ideas had become institutionalized. Aggressive merchandising led by empowered associates and the trademark greeters, for example, remained part of the Wal-Mart profile. In addition, there was a focus on energy adding "Retailtainment," including live concert broadcasts in the home entertainment departments, exclusive promotional events around video releases, and exhibits by local organizations. Equity was built into private-label brands, such as Ol' Roy dog food (which has surpassed Purina as the world's top-selling dog food), White Cloud tissues and diapers, and the Sam's Choice and Great Value product lines.

Low prices and cost containment have continued to be the focus—some say the obsession—of Wal-Mart management. The customer promise of "Low Prices, Always" drives the culture and the strategy. Suppliers are continuously and aggressively challenged to reduce costs. Wal-Mart will set demanding cost reduction goals, on occasion showing suppliers how to achieve them. Operations are continuously made more efficient. The resulting cost savings are passed on to customers, as Wal-Mart does not support suppliers' premium-price brand policies. The firm's private-label lines are often sourced directly from foreign factories, creating significant cost advantages and disrupting price norms in many categories. Wal-Mart views itself, first and foremost, as the customer's purchasing agent, and its goal is to reduce prices. By some estimates, Wal-Mart saves consumers $20 billion a year.

Wal-Mart has significant detractors as well. One set of arguments, summarized in a *Business Week* cover story questioning whether Wal-Mart is too powerful, relate to jobs. Wal-Mart has been accused of hastening the move of jobs abroad, as its focus on costs led the company to buy over $12 billion in goods from China alone in 2002. Some even argue that suppliers, in order to meet Wal-Mart's cost targets, are forced to move jobs to China and elsewhere. In addition, it is estimated that for every supercenter that Wal-Mart opens, two supermarkets will close. When Wal-Mart went into Oklahoma City, for example, thirty supermarkets closed. Because of the loss of local businesses, many communities have resisted Wal-Mart's entry. Even the jobs that Wal-Mart adds are said to be inferior, as the company's anti-union, low-pay policy has been hypothe-sized to hold down wages in retail America and throughout local regions. On average, a Wal-Mart sales clerk in 2001 made less than $14,000, which was below the poverty line for a family of three. Dozens of lawsuits related to overtime pay and sex discrimi-nation have been filed against the firm. Sam Walton's values of "Made in America" and "respect for the individual" seem to some a distant memory.

Wal-Mart also faces some more intangible concerns. Because it controls over 15 percent of all non-subscription magazine and video/DVD sales, some fear that the firm wields an unwelcome and arbitrary influence on culture. Wal-Mart elects to stock some magazines while banning or hiding the covers of others (a nearly naked woman on the cover of *Rolling Stone* is acceptable, but not on the front of *Glamour* and *Redbook*), and it sells only videos that meet family-friendly standards. As a result, some movie pro-ducers have felt compelled to create a "Wal-Mart version" of their films. Further, Wal-Mart's market power is so high that some people fear it has an inordinate influence on product design (for example, a particular design direction may be deemed by Wal-Mart as too costly for its customers). In a wide variety of product areas, manufacturers can-not afford to deviate from specifications set by Wal-Mart.

Wal-Mart has plans to expand dramatically as the first decade of the twenty-first century continues. The primary vehicle for this growth will be Wal-Mart super-centers, often located in malls where sites are available at distressed prices, face fewer zoning issues, and precipitate less neighborhood opposition. The obsession with low prices, costs, and efficiency will not change. In fact, suppliers have been given a deadline to attach radio-frequency identification tags to all packages and pal-lets in order to create a new level of efficiency. There will be a continued emphasis on the growth of private-label goods, which were estimated to represent 20 percent of Wal-Mart's sales in 2003. A program to upgrade Sam's Club by adding pharmacy, optical, one-hour photo, fuel, and other services is under way.

FOR DISCUSSION

Grocery stores and general merchandise stores must look forward to more intense challenges from Wal-Mart in the future. Such firms need to understand Wal-Mart and how it competes. What Wal-Mart strategies led to success? What was the role of Sam Walton? What is the company's likely future direction beyond its stated intentions? Would it make sense for Wal-Mart to extend its brand into stand-alone grocery stores (such as Safeway) or convenience stores (for example, 7-Eleven)?

Consider two competitors, Costco and Wegmans, who must design a strategy that will lead to success in the Wal-Mart environment.

Wegmans

There are sixty-five Wegmans Food Markets in New York, Pennsylvania, and Maryland. Wegmans is healthy, with sales in 2003 of $3.3 billion (up 9 percent from the prior year) and operating earnings at 7.5 percent. However, thirty-nine of these stores are within twenty miles of a Wal-Mart Supercenter, and expansion plans in Baltimore and Washington, D.C., involve more competition with Wal-Mart.

1. What are the strengths and weaknesses of Wal-Mart from the perspective of Wegmans?
2. Are there market segments that would be attracted to Wegmans, and are they large enough to support a viable business?
3. What strategies should Wegmans avoid?
4. What strategies will allow Wegmans to thrive or at least survive in the face of Wal-Mart's strengths? How should Wegmans exploit the Wal-Mart resentment factor?

Costco

Costco started in 1981, just a few years before Sam's Club appeared. It had fewer stores than Sam's Club (312 compared to 532) but more sales ($34.4 billion versus an estimated $32.9 billion) because the average Costco store generates nearly double the revenue of a Sam's Club. Unlike Sam's Club, which focuses on price, Costco offers upscale brands like Callaway golf clubs, Starbucks coffee, and expensive jewelry, and thus it attracts a different kind of shopper. Sam's Club is attempting to attack Costco by adding upscale brands and integrating more closely with Wal-Mart in order to achieve more buying power and logistical efficiencies.

1. What are the strengths and weaknesses of Sam's Club from the perspective of Costco?
2. Are there market segments that would be attracted to Costco, and are they large enough to support a viable business?
3. How should Costco react to the Wal-Mart threat?

Sources: Wal-Mart, Costco, and Wegmans company Web sites in 2003; Wal-Mart annual report for 2002; Anthony Bianco and Wendy Zellner, "Is Wal-Mart Too Powerful?" *Business Week,* October 6, 2003, pp. 100–110.

ALTERNATIVE BUSINESS STRATEGIES

CHAPTER EIGHT

Creating Advantage— Synergy and Vision versus Opportunism

Vision is the art of seeing things invisible.
—*Jonathan Swift*

All men can see the tactics whereby I conquer, but what none can see is the strategy out of which great victory is evolved.
—*Sun-Tzu, Chinese military strategist*

Don't manage, lead.
—*Jack Welch, GE*

Our attention now shifts from strategic analysis to the development of a business strategy. What strategic alternatives should be considered? Which one is optimal? These questions will be the focus of Chapters 8 through 12. One goal will be to provide a wide scope of available strategic alternatives in order to increase the likelihood that the best choices will be considered. Even a poor decision among superior alternatives is preferable to a good decision among inferior alternatives.

This chapter discusses the concept and creation of a sustainable competitive advantage (SCA), the key to a successful strategy. It then turns to the challenge of creating and leveraging synergy as one basis for a SCA. Finally, two very different routes to developing winning strategies are presented: strategic vision and strategic opportunism. Chapters 9, 10, and 11 discuss a variety of strategic options, including quality, focus, value, innovation, and being global. Chapter 12 then introduces strategic position—the face of the business strategy, both internally and externally. In the next section of the book, Chapters 13, 14, and 15 discuss growth strategies. The final section covers organizational issues.

THE SUSTAINABLE COMPETITIVE ADVANTAGE

As defined earlier in this book, a sustainable competitive advantage is an element (or combination of elements) of the business strategy that provides a meaningful advantage over both existing and future competitors (see Figure 8.1). Wal-Mart has a cost advantage because of its scale economies, market power and logistical efficiencies, value reputation, and site location assets. Southwest Airlines has a fun personality and a point-to-point model that provides for convenient, reliable, uncomplicated travel. Dell Computers' efficient direct-sales model makes customized computers easy to order and service and generates personal contact with Dell people.

An SCA needs to be both meaningful and sustainable. It should be substantial enough to make a difference; a marginal superiority in quality, especially when "good" quality is good enough for most customers, will not generate an SCA. Meanwhile, sustainability (in the absence of an effective patent) means that any advantage needs to be supported and enhanced over time. There needs to be a moving target for competitors. For example, Gillette maintained its technological superiority in razors over a long time period with innovation after innovation making copying its competitive advantage difficult.

An SCA will in part depend on the functional strategies and programs, how you compete. Wal-Mart's discount store, Southwest's point-to-point system, and the Dell direct-sales model all have SCAs based in part on their functional strategies and programs. In these cases and others, however, an effective SCA will also involve other aspects of the business strategy—assets and competencies, the value proposition, and the selection of the product market.

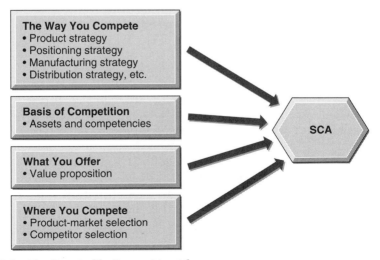

Figure 8.1   The Sustainable Competitive Advantage

The Basis of Competition: Assets and Competencies

The assets and competencies of an organization represent the most sustainable element of a business strategy, because these are usually difficult to copy or counter. There is no point in pursuing a quality strategy, for example, without the design and manufacturing competencies needed to deliver quality products. Anyone can try to distribute cereal or detergent through supermarkets, but few have the competencies in logistics, shelf space management and promotions or relationships with chain executives that make product distribution efficient and effective. Similarly, a department store's premium-service positioning strategy will not succeed unless the right people and culture are in place and are supported. Who you are, in other words, is as important as what you do.

As discussed in Chapter 4, several questions can help to identify relevant assets and competencies. What are the key motivations of the major market segments? What are the large value-added components? What are the mobility barriers? What elements of the value chain can generate an advantage? What assets and competencies are possessed by successful businesses and lacking in unsuccessful businesses?

What You Offer—The Value Proposition

An effective SCA should be visible to customers and provide or enhance a value position. The key is to link an SCA with the positioning of a business. A product's reliability may not be apparent to customers, but if it can be made visible through advertising or product design, it can support a reliability positioning strategy. Maytag is an example of a firm whose reliability positioning is supported by advertising that communicates the SCA provided by its product design and performance.

A reputation for delivering a value proposition can be a more important asset than the substance that underlies that reputation. A business with such a reputation can falter for a time, and the market will either never become aware of the weakness or will forgive the firm. Conversely, competitors often have a much easier time in matching the quality or performance of a market offering than it convincing customers that it indeed has done so. Enduring impressions like these are why a visible value proposition that is meaningful to customers is strategically valuable.

A solid value proposition can fail if a key ingredient is missing. Procter & Gamble's Pringles potato chips had a host of assets, such as a consistent product, long shelf life, a crushproof container, and national distribution. The problem was that these attributes were valued only if the taste was perceived to be good. As a result, Pringle's ability to penetrate the snack market was limited for decades until it made progress in terms of both actual and perceived taste. Kingsford Charcoal failed in the barbeque sauce market simply because there was no room for a third entrant in the premium segment.

Where You Compete: The Product Market Served

An important determinant for an SCA is the choice of the target product market. A well-defined strategy supported by assets and competencies can fail because it does not work in the marketplace. One way to create marketplace value is to be relevant to customers. As noted in Chapter 5, it does no good to offer the best minivan in the market if most of your target customers now want to buy SUVs.

The scope of the business also involves the identity of competitors. Sometimes an asset or competency will form an SCA only given the right set of competitors. Thus, it is vital to assess whether a competitor or strategic group is weak, adequate, or strong with respect to assets and competencies. The goal is to engage in a strategy that will match up with competitors' weak points in relevant areas.

SCAs Versus Key Success Factors

What is the difference between key success factors (KSFs), introduced in Chapters 2 and 5, and SCAs? A KSF is an asset or competence needed to compete. An SCA is an asset or competence that is the basis for a continuing advantage. For example, an automobile firm needs to have adequate distribution given is business model and objectives, so distribution is a KSF. Lexus has turned its dealer network into an SCA, however, because it is capable of delivering a superior customer experience. A KSF for value-priced economy cars is the ability to control costs in order to create profit margins. Hyundai's ability in this regard is markedly superior to its competitors, and thus it becomes an SCA.

To be a winner at poker requires skill, nerve, and money. In also requires a player to ante—to put up a certain amount of money just to see the cards and engage in betting. A KSF can be an ante in terms of the marketplace. Generating a superior quality car may have been an SCA for Lexus or Mercedes and a point of differentiation in the mid-1990s. As Jaguar, BMW, and Cadillac improve their own quality, though, the quality dimension starts to be an attribute all luxury cars are assumed to have, and thus a KSF but not a basis for an SCA. Instead of winning the competitive hand, a KSF merely buys an organization a seat at the table.

In the branding arena, Keller talks about points of parity (POPs) and points of differentiation (PODs), which provide additional insight into this distinction.[1] PODs are strong, favorable, and unique brand associations based on some attribute or benefit associations. Ikea, for example, provides home furnishings at accessible prices with unique designs and by having customers handle and assemble the products. A POP, in contrast, is an association that is not necessarily unique to the brand. POPs may be necessary to present a credible offering with a certain category, as in the case of ATMs and convenient hours for a bank. A POP might also be designed to negate a competitor's point of distinction. Snackwell's, for example, seeks to create parity with regard to taste, thereby negating the taste POD of its competitors and leading customers to base their selection on Snackwell's POD (namely, calorie and fat control). An SCA is analogous to a POD, whereas a KSF can be analogous to either a POP or a POD.

What Business Managers Name as Their SCAs

Managers of 248 distinct businesses in the service and high-tech industries were asked to name the SCAs of their business.[2] The objectives were to identify frequently employed SCAs, to confirm that managers could articulate them, to determine whether different managers from the same businesses would identify the same SCAs, and to find how many SCAs would be identified for each business. The responses were coded into categories. The results, summarized in Figure 8.2, provide some suggestive insights into the SCA construct.

The wide variety of SCAs mentioned, each representing distinct competitive approaches, is shown in the figure. Of course, the list did differ by industry. For high-tech firms, for example, name recognition was less important than technical superiority, product innovation, and installed customer base. The next two chapters discuss several SCAs in more detail.

Most of the SCAs in Figure 8.2 reflect assets or competencies. Customer base, quality reputation, and good management and engineering staff, for example, are business assets, whereas customer service and technical superiority usually involve sets of competencies.

For a subset of ninety-five of the businesses involved, a second business manager was independently interviewed. The result suggests that managers can identify SCAs with a high degree of reliability. Of the ninety-five businesses, seventy-six of the manager pairs gave answers that were coded the same and most of the others had only a single difference in the SCA list.

Another finding is instructive—the average number of SCAs per business was 4.58, suggesting that it is usually not sufficient to base a strategy on a single SCA. Sometimes a business is described in terms of a single competency or asset, implying that being a quality-oriented business or a service-focused business explains success. This study indicates, however, that it may be necessary to have several assets and competencies.

Strategic Options—Routes to an SCA

As noted in Chapter 1, even given the specification of a product-market investment plan, a business strategy will still involve choices that can usefully be conceptualized and labeled as strategic options. A *strategic option* is a particular value proposition for a product market with supporting assets and competencies and functional area strategies and programs. The value proposition can involve social, emotional and self-expressive benefits as well as functional benefits. Most successful strategies involve more than one strategic option. For example, as noted in Chapter 1, Virgin Atlantic Airways combines a value strategy with one based on innovation and customer intimacy. Thus, a strategic option is a building block for a business strategy and a business strategy can be viewed as a set of integrated strategic options.

Figure 8.3 lists some of the strategic options that will be discussed in the coming chapters. Chapter 9 will introduce the quality option, as well as others related to a product attribute, product design, product line breadth, corporate social responsibility, brand familiarity, and customer intimacy. Chapter 10 describes the value, focus and innovation options, and Chapter 11 considers the global option in detail. Of course, each option will have many variants depending on the industry and context. This list is far from complete, but the descriptions of these options will provide insights into others as well.

		High-Tech	Service	Other	Total
1.	Reputation for quality	26	50	29	105
2.	Customer service/product support	23	40	15	78
3.	Name recognition/high profile	8	42	21	71
4.	Retain good management and engineering staff	17	43	5	65
5.	Low-cost production	17	15	21	53
6.	Financial resources	11	26	14	51
7.	Customer orientation/feedback/ market research	13	26	9	48
8.	Product-line breadth	11	23	13	47
9.	Technical superiority	30	7	9	46
10.	Installed base of satisfied customers	19	22	4	45
11.	Segmentation/focus	7	22	16	45
12.	Product characteristics/differentiation	12	15	10	37
13.	Continuing product innovation	12	17	6	35
14.	Market share	12	14	9	35
15.	Size/location of distribution	10	11	13	34
16.	Low price/high-value offering	6	20	6	32
17.	Knowledge of business	2	25	4	31
18.	Pioneer/early entrant in industry	11	11	6	28
19.	Efficient, flexible production/ operations adaptable to customers	4	17	4	25
20.	Effective sales force	10	9	4	23
21.	Overall marketing skills	7	9	7	23
22.	Shared vision/culture	5	13	4	22
23.	Strategic goals	6	7	9	22
24.	Powerful well-known parent	7	7	6	20
25.	Location	0	10	10	20
26.	Effective advertising/image	5	6	6	17
27.	Enterprising/entrepreneurial	3	3	5	11
28.	Good coordination	3	2	5	10
29.	Engineering research and development	8	2	0	10
30.	Short-term planning	2	1	5	8
31.	Good distributor relations	2	4	1	7
32.	Other	6	20	5	31
	Total	315	539	281	1,135
	Number of businesses	68	113	67	248
	Average number of SCAs	4.63	4.77	4.19	4.58

Figure 8.2   Sustainable Competitive Advantages of 248 Businesses

Figure 8.3   Strategic Options

THE ROLE OF SYNERGY

Synergy between business units can provide an SCA that is truly sustainable because it is based on the characteristics of a firm that are probably unique. A competitor might have to duplicate the organization in order to capture the assets or competencies involved.

A core element in the GE strategic vision was to achieve synergy across many businesses.[3] GE's Jack Welch called it "integrated diversity." The concept was that a GE business can call on the resources of the firm and of other GE businesses to create advantage. For example, the SCAs of General Electric in the CT scanner (an X-ray-based diagnostic system) business are in part based on its leadership in the X-ray business, in which it has a huge installed base and a large service network, and in part based on the fact that it operates other businesses involving technologies used in CT scanners.

A cornerstone of the IBM strategy under Lou Gerstner was to create synergy by pushing core technologies across more product lines.[4] The intent was to leverage the IBM size, scale, and technologies. This vision was a far cry from that of Gerstner's predecessors, who planned to break IBM up into autonomous business units.

Sony exploits the synergy of its many product groups by showcasing them together in stores (such as one on Chicago's Michigan Avenue) and even on several Celebrity Cruise ships. The ships are outfitted with Sony entertainment products, including television sets, movie theaters, and sound equipment. The result is an integrated package that has the cumulative impact of reinforcing Sony's role of providing high quality and technologically advanced entertainment.

Synergy means that the whole is more than the sum of its parts. In this context, it means that two businesses (or two product-market strategies) operating together will be superior to the same two businesses operating independently. In terms of products, positive synergy means that offering a set of products will generate a higher return over time than would be possible if each of the products were offered separately. Similarly, in terms of markets, operating a set of markets within a business will be superior to operating them autonomously.

As a result of synergy, the combined businesses will have one or more of the following:

1. Increased customer value and thus increased sales.
2. Lower operating costs.
3. Reduced investment.

Generally the synergy will be caused by exploiting some commonality in the two operations, such as:

- Customers and sometimes customer applications (potentially creating a systems solution).
- A sales force or channel of distribution.
- A brand name and its image.
- Facilities used for manufacturing, offices, or warehousing.
- R&D efforts.
- Staff and operating systems.
- Marketing and marketing research.

Synergy is not difficult to understand conceptually, but it is slippery in practice, in part because it can be difficult to predict whether synergy will actually emerge. Often two businesses seem related, and sizable potential synergy seems to exist but is never realized. Sometimes the perceived synergy is merely a mirage or wishful thinking, perhaps created in the haste to put together a merger. At other times, the potential synergy is real, but implementation problems prevent its realization. Perhaps there is a cultural mismatch between two organizations, or the incentives are inadequate. The material on implementation in Chapter 16 is directly relevant to the problem of predicting whether potential synergy will be realized.

Alliances

Obtaining instant synergy is a goal of alliances. Pairing McDonald's with Texaco, for example, has provided traffic and added value for Texaco and valuable locations for

McDonald's. Sega has used alliances to gain access to new technology and to exploit its own core graphics technology.[5] Sega has partnered with AT&T in communications, Hitachi in chips, Yamaha in sound, JVC in game machines, and Microsoft in software.

Alliances are often the key to a successful Internet strategy. Yahoo!, AOL, and Amazon have hundreds of major alliances and thousands of smaller ones that combine to help them reach their goals of driving Internet traffic and offering differentiated value to their visitors. Chapter 11, Global Strategies, covers the difficult process of putting together alliances and joint ventures and making them work.

Core Assets and Competencies

A firm's asset or competency that is capable of being the competitive basis of many of its businesses is termed a core asset or competency and can be a synergistic advantage. Prahalad and Hamel suggest a tree metaphor, in which the root system is the core asset or competency, the trunk and major limbs are core products, the smaller branches are business units, and the leaves and flowers are end products.[6] You may not recognize the strength of a competitor if you simply look at its end products and fail to examine the strength of its root system. Core competence represents the consolidation of firm-wide technologies and skills into a coherent thrust. A core asset, such as a brand name or a distribution channel, merits investment and management that span business units.

Consider, for example, the core competencies of Sony in miniaturization, 3M in sticky-tape technology, Black & Decker in small motors, Honda in vehicle motors and power trains, NEC in semiconductors (which underlies its attack on both the computer and communications businesses), and Canon in precision mechanics, fine optics, and microelectronics. Each of these competencies underlies a large set of businesses and has the potential to create more. Each of these firms invests in competence in a variety of different ways and contexts. Each would insist on keeping its primary work related to the core competency in-house. Outsourcing would risk weakening the asset, and each firm would rightfully insist that there is no other firm that could match its state-of-the-art advances.

Capabilities-Based Competition

Capabilities-based competition suggests that the key building blocks of business strategy are not products and markets but, rather, competencies in business processes.[7] Investment in building and managing a process that outperforms competition and can be applied across businesses can lead to a sustainable advantage. Therefore, strategy development must identify the most important processes within the organization, specify how they should be measured, identify target performance levels, relate performance to achieving superior customer value and competitive advantage, and assign cross-functional teams to implement them.

One such process is the new product development and introduction process. Japanese automobile firms that have reduced the process from five years to three years while making it more responsive to the needs of the market have achieved a huge advantage. Another is the management of international operations, considered an SCA by IDV, the spirits subsidiary of Grand Metropolitan. Still another is the order and logistics process in retailing. By developing dramatic improvements in its order and logistics process through distribution center innovations, a dedicated trucking system, and computerized ordering, Wal-Mart developed huge cost and inventory handling advantages over its competition.

Developing superior capabilities in key processes involves strategic investments in people and infrastructure to gain advantage. True process improvement does not occur without control and ownership of the parts of the process. Thus, the virtual corporation, which draws pieces from many sources in response to the organizational task at hand, is not a good model for capabilities-based competition.

STRATEGIC VISION VERSUS STRATEGIC OPPORTUNISM

There are two very different approaches to the development of successful strategies and sustainable competitive advantages. Each can work, but may require very different systems, people, and culture. Strategic vision takes a long-term perspective; the focus is on business strategies that are expected to be successful over a long time period. Strategic opportunism emphasizes strategies that make sense today. The implicit belief is that the best way to have the right strategy in place tomorrow is to have it right today.

Strategic Vision

To manage a strategic vision successfully, a firm should have four characteristics:

1. *A clear future strategy* with a core driving idea and a specification of the competitive arena, functional area strategies, value proposition, and competitive advantage that will define the business.
2. *Buy-in throughout the organization.* There should be a belief in the correctness of the strategy, an acceptance that the vision is achievable and worthwhile, and a real commitment to making that vision happen.
3. *Assets, competencies, and resources to implement* the strategy should be in place, or a plan to obtain them should be under way.
4. *Patience.* There should be a willingness to stick to the strategy in the face of competitive threats or enticing opportunities that would divert resources from the vision.

A strategic vision provides a sense of purpose. Saturn's commitment to building a world-class car and respecting customers' intelligence had the potential to inspire. In contrast, it is hard to get energized to increase ROI by 2 points or sales by 10 percent so shareholders will be wealthier. Strategic vision also provides the rationale for investment that may require years to achieve a payoff. The ability of Costco to stick to a price-value position throughout its operations is one reason it has developed effective programs and resources.

Managing a strategic vision requires a certain kind of organization and management style, as summarized in Figure 8.4. A strategic vision is based on a forward-looking, long-term perspective—the planning horizon extends into the future two, five, or more than ten years, depending on the business involved. The goal of the supporting

Organizational Characteristics	Strategic Vision	Strategic Opportunism
Perspective	• Forward-looking	• Present
Strategic Uncertainties	• Trends affecting the future	• Current threats and opportunities
Environmental Sensing	• Future scenarios	• Change sensors
Information System	• Forward-looking	• On-line
Orientation	• Commitment	• Flexibility
	• Build assets	• Adaptability
	• Vertical integration	• Fast response
Leadership	• Charismatic	• Tactical
	• Visionary	• Action oriented
Structure	• Centralized	• Decentralized
	• Top-down	• Fluid
People	• Eye on the ball	• Entrepreneurial
Economic Advantage	• Scale economies	• Scope economies
Signaling	• Strong signals sent to competitors	• Surprise moves

Figure 8.4   Organizational Differences

information system and analysis effort is thus to understand the likely future environment. Experts who have insights into key future events and trends can be helpful. Scenario analysis, technological forecasting, and trend analysis should be part of the analysis phase of strategy development.

The organization needs to be capable of building assets that may not have immediate payoff. A top-down, centralized structure with a reward system that supports the vision is helpful, as is a strong, charismatic leader who can sell the vision to relevant constituencies inside and outside the organization.

A vision of being a synergistic, technology-driven firm has helped Corning develop from a consumer products firm to a leader in such areas as fiber optics and liquid-crystal displays.[8] Corning's strategy involves investing heavily in technology, sharing the technology across business units, and forming technology and marketing alliances. The goal is to leverage technological developments to maximize the impact on the whole organization.

A strategic vision can take many forms. Jack Welch of GE had a vision of being the first or second largest competitor in each business area and he dramatically changed GE as a result. Mercedes, Tiffany, and Nordstrom at one point were guided by a vision of being the best in their field in terms of delivering quality products and services. The vision of Sharp is to succeed by being a technological innovator, especially in optoelectronic technologies.

Strategic Stubbornness

The risk of the strategic vision route, as suggested by Figure 8.5, is that the vision may be faulty and its pursuit may be a wasteful exercise in strategic stubbornness. There are a host of pitfalls that could prevent a vision from being realized. Three stand out.

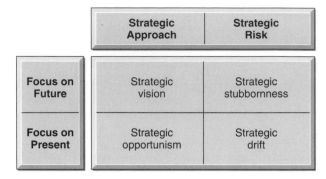

	Strategic Approach	Strategic Risk
Focus on Future	Strategic vision	Strategic stubbornness
Focus on Present	Strategic opportunism	Strategic drift

Figure 8.5   Vision versus Opportunism

Implementation Barriers

The picture of the future may be substantially accurate, but the firm may not be able to implement the strategy required. That was, in part, the problem with the efforts of GE and others to crack the computer market in the 1960s and with the attempt of Sony to promote its beta VCR format as the industry standard in the early days of the VCR.

Faulty Assumptions of the Future

The vision might be faulty because it is based on faulty assumptions about the future. For example, the concept of a one-stop financial services firm that drove the vision of American Express, Sears, Merrill Lynch, and others was based, in part, on the erroneous assumption that customers would see value in a one-stop financial service. It turned out that consumers preferred to deal with specialists. GE's concept of factory automation was similarly faulty, as it discovered after some big losses. Customers wanted hardware and software components, not a factory system.

A Paradigm Shift

A third problem occurs when there is a paradigm shift. For example, changes in technology might cause the nature of a business to change. Thus, computers changed from mainframes to minicomputers, personal computers, portables, workstations, and servers. In the semiconductor industry, the vacuum-tube business first gave way to transistors and then, in sequence, to semiconductors, integrated circuits, and microprocessors. In both cases, each new paradigm brought with it a remarkable change in the cast of characters. It was extremely rare for a leader in one paradigm to be a leader in the next. In fact, it was common to see industry leaders fade sharply in the face of the new paradigms.

New operating models can also change the paradigm. Starbucks and others have changed the way coffee is purchased and consumed, leaving those selling canned coffee in supermarkets to fight in a declining, unprofitable segment. Dell has changed the way both individuals and organizations buy their computers, leaving those selling through retail channels at a disadvantage. Nucor changed the steel industry by creating dispersed minimills that used scrap steel as raw material, leaving the big steel companies to compete on price and watch their sales decline and profits disappear. In each case, it is no coincidence that the new paradigm has been dominated by new entries or by entries that had been considered insignificant niche players by the leading companies. This movement of industry profits and firm value away from an established way of doing business has been termed "value migration" by management consultant Adrian Slywotzky.[9]

Why Are Organizations Stubborn?

Organizational stubbornness, which is especially prevalent among successful firms, has several causes. First, there is the ironic penalty of success. Success should tend to provide resources that can be used to create a new-paradigm business. However, success instead tends to reinforce the old vision and efforts to refine it by reducing costs and improving service. The result is that operational improvements often mask the fundamental shifts. Kenichi Ohmae has observed that Japanese firms have a "winning by working harder" obsession that has not only discouraged change, but also made whole industries unprofitable.[10] For example, Japanese firms have created enormous overcapacity in shipbuilding, automobiles, and other industries and have engaged in destructive price competition in order to "win."

Second, and closely related, the new paradigm will probably require a different organization, and, in particular, a different culture. It is not easy to change a culture, especially when an organization has successfully developed and nurtured that culture to suit the old vision. According to two leading organizational theorists, Michael Tushman and Charles O'Reilly, the strength of the existing culture and the difficulty of change were two key reasons that business transformation at British Airlines, IBM, and Sears occurred only after traumatic financial losses.[11]

Third, why participate in killing the golden goose? Any new-paradigm success will often directly cannibalize the old-vision business. And there is always the chance that the new paradigm will not arrive if the industry leader does not help. Xerox, for example, had a virtual monopoly on copiers in the 1960s, and because of its lease strategy, had a money flow that was difficult to spend. There were therefore significant nonincentives for Xerox to invent a small office copier. This delayed innovation, but it also left room for Canon and others to later change the photocopier world forever.

The power of a vision is based on the commitment that accompanies it. This commitment, together with a focus on the future instead of the past, can result in pursuing a faulty vision beyond the point at which the probability of success is high. The trick is to maintain the commitment and patience in the face of adversity, while at the same time not allowing a failed vision to use up resources on a futile attempt at a miracle recovery.

Strategic Opportunism

Strategic opportunism is driven by a focus on the present. The premise is that the environment is so dynamic and uncertain that it is not feasible to aim at a future target. Unless a business is structured to have strategic advantages in the present, it is unlikely to be strategically successful in the future.

Strategic opportunism provides several advantages. One is that the risk of missing emerging business opportunities is reduced. Firms such as Purina in pet foods, General Mills in cereals, and Ziff-Davis Media in special interest computer publishing all seek emerging niche segments and develop brands tailored to specialty markets. Thus, Purina brands such as Deli-Cat, Kaboodle, and Cat Chow Senior Formula; General Mills brands such as Triangles, Oatmeal Crisp, Sprinkle Spangles, and Cinnamon Toast Crunch; and Ziff-Davis brands like *eWeek, Sync,* and *PC Magazine* all are designed to appeal to a current taste or trend. The risk of strategic stubbornness is also reduced.

Strategic opportunism also tends to generate a vitality and energy that can be healthy, especially when a business has decentralized R&D and marketing units that generate a stream of new products. Within 3M, for example, new businesses are continually created and evaluated with respect to their prospects. HP is another firm that believes in decentralized entrepreneurial management. These decentralized firms are often close to the market and technology and are willing to pursue opportunities.

Strategic opportunism results in economies of scope, with assets and competencies supported by multiple product lines. Nike, which applies its brand assets and competencies in product design and customer sensing to a wide variety of product markets, is a good example. A key part of the Nike strategy is to develop strong emotional ties and relationships with focused segments through its product design and brand name strengths. The organization is extremely sensitive to emerging segments (such as outdoor basketball) and the need for product refinements and product innovation. Nike has strategic flexibility, which characterizes successful strategically opportunistic firms.

As Figure 8.4 suggests, the prototypical business driven by strategic opportunism is very different from a business guided by a strategic vision. The strategic uncertainties are very different. What trends are most active and critical now? What is the current driving force in the market? What are the strategic problems facing the business that need immediate correction? What technologies are ready to be employed? What are current strategic opportunities and threats? What are competitors doing in the market and in the lab? What strategy changes are occurring or will soon occur?

The supporting information system and analysis are also different. To support strategic opportunism, companies must monitor customers, competitors, and the trade to learn of trends, opportunities, and threats as they appear. Information gathering and analysis should be both sensitive and on-line. Frequent, regular meetings to analyze the most recent developments and news may be helpful. The organization should be quick to understand and act on changing fundamentals.

The hallmark of an organization that emphasizes strategic opportunism is strategic flexibility and the willingness to respond quickly to strategic opportunities as they emerge. The organization is adaptive, with the ability to adjust its systems, structure, people, and culture to accommodate new ventures. The strategy is dynamic, and change is the norm. New products are being explored or introduced and others are de-emphasized or dropped. New markets are entered and disinvestment occurs in others. New synergies and assets are being created. The people are entrepreneurial, sensitive to new opportunities and threats, and fast to react.

Strategic Drift

The problem with the strategic opportunism model is that, as suggested by Figure 8.5, it can turn into strategic drift. Investment decisions are made incrementally in response to opportunities rather than directed by a vision. As a result, a firm can wake up one morning and find that it is in a set of businesses for which it lacks the needed assets and competencies and that provide few synergies.

At least three phenomena can turn strategic opportunism into strategic drift. First, a short-lived, transitory force may be mistaken for one with enough staying power to make a strategic move worthwhile. If the force is so short-lived that a strategy does not pay off or does not even have a chance to get into place, the result will be a strategy that is not suitable for the business or the environment.

Second, opportunities to create immediate profits may be rationalized as strategic when, in fact, they are not. For example, an instrumentation firm might receive many requests from some of its customers for special-purpose instruments that could conceivably be used by other customers but that have little strategic value for the company. Such opportunities might result in a sizable initial order, but could divert R&D resources from more strategic activities.

Third, expected synergies across existing and new business areas may fail to materialize owing to implementation problems, perhaps because of culture clashes or because the synergies were only illusions in the first place. A drive to exploit core assets or competencies might not work. As a result, new business areas would be in place without the expected sustainable advantages.

Strategic drift not only creates a business without needed assets and competencies, but it can also result in a failure to support a core business that does have a good vision. Without a vision and supporting commitment, it is tempting to divert investment into seemingly sure things that are immediate strategic opportunities. Thus, strategic opportunism can be an excuse to delay investment or divert resources from a core vision.

One example of strategic drift is a firm that designed, installed, and serviced custom equipment for steel firms. Over time, steel firms became more knowledgeable and began buying standardized equipment mainly on the basis of price. Gradually, the firm edged into this commodity business to retain its market share. The company finally realized it was pursuing a dual strategy for which it was ill suited. It had too much overhead to compete with the real commodity firms, and its ability to provide upscale service had eroded to the point that it was now inferior to some niche players. Had there been a strategic vision, the firm would not have fallen into such a trap.

Another is a discounter that did well when operating a limited product line in a local market with a low-cost message. The customer value was clear and the hands-on management style was effective. However, when the firm expanded its geographic and product scope even going into groceries, the management systems were no longer adequate and the value proposition become fuzzy as well. It had drifted into a business requiring assets and competencies it did not have.

Vision Plus Opportunism

Many businesses attempt to have the best of both worlds by engaging in strategic vision and strategic opportunism at the same time. Strategic opportunism can supplement strategic vision by managing diversification away from the core business and by managing the route to achievement of a firm's vision. Thus, if Weight Watchers' vision is to exploit brand associations by extending its name to other product categories, strategic opportunism can describe the process of selecting the extensions and the order in which they are pursued.

The combination can and does work. However, there are obvious risks and problems. One is that strategic vision requires patience and investment and is vulnerable to the enticements represented by the more immediate return that is usually associated with strategic opportunism. It is difficult to maintain the persistence and discipline required by strategic vision in any case, even without the distractions of alternative strategies that have been blessed as part of the thrust of the organization.

The organizational problems are worse. It is difficult for one organization to use both approaches well because the systems, people, structure, and culture that are best for one approach are generally not well suited to the other. To create an organization that excels at or even tolerates both is not easy.

A DYNAMIC VISION

An attractive strategy is to have a *dynamic* vision that can change in anticipation of emerging paradigm shifts. This is a difficult goal, and few managers and firms have been able to pull it off. But the payoff is huge. And some firms, such as Nucor, Charles Schwab, and Microsoft, have succeeded.

In the 1970s, facing price pressures from fully integrated steel firms plus efficient Japanese brands, Nucor developed a strategy of producing joists (higher-value products used in construction) in rural minimills that employed nonunionized labor and used scrap steel as raw material. For a decade, this model made Nucor a strategic and financial success. By the mid-1980s, however, others had started to copy the strategy, scrap steel was no longer as plentiful, and aluminum had made serious inroads into traditional steel markets. In response to these changes, Nucor again reinvented the paradigm by focusing on flat-rolled, up-market products, using a scrap-steel substitute, and drawing on iron ore in Brazil and a processing plant in Trinidad.[12]

Charles Schwab shifted from being a discount broker for individual investors to being an innovative supplier of no-load, no-transaction-fee mutual funds under the Schwab OneSource brand. It has now enlisted an army of fee-only financial advisers called Schwab Institutional to guide investors who are attracted to the Schwab investment options. Microsoft's focus progressed from operating systems to applications to the Internet. Both Schwab and Microsoft did not abandon the old vision, but rather augmented it with a new direction. The Schwab story will be revisited in Chapter 12.

How do you change a vision? Certainly it requires a will to change, an ability to anticipate paradigm shifts and create the new vision via an insightful and forward-looking strategic analysis, and an ability to change the organization and particularly the culture. The strategic analysis phase has already been covered. The organizational elements will be discussed in Chapter 16. The next two sections will discuss two perspectives that provide paths relevant to changing a vision: strategic intent and strategic flexibility.

Strategic Intent

Hamel and Prahalad have suggested that some firms have strategic intent, which couples strategic vision with a sustained obsession with winning at all levels of the organization.[13] They note that this model explains the successful rise to global leadership of companies such as Canon, Komatsu, Samsung (see box), and Honda. Thus, Canon was out to "beat Xerox," Komatsu to "encircle Caterpillar," and Honda to become a "second Ford."

A strategic intent to achieve a successful strategy has several characteristics in addition to strategic vision and an obsession with success. First, it should recognize the essence of winning. Coca-Cola's strategic intent has included the objective of putting a Coke within "arm's reach" of every consumer in the world because distribution and accompanied visibility are the keys to winning. NEC decided it needed

SAMSUNG AND MICROWAVE OVENS

In 1977, Samsung decided to make microwave ovens even though major established competitors with seemingly unbeatable SCAs were making millions of ovens per year.[14] During the next four years, it saw its first two prototypes melt down, redesigned its product again and again, bought the last magnetron factory from the United States, and received its first order for 240 ovens from Panama. In 1980, a J. C. Penney order requiring Samsung to build a unit 25 percent less expensive than existing ones necessitated still another redesign. In 1983, GE, under pressure from Japanese firms, turned to Samsung to source some of its products, Samsung's labor costs of $1.47 contrasted sharply with GE's $52.00. By the late 1980s, Samsung was building more than 4 million units per year and had cornered more than one-third of the U.S. market.

It is clear that Samsung had a strategic intent to enter the microwave oven market. Its goals during the first decade were production and meeting whatever customer needs were required to gain sales. Financial return was of no consequence. An enormous investment was made in design, manufacturing, and engineering. To make it happen a large, competent staff carefully analyzed how competitors had solved problems and what customers expected. The firm was very responsive to customer needs even when it met sizable losses. It capitalized on its cost advantage and the willingness of production and engineering personnel to work 68-hour weeks. Samsung virtually willed its own remarkable success.

to acquire the technologies that would allow it to exploit the convergence of computing and telecommunications. That became its guiding theme.

Second, strategic intent involves stretching an organization with a continuing effort to identify and develop new SCAs or to improve those that exist. Thus, it has a dynamic, forward-looking perspective. What will our advantage be next year and two years after that? Consider Matsushita, Toshiba, and the other Japanese television manufacturers. They first relied on the advantage of low labor cost. By serving private-label needs, they added economies of scale. The next step was to build advantages in quality, reliability, features, brand name, and distribution. In contrast, an analysis of their strengths and weaknesses might have led to the conclusion that they should focus on a low-cost niche.

Third, strategic intent often requires real innovation, a willingness to do things very differently. Savin entered the U.S. copier market with a product that could be sold through dealers instead of leased and was simple, low priced, and reliable. As a result, Xerox's huge advantage in sales and service and its ability to finance leased equipment were neutralized. Honda made real advances in motor design in order to attack the large motorcycle market.

An obsession with winning can be created even without a competitor. Peter Johnson told how he created a phantom competitor when running Trus Joist, a maker of structural components for buildings, which had a patent-based monopoly.[15] The phantom competitor developed low-cost options and generated creative options for breaking into the business. As a result, Trus Joist was stimulated to innovate in an adjacent market.

Strategic intent provides a long-term drive for advantage that can be essential to success. It provides a model that helps break the mold, moving a firm away from simply doing the same things a bit better and working a bit harder than the year before. It has the capability to elevate and extend an organization, helping it reach levels it would not otherwise attain.

Strategic Flexibility

Strategic intent usually represents a commitment to attaining an SCA. However, in some dynamic industries, an SCA can be a moving target that is difficult to attain proactively because there are too many uncertainties to make the necessary predictions about customer needs, technology, competitive posture, and so on. In those contexts, the answer is to attain strategic flexibility, so that the business will be ready when a window of opportunity arises.

Strategic flexibility (the ability to adjust or develop strategies to respond to external or internal changes) can be achieved in a variety of ways, including participating in multiple product-markets and technologies, having resource slack, and creating an organizational system and culture that supports change.

Participation in multiple product-markets or technologies means that the organization is already "on the ground" in different arenas. Thus, if it appears that demand will shift to a new product-market or that a newer technology will emerge, the organization can just expand its current product-market rather than start from zero with all the risks and time required. An organization may also participate in business areas with weak returns in order to gain the strategic flexibility to deal with possible market changes. For example, GM's investment in Saturn resulted in a very modest return. However, having Saturn could allow GM some very nice competitive options if gas supplies were curtailed by OPEC or by a war.

Investing in underused assets provides strategic flexibility. An obvious example is maintaining liquidity (as with Toyota's $20 billion cash hoard) so that investment can be funneled swiftly to opportunity or problem areas. Maintaining excess capacity in distribution, organizational staffing, or R&D can also enhance a firm's ability to react quickly.

An organizational culture that supports change will create strategic flexibility. A change-enhancing culture starts with being good at detecting opportunities and threats, perhaps drawing on the external information system described in Chapter 6. It will also include an entrepreneurial style, supported by organizational structures and reward systems, that encourages managers to exploit opportunities with action-oriented strategies. There has to be some ability to tolerate a "ready, fire, aim" mentality.

A Note of Caution

A strategic vision requires real persistence in the face of tempting distractions. It also requires discipline and eye-on-the-ball focus. Visions that are excessively dynamic are no longer visions at all. There is a very real risk of capsizing when trying to catch the wave.

LESSONS FROM U.S. BUSINESS BLUNDERS

An analysis of some egregious business blunders revealed four fatal misconceptions:[16]

1. Labor costs are killing us. In fact the labor content is often only a small percentage of value added. Furthermore, the most efficient factories have more costly labor input; they just use and motivate it better.

2. You can't make money at the low end. Actually last year's low end from radios to semiconductors often forms the technological, manufacturing, and marketing basis for next year's high end.

3. We can't sell it. U.S. firms attempted to sell products from microwave ovens (the major appliance firms) to fax machines (Xerox, first introduced the fax) using marketing methods familiar to them, rather than approaches attuned to the innovation.

4. It's cheaper to buy it (a new business area) than grow it. Treating businesses as stand-alone units to be bought or sold discourages unit synergy, diverts attention to external investment (the grass is always greener on the other side), and treats investment needed for survival as just another capital budgeting decision.

KEY LEARNINGS

- To create an SCA, a strategy needs to be valued by the market and supported by assets and competences that are not easily copied or neutralized by competitors. The most common SCAs are quality reputation, customer support, and brand name.

- Synergy is often sustainable because it is based on the unique characteristics of an organization.

- Strategic opportunism focuses on the present and emphasizes current opportunities and strategic choices, whereas strategic vision has a long-term perspective and avoids changes in strategy. Opportunism can lead to strategic drift, while a vision-based approach can lead to strategic stubbornness.

- Strategic intent couples strategic vision with a sustained obsession. Strategic flexibility provides a way for organizations to exploit strategic opportunities and manage strategic problems.

FOR DISCUSSION

1. What is a sustainable competitive advantage? Identify SCAs for Dell, P&G, Tide, and Citibank.

2. Pick a product class and several major brands. What are each brand's points of parity and point of difference? Relate POPs to KSFs, and the POD to SCAs.

3. What is synergy? What are the sources of synergy? Give examples. Why is it so elusive?

4. What is strategic vision, and how does it differ from strategic opportunism? What are strategic drift and strategic stubbornness, and why do they occur? Can you name any examples besides those mentioned in the chapter? Were faulty strategic decisions the real problem, or was there a deeper organizational flaw? What is a dynamic vision, and is it feasible? Did Schwab really exhibit dynamic vision?

5. Compare strategic vision with strategic intent. Illustrate with examples.

6. Illustrate with examples strategic flexibility.

NOTES

1. Kevin Lane Keller, *Strategic Brand Management,* 2nd edition,Upper Saddle River, New Jersey: Prentice-Hall, 2003, pp. 131–136.

2. David A. Aaker, "Managing Assets and Skills: The Key to a Sustainable Competitive Advantage," *California Management Review,* Winter 1989, pp. 91–106.

3. Noel M. Tichy, "Revolutionize Your Company," *Fortune*, December 13, 1993, pp. 114–118.

4. Louis V. Gertner, Jr., *Who Says Elephants Can't Dance?*, New York: Harper Business, 2002.

5. Neil Gross and Robert D. Hof, "Sega!" *Business Week*, February 21, 1994, pp. 66–71.

6. C.K. Prahalad and Gary Hamel, "The Core Competence of the Corporation," *Harvard Business Review*, May–June 1990, pp. 79–91. This book uses the phrase "core assets and competencies," which is an extension of the term "core competencies" used in Prahalad and Hamel's article.

7. George Stalk, Philip Evans, and Lawrence E. Shulman, "Competing on Capabilities: The New Rules of Corporate Strategy," *Harvard Business Review*, March–April 1992, pp. 57–69.

8. Keith H. Hammonds, "Corning's Class Act," *Business Week*, May 13, 1991, pp. 68–76.

9. Adrian J. Slywotzky, *Value Migration*, Boston: Harvard Business School Press, 1996.

10. Kenichi Ohmae, "Companyism and Do More Better," *Harvard Business Review*, January–February 1989, pp. 125–132.

11. Michael L. Tushman and Charles A. O'Reilly III, *Winning through Innovation: A Practical Guide to Leading Organizational Change and Renewal*, Boston: Harvard Business School Press, 1997.

12. Slywotzky, *Value Migration*.

13. Gary Hamel and C.K. Prahalad, "Strategic Intent," *Harvard Business Review*, May–June 1989, pp. 63–76.

14. Ira C. Magaziner and Mark Patinkin, "Fast Heat: How Korea Won the Microwave War," *Harvard Business Review*, January–February 1989, pp. 83–92.

15. Peter T. Johnson, "Why I Race against Phantom Competitors," *Harvard Business Review*, September–October 1988, pp. 106–112.

16. Thomas A. Stewart, "Lessons from U.S. Business Blunders," *Fortune*, April 23, 1990, pp. 128–138.

CHAPTER NINE

Strategic Options

Ever since Morton's put a little girl in a yellow slicker and declared, "When it rains, it pours," no advertising person worth his or her salt has had any excuse to think of a product as having parity with anything.
—*Malcolm MacDougal, Jordan Case McGrath*

If you don't have a competitive advantage, don't compete.
—*Jack Welch, GE*

You can't depend on your eyes when your imagination is out of focus.
—*Mark Twain*

A business strategy, as defined in Chapter 1, involves four components: the product-market investment decision, the customer value proposition, the organization's assets and competencies, and functional strategies and programs. For a given industry and organizational context, a strategist will have innumerable ways to compete. Alternative markets, submarkets, product extensions and new product arenas can always be considered. A bewildering variety of customer value propositions, each with its own nuances and spins, will represent strategy variants. Hundreds of conceivable assets and competencies can be developed, nurtured, exploited, and combined, and there are potentially thousands of viable functional strategies and programs.

Usually, however, business strategies cluster around a limited number of strategic options—particular value propositions for a product market, supported by assets and competencies and functional strategies and programs. Common strategic options include quality, focus (on a product or market), value, innovation, customer intimacy, or being global. Each of these options needs to be adapted to a given context, but all should offer a clear value proposition to customers and be supported by assets and competencies and functional strategies and programs.

Understanding these strategic options will help guide you in evaluating and developing business strategies. To succeed, you will need to be creative and cast a wide net; having a set of potentially viable options can help make sure that you consider all of the promising alternatives. In addition, when you have a sense of the available choices, you will be more thorough and realistic in appraising whether a proposed strategic option is likely to succeed. Finally, knowing the keys to success of the various options will enhance the development of programs to implement a business strategy.

A business may select more than one strategic option—choosing to walk and chew gum at the same time, so to speak. It is not an either/or situation. In fact, most successful strategies will represent an integration of several strategic options. A solid understanding of each, however, can guide you not only in making the decision which to include but also in specifying their respective roles and priorities in the overall strategy. Which should be dialed up? How should various options interact? The way they combine can be a key to success.

BUSINESS STRATEGY CHALLENGES

Which strategic option or set of options should form the basis for a business strategy? To answer this question, each option should be challenged with respect to whether it contains a real and perceived value proposition and whether it is relevant, sustainable, and feasible. The goal of this analysis is to identify not only the potential impact of the strategic option, but also its limitations and feasibility.

Is There a Real Customer Value Proposition?

A successful business strategy needs to add value for the customer, and this value needs to be real rather than merely assumed. The one-stop financial service vision, for example, had much less value to customers than was hoped when it was first tried in the early 1980s. This example of synergy that never materialized will be told in Chapter 14. Similarly, Bayer tried to apply its familiar brand name on non-aspirin products, only to find that the value of the Bayer name diminished greatly outside of the aspirin category.

Value is more likely to be real if it is driven from the customer's perspective rather than from that of the business operation. How does the point of differentiation affect the customer's experience of buying and using the product? Does it serve to reduce cost, add performance, or increase satisfaction? The concepts of unmet needs and customer problems, outlined in Chapter 3, are relevant. Does market research confirm that value is added from the customer's perspective?

Is There a Perceived Customer Value Proposition?

Further, the value proposition must be recognized and perceived as worthwhile by the customers. Delivering a value proposition is pointless unless customers know about it and believe it. For example, a customer may be unaware that Burger King has a convenient ordering process, or that Subaru has a superior braking system. This may occur because customers have not have been exposed to the information, because the information was not packaged in a memorable and believable way, or because the attribute or service was not considered to be relevant or of value.

The perceived value problem is particularly acute when the customer is not capable of judging the added value easily. Customers, for example, cannot evaluate airline safety or the skill of a dentist without investing significant time and effort. Instead the customer will look for signals, such as the appearance of the aircraft or the professionalism of the dentist's front office. The firm's task, then, is to manage the signals or cues that imply added value.

Is the Strategy Relevant to Customers?

A business has to make what customers want to buy. The product or service has to be considered relevant to the markets in which the business chooses to compete. As noted in the discussion of relevance in Chapter 5, it does no good to make the best SUV if customers are interested in hybrid cars. If a business has a value proposition that is of secondary interest to customers, the latter may look elsewhere even if the business is executing its value proposition effectively. If the products are considered passé or inferior, the business will lack relevance.

Is the Strategy Sustainable?

The strategy's point of difference from competitors needs to be not only perceived but sustainable. This is often a tough challenge, because most points of differentiation are easily copied. One route to a sustainable advantage is to own an important product dimension, perhaps with the aid of a branded differentiator (such as the Cadillac Northstar engine or the GM On Star guidance system). A second route would be creating a program of continuous investment and improvement that enables the strategy to remain a moving target, always ahead of competitors or poised to leapfrog them. Third, a business could create points of differentiation that are based on unique assets and competencies of the organization, which are inherently difficult to copy.

Overinvestment in a value-added activity may pay off in the long run by discouraging competitors from duplicating a strategy. For example, competitors might be deterred from developing a service backup system that is more extensive than current customers expect. The same logic can apply to a broad product line. Some elements of that line might be unprofitable, but still might be worth retaining if they plug holes that competitors could use to provide customer value.

Is the Strategy Feasible?

It is one thing to create the perfect strategy with respect to customers, competitors, and the marketplace. It is another to execute that strategy effectively. The strategy may require assets and capabilities that are currently inadequate or do not exist, and programs to develop or upgrade them may turn out to be unrealistic. Alliance partners to fill the gap may be difficult to find or to work with. Further, an objective analysis of the customer trends, competitor strengths, or market dynamics may reveal that any strategic success will be short-lived.

STRATEGIC OPTIONS

While there are an infinite number of business strategy variants in any context, certain strategic options tend to be used most often. In this chapter and the two that follow, five of these options—quality, value, focus, innovation, and being global—will be discussed in some detail. Each is frequently employed, has led to performance successes, and is associated with a body of knowledge and experience. Further, the resulting analysis of these few will provide a feel for the types of issues and questions associated with any strategic option.

A snapshot of some of the other strategic options that can be considered follows, to provide a glimpse of the scope of choices available to the business strategist. The ultimate goal of developing brilliant strategies will be reached only when brilliant options are considered. It does little good to be an expert at selecting among mediocre alternatives.

Product Attribute

If a product or service attribute is central to the purchase and use of an offering, one strategic option is to dominate or even own that attribute. Volvo has long owned safety by designing its cars and positioning its brand so that it has extremely strong credibility on that dimension. Pringles offers both a product form and package that allows convenient, compact storage of the product. Heinz has catsup that pours slowly because it is so thick and rich. Some airlines offer business-class passengers more comfortable sleeping space. In each case, the attribute is relevant to customers, and the brands are clearly positioned on that attribute.

If such an option is to be viable over time, it needs to be protected against competitors. Having patent protection is one route. Dolby Laboratories has created a position based on an ever-expanding set of patents to support its sound offerings. Another route is to have a programmatic investment strategy in order to maintain the real and perceived edge. Thus, Volvo has an investment program and clear design philosophy to ensure that it can deliver on its safety promise.

Another route to owning an attribute over time is to brand it and then actively manage that brand and its promise. For example, in 1999, the Westin Hotel Chain created the "Heavenly Bed," a customer designed mattress set (by Simmons) that became a branded differentiator for the chain. The Heavenly Bed was meaningful in that it addressed the fundamental purpose of a hotel room—to provide a good night's sleep. It also had an impact. During the first year of its life, hotel sites that featured the Heavenly Bed had a 5 percent increase in customer satisfaction, noticeably improved perceptions of cleanliness, room décor, and maintenance, and increased occupancy. Westin has actively managed the Heavenly Bed brand. The bed can now be purchased, and the concept has been extended into the Heavenly Bath, giving core loyal customer another reason to believe and to talk about Westin to friends.

Product Design

An offering can appeal to a person's aesthetics, providing substantial self-expressive as well as functional benefits. Jaguar has long pursued this strategy and is somewhat unique among competitors that look all too similar, as if they all use the same wind tunnel. W Hotels have a unique look and feel (which extends to their rooms) that appeals to fashion-forward travelers. The translucent Apple iMac showed that even computers could have design flair. (Steve Jobs has been quoted as saying, "Design is the soul of a manmade creation.") The Volkswagen Beetle came back with a new design that retained the original Beetle look and its authentic personality.

Pursuing a design option requires the firm to really have a passion for design and to support a home for a creative design team. Creating such a culture and infrastructure is a key to success for firms like Jaguar, W Hotels, and Apple, as well as other design driven firms such as Disney and Ralph Lauren. Because achieving a home for design can be difficult, another route is to create an alliance with a design firm, which allows access to best-of-breed designers when needed. Outsourcing can succeed if the firm manages the alliance properly and establishes exclusive ownership of the output.

Product Line Breadth

A compelling value proposition can be based on product-line breadth. Best Buy provides a one-stop shopping experience for electronic goods. Menu variety is one reason behind the success of Subway. Sony, because it makes a complete line of home entertainment products, offers customers total system design and a single source for upgrades and service.

Especially in the business-to-business space, many firms are trying to move from being component suppliers to being systems solution players. One reason is that a systems-based organization will be more likely to control the customer relationship. Another is a need to capture greater margins, because components can tend to become commodities. Simply bundling products, though, is rarely enough. To deliver value to the customer, a firm must offer not only product breadth but a systems orientation and expertise.

Corporate Social Responsibility

BP is serious about its motto of "Beyond Petroleum," aggressively promoting conservation and investing in cleaner energy sources. The Body Shop built up a following through its visible endorsement of Third World ecology and other causes. Ben & Jerry's has supported environmental causes in a colorful way that has enhanced the company's image. The Ronald McDonald House and the Avon Breast Cancer Crusade provide unmistakable expressions of organizational values. The "HP way" involved a commitment to employees, customers, suppliers, and the community to which people could relate.

CEOs believe that corporate social responsibility (CSR) can pay off. In one survey, more than 90 percent thought that socially responsible management creates shareholder value.[1] In another study, 300 firms judged to have high commitment to CSR had a slightly higher stock return during a two year period beginning in October 2000.[2] Perhaps providing a more direct measurement, a UK study compared the marketplace performance of three energy companies. Two of these, BP and Shell, were perceived as environmentally friendly while the third, Esso, had visibly taken the position that renewable energy was not a viable solution and that the Kyoto international accords on the environment were flawed. Greenpeace subsequently attacked Esso with a high-profile "StopEsso" campaign. A subsequent Greenpeace poll found that the proportion of British gasoline buyers who said they regularly used Esso stations dropped by 7 percent during the year of the campaign.[3]

There are good reasons why CSR could influence profitability. Many people fundamentally want to have a relationship with good people who can be trusted, and they perceive that CSR programs reflect a firm's values. A strong and visible CSR program can deliver self-expressive benefits, particularly for the core group of customers who have strong feelings about environmental issues. Certainly, many drivers of Toyota's Prius, the leading gas-electric hybrid car, achieve significant self-expressive benefits. In fact, the glamorous CEO of The Body Shop Japan drives a Prius as a statement about both herself and her firm. With Prius as the flagship of dozens of environmental programs, Toyota has taken the leadership position with respect to CSR, at least in North America and the Far East. A CSR program can also be defensive; in that it can help a firm deal with an accident or criticism by activists based on social responsibility issues.

Ad hoc programs, though, are not the way to pursue CSR. Rather, the programs need to be focused, meaningful, consistent over time, and hopefully branded. All firms will give lip service and some resources toward CSR. The firms that stand out, such as Toyota and BP, however, have a real commitment—even a passion—and find ways to make it visible.

There are challenges in pursuing a CSR strategy. One, perhaps the most serious, involves creating unreasonable expectations. If a firm is visible and active with regard to CSR, people will expect it to be flawless. Given the complexity of the issues, however, a firm can be making strides and still be criticized. BP can make significant investments in renewable energy relative to its competitors, for example, but some may correctly point out that the investment is still small relative to BP's size. Nike can make progress in addressing the labor practices of its offshore suppliers, but still draw fire because problems remain. Another challenge is to make CSR programs visible and relevant to customers, many of whom will find a firm's CSR activities too far removed from its offering's attributes and benefits.

Brand Familiarity

Simple brand familiarity can create a reason to buy, as well as a basis for a customer relationship. It is remarkable how much familiarity can influence. Taste tests of such products as colas and peanut butter show that a recognized name can affect evaluations even if the subject has never purchased or used the brand. Name awareness can signal presence, commitment, and substance—attributes that can be very important, even to industrial buyers of big-ticket items and consumer buyers of durable goods. The logic is that if a name is recognized, there must be a reason. The "Intel Inside" campaign has earned a significant price premium for Intel by creating a perception of advanced technology, even though the ads do not communicate anything about the company or the product. This remarkable success represents the pure power of awareness.

Brand awareness is an asset that can be extremely durable and thus sustainable. It can be very difficult to dislodge a brand that has achieved a dominant awareness level. Customers' awareness of the Datsun brand, for example, was as strong as that of its successor, Nissan, four years after the firm changed its name.[4] An awareness study on blenders over twenty years after GE stopped making the product found that the GE brand was the second most preferred brand.[5] Another study of familiarity asked homemakers to name as many brands as they could; they averaged twenty-eight names each. The ages of the brands named were surprising: more than 85 percent were over 25-years-old, and 36 percent were over 75-years-old.[6]

The fragmentation and clutter in mass media make the task of building awareness and presence economically even more formidable. Even for brands such as Sony, GE, or Ford, which have a broad product and sales base, maintaining visibility is a challenge. The key is to become skilled at operating outside the normal media channels by using event promotions, publicity, sampling, and other attention-grabbing approaches. For example, consider the impact of Samsung's Olympic sponsorship, the Niketown showcase stores, and Swatch hanging a 165-yard-long watch from skyscrapers in Frankfurt and Tokyo. All of these firms were able to increase their awareness levels much more effectively than if they had relied only on mass media advertising.

Customer Intimacy

All firms place an emphasis on the customer. A few, however, create an experience that connects the offering to the customer on a more involved and passionate level. For these firms, customer intimacy is a strategic option. Starbucks' vision of a "third place" (after home and office) where people feel comfortable and secure represents an experience that many customers view as a high point in their day. Some local hardware stores create offerings, specialized services, and personal customer relationships that allow them to prosper while competing with "big boxes" such as Home Depot or Wal-Mart. Nordstrom has generated a customer link by offering personalized service and a shopping experience that often delights rather than merely satisfies. Sony and 3M have similarly connected by providing products that generate a "Wow!" response.

Firms that create intimacy understand customers at a deep level. They deliver an experience that is satisfying on several levels, going beyond functional benefits to provide emotional, social, and self-expressive benefits. The open-road experience associated with Harley-Davidson, for example, has important social and self-expressive elements. The result is an intensely loyal customer base that will talk about the brand and the experience, not just to others in the "club" but also to those who should be.

The key to really turning on customers and achieving intimacy might be resolving unmet needs in the marketplace—finding answers to annoyances that customers have tolerated because there was no option. For example, the automobile buying experience was distasteful before Saturn and Lexus introduced a very different buying experience which became a basis for a new customer relationship. Intimacy can also come from delight at an unexpected experience, such as the massages that come with Virgin's first-class seats, the piano in a Nordstrom store, or the Harley-Davidson biking parties. Or it could develop from an over-the-top product, such as Krispy Kreme doughnuts, In-N-Out hamburgers, or Apple's iMac.

The highly loyal, even fanatical customer base sometimes created through an intimacy strategy needs active programs to nurture and support it. Harley-Davidson, for example, supports its Harley Owners' Groups (HOGs) with local and national events, clothing and accessories, and a Web site with a host of supporting services, including a trip planner and online photo center. Virgin continually adds new features and services designed to support its image of being creative and willing to ignore convention in pursuit of enjoyable customer experiences.

This list of strategic options could be extended in any given context. For now, in the balance of this chapter and in the next two, we will explore five options in more detail: quality, value, innovation, focus, and being global.

THE QUALITY OPTION

Perceived quality can be the driver of a business strategy as the Lexus case shows. But the Schlitz story illustrates how a failure to deliver can be disastrous.

Lexus—A Passion for Excellence

For more than a decade, Lexus has been among the leaders on a variety of objective quality indicators. In particular, Lexus in the United States regularly captures the top spot in the J.D. Power ratings of initial customer satisfaction, long-term dependability, and the most appealing premium luxury car. In 2002, in the first Power survey in Germany, Lexus was again the top nameplate, placing ahead of the famed German brands. Lexus was also named the finest luxury sedan in America by the AMCI organization, which evaluates cars on 193 dimensions involving appointments, performance, utility, and defects. These successes exemplify an incredible quality performance over a long time period.[7]

Among the many reasons behind the Lexus achievement, several stand out. First, the Lexus concept was based on quality from its inception. Toyota launched Lexus in the early 1980s as a brand that would take automobile design, manufacturing, and retailing to a new level. Second, the brand delivered on the concept, as Lexus drew on assets and competencies developed by Toyota to make cars that were more reliable and had fewer defects. Third, a new dealer network offered the potential to break from industry norms and provide a pleasant buying experience. Fourth, the positioning of the Lexus brand (with the classic "relentless pursuit of perfection" tagline) delivered the quality message consistently over the years.

The challenge facing Lexus now is that despite its success with a quality mission and message, it has failed to develop much personality in comparison to BMW,

Mercedes, Jaguar, and Cadillac. When the latter brands gradually closed the quality gap over the years, the Lexus message became less compelling. In response, Lexus belatedly has tried to inject some emotional and self-expressive benefits, as demonstrated by its modified tagline, "The passionate pursuit of perfection." It has not been an easy task.

Schlitz: When Perceived Quality Falters

The story of Schlitz beer dramatically illustrates the strategic power of perceived quality and how fragile it is. From a strong number two position in 1974 (17.8 million barrels of beer annually) supported by a series of well-regarded "go for the gusto" ad campaigns, Schlitz fell steadily until the mid-1980s, when it had all but disappeared (with sales of only 1.8 million barrels). The stock market value fell more than a billion dollars.

The collapse can be traced to a decision to reduce costs by converting to a fermentation process that took four days instead of twelve, substituting corn syrup for barley malt, and using a different foam stabilizer. Word of these changes got into the marketplace. In early 1976, when bottles of flaky, cloudy-looking Schlitz beer appeared on the shelves, the condition was eventually traced to the new foam stabilizer. Worse still, in early summer of that same year, an attempted fix caused the beer to go flat after a few months on the shelf. In the fall of 1976, 10 million bottles and cans of Schlitz were "secretly" recalled and destroyed. Despite a return to its original process and aggressive advertising, Schlitz never recovered.

A quality strategy means that the brand—whether it is for hotels, cars, or computers—will be perceived as superior to other brands in its reference set. The point of superiority is not limited to an attribute or service but spans the offerings, delivering exceptional quality across products and individual attributes. Usually, such superiority will be associated with a price premium.

The reference set could be premium offerings, as it was in the case of Lexus, but superiority can also be demonstrated with respect to value offerings. Thus, Target may be regarded as higher in quality than other discount retailers, although no one would confuse it with Bloomingdale's or Nordstrom. It will simply be judged on a different set of criteria, including ease of parking, waiting time at checkout, courtesy of the checkout person, and whether desired items are in stock. In much the same manner, Gillette's Good News is the quality option among disposable blades.

Superiority will be defined by customers. In nearly all contexts, a single overall indicator of quality exists, is relevant to customers, and in fact drives other, more specific dimensions of performance. To understand what drives perceived quality and to actively manage it, however, you will need to determine the underlying dimensions in any given context.

Figure 9.1 lists several dimensions of quality that are often relevant. Of course, each of these dimensions has multiple components (for example, performance for a printer will involve attributes such as speed, resolution, and capacity). Further, the list itself will depend on the context. The dimensions of quality in a service or software context will differ from those in a product context.

In a service context—such as a bank, restaurant, or theme park—research has shown that quality is based in large part on the perceived competence, responsiveness,

1. **Performance.** What are the specifications? How well is the task performed? Does the lawn mower cut grass well? Does the bank handle transactions with speed and accuracy?

2. **Conformance to specifications.** Does the product or service perform reliably and provide customer satisfaction?

3. **Features.** Does the airline offer the latest movie technology, the most comfortable seats, and the best frequent-flier plan?

4. **Customer support.** Does the firm support the customer with caring, competent people and efficient systems?

5. **Process quality.** Is the process of buying and using the product or service pleasant, rather than frustrating and disappointing?

6. **Aesthetic design.** Does the design add pleasure to the experience of buying and using the product or service?

Figure 9.1   Quality Dimensions

and empathy of the people with whom customers interact.[8] A successful organization therefore must deliver consistently on those dimensions. Delivering service quality, however, also means managing expectations. If expectations are too high, the service experience might be unsatisfactory even if it is at a high level. Generating clarity about the service promise, whenever possible, will thus be helpful.

Because negative experiences are more salient than positive ones, avoiding them is often as important as creating positive ones. The challenge is to seek points of annoyance and attempt to reduce their incidence and intensity. For example, in order to make even waiting in line at their respective locations bearable, Disney provides entertainment with its delightful characters, and Schwab provides stock news.

In the software and information-products industry, the products need to work, but perceptions of quality are often driven by three other factors as well. First, the experience should not be frustrating: the product should be easy to install and use, even for those who are new to it. Second, the performance of the customer support center is crucial. A good support experience will not only decrease user frustration but also help create a personal relationship by exhibiting concern and competence. Third, software users do not want to be left behind. They want a continuous stream of novel features and upgrades—not merely cosmetic changes, but real improvements that work.[9]

One trend is a greater emphasis on the *process* customers experience rather than the output of the experience, because often the output is harder to differentiate. Any part of the total customer-facing process may receive a quality focus, including the customer's information-gathering, transaction, and post-purchase experiences. One result can be the creation of branded features (such as Amazon's One-Click) or offering a simplified, less frustrating buying experience (as Dell does online, and Nordstrom and Home Depot do in their stores).

Understanding what drives quality in a given segment is a critical step in creating a quality program and monitoring its effectiveness. One risk in focusing on specific dimensions, however, is that the resulting measures can be counterproductive. For example, a company sought to improve the quality of its phone service by measuring the percentage of calls answered after the first ring. Unfortunately, the pressure to answer promptly caused agents to become abrupt and impatient with callers, and thus customer satisfaction suffered. The saying "be careful what you wish for" is especially true in performance measurement.

Perceived Quality and Financial Performance

Perceived quality is a powerful construct. Image studies regularly show that customers who attribute high quality to a brand also will believe that it excels on a wide variety of attribute dimensions. Not surprisingly, quality is also associated with brand choice. The J.D. Power organization, which surveys customers' quality perceptions of automobiles, has found that its results influenced 40 percent of buyers.[10] Most important of all, though, perceived quality has been found to be related to financial performance.

An analysis of a database of some 3,000 businesses found that firms in the highest twentieth percentile with respect to perceived quality averaged twice the ROI of those in the bottom twentieth percentile.[11] Perceived quality was found to affect ROI directly because the cost of retaining customers is reduced, and indirectly because it allows a higher price to be charged and enhances the market share. The finding of higher market share suggests that a quality strategy does not have to involve a focus on narrow, ultra-high premium niches.

Perceived quality has also been shown by Aaker and Jacobson to drive stock return, a measure that truly reflects long-term performance.[12] They analyzed annual measures of perceived quality obtained from the Total Research EquiTrend database for thirty-five brands (including IBM, Hershey, Pepsi, and Sears) for which brand sales were a substantial part of firm sales. The impact on stock return of perceived quality, they found, was nearly as strong as the impact of ROI. Given that ROI is an established and accepted influence on stock return, the performance of perceived quality is noteworthy. It means that investors are able to detect and respond to programs that affect intangible assets such as perceived quality. Figure 9.2 shows the dramatic relationship between perceived quality and stock return.

Total Quality Management

To pursue a quality strategic option successfully, a business must distinguish itself with respect to delivering quality to customers. To accomplish this goal, it needs a

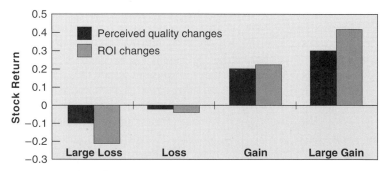

Figure 9.2 Perceived Quality and Stock Return

quality-focused management system that is comprehensive, integrative, and supported throughout the organization. Such a total quality management (TQM) system[13] should incorporate a host of tools and precepts, including the following:

- The commitment of senior management to quality, as evidenced by a substantial time commitment and an emphasis on TQM values.
- Cross-functional teams empowered to make changes by initiating and implementing quality improvement projects.
- A process (rather than results) orientation. The goal is not a one-time quality enhancement, but to develop processes that will lead to quality improvements on an ongoing basis. Teams should use problem-solving tools and methods to develop programs.
- A set of systems, such as suggestions systems, measurement systems, and recognition systems.
- A focus on the underlying causes of customer complaints and areas of dissatisfaction. One approach used in TQM is to explore a problem in depth by repeatedly asking, "Why?" This process has been dubbed the five whys.
- The tracking of key quality measures—including customer satisfaction, the ultimate quality measure.
- The involvement of suppliers in the system through supplier audits, ratings, and recognition, as well as joint team efforts.

Signals of High Quality

Most quality dimensions, such as performance, durability, reliability, and serviceability, are difficult if not impossible for buyers to evaluate. As a result, consumers tend to look for attributes that they believe indicate quality. The fit-and-finish dimension can be such a quality signal. Buyers assume that if a firm's products do not have good fit and finish, they probably will not have other, more important attributes. An electronics firm, for example, found that its speed of responding to information requests affected its perceived product quality. In pursuing a quality strategy, it is usually critical to understand what drives the perception of quality and then focus on small but visible elements. Research has shown that in many product classes, a visible key dimension can be pivotal in affecting perceptions about more important dimensions that are very difficult to judge.[14] Some examples for different markets are as follows:

- ***Broadband suppliers.*** A professional attitude on the part of the installation team means quality.
- ***Tomato juice.*** Thickness means high quality.
- ***Cleaners.*** A lemon scent can signal cleaning power.
- ***Supermarkets.*** Produce freshness means overall quality.
- ***Cars.*** A solid door-closure sound implies good workmanship and a safe body.
- ***Clothes.*** Higher price means higher quality.

QUALITY AT SHERATON

A team of two dozen people developed a service improvement program at Sheraton labeled the Sheraton Guest Satisfaction System.[15] The system has several elements:

- *Customer-satisfaction goals.* Employees are expected to be friendly, acknowledge a guest's presence, answer guests' questions, and anticipate their problems and needs. Staff performance in these areas is measured, and good employees are rewarded with prizes and recognition.
- *Hiring.* Responses to videos of potentially problematic incidents help personnel select staff who really empathize with people.
- *Training.* A series of training programs that include role-playing exercises help staff cope with difficult situations.
- *Measurement.* Quarterly reports are based on guest questionnaires that rate factors such as bed comfort and room lighting, as well as interactions with employees.
- *Ongoing meetings.* Performance is assessed, problems are corrected, and improvement programs are developed.
- *Rewards.* The top-performing and most improved hotels each quarter become members of Sheraton's "Chairman's Club."

In the service context, the most important attributes, such as the competence of those providing the service, are extremely difficult to evaluate—consider, for example, how true this is for surgeons, librarians, airline pilots, dentists, or bankers. Customers cope by looking at those dimensions that are easily evaluated, such as the physical appearance of personnel or a facility. The chairman of one airline was quoted as saying, "Coffee stains on the flip-down trays mean [to the passengers] that we do our engine maintenance wrong."[16] It is thus crucial to understand not only what customers believe is important with respect to quality, but also what drives those perceptions.

KEY LEARNINGS

- Strategic options—that is, particular value propositions for a product market with supporting assets and competencies and functional strategies and programs—form the basis for successful business strategies.
- To be successful, strategic options should contain both real and perceived value propositions and be relevant, sustainable, and feasible.
- Among the many possible strategic options can be based on a product attribute, product design, product line breadth, corporate social responsibility (CSR), brand familiarity, customer intimacy, quality, value, innovation, focus, and being global.

- One common strategic option is to create an offering with real and perceived superiority in quality to reference competitors in the eyes of customers. Quality dimensions will depend on the context but could include performance, conformance to specifications, features, customer support, and process quality.
- Research has shown that perceived quality drives both ROI and stock return.

FOR DISCUSSION

1. Consider three of the following strategic options: product attribute, product design, product-line breadth, corporate social responsibility, brand familiarity, customer intimacy, and quality. For each of these three strategic options, think of two firms not mentioned in the book that have pursued them. Which of the two firms has done better with respect to the five business strategy challenges? Discuss why and how that firm was able to do better.

2. Evaluate the quality strategy of Lexus with respect to the business strategy challenges. How might Lexus add more personality and emotion to its brand? Think of role models that have achieved a quality reputation and a strong personality.

3. Pick a product or service offering. How would you develop a set of customer survey questions that would measure its quality on an ongoing basis? How would you administer the survey?

NOTES

1. Stan L. Friedman, "Corporate America's Social Conscience," *Fortune,* June 23, 2003, p. S6.
2. Ibid., p. S4.
3. "Esso—Should the Tiger Change Its Stripes?" *Reputation Impact,* October 2002, p. 16.
4. David A. Aaker, *Managing Brand Equity,* New York: Free Press, 1991, p. 57.
5. "Shoppers Like Wide Variety of Houseware Brands," *Discount Store News,* October 24, 1988, p. 40.
6. Leo Bogart and Charles Lehman, "What Makes a Brand Name Familiar?" *Journal of Marketing Research,* February 1973, pp. 17–22.
7. Lexus Web site, 2003.
8. Valarie A. Zeithaml, Leonard L. Berry, and A. Parasuraman, "Communication and Control Processes in the Delivery of Service Quality," *Journal of Marketing,* April 1988, pp. 35–48; and A. Parasuraman, Leonard L. Berry, and Valarie A. Zeithaml, "Guidelines for Conducting Service Quality Research," *Marketing Research,* December 1990, pp. 34–44.
9. C.K. Prahalad and M.S. Krisnan, "The New Meaning of Quality in the Information Age," *Harvard Business Review,* September–October 1999, p. 110.

10. Lawrence Ulrich, "Toyota, Lexus Lead in Quality," www.auto.com/industry, June 16, 2003.

11. Robert Jacobson and David A. Aaker, "The Strategic Role of Product Quality," *Journal of Marketing*, October 1987, pp. 31–44.

12. David A. Aaker and Robert Jacobson, "The Financial Information Content of Perceived Quality," *Journal of Marketing Research*, May 1994.

13. For a summary of total quality management in the United States, see the special issue on this subject in *California Management Review*, Spring 1993.

14. A. Parasuraman, Leonard L. Berry, and Valarie A. Zeithaml, "Guidelines for Conducting Service Quality Research," *Marketing Research*, December 1990, pp. 34–44.

15. David Walker, "At Sheraton, the Guest Is Always Right," *Ad Week's Marketing Week*, October 23, 1989, pp. 20–21.

16. Tom Peters and Nancy Austin, *A Passion for Excellence*, New York: Random House, 1985, p. 77.

CHAPTER TEN

Strategic Options: Value, Focus, and Innovation

What matters in the new economy is not return on investment, but return on imagination.
  Gary Hamel

The first man gets the oyster, the second man gets the shell.
—*Andrew Carnegie*

Never follow the crowd.
—*Bernard M. Baruch*

*I*n this chapter, we will continue detailing strategic options that are widely used, that have led to success over a long time period, and for which some experience and insight is available. These include the value, innovation, and focus options. In each case, although positioning is important, the strategy needs more: commitment, ongoing investment, and programmatic management over time. The culture and values of the organization need to support the strategy. The soundest strategy from a marketplace view will ultimately falter if the organization is not compatible and supportive.

THE VALUE OPTION

Southwest Airlines

Southwest Airlines was founded in 1971, with three planes serving three Texas cities, as a low-fare airline whose goal was to make air travel efficient and pleasant. Its airfares were so aggressively low from the start that Southwest often competed as much with automobile travel as with other airlines. Even as it has grown, Southwest's point-to-point, no-frills approach has made it the consistent price leader in the markets it serves. The brand personality allows the staff to crack jokes and host games, injecting fun into what could be a boring time and further distinguishing Southwest from its competitors. The relationship of the staff to customers and its outstanding on-time record has helped Southwest win numerous customer satisfaction honors over the years.

The low-fare position often came under attack by aggressive and sometimes desperate competitors, who failed because Southwest had established a sustainable cost advantage supported by its no-frills operation. Southwest has no assigned seats, peanuts as meal service, and wages that are below the industry average. The company also shuns fancy hubs, reservation systems, and global schedules. Because of its service model, Southwest could turn around planes more quickly, which resulted in more trips and scale economies. The business model and brand personality were supported by a culture that valued cost containment and customer service.

Competitors such as Delta and American could not cut services that their customers expected, nor could they adapt their strategies, which were based on a hub/reservation/meals system. As a result, the no-frills strategy turned Southwest into an industry winner, separating it from its struggling competitors.

Dell Computer

Dell was founded in 1984 by Michael Dell on a simple direct-model concept—selling computers based on industry standards, assembled to order, directly to customers at low prices.[1] The direct sales model created visible credibility for a low-cost value position. There are no retailer or other intermediary markups, as retailers and other resellers are eliminated. In addition, business customers understand that Dell's cost structure benefits from minimal inventory and warehousing costs—Dell turns inventory every four days. Thus there is logic behind the low-cost claim.

Dell has never been the only firm selling computers direct, but it has emerged as superior on key components of the business model. Dell always seems to be ahead in terms of efficiencies in logistics, distribution, and manufacturing, especially after developing a volume advantage over its direct competitors that has resulted in significant scale economies. Part of this is due to a low-cost culture. Dell President Kevin Rollins has noted, "There are some organizations where people think they're a hero if they invent a new thing. Being a hero at Dell means saving money."[2]

The direct-selling business model provides advantages to Dell's customers besides lower costs. First, because the computer is assembled after the order is received, it can be customized to exactly what the customer needs and wants. Second, because finished computers do not sit in warehouses or on retail shelves, the latest technologies can be applied to each computer as they become available. Third, in the direct model the customer interacts with the company, thereby allowing Dell to demonstrate its customer service values. Roughly 90 percent of Dell's employees have some customer contact, and the company has excelled over the years in making its sales and service system live up to the "Simple as Dell" promise.

Ford and the Experience Curve

Ford introduced the Model T in 1908, and by the mid-1920s it had sold 15 million. It was a car that was reliable, easy to operate, and remarkably inexpensive.[3] The

Model T began its life priced at $850 (around $17,000 in modern dollars), but the price fell continuously until in 1922 it cost less than $300. As a result, the demand for automobiles expanded, affecting the work and lifestyle of the time.

The car could be value priced because of the mass production that Ford pioneered. Model Ts all used the same chassis, were almost all the same color (black), and were designed to be easy to build. As a result, production costs declined according to an 85 percent experience curve (that is, costs fell roughly 15 percent every time cumulative production doubled). Figure 10.1 presents the pattern. The experience-curve effect was created in part because of the building of the huge River Rouge plant, a reduction in the proportion of management staff (from 5 percent to 2 percent of all employees), extensive vertical integration, and the creation of the integrated, conveyor-driven mechanized production process.

In the early 1920s, however, consumers began to request heavier, closed-body cars that offered more comfort. The Model T design could not be adapted, and in 1927 Ford had to shut down operations for nearly a year to retool. The focus on cost reduction and exploiting the experience curve, it turned out, limited the company's ability to respond to changing times and competition. The standardized product, extensive vertical integration, and single-minded devotion to production improvements had clear experience-curve advantages, but they also tended to create an organization whose goals and thrust were intimately involved with preserving the status quo, the existing product. There is no free lunch.

In nearly every market, from appliances to economy sedans to toothpaste to booksellers to brokerage services, there will be a segment that is motivated by price. Even in high-end markets such as luxury sports sedans, some brands (Acura, for example) will stake out a value position. Whether it comprises 10 percent or 80 percent of the market, the price segment will usually be a significant one.

Ignoring the value segment can be risky because even healthy markets can evolve into situations where price grows in importance. In consumer electronics, appliances, and other product arenas, competitors have created overcapacity,

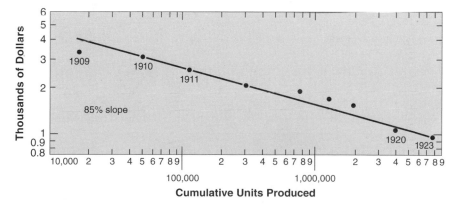

Figure 10.1   Price of Model T, 1909–1923 (Average List Price in 1958 Dollars)

causing a need to create or maintain a critical mass in the market. Power retailers with their own brands as competitive tools are another potential contributing force. Thus, ignoring the value segment may not be an option. It may be necessary to participate, perhaps with a value brand or as a private label supplier, in order to maintain scale economies.

As Figure 10.2 suggests, to compete successfully in the value arena it is necessary to:

- have a cost advantage (or at least avoid a cost disadvantage),
- make sure the quality perception does not erode to the point that the offering is considered unacceptable, and
- create a cost culture in the organization.

Creating a Cost Advantage (or Avoiding a Cost Disadvantage)

Although there is a tendency to think of low cost as a single approach, there are actually many dimensions to cost control and thus many routes to a cost reduction. The successful low-cost firms are those that can harness multiple approaches, including the use of no-frills products/services, operational efficiency, scale economies, and the experience curve.

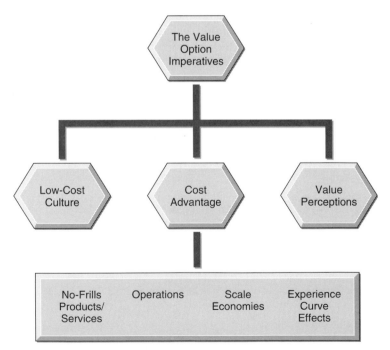

Figure 10.2   The Value Option

No-Frills Product/Service

One direct approach to low cost is simply removing all frills and extras from a product or service. Membership warehouses, such as Costco, Home Depot, and Sam's, all provide settings with limited amenities and personal service. No-frills airlines, legal services clinics, and discount brokers follow the same general principle.

A no-frills product, such as Hyundai automobiles, will omit features and use materials and components that are adequate but may lack the aesthetic appeal of competitors. Value furniture lines that use pressed wood create significant sustainable cost advantages. Japanese competitors have entered several established industries, including copiers, by designing reliable, simple products that use fewer and readily available (as opposed to customized) parts.

A major risk, especially in the service sector, is that competitors will position themselves against a no-frills offering by adding just a few features. Motel 6 pioneered the concept of economy lodging in the early 1960s by giving the world a $6 hotel room with no phone or TV set. The industry has attracted a host of competitors since that time, many promising just a bit more in terms of creature comforts. The result of such strategies can be a feature war.

Operations

Enduring cost advantages can also be created through efficiencies in operations. They can be based on government subsidies, process innovation, distribution efficiency (as in Dell's direct sales model), access to target markets (USAA insurance is available only to military personnel), outsourcing competencies, and the management of overhead.

To obtain significant operational economies, it is useful to examine the value chain and look for inherently high cost components that could be eliminated or reduced by changing the way that the business operates. The best example is the disintermediation of channel members. By selling direct, Dell and Amazon strip large components out of the value chain. For instance, in the conventional bookstore model, about 30 percent of sold books are returned, representing a huge dead weight on costs. In the Amazon model, that proportion is reduced to 3 percent—an enormous potential savings.[4]

Another place to find operations-based cost savings is in the interface with a supplier or customer. Uniqlo (a Japanese Gap-like retailer) links its store sales and inventory to its factories in China to create breathtaking efficiencies. P&G realized that retailers were buying products and shipping them across country, or storing them for months just to take advantage of short-term price deals, leading to grossly inefficient ordering and warehousing practices.[5] In response, P&G embarked on an ongoing partnership with Wal-Mart to optimize the system. One result was a continuous replenishment system for reordering, shipping, and restocking that would minimize shipping and warehouse costs, inventory, and out-of-stock conditions. Another was a revision of the trade discount policy to remove incentives to engage in unproductive gaming of promotions. Ten years after the partnership program began, stockkeeping units were down 25 percent, sales staffing was down 30 percent, inventory was down 15 percent, and the program was expanded to all major P&G customers.

Making operations more efficient can be a battle. Firms successful at reducing costs plan and implement incremental improvements over time. The devil is in the details. Each component of operations needs to be considered an opportunity. The Japanese firms have long excelled at relentlessly making small improvements toward improving the cost position, it is that persistence that is needed. Continuous improvement in efficiency, as Southwest and Dell strive for, can create an ongoing competitive advantage.

There is always resistance to change, especially to major shifts in processes and perspectives. So a change agent is often needed. The catalyst can be a person who comes in and makes sure that cost reduction is a priority and that all aspects of the organization are involved, or sometimes it can be an acquisition. A merger or acquisition can reduce costs not only by eliminating redundancies but by removing barriers to change. The result can be a much leaner operation than was once in place.

Scale Economies

The scale effect reflects the natural efficiencies associated with size. Fixed costs such as advertising, sales force overhead, R&D, staff work, and facility upkeep can be spread over more units. Furthermore, a larger operation can support specialized assets and activities (such as market research, legal staff, and manufacturing-engineering operations) dedicated to a firm's needs. During its early days, Amazon maintained that the fixed costs of warehousing and technology would ultimately create a sustainable cost advantage, but only when the scale of its operations reached billions of dollars. The firm was ultimately proved correct.

An empirical study of the performance of 109 food, beverage, and consumer-products companies of different sizes demonstrates the phenomenon of scale economies.[6] Figure 10.3 shows the financial performance of small firms (49 firms with sales less than $1 billion) versus "tweeners" (40 firms with sales between $1 billion and $7 billion) and large firms (20 firms with sales over $7 billion). The performance is significantly better for the larger firms and worse for the smaller firms. Further analysis, however, shows that the small tweeners (sales less than $2.5 billion) did significantly better than the large tweeners. One possible reason is that the cost of increased complexity served to counter scale economies for the large tweeners.

When a business is too small to support needed assets or operations, the result can be a a severe competitive disadvantage. The solution might be to prune or consolidate business units. Scale economy effects are particularly relevant in brand management, where each brand may seek a share of limited resources. Nestlé, Unilever,

	Small	Tweeners	Large
Operating-profit growth rate	(2.8%)	3.4%	9.6%
Return on assets	7.1%	9.0%	15.7%
Shareholder return over five years	(1.2%)	3.8%	6.2%

Figure 10.3   Financial Performance by Firm Size

P&G, HP, UBS, and other firms are deleting, consolidating, and prioritizing brands in their portfolios in order to make sure that the important brands are fully funded.

In retailing, scale can be obtained by combining business units. Yum! has introduced dual branded stores from its stable of KFC, Pizza Hut, Taco Bell, Long John Silver's, and A&W. Such dual brand outlets can compete with McDonald's and Burger King for expensive sites that require a large annual sales volume.

The Experience Curve

The experience curve, empirically verified in thousands of studies, suggests that as a firm accumulates experience in building a product, its costs in real dollars will decline at a predictable rate. When the experience curve applies, the first market entry attaining a large market share will have a continuing cost advantage. The experience curve effect is based on the fact that over time people will learn to do tasks faster and more efficiently, that technological process improvements will occur, and that products will be redesigned to be simpler to build.

Several issues need to be understood in working with the experience curve concept. First, multiple products with overlapping experience curves can complicate the situation. For example, when several products share a component, the associated experience curve will have a sharper slope. Second, the experience curve is not automatic. It must be proactively managed with efficiency-improvement goals, quality circles, product design targets, and equipment upgrading. Further, a late entry can often gain the same advantage as the more experienced vendors simply by accessing the most recent design. Third, if the technology or market changes, the experience curve may become obsolete. Fourth, the experience curve model implies that cost improvements, whatever their source, should be translated into low prices and higher share so that the business can stay ahead on the experience curve. Lower prices can trigger price wars, however, leading to reduced margins.

A key to strategy development is recognizing when the experience curve model will apply. When an industry is mature, the experience curve becomes flat, and doubling a firm's cumulative experience takes so long that the model is less useful. If the value added is low, the experience curve will also have little impact. If a purchased raw material, such as wheat or sulfur, is 80 percent of the offering's cost, there is very little role for experience to play. Some of the most successful applications of the experience curve have been in continuous-process manufacturing contexts (such as semiconductors) or in capital-intensive heavy industries (such as steel).

Perceived Value

Creating a credible value story—the perception that there is real value in the offering—requires substance. The core is a perceived price point that will deliver value. In this respect, the way that customers process price information is important. What price element is most visible? Grocery stores have long learned that customers tend to be knowledgeable about a few categories and brands. Similarly, the major book chains pay close attention to best-selling books, because those are the ones most likely to receive a price comparison. Car manufacturers are concerned most with base prices and much less for accessories and options, because prices for the latter will be harder to compare.

Managing prices is tricky, because price is often a quality cue and customers may perceive low price as a signal for inferior quality. If the quality is perceived to be unacceptably low, the offering will be deemed irrelevant to the customer's needs. This is particularly troublesome for offerings in categories where it is difficult to judge actual quality (perfume or motor oil, for example).

One responsive approach is to make cost (and thus price) differences as visible and understandable as possible. Dell's direct sales model, Southwest's point-to-point travel and no-frills service, Ford's mass production, the scale economies of Amazon and Wal-Mart, and the warehouse feel of Ikea, Home Depot, and Costco are all transparent to customers, and thus reduce the risk of a perceived quality problem.

Another approach is to manage the relevance issue by positioning the offering with respect to the appropriate product category and set of competitors. Acura, which aspires to be considered alongside BMW and Lexus, needs to manage its product category associations so it is not perceived as a sub-luxury car. Product design, advertising, and the retail experience are among the tools available to Acura to accomplish this goal.

A Low-Cost Culture

A successful low-cost strategy is usually multifaceted and supported by a cost-oriented culture. Performance measurement, rewards, systems, structure, top management values, and culture are all fronts where cost reduction should be stressed. The single-minded focus needed is comparable to that required for total quality management. Such a commitment is evident at Dell, Southwest, Wal-Mart, and other firms that have succeeded with a value strategy.

There are many examples of firms that decided to go into the low-cost world and failed because their cultures never could adapt. One large supermarket chain decided to create a discount beverage chain. When the chain failed to deliver on the promise and still be profitable, an analysis determined that the people and processes were not compatible with the cost structure needed to succeed in that market. A successful discount operation almost always requires a new organization with different culture, processes, and people.

FOCUS

Shouldice Hospital

Shouldice Hospital near Toronto only does hernia operations.[7] Since its founding in 1945, nearly 300,000 operations have been conducted, with a 99 percent success rate. Measured by how often repeat treatment is needed, Shouldice is ten times more effective than are other hospitals. The surgical procedure used is branded as the Shouldice Technique.

The experience of the doctors and staff are appealing, but so are the Shouldice setting and its recovery program. Located on a country estate, the hospital has a calming ambiance and facilities tailored to needs of recovering hernia patients. Patients walk to watch TV, to eat, and even to and from the operating room, because walking is good therapy for hernias. There is thus no need to deliver food to rooms, or to have wheelchair facilities. The length of a hospital visit at Shouldice is around half the norm elsewhere. No general anesthesia is administered, because local anesthesia is safer and cheaper for hernia operations.

By concentrating on one narrow segment of the medical market, Shouldice has developed a hospital that is proficient, inexpensive, and capable of delivering an extraordinary level of patient satisfaction. Ex-patients are so pleased that the Shouldice Hospital annual reunion attracts some 1,500 "alumni."

Krispy Kreme

Krispy Kreme was a wholesale seller of doughnuts until at one plant, a manager cut a hole into a wall in order to sell product to passers-by who were attracted by the aroma. The firm soon started opening stores, and quickly the retail business became not only profitable but a marketing vehicle. Krispy Kreme (called the hottest brand in America by a *Fortune* writer) is growing at 25 percent per year and has seen its stock quadruple during a falling stock market.[8] Even more impressive, the product is doughnuts at a time when healthy eating is getting all the press.

The Krispy Kreme retail experience, like that of Starbucks, defines the brand and fuels the loyalty of the core customer group. It starts with the doughnuts, which are special when they are hot. Many customers are fanatics, raving about the taste and going way out of their way to find a Krispy Kreme location. When a new store opens, people line up to get the warm, glazed doughnuts. But the experience, like that of Starbuck's, goes beyond the product. There is the "hot light" that signals new doughnuts are coming out, the incredible aroma in the store, and the theatrical benefit of watching the doughnut production line (a visible demonstration of freshness). On top of everything else, there is the chance to share Krispy Kreme stories with others. This isn't just any doughnut store. And it would not have happened without the firm's focus on the doughnuts and the store experience.

Castrol Motor Oil

Castrol Motor Oil is a very successful brand in the shadow of competitors such as Quaker State, Pennzoil, Shell, Mobil, and private-label brands from power retailers. There are two keys to Castrol's strategy. First, it focuses on male car owners who change their own oil. Castrol has no distribution in service stations, but that is not a liability for its chosen segment. The brand personality and communication efforts used by Castrol to match its macho, independent customer profile are very different from those needed by the major players in order to reach a broader market. Second, Castrol engages in a very dynamic product and package policy, creating niche offerings and keeping retailers off balance.

A focus strategy concentrates on one part of the market or product line and can emerge in virtually any arena. Calvin Klein clothes and Portman Hotels focus on the upscale segment; for example, Portman will pick up guests at the airport in a Rolls-Royce. An industrial distributor may focus on large-volume users or even a single user. A clothing store might offer torrid fashions for plus-sized teen girls. Armstrong Rubber has performed well over the years by focusing on replacement tires. Voyager MC makes two-piece golf clubs that can be taken on airplanes for golfers who travel. Regional beers such as Lone Star in Texas focus on a limited geographic area, allowing the use of regional humor and dialects and local promotions.

Focus strategies concentrate resources, provide a way to compete when resources are limited, and add credibility to a positioning strategy (see Figure 10.4).

Concentrating Resources and Energy

Because a focus strategy by its nature tends to avoid strategy dilution or distraction, it is more likely to lead to a sustainable advantage. When internal investments, programs, and culture have all been directed toward a single end and there is buy-in on the part of everyone in the organization, the result will be assets, competencies, and functional strategies that match market needs. In most cases, expansion of the product line or market results in compromises and a diluted ability to deliver on the business model. It is no accident that specialized retailers such as The Limited, Williams-Sonoma, Toys "R" Us, and Victoria's Secret have been much more successful than department stores and others that are spread thin. One reason is the strategic and operational advantages of focusing.

Product focus can result in technical superiority. In most businesses, the key people have expertise or interest in a limited product arena. Those who are the driving force behind a fashion firm, for instance, may be interested primarily in women's high fashion. A consumer electronics firm may be founded and run by someone who is very interested in audio quality. When the products of a firm capture the imagination of its key people, the products tend to be exciting, innovative, and high quality. As the product line broadens, however, the products tend to be me-too products, which do

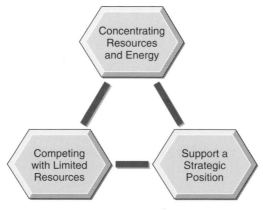

Figure 10.4   A Focus Strategy

not provide value and detract from the base business. In such situations, the willpower to maintain focus by resisting product expansion may pay off.

The potential of enhancing an SCA by using a focus strategy must be balanced by the fact that it naturally limits the potential business. As a result, profitable sales may be missed. Furthermore, the focused business will often have to compete with larger companies that will enjoy scale economies. Thus, it is crucial for the focus to be closely tied to a strategy with meaningful SCAs. Because of the appeal of a larger business and the perceived need to increase scale, it can take discipline to stick to a focus strategy.

Competing with Limited Resources

A business that simply lacks the resources to compete in a broad product market must focus in order to generate the impact needed to compete effectively. Such a limitation can occur, for example, when an automobile or airplane manufacturer faces heavy product development and tool costs, or a consumer products firm cannot afford to support multiple brands.

A focus strategy provides the potential to bypass competitors' assets and competencies. For example, in packaged-foods industries (such as cereal), the ability to establish brand names and distribute branded products is a key success factor. However, firms can also do well by focusing on private-label manufacture, in which cost-control considerations dominate. These firms insulate themselves from the major manufacturers, who would compromise their own brands by producing private labels.

Although the payoff of a small niche may be less than that of a large, growing market, the competition may often also be less intense. The majority-fallacy concept states that appraisals of large, attractive segments overlook or minimize the likelihood that many competitors will be attracted to the segment resulting in destructive overcapacity. A more modest product-market scope involving smaller market potential may thus be a preferable choice.

Supporting a Strategic Position

A focus strategy may also provide a positioning tool. The association of a business with a narrow product line, segment, or geographic area can serve to provide a useful identity. For example, Neiman Marcus competes only in the very high-priced end of its industry and therefore appeals to a very narrow segment. Any effort to compete in a broader product market, even if feasible, would risk damaging the exclusive image it has developed for its existing stores. The Raymond Corporation is known for its limited product line of lift trucks suitable for navigating the narrow spaces in warehouses.

A focus strategy can translate into a value proposition for customers that supports the strategic positioning. First, a focused firm will have more credibility than a firm that makes a wide array of products, as demonstrated by Shouldice Hospital in hernia surgeries, Williams-Sonoma in cooking, and the In-N-Out chain in making hamburgers. If you are really interested in the best, you will go to a firm that specializes in and has a passion for the business. Second, the bond between the loyal user and the brand will tend to be greater when the brand is focused. The reunions of Shouldice Hospital patients and the passion of Krispy Kreme customers would not happen without a focus strategy.

INNOVATION

Sony

Sony is one of the strongest brands not only in Japan, but throughout the world. In the United States, the Harris Poll each year since 1995 has asked people to name what they believe are the top three product or service brands. In 2002, Sony was the most often-named brand for the third year in a row; during the seven years of measurement, Sony has never placed lower than third.[9]

One reason behind Sony's brand strength is its disciplined focus on innovation, as it strives continuously to deliver astonishing technology. Sony marketing executive T. Scott Edwards has noted that the Sony "value proposition is innovation. Part of innovation is constantly providing consumers with news. Primarily we do that with new products."[10] Sony France once had a tagline, "If you can dream it, we can make it," that captured the innovative spirit of the organization.

Rather unique among Japanese firms, the Sony corporate brand is supported by a host of strong product brands. Some of these brands, such as Walkman, Handycam, and Aibo (a personal entertainment robot), have helped define a product category that is associated with Sony. Others, such as Trinitron and Wega (television), Xplod (mobile entertainment), Playstation (games), Clie (handheld PDA), Cyber-shot (digital camera), and VAIO (notebook computer), represent significant relevant product advances that are owned by the Sony brand. For example, in 2003 VAIO became (along with PowerBook) one of the strongest brands in the portable computer space, despite being a late entry in part because of its dramatic design.[11]

The support that these brands received from and delivered to the Sony brand has been documented by the Dentsu advertising agency. The agency asked a sample of Japanese in 2000 about the extent to which they agreed with two statements: "The brand contributes toward Sony's image," and "I would choose it because it's a Sony." The subbrands PlayStation, Handycam, VAIO, and Walkman demonstrated a strong two-way flow of influence, supporting the Sony image while the corporate brand helped make the subbrand more attractive. For other subbrands, however, the influence was neither always symmetric nor strong. Aibo contributed to the Sony brand but relied less on the Sony connection for its own worth. Trinitron and Clie, in contrast, drew on the Sony brand strength but were relatively low on helping to support the Sony brand. Sony Life, an insurance brand used in the Japanese market that does not fit the Sony image or identity, was perceived as disconnected from the Sony brand in that it neither helped nor benefited from the corporate brand name.

Procter & Gamble

P&G considers itself an innovation company. Spending more than 4 percent of its sales on R&D, it has over 8,000 scientists working in twenty-two research centers.

The output is visible to customers in the form of both improved products and new products that define categories.

Tide, one of P&G's eight billion-dollar brands, has been the beneficiary of hundreds of improvements since it was first introduced in 1948. Many of these have been made visible to the consumer through the branding of such variants as Tide Liquid, Tide with Bleach, Tide HE (for use with high-efficiency washers), and Tide Rapid Action Tabs. The result is a brand that leads its category, presents ongoing energy to its customers, and is a moving target to its competitors.

Breakthrough innovations from the P&G research labs have contributed to the creation of many new product categories and subcategories. It all started with Ivory ("99 and $^{44}/_{100}$ pure, it floats") in 1881. Since then there has been Pert (combining shampoo and conditioner), Crest fluoride toothpaste, Pringles (a new form of potato chip), Pampers disposable diapers, and more recently Dryel (a home dry cleaning product), Febreze (a fabric spray and with unique order eliminating qualities), and Swiffer (a sweep system to capture dust).

The firm's technology success is based in part on three characteristics.[12] First, a deep understanding of consumers drives the research. P&G professionals routinely spend days with families to learn about their habits and needs. Second, research on technologies is leveraged across multiple product arenas. Advances in perfumes and odor management, for example, can be applied to products ranging from Tide, Febreze, and Downey to Pantene and Giorgio of Beverly Hills. P&G's baby care, feminine hygiene, and tissue/towel businesses are all based on advances related to absorbent structures and materials. Third, the ability to link consumer needs with technology is a key P&G skill. The organization does not generate technology haphazardly, and then look for an application.

Innovation may be the most widely used business strategy option. It is hard to find a firm that does not want to be truly creative in ways that touch the customer. Innovation is a sought-after ability because it goes to the heart of the offering—how can the product and its delivery to customers be improved so that the value proposition and point of differentiation are enhanced?

For most firms, innovation means incremental improvement. They offer the same product or service, but add elements through creative engineering supported by investments. P&G's major brands (such as Tide, Pampers, Bounty, and Crest) have all seen continuous improvement over the years, but the basic function of each product remains the same, and customers regard the improvements as incremental. Some firms, however, occasionally engage in disruptive innovation (a concept introduced in Chapter 6) by creating new products that define new product categories or subcategories. Both P&G and Sony have been able to do this several times, an accomplishment that sets them apart from most companies.

While many firms strive for innovation, not all achieve it. Success requires a true commitment to innovation that survives pressures for short-term results. This commitment must be well managed so that the right people are given the right environment. Further, the organization must be competent at turning innovation (whether it comes from R&D, marketing, the customer, or wherever) into commercial products and must be willing to take chances and be wrong.

The stimulation of strong competitors is often behind many innovative firms. Two of the eleven firms in the Collins list of "good to great" companies that prospered by innovating were pushed by strong competitors. Nucor found new methods of steel production in the face of aggressively priced foreign suppliers. Kimberly-Clark sold off its mills and decided to compete directly with P&G in branded paper products by innovating behind brands like Huggies, Depends, and Kleenex.[13]

Innovation and the Value Proposition

Innovation provides value to customers along several dimensions. An incremental innovation usually enhances the value proposition by providing a new or improved attribute or feature. The confidence in purchasing the product or service, as well as the satisfaction in using it, will thus be enhanced. The value to the customer goes beyond the specific benefits, however, because an organization perceived as innovative is usually seen to have other desirable characteristics that can affect purchase and loyalty. An innovative firm, for example, is often seen as having credibility in its product arena, which translates into trust and confidence. In some contexts, there are even prestige and self-expressive benefits in being seen as the innovator.

Firms such as Sony that create new categories or subcategories (as opposed to incremental improvements) are likely to generate additional benefits. First, the perception of being innovative is likely to be stronger. Second, to the extent that a new product category or subcategory is defined, the innovation has the potential to affect whether competitor brands will be considered relevant. Sony demonstrated this capability by defining the Walkman space. Third, such innovations can generate first-mover positions, giving the firm a perception of authenticity and the powerful associations that accompany it. The first-mover advantage is worth exploring further.

The First-Mover Advantage

As noted in the preceding paragraph, innovation can create a first-mover advantage. Competitors will be playing catch-up technologically. If they copy the innovation, they risk being left behind again as advancements continue. In the meantime, the innovator can create customer loyalty based on several factors. One of these is simple familiarity; if the first mover's product or service is satisfactory, there may be no incentive to try something different. Alternatively, a customer may have been enticed or required to make a long-term commitment to the product or service. It then becomes not just risky, but expensive and inconvenient to change.

To capture a first-mover advantage, it is important to hit the market first and invest to build position. While high initial prices may be an attractive way to capture margin and recover development costs, a low-price strategy may serve to build share and thus construct a more daunting barrier to followers. Followers will have the benefit of seeing the innovation, but will often need to create a significantly better offering to have a chance of dislodging the first mover among its user base. Making that user base as large as possible maximizes the challenge.

RESEARCH ON EARLY MARKET LEADERS

It turns out that true market pioneers often do not survive—frequently because they entered before the technology was in place, or because they got blown away by larger competitors.[14] In contrast, Golder and Tellis found that early market leaders (that is, firms which assume market leadership during the early product growth phase) had a minimal failure rate, an average market share almost three times that of market pioneers, and a high rate of market leadership.[15] The authors noted that successful early market leaders tended to share the following characteristics:

- *Envisioning the Mass Market.* While pioneers such as Ampex in video recorders or Chux in disposable diapers charged high prices, the early market leaders (Sony and Matsushita in video recorders, or P&G in diapers) priced their offerings at a mass market level. Timex in watches, Kodak in film, Gillette in safety razors, Ford in automobiles, and L'eggs in women's hosiery all used a vision of the mass market to fuel their success.

- *Managerial Persistence.* The technological advances of early market leaders often took years of investment. P&G needed a decade of research to create the successful Pampers entry, and the Japanese firms spent twice as long developing the video recorder.

- *Financial Commitment.* The willingness and ability to invest is a crucial factor when the payoff is in the future. For example, when Rheingold Brewery introduced Gablinger's light beer, it had a promising start, but financial downturns in other sectors caused the firm to withdraw resources from the brand. In contrast, Philip Morris invested substantially in Miller Lite for five years in order to achieve and retain a dominant position.

- *Relentless Innovation.* It is clear that long-term leadership requires continuous innovation. Gillette learned its lesson in the early 1960s when the U.K. firm Wilkinson Sword introduced a stainless steel razor blade that lasted three times longer than Gillette's carbon steel blade. Gillette, after experiencing a sharp market share drop, returned to its innovative heritage and developed a new series of products.

- *Asset Leveraging.* Early market leaders often also hold dominant positions in a related category, allowing them to exploit their distribution clout and a powerful brand name to achieve shared economies. Diet Pepsi and Coke's Tab, for example, were able to use distribution and branding advantages to take over the diet cola market from the pioneer, Royal Crown Cola.

- *Follower Advantages.* Some firms deliberately engage in follower strategies in order to achieve reduced R&D investment, to make sure of the product's acceptance, and to learn about how customers buy and use the product. The follower can make sure the timing is right. Recall, for example, how Apple's Newton PDA was premature and struggled, whereas later competitors found a ready market.

KEY LEARNINGS

- A value position needs to be communicated effectively and supported by a cost advantage, which can be based on a no-frills offering, operations, scale economies, and/or the experience curve.

- A focus strategy avoids diluting or distracting from the implementation of strategy, provides a way to compete when resources are limited, can contribute to a positioning strategy, reduces competitive pressures, and can connect with customers. Following a focus strategy requires discipline to avoid expanding the offering.

- Innovation can generate a value proposition, enhance credibility, be prestigious, and create a first-mover advantage.

FOR DISCUSSION

1. Compare the value strategies of Dell and Southwest. How are they similar? How are they different? What are the bases for the value proposition in each case? Why has the advantage been sustainable?

2. Develop expansion options for Shouldice Hospital and/or Krispy Kreme.

3. Have Shouldice Hospital and Krispy Kreme generated first-mover advantages? How? What is to stop Kaiser or Dunkin' Donuts, respectively, from following them? Why haven't the latter firms done so? Where do you see the competition for Shouldice and Krispy Kreme coming from?

4. Compare and contrast the innovation strategies of Sony and P&G. Which has engaged in disruptive innovation (introduced in Chapter 6)? Which is better described as having sustaining innovations? Sony prides itself on being technology driven (almost ignoring the customer), while P&G is customer driven. What is the difference? Who is right?

NOTES

1. Sources: Dell Annual Reports, 2000, 2001, 2002; Dell Online, HBS Case 596-058; Matching Dell, HBS Case 9-799-158; Andy Serwer, "Dell Does Domination," *Fortune*, January 21, 2002, p. 71; Brad Stond, "Dell's New Toy," *Newsweek*, November 18, 2002; and an interview with Dell's Global Brand Team, April 2003. Thanks to Scott Helbing, Global Brand Manger of Dell, for helpful comments.

2. Andrew Park, "What You Don't Know About Dell," *Business Week*, November 3, 2003, p. 79.

3. William J. Abernathy and Kenneth Wayne, "Limits of the Learning Curve," *Harvard Business Review*, September–October 1974, pp. 109–119. Figure 10.1, which is used with permission, is sourced from this article.

4. Timothy M. Saseter, Patrick W. Houston, Joshua L. Wright, and Juliana U. Park, "Amazon: Extracting Value from the Value Chain," *Strategy and Business,* First Quarter 2000, pp. 94–105.

5. Material is drawn in part from Lawrence D. Milligan, "Keeping It Simple, The Evolution of Customer-Business Development at Procter & Gamble," remarks made at the American Marketing Association Doctoral Symposium, Cincinnati, July 1997.

6. Swandler Pace & Co., "Does Size Really Matter?", *Research Note,* Vol. 10, Issue 3, 1997.

7. William H. Davidow and Bro Utal, "Service Companies: Focus or Falter," *Harvard Business Review,* July–August 1989, pp. 77–85.

8. Andy Serwer, "The Hole Story," *Fortune,* July 7, 2003.

9. Humphrey Taylor, "Sony Retains Number One Position in The Harris Poll Annual 'Best Brand' Survey for Third Year in a Row." Harris Poll, July 2002.

10. Kenneth Hein, "When is Enough Enough?", *Brand Week,* December 2, 2002, p. 27.

11. According to research conducted by Techtel in 2003.

12. P&G Web site, 2003, Innovation section.

13. Jim Collins, *Good to Great,* New York: HarperBusiness, 2003, chapter 2.

14. Peter N. Golder and Gerard J. Tellis, "Pioneer Advantage: Marketing Logic or Marketing Legend?" *Journal of Marketing Research,* May 1993, pp. 158–170.

15. Gerard J. Tellis and Peter N. Golder, "First to Market, First to Fail? Real Causes of Enduring Market Leadership," *Sloan Management Review,* Winter 1996, pp. 65–75.

CHAPTER ELEVEN

Global Strategies

Most managers are nearsighted. Even though today's competitive landscape often stretches to a global horizon, they see best what they know best: the customers geographically closest to home.
—*Kenichi Ohmae*

A powerful force drives the world toward a converging commonality, and that force is technology. ... The result is a new commercial reality—the emergence of global markets for standardized consumer products on a previously unimagined scale of magnitude.
—*Theodore Levitt*

My ventures are not in one bottom trusted, nor to one place.
—*William Shakespeare, The Merchant of Venice*

*M*any firms find it necessary to develop global strategies in order to compete effectively. A global strategy is different from a multidomestic or multinational strategy, in which separate strategies are developed for different countries and implemented autonomously. Thus, a retailer might develop different store groups, in several countries, that are not linked and that operate autonomously. A multidomestic operation is usually best managed as a portfolio of independent businesses, with separate investment decisions made for each country.

A global strategy, in contrast, represents a worldwide perspective in which the interrelationships between country markets are drawn on to create synergies, economies of scale, strategic flexibility, and opportunities to leverage insights, programs, and production economies.

A global strategy can result in strategic advantage or neutralization of a competitor's advantage. For example, products or marketing programs developed in one market might be used in another. Or a cost advantage may result from scale economies generated by the global market or from access to low-cost labor or materials. Operating in various countries can lead to enhanced flexibility as well as meaningful sustainable competitive advantages (SCAs). Investment and operations can be shifted to respond to trends and developments emerging throughout the world or to counter competitors that are similarly structured. Plants can be located to gain access to markets by bypassing trade barriers.

Even if a global strategy is not appropriate for a business, making the external analysis global may still be useful. A knowledge of competitors, markets, and trends from other countries may help a business identify important opportunities, threats, and strategic uncertainties. A global external analysis is more difficult, of course, because of the different cultures, political risks, and economic systems involved.

A global strategy requires addressing a set of issues that include the following:

1. Should the firm become global by entering new countries?
2. What countries should be entered, and in what sequence?
3. To what extent should products and service offerings be standardized across countries?
4. To what extent should the brand name and marketing activities (such as brand position, advertising, and pricing) be standardized across countries?
5. How should the brand be managed globally?
6. To what extent should strategic alliances be used to enter new countries?

Each of these issues will be explored in turn. The next section, in which the motivations for global strategies are presented, will be followed by discussions of how to select which countries to enter, standardization versus customization, global brand management, and the use of alliances in developing global strategies.

MOTIVATIONS UNDERLYING GLOBAL STRATEGIES

A global strategy can result from several motivations in addition to simply wanting to invest in attractive foreign markets. The diagram of these motivations shown in Figure 11.1 provides a summary of the scope and character of global strategies.

Obtaining Scale Economies

Scale economies can occur from product standardization. The Ford world-car concept, for example, allows product design, tooling, parts production, and product testing to be spread over a much larger sales base. Standardization of the development and execution of a marketing program can also be an important source of scale economies. Consider Coca-Cola, which since the 1950s has employed a marketing strategy—the brand name, concentrate formula, positioning, and advertising theme—that has been virtually the same throughout the world. Only the artificial sweetener and packaging differ across countries.

Scale economies can also occur from standardization of marketing, operations, and manufacturing programs. Brands that share advertising (even when it is adjusted for local markets) spread the production and creative effort over multiple countries

Figure 11.1   Global Strategy Motivations

and thus a larger sales base. A firm similarly benefits when fixed costs involving IT and production technologies can be distributed over countries.

Desirable Global Brand Associations

Brand names linked to global strategies can have useful associations. For customers and competitors, a global presence automatically symbolizes strength, staying power, and the ability to generate competitive products. Such an image can be particularly important to buyers of expensive industrial products or consumer durables such as cars or computers because it can lessen concern that the products may be unreliable or rendered obsolete by technological advances. Japanese firms such as Yamaha, Sony, Canon, and Honda operate in markets in which technology and product quality are important, and they have benefited from a global brand association.

Access to Low-Cost Labor or Materials

Another motivation for a global strategy is the cost reduction that results from access to the resources of many countries. Substantial cost differences can arise with respect to raw materials, R&D talent, assembly labor, and component supply. Thus, a computer manufacturer may purchase components from South Korea and China, obtain raw materials from South America, and assemble in Mexico and five other countries throughout the world in order to reduce labor and transportation costs. Access to low-cost labor and materials can be an SCA, especially when it is accompanied by the skill and flexibility to change when one supply is threatened or a more attractive alternative emerges.

INDICATORS THAT STRATEGIES SHOULD BE GLOBAL

- Major competitors in important markets are not domestic and have a presence in several countries.
- Standardization of some elements of the product or marketing strategy provides opportunities for scale economies.
- Costs can be reduced and effectiveness increased by locating value added activities in different countries.
- There is a potential to use the volume and profits from one market to subsidize gaining a position in another.
- Trade barriers inhibit access to worthwhile markets.
- A global name can be an advantage and the name is available worldwide.
- A brand position and its supporting advertising will work across countries and has not been preempted.
- Local markets do not require products or service for which a local operation would have an advantage.

Access to National Investment Incentives

Another way to obtain a cost advantage is to access national investment incentives that countries use to achieve economic objectives for target industries or depressed areas. Unlike other means to achieve changes in trade, such as tariffs and quotas, incentives are much less visible and objectionable to trading partners. Thus, the British government has offered Japanese car manufacturers a cash bonus to locate a plant in the United Kingdom. The governments of Ireland, Brazil, and a host of other countries offer cash, tax breaks, land, and buildings to entice companies to locate factories there.

Cross-Subsidization

A global presence allows a firm to cross-subsidize, to use the resources accumulated in one part of the world to fight a competitive battle in another.[1] Consider the following: One firm uses the cash flow generated in its home market to attack a domestically-oriented competitor. For example, in the early 1970s, Michelin used its European home profit base to attack Goodyear's U.S. market. The defensive competitor (i.e., Goodyear) can reduce prices or increase advertising in the United States to counter, but by doing so, it will sacrifice margins in its largest markets. An alternative is to attack the aggressor in its home market, where it has the most to lose. Thus, Goodyear carried the fight to Europe to put a dent in Michelin's profit base.

The cross-subsidization concept leads to two strategic considerations:[2]

- To influence an existing or potential foreign competitor, it is useful to maintain a presence in its country. The presence should be large enough to make the threat of retaliation meaningful. If the share is only 2 percent or so, the competitor may be willing to ignore it.

- A home market may be vulnerable even if a firm apparently controls it with a large market share. A high market share, especially if it is used to support high prices and profits, can attract foreign firms that realize the domestic firm has little freedom for retaliation. A major reason for the demise of the U.S. consumer electronics industry was that U.S. firms were placed at a substantial disadvantage compared with global competitors that had the option to cross-subsidize.

Dodge Trade Barriers

Strategic location of component and assembly plants can help gain access to markets by penetrating trade barriers and fostering goodwill. Peugeot, for example, has plants in twenty-six countries from Argentina to Zimbabwe. Locating final-assembly plants in a host country is a good way to achieve favorable trade treatment and goodwill, because it provides a visible presence and generates savings in transportation and storage of the final product. Thus, Caterpillar operates assembly plants in each of its major markets, including Europe, Japan, Brazil, and Australia, in part to bypass trade barriers. An important element of the Toyota strategy is to source a significant portion of its car cost in the United States and Europe to deflect sentiment against foreign domination.

Access to Strategically Important Markets

Some markets are strategically important because of their market size or potential or because of their raw material supply, labor cost structure, or technology. It can be important to have a presence in these markets even if such a presence is not profitable. Because of its size, the U.S. market is critical to those industries in which scale economies are important, such as automobiles or consumer electronics.

Sometimes a country is important because it is the locus of new trends and developments in an industry. A firm in the fashion industry may benefit from a presence in countries that have historically led the way in fashion. Or a high-tech firm may want to have operations in a country that is in the forefront of the relevant field. For example, an electronics firm without a Silicon Valley presence will find it difficult to keep abreast of technology developments and competitor strategies. Sometimes adequate information can be obtained by observers, but those with design and manufacturing groups on location will tend to have a more intimate knowledge of trends and events.

WHAT COUNTRY TO ENTER?

Once a firm has decided to become global, deciding what country or countries to enter—and in what sequence—is a key challenge. Entering any new market can be risky and take away resources that could be used to make strategic investments elsewhere. A frequently unforeseen consequence of global expansion is that healthy markets, especially the home market, are put at risk by this diversion of resources. It is thus important to select markets for which the likelihood of success will be high and the resource drain minimized.

Market selection starts with several basic dimensions:

- Is the market attractive in terms of size and growth? Are there favorable market trends? For many companies, China and India often appear attractive because of their sheer size and growth potential.

- How intense is the competition? Are other firms well entrenched with a loyal following, and are they committed to defending their position? Tesco, a major retailer in the United Kingdom, found that expansion to France was unattractive because of the established competition, whereas eastern European countries had much less formidable competition. As a result, Hungary was the first country in continental Europe that Tesco entered.[3]

- Can the firm add value to the market? Will the products and business model provide a point of differentiation that represents a relevant customer benefit? Tesco has developed an Internet-based home delivery system for grocery retailers that adds value in many markets, including the United States.[4]

- Can the firm implement its business model in the country, or do operational or cultural barriers exist? How feasible is any adaptation that is required? Marks & Spencer, a U.K. retailer spanning food, clothing, and general merchandise, attempted to export its offerings and the look and feel of its stores to the Continent, only to find that these offerings had little appeal to Europeans.

- Can a critical mass be achieved? It is usually fatal to enter countries lacking the sales potential needed to support the marketing and distribution effort needed for success.

Understanding the four types of distance between a firm and the target country can be helpful in making these judgments, particularly the last two.[5] Geographic distance includes not only the physical distance but whether there is a common border, sea or river access, or a different climate. Administrative distance involves government policies, as well as possible restrictions on trade, monetary weakness, or political hostility. Cultural distance refers to dissimilar languages, ethnicities, religions, and social norms. Economic distance means disparities in consumer incomes, national infrastructure, and the costs of natural and human resources.

These multiple forms of distance, particularly cultural and administrative distance, help explain why firms attracted to China's enormous potential are finding it difficult to enter successfully. In one survey, more than half of the firms admitted that their business performance in China had been "worse than planned."[6] Culturally, the language problem, the importance of personal connections, and consumer preferences for home-country brands all affect the success of foreign entrants into China. Administrative barriers such as market access restrictions, high taxes, and customer duties also inhibit entering firms, as does corruption (which can be significant).

A strategy of entering countries sequentially has several advantages. It reduces the initial commitment, allows the product and marketing program to be improved based on experience in preceding countries, and provides for the gradual creation of a regional presence. Other factors, however, argue that global expansion should be done on as wide a front as possible. First, economies of scale, a key element of successful global strategies, will be more quickly realized and will be a more significant factor. Second, the ability of competitors to copy products and brand positions—a very real threat in most industries—will be inhibited because a first-mover advantage will occur in more markets. Third, standardization, a topic to which we now turn, is more feasible.

STANDARDIZATION VERSUS CUSTOMIZATION[7]

Standardized brands gained widespread credence as a strategy because of Ted Levitt's classic 1983 Harvard Business Review article, "The Globalization of Markets," which gave three reasons why it would succeed.[8] First, the forces of communication, transport and travel were breaking down the insulation of markets, leading to a homogeneity of consumer tastes and wants. Second, the economics of simplicity and standardization—especially with respect to products and communication—represented compelling competitive advantages against those who held on to localized strategies. Third, customers would sacrifice preferences in order to obtain high quality at lower prices. The article provided an academic underpinning to the logical premise that standardization should be the goal of a global business.

Pringles, Visa, MTV, Sony, Dove, Vodafone, BP, DeBeers, Nike, McDonald's, Pantene, Disney, and IBM are the envy of many brand builders because they seem to have generated global businesses with a high degree of similarity in terms of brand, position, advertising strategy, personality, product, packaging, and look and feel. Pringles, for example, stands for "fun," a social setting, freshness, less greasiness, resealability, and the whole-chip product everywhere in the world. Further, the Pringles package, symbols, and advertising are almost the same globally. Disney's brand of magical family entertainment is implemented by theme parks, movies, and characters that are remarkably consistent across countries.

These "standardized" brands are often not as identical worldwide as one might assume. McDonald's has disparate menus, advertising, and retail architectures in various countries. Pringles uses different flavors in different countries, and advertising executions are tailored to local culture. Heineken is the premium beer to enjoy with friends everywhere—except at home in the Netherlands, where it is more of a mainstream beer. Visa even has had different logos in some countries (such as Argentina), and Coke has a sweeter product in areas like southern Europe. Regardless of these variations, however, brands that have moved toward the global end of the local global spectrum demonstrate some real advantages.

A standardized brand can achieve significant economies of scale. For example, when IBM decided to exchange some three dozen advertising agencies for one in order to create a single global campaign (even if it needed some adapting from market to market), one motivation was to achieve efficiencies. The task of developing packaging, a Web site, a promotion, or a sponsorship will also be more cost-effective when spread over multiple countries. Economies of scale across countries can be critical for sponsorships with global relevance, such as the World Cup or the Olympics.

Perhaps more important though, is the enhanced effectiveness that results from better resources. When IBM replaced its roster of agencies with Ogilvy & Mather, it immediately became the proverbial elephant that can sit wherever it wants. As the most important O&M client, it gets the best agency talent from top to bottom. As a result, the chances of a well-executed breakout campaign are markedly improved.

Cross-market exposure produces further efficiencies. Media spillover, where it exists, allows the standardized brand to buy advertising more efficiently. Customers who travel can get exposed to the brand in different countries, again making the campaign work harder. Such exposure is particularly important for travel-related products such as credit cards, airlines, and hotels.

A standardized brand is also inherently easier to manage. The fundamental challenge of brand management is to develop a clear, well-articulated brand identity (what you want your brand to stand for) and to find ways to make that identity a driver of all brand-building activities. The absence of multiple strategies makes this task less formidable with a global brand. In addition, simpler organizational systems and structures can be employed. Visa's "worldwide acceptance" position is much easier to manage than dozens of country-specific strategies.

The key to a standardized brand is to find a position that will work in all markets. Sprite, for example, has the same position globally—honest, no hype, refreshing taste. It is based on the observation that kids everywhere are fed up with hype and empty promises and ready to trust their own instincts. The Sprite advertising tagline ("Image is nothing. Thirst is everything. Obey your thirst.") resonates around the world. In one scene from a Sprite ad, kids are discussing why their basketball hero would drink Sprite. After his friends speculate about its ability to make players jump higher and perform other athletic feats, one concludes, "I heard Grant Hill drinks it when he gets thirsty."

Several generic positions seem to travel well. One is being the "best," the upscale choice. High-end premium brands such as Mercedes, Montblanc, Heineken, and Tiffany's can cross geographic boundaries because the self-expressive benefits involved apply in most cultures. Another is the country position. For example, the "American" position of brands such as Coke, Levi's, Baskin-Robbins, KFC, and Harley-Davidson will work everywhere (with the possible exception of the United States). A purely functional benefit such as Pampers' dry, happy baby can also be used in multiple markets. Not all brands that are high-end or American or have a strong functional benefit, however, can be global.

Standardization can come from a centralized decision to create a global product. Canon, for example, developed a copier that had a common design throughout the world in order to maximize production economies. Unfortunately, the copier could not use the standard paper size in Japan, resulting in substantial customer inconvenience. The risk inherent in a truly global standardization objective is that the result will be a compromise. A product and marketing program that almost fits most markets may not be exactly right anywhere; such a result is a recipe for failure or mediocrity.

Another strategy is to identify a lead country, a country whose market is attractive because it is large or growing or because the brand has a natural advantage there. A product is tailored to maximize its chances of success in that country, then exported to other markets (perhaps with minor modification or refinements). A firm may have several lead countries, each with its own product. The result is a stable of global brands, with each brand based in its own home country. Nissan has long taken this approach, developing a corporate fleet car for the United Kingdom, for example, and then offering it to other countries. Lycra, a 35-year-old ingredient brand from DuPont, has lead countries for each of the product's several applications all under the global tagline "Nothing moves like Lycra." Thus, the Brazilian brand manager is also the global lead for swimsuits, the French brand manager does the same for fashion, and so on.

Global Leadership Not Standardized Brands

The fact is that a global brand is not always optimal or even feasible. Yet, attracted by the apparent success of other brands, many firms are tempted to globalize their own brand. Too often the underlying reason is really executive ego and a perception that globalization is the choice of successful business leaders.

Such decisions are often implemented by a simple edict—that only global programs are to be used. The consolidation of all advertising into one agency and the development of a global advertising theme are typically cornerstones of the effort. Even when having a standardized brand is desirable, though, a blind stampede toward that goal can be the wrong course and even result in significant brand damage. There are three reasons.

First, economies of scale and scope may not actually exist. The promise of media spillover has long been exaggerated, and creating localized communication can sometimes be less costly and more effective than adapting "imported" executions. Further, even an excellent global agency or other communication partner may not be able to execute exceptionally well in all countries.

Second, the brand team may not be able to find a strategy to support a global brand, even assuming one exists. It might lack the people, the information, the creativity, or the executional skills and therefore end up settling for a mediocre approach. Finding a superior strategy in one country is challenging enough without imposing a constraint that the strategy be used throughout the world.

Third, a standardized brand simply may not be optimal or feasible when there are fundamental differences across markets. Consider the following contexts where a global brand would make little sense:

- *Different market share positions.* Ford's European introduction of a new van, the Galaxy, into the United Kingdom and Germany was affected by its market share position in each country. As the number-one car brand in the United Kingdom with a superior quality image, Ford sought to expand the Galaxy's appeal beyond soccer moms to the corporate market. So the UK Galaxy became the "non-van," and its roominess was compared to first-class airline travel. In Germany, however, where Volkswagen held the dominant position, the Galaxy became the "clever alternative."

- **Different brand images.** Honda means quality and reliability in the United States, where it has a legacy of achievement based on the J.D. Powers ratings. In Japan, however, where quality is much less of a differentiator, Honda is a car-race participant with a youthful, energetic personality.

- **Preempted positions.** A superior position for a chocolate bar is to own associations with milk and the image of a glass of milk being poured into a bar. The problem is that different brands have preempted this position in different markets (for example, Cadbury in the United Kingdom, and Milka in Germany).

- **Different customer motivations.** In Finland, after finding that users were apprehensive about perceived machine complexity, Canon became the copier that empowered the user, making him or her the boss. In Germany and Italy, however, more traditional attribute-oriented messages did better.

- **Names and symbols may not be available or appropriate everywhere.** The Ford truck name Fiera means "ugly old woman" in some Spanish-speaking countries. Procter & Gamble's Pert Plus needed to be sold as Rejoy in Japan, Rejoice in much of the Far East, and Vidal Sassoon in the United Kingdom because the Pert Plus name had been preempted.

A global business strategy is often misdirected. The priority should be developing non-standardized brands (although such brands might result) but standardized brand *leadership*, strong brands in all markets. Effective, proactive global brand management should utilize the people, systems, culture, and structure of an organization to allocate brand-building resources globally, create global synergies, and develop a global brand strategy that will coordinate and leverage the strategies in individual countries.

GLOBAL BRAND MANAGEMENT

A study of some fifty global firms, conducted by David Aaker and Erich Joachimsthaler and extended by the Dentsu advertising agency, concluded that an effective global brand management system needs to address four challenges— developing a communication system to facilitate the sharing of insights and experiences, creating a global brand planning system, form an organizational structure that will resist the "I am different" syndrome, and finding ways to achieve brilliance in brand-building (see Figure 11.2).[9]

Global Brand Communication System

A cross-country communication system that shares insights, methods, and best practices is the most basic and nonthreatening element of global brand management. A customer insight that may be obvious in one country might be more subtle and difficult to

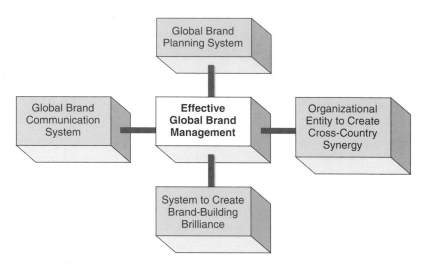

Figure 11.2 Effective Global Brand Management

access in another. For most companies, a cross-country system includes a person or small team that identifies and disseminates experiences, supplemented by global meetings where involved managers can exchange experiences (both formally and informally). Intranets often play an active role in the process, with the principal challenges being how to encourage people to express their experiences and preventing information overload. Mobil (now Exxon) addressed these challenges by having each intranet sponsored by a senior manager and directed by a leader/facilitator who provides the necessary energy, ideas, and continuity.

Global Brand Planning System

Every country manager needs to use the same vocabulary and planning template when developing strategies. Without this commonality, there is little chance of creating synergy across countries. The planning template (such as the one developed in this book, in Appendix A) should include some basic elements of strategic analysis, self-analysis, a business strategy, tactical plans, and goals and measurement.

Organizational Brand Planning Structure

The goal of achieving significant global synergies is usually inhibited by local biases usually supported by a well-established decentralized structure and culture. Country managers often believe that context is unique, so consumer insights and best practices from other markets do not apply. They further believe that others lack the background to understand the subtle ways in which their country differs from others.

To have any hope of creating synergy and leveraging programs to achieve market success in the face of such biases, someone or some group needs to be in charge of the global brand. A global brand manager serves this role in some firms. There might also be a global brand team, with cross-country representation that can play either a leadership or supporting role.

Whether the global brand is represented by a person or a team, the people involved need three key ingredients for success, or at least access to these ingredients. The first is an in-depth knowledge of the local markets, including trends, competitor

DYSFUNCTIONAL GLOBAL BRAND MANAGEMENT STYLES

When the centralized brand group lacks one or more of the three success ingredients, the brand management process is at risk of falling into one of the following models:

- *Uninformed dictator model.* In this model, a person with organizational power (sometimes the CEO) becomes a convert to brand power and standardization. This reborn brand champion, however, lacks market and/or product knowledge and, most importantly, patience. As a result, he or she is prone to make arbitrary decisions without research or analysis. Perhaps, for example, a hasty decision is made to change a brand name or position after an acquisition, or whenever a brand appears inconsistent across markets. If such a decision damages the brand (or even if it is not supported within the organization), the ability and willingness of employees to support the brand going forward can be affected as well.

- *Brand bureaucracy model.* The brand group in this model lacks adequate market knowledge and is seriously deficient in authority and/or resources. The team becomes little more than a logo cop charged with making sure that the visual presentation is correct and perhaps sending out forms to be filled in by the business units. This model can work for a while, especially when the visual presentation is clearly confused across markets. But over time, the team is often ignored as others recognize its lack of influence.

- *All hat, no cattle model.* This expression comes from the old West popularized by cowboy movies where people with no resources (cattle) talk big (and wear "big" hats) while others with thousands of head of cattle talk softly. In much the same way, management sometimes decides that brands are important, but fails to provide the brand team with enough authority and/or resources. As a result, regardless of how capable the people are or how much market and product knowledge they have, the brand team cannot influence autonomous business units, hire outside brand experts, or really do anything of significance. As a result, the organization gets frustrated or suspects that top management is only giving lip service to the brands. This model is all too common in Japanese firms.

- *Anarchy model.* In the anarchy model, the organization has an extremely decentralized structure, with little guidance or cross-country communication. Market understanding, product knowledge, and strategic talent are sprinkled unevenly throughout the organization. Some business units will do well, but the organization as a whole will be underleveraged, and most countries will be vulnerable to underperformance.

dynamics, segmentation, and customer motivations. The second is an understanding of the product or service, its underlying technology, and how the offering might be extended. The third is real authority and resources, as well as the ability to participate in the development of country-specific business strategies.

The global brand manager or team can influence country strategies in a variety of ways. The best approach in a particular case will depend on the maturity of the global operation and the extent to which the decentralized culture is ingrained. At one extreme is the centralized command-and-control model, where external analysis and strategy are centralized and the country mangers are simply implementers. At the other is the anarchy model, one of five dysfunctional models described in the insert. In between are the service provider, consultant, and facilitator models.

Service provider model. The central brand group will be a partner and service provider. It will select and manage the single advertising agency, for example, but the objectives for the communication will be initiated from the country and be jointly determined. The centralized group will control some of the brand-building budget, perhaps including sponsorships and corporate advertising.

Consultative model. The central brand group learns about the markets, competitors, and customers and develops insights and brand options. It would then meet with the business units, provide insights, and make suggestions as to what brand strategy should be considered and what brand-building programs are likely to be effective.

Facilitator model. The central group becomes a facilitator in helping the business units work within a defined brand management process to develop sound strategies and would have less responsibility for knowing the markets and making strategy suggestions. Least threatening, this model is usually the best choice when introducing global brand management into an organization.

Delivering Brilliance in Brand Strategy Implementation

Global brand leadership, especially in these days of media clutter, requires implementation brilliance—"good enough" is *not* good enough. The dilemma is how to achieve brilliance in local markets while still gaining synergy and leverage as a global organization. Here are some guidelines:

- Consider what brand-building paths to follow for example, advertising versus sponsorship, retail presence, or promotions. The genius may not be in execution per se but in the selection of the vehicles.

- Get the best and most motivated people to work on the brand. Some agency-client tension can be helpful in this regard; Audi, for instance, uses multiple agencies.

- Develop multiple options. In general, the more attempts you make at brilliance, the higher the probability that it will be reached. Procter & Gamble finds exceptional ideas by empowering its country brand teams to develop breakthrough brand-building programs. When one is found (such as Pantene Pro-V's "Hair so healthy it shines"), it is rolled out country by country.

- Measure the results. Measurement drives excellence, and a global brand measurement system is fundamental to excellence.

STRATEGIC ALLIANCES

Strategic alliances play an important role in global strategies because it is common for a firm to lack a key success factor for a market. It may be distribution, a brand name, a sales organization, technology, R&D capability, or manufacturing capability. To remedy this deficiency internally might require excessive time and money. When the uncertainties of operating in other countries are considered, a strategic alliance is a natural alternative for reducing investment and the accompanying inflexibility and risk.

For example, IBM, which has relatively few alliances in the United States, has teamed up with just about everyone possible in Japan.[10] It has links with Ricoh in distribution of low-end computers, with Nippon Steel in systems integration, with Fuji Bank in financial systems marketing, with OMRON in integrated computer manufacturing, and with NTT in value-added networks. There is even a book in Japanese entitled *IBM's Alliance Strategy in Japan*. As a result, IBM is considered a major insider in the Japanese market, and it competes across the board in all segments and applications.

Strategic alliance is thus becoming a key part of global competition. Kenichi Ohmae, a Japanese management guru, has said that:

> Globalization mandates alliances, makes them absolutely essential to strategy. Uncomfortable, perhaps—but that's the way it is. Like it or not, the simultaneous developments that go under the name of globalization make alliances—entente—necessary.[11]

A strategic alliance is a collaboration leveraging the strengths of two or more organizations to achieve strategic goals. There is a long-term commitment involved. It is not simply a tactical device to provide a short-term fix for a problem—to outsource a component for which a temporary manufacturing problem has surfaced, for example. Furthermore, it implies that the participating organizations will contribute and adapt needed assets or competencies to the collaboration and that these assets or competencies will be maintained over time. The results of the collaboration should have strategic value and contribute to a viable venture that can withstand competitive attack and environmental change.

A strategic alliance provides the potential for accomplishing a strategic objective or task—such as obtaining distribution in Italy—quickly, inexpensively, and with a relatively high prospect for success. This is possible because the involved firms can combine existing assets and competencies instead of having to create new assets and competencies internally.

Forms of Strategic Alliances

A strategic alliance can take many forms, from a loose informal agreement to a formal joint venture. The most informal arrangement might be simply trying to work together (selling our products through your channel, for example) and allowing systems and organizational forms to emerge as the alliance develops. The more informal the arrangement, the faster it can be implemented and the more flexible it will be. As conditions and people change, the alliance can be adjusted. The problem is usually commitment. With low exit barriers and commitment, there may be a low level of strategic importance and a temptation to back away or to disengage when difficulties arise.

A formal joint venture involving equity and a comprehensive legal document, on the other hand, has very different risks. When equity sharing is involved, there is often worry about control, return on investment, and achieving a fair percentage of the venture. A major concern is whether such a permanent arrangement will be equitable in the face of uncertainty about the relative contributions of the partners and the eventual success of the endeavor. Also, one or more of the firms involved may tend to drag their heels and the venture may lose a window of opportunity. Another concern is that equity positions and the accompanying limits on each partner's contribution can result in a lack of needed flexibility as conditions change. Furthermore, the parties involved may rely excessively on legal documents to preserve the health of the alliance.

Motivations for Strategic Alliances

Strategic alliances can be motivated by a desire to achieve some of the benefits of a global strategy, as outlined in Figure 11.1. For example, a strategic alliance can:

- *Generate scale economies.* The fixed investment that Toyota made in designing a car and its production systems was spread over more units because of a joint venture with GM in California.
- *Gain access to strategic markets.* The Japanese firm JVC provided VCR design and manufacturing capability but needed a relationship with Thompson to obtain help in accessing the fragmented European market.
- *Overcome trade barriers.* Inland Steel and Nippon Steel jointly built an advanced cold-steel mill in Indiana. Nippon supplied the technology, capital, and access to Japanese auto plants in the United States. In return, it gained local knowledge and, more important, the ability to get around import quotas.

Perhaps more commonly, a strategic alliance may be needed to compensate for the absence of or weakness in a needed asset or competency. Thus, a strategic alliance can:

- *Fill out a product line to serve market niches.* Ford, General Motors, and Chrysler have, for example, relied on alliances to provide key components of its product line. Ford's long-time relationship with Mazda has resulted in many Ford models, as well as access to some Far East markets. When Mazda decided not to build a minivan, Ford turned to Nissan for help. One firm simply cannot provide the breadth of models needed in a major market such as the United States.
- *Gain access to a needed technology.* While JVC gained access to the European market, its European partner accessed a competitive VCR source.

- *Use excess capacity.* The GM/Toyota joint venture used an idle GM plant in California.

- *Gain access to low-cost manufacturing capabilities.* GE sourced its microwave ovens from Samsung in South Korea.

- *Access a name or customer relationship.* NGK bought an interest in a GE subsidiary whose product line had become obsolete in order to access the GE name and reputation in the U.S. electrical equipment market. A U.S. injection molder joined with Mitsui in order to help access Japanese manufacturing operations in the United States that preferred to do business with Japanese suppliers.

- *Reduce the investment required.* In some cases, a firm's contribution to a joint venture can be technology, with no financial resources required.

The Key: Maintaining Strategic Value for Collaborators

A major problem with strategic alliances occurs when the relative contribution of the partners becomes unbalanced over time and one partner no longer has any proprietary assets and competencies to contribute. This has happened in many of the partnerships involving U.S. and Japanese firms in consumer electronics, heavy machinery, power-generation equipment, factory equipment, and office equipment.[12]

The result, when the U.S. company has become de-skilled or hollowed out and no longer participates fully in the venture, can be traced in part to the motivation of the partners. Japanese firms are motivated to learn skills; they find it embarrassing to lack a technology and they work to correct deficiencies. U.S. firms are motivated to make money by outsourcing elements of the value chain in order to reduce costs. They start by outsourcing assembly and move on to components, to value-added components, to product design, and finally to core technologies. The U.S. partner is then left with just the distribution function, whereas the Japanese firm retains the key business elements, such as product refinement, design, and production.

Hamel, Doz, and Prahalad studied fifteen strategic alliances and offered suggestions as to how a firm might protect its assets and competencies from its alliance partner.[13] One approach is to structure the situation so that learning takes place and access to missing competencies and assets occurs. Compare, for example, the joint Toyota/GM manufacturing facility, where GM is involved in the manufacturing process and its refinements, to Chrysler's effort to sell a Mitsubishi car designed and manufactured in Japan. In the latter case, Mitsubishi eventually developed its own name and dealer network and now sells its car directly. When the motivation for an alliance is to avoid investment and achieve attractive short-term returns instead of to develop assets and competencies, the alliance will break down.

Another approach is to protect assets from a partner by controlling access. Many Japanese firms have a coordinated information transfer. Such a position avoids uncoordinated, inappropriate information flow. Other firms put clear conditions on access to a part of the product line or a part of the design. Motorola, for example, releases its microchip technology to its partner, Toshiba, only as Toshiba delivers on its promise to increase Motorola's penetration in the Japanese market. Still others keep improving the assets involved so that the partner's dependence continues. Of course, the problem of protecting assets is most difficult when the asset can be communicated by a drawing. It is somewhat easier when a complex system is involved—when, for example, the asset is manufacturing excellence.

The problem of protection is reduced substantially when the two partners bring complementary assets into the alliance that are core competencies of each and are the bases of other business areas. Thus, the danger that one will wither is low. Clintee International formed a joint venture between Baxter (a health-care giant) and Nestlé (the food and nutrition products firm) and realized more than $400 million in sales just three years later. Baxter was strong in the parenterals business, which included products that delivered nutrition intravenously or through a catheter, and it had experience with medical markets, mainly in the United States. Nestlé had a strong background in basic nutrition, a growing interest in adult nutrition products, a strong R&D capability, and a presence in world markets. Neither firm was likely to see its core strengths dissipated in the context of the joint venture.

Making Strategic Alliances Work

Even if an alliance is strategically sound, a host of operational problems can arise. One study of thirty-seven joint ventures uncovered a variety of management problems.[14] In one case, the partners differed in terms of priorities for short-term versus long-term objectives. In another, a British firm could not understand a U.S. partner's obsession with numbers and analysis. In still another, a sensitive decision about the location of a new plant became political.

With strategic alliances, at least two sets of business systems, people, cultures, and structures need to be reconciled. In addition, the culture and environment of each country must be considered. The Japanese, for example, tend to use a consensus-building decision process that relies on small group activity for much of its energy; this approach is very different from that of managers in the United States and Europe. Furthermore, the interests of each partner may not always seem to be in step. Many otherwise well-conceived alliances have failed because the partners simply had styles and objectives that were fundamentally incompatible.

There are several keys to making a collaboration work. Perhaps the most important is that it be well planned to provide ongoing mutual benefit. Partners should make sure they have real assets and competencies that combine to provide strategic advantage. These assets and competencies should continue to be relevant to the venture and to be maintained by the partners over time. If there is a significant ongoing strategic motivation reinforced by success, problems are more likely to be manageable.

When a joint venture is established as a separate organization, research has shown that the chances of success will be enhanced if:

- The joint venture is allowed to evolve with its own culture and values—the existing cultures of the partners will probably not work even if they are compatible with each other.

- The management and power structure from the two partners is balanced.
- Venture champions are on board to carry the ball during difficult times. Without people committed to making the venture happen, it will not happen.
- Methods are developed to resolve problems and to allow change over time. It is unrealistic to expect any strategy, organization, or implementation to exist without evolving and changing. Partners and the organization thus need to be flexible enough to allow change to occur.

Alliances are a widespread part of business strategy (the top 500 global businesses have an average of sixty major alliances each) but need to be actively managed. One study of some 200 corporations found that the most successful at adding value through alliances employed staff who coordinated all alliance-related activity within the organization.[15] This function would draw on prior experiences to provide guidance to those creating and managing new alliances. Lotus, for example, has "thirty-five rules of thumb" to manage alliances from creation to termination. The dedicated alliance staff would also increase external visibility (an alliance announcement has been found to influence stock price), coordinate internal staffing and management of alliances, and help identify the need to change or terminate an alliance.

KEY LEARNINGS

- A global strategy considers and exploits interdependencies between operations in different countries.
- Among the motivations driving globalization are obtaining scale economies, accessing low-cost labor or materials, taking advantage of national incentives to cross-subsidize, dodging trade barriers, accessing strategic markets, and creating global associations.
- A brand with extensive commonalities across countries can potentially yield economies of scale, enhanced effectiveness because of better resources involved, cross-market exposure, and more effective brand management.
- The selection of a country to enter should involve an analysis of the attractiveness of the market and the ability of the firm to succeed in that market.
- A standardized brand is not always optimal. Economies of scale may not exist, the discovery of a global strategy (even assuming it exists) may be difficult, or the context (for example, different market share positions or brand images) may make such a brand impractical.
- Global brand management needs to include a global brand communication system, a global brand planning system, a global management structure, and a system to encourage excellence in brand building. The brand group can operate under a command-and-control, service provider, consultative, or facilitator style.

- Strategic alliances (long-term collaboration leveraging the strengths of two or more organizations to achieve strategic goals) can enable an organization to overcome a lack of a key success factor, such as distribution or manufacturing expertise.

- A key to the long-term success of strategic alliances is that each partner contributes assets and competencies over time and obtains strategic advantages.

FOR DISCUSSION

1. Pick a product or service that is offered in a limited number of countries. Assess the advantages of expanding to a more global presence.

2. For a particular product or service, how would you evaluate the countries that would represent the best prospects? Be specific. What information would you need, and how would to obtain it? Prioritize the criteria that would be useful in deciding which countries to enter.

3. What is the advantage of a global brand team? What are the problems of using a team to devise and run the global strategy? When should a team lead, and when should it take on a supporting role? Would your answer differ for BP versus P&G? Why?

4. For a firm such as Bank of America, P&G, or Ford, how would you go about creating blockbuster brand-building programs—for example, sponsorships, promotions, or advertising? How would you leverage those programs?

5. Select a company. How would you advise it to find an alliance partner to gain distribution into China? What advice would you give regarding the management of that alliance?

NOTES

1. Gary Hamel and C.K. Prahalad, "Do You Really Have a Global Strategy?" *Harvard Business Review*, July–August 1985, pp. 139–148.

2. Ibid.

3. Victoria Griffith, "Welcome to Your Glocal Superstore," *Strategy+Business*, Vol. 26, 2002, p. 95.

4. Ibid.

5. Pankaj Ghemawat, "Distance Still Matters," *Harvard Business Review*, September 2001, pp. 137–147.

6. Ghemawat, op. cit., p. 144.

7. The material in this section draws from Chapter 10 of the book *Brand Leadership* by David A. Aaker and Erich Joachimsthaler (New York: The Free Press).

8. Theodore Levitt, "The Globalization of Markets," *Harvard Business Review*, May–June 1983, pp. 92–102.

9. David A. Aaker, "The Lure of Global Branding," (with Erich Joachimsthaler), *Harvard Business Review,* November–December 1999.

10. Kenichi Ohmae, "The Global Logic of Strategic Alliances," *Harvard Business Review,* March–April 1989, pp. 143–154.

11. Ibid.

12. David Lei and John W. Slocum, Jr., "Global Strategy, Competence-Building and Strategic Alliances," *California Management Review,* Fall 1992, pp. 81–97.

13. Gary Hamel, Yves L. Doz, and C. K. Prahalad, "Collaborate with Your Competitors—and Win," *Harvard Business Review,* January–February 1989, pp. 133–139.

14. J. Peter Killing, "How to Make a Global Joint Venture Work," *Harvard Business Review,* March–April 1986, pp. 78–86.

15. Jeffrey H. Dyer, Prashant Kale, and Harbir Singh, "How to Make Strategic Alliances Work," MIT *Sloan Management Review,* Summer 2001, pp. 37–43.

CHAPTER TWELVE

Strategic Positioning

You do not merely want to be considered just the best of the best. You want to be considered the only ones who do what you do.
—*Jerry Garcia, The Grateful Dead*

You cannot make a business case that you should be who you're not.
—*Jeff Bezos, Amazon*

The secret of success is constancy of purpose.
—*Benjamin Disraeli*

Strategic position, the face of the business strategy, specifies how the business aspires to be perceived (by its customers, employees, and partners) relative to its competitors and market. Strategic initiatives and communication programs are driven by strategic position, and it is the guiding beacon for organizational culture and values. For all of these reasons, it is crucial to get the strategic position right. In particular, as suggested by Figure 12.1, a strategic position should be:

- **Strategic.** It should reflect a long-term effort to gain advantage in the market over competitors, and it should not be changed until the strategy itself is changed. In contrast, an advertising campaign and a tagline reflect a communications objective, which is tactical and may change within the life of a business strategy.
- **The face of the business strategy.** Unlike an image, which reflects current associations held by customers, the strategic position is under the control of the firm. Indeed, the strategic position is too important to be left in the hands of customers, who lack knowledge of the business strategy going forward. Positioning should reflect business strategy.

- ***Defined relative to competitors and to the market.*** Because the business does not exist in a vacuum, it must not only decide what its scope should be but have a point of differentiation from its competition. If a desired strategic position of innovation has been adopted by competitors, the business must create a spin on innovation that is ownable and differentiated—for example, innovation that provides customer benefit (rather than merely stretching technological boundaries).

- ***Logically and/or emotional resonant with customers and relevant to the market.*** A strategic position that is liked and admired can fail if it ceases to be meaningful.

THE ROLE OF THE STRATEGIC POSITION

The need to articulate a strategic position introduces discipline and clarity into the strategy formulation process. The ultimate strategy is usually more precise and elaborate as a result. The strategic position has other, more explicit, roles to play as Figure 12.1 indicates.

One role is to drive and guide strategic initiatives throughout the organization, from operations to product offering to R&D project selection. The overall thrust

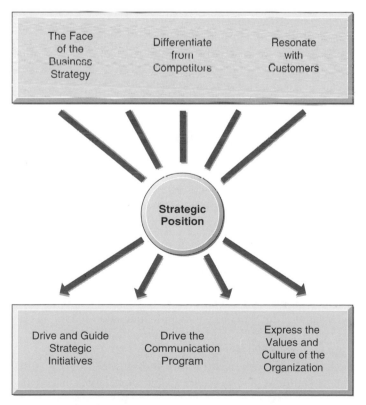

Figure 12.1 Strategic Positions

captured by the strategic position should imply certain initiatives and programs. For example, given that we want to be an e-business firm, what tools and programs will customers expect from us? Initiatives and programs that do not advance the strategic position should be dialed down or killed.

A second role is to drive the communication program. A strategic position that truly differentiates the product and resonates with customers will provide not only punch and effectiveness to external communication, but consistency over time because of its long-term perspective.

A third role is to support the expression of the organization's values and culture to employees and business partners. Such internal communication is as vital to success as reaching out to customers. Lynn Upshaw, a San Francisco communication consultant, suggests asking employees and business partners two questions:

- Do you know what the business stands for?
- Do you care?

Unless the answers to these questions are yes, that is, employees and business partners understand and believe in the business strategy, the strategy is unlikely to fulfill its potential. Too many businesses drift aimlessly without direction, appearing to stand for nothing in particular. Lacking an organizational sense of soul and a sound strategic position, they always seem to be shouting "on sale," attached to some deal, or engaging in promiscuous channel expansion.

The strategic position for a business is analogous to the core identity (and related aspirational associations) for a brand, as described in the books *Building Strong Brands* and *Brand Leadership*.[1] In some cases the two concepts are identical, but in others a strategic position can be broader as it applies to a business strategy rather than a brand strategy.

Strategic position can dramatically affect the prospects of a business, as demonstrated by the experiences of Virgin Atlantic Airlines, IBM, and Charles Schwab.

Virgin Atlantic Airlines

In 1970, Richard Branson and a few friends founded Virgin as a small mail-order record company in London, England. By the mid-1980s, this modest beginning had led to a chain of record shops and the largest independent music label in the United Kingdom, with artists as diverse and important as Phil Collins, the Sex Pistols, Boy George, and the Rolling Stones. The 1990s saw the retail business grow to include over 100 Virgin "megastores" sprinkled around the world. Many, such as the Times Square store, made a significant brand statement with their signage, size, and interior design.

In February 1984, Branson, who found air travel boring and unpleasant, decided to start Virgin Atlantic Airlines to make flying fun and enjoyable for all classes, not just first-class passengers. Defying the odds (and vigorous attempts by British Airways to crush it), Virgin has prospered. By the end of the 1990s, it had become the number two airline in most of the markets and routes it serves. Not only that, it enjoyed the same consumer awareness and reputation as much larger international carriers including service-oriented airlines such as Singapore Airlines, which is consistently rated high with respect to trust, innovation, and service. Virgin Atlantic's success is due in part to its strategic positioning along several dimensions: service quality, value for money, being the underdog, and an edgy personality.

Extraordinary Service Quality

There are thousands of moments of truth in the airline business when the customer experiences service quality (or the lack of it) firsthand. In this context Virgin has performed extraordinarily, not only delivering on the basics but often dazzling with original "wow"-type experiences. Virgin pioneered sleeper seats in 1986 (British Airways followed nine years later with the cradle seat), limo service at each end of the flight (or motorcycle service for those flying light), in-flight massages, child safety seats, individual TVs for business class passengers, drive-through check-in at the airport, and new classes positioned above the normal service levels of coach and business class. It offers first-class passengers a new tailor-made suit to be ready at their destination, masseurs or beauty therapists, and a facility to shower, take a Jacuzzi, and even nap.

Value for Money

Virgin Atlantic's Upper Class is priced at the business-class level but equivalent to many other airlines' first-class service. Mid Class is offered at full-fare economy prices, and most Virgin Economy tickets are available at a discount. While this lower price point offers a clear consumer advantage, however, Virgin does not emphasize the price position in its promotion. Cheapness *per se* is not the message at Virgin

The Underdog

Virgin's business model is straightforward. The company typically enters markets and industries that have large, established players (such as British Airways, Coca-Cola, Levi Strauss, British Rail, and Smirnoff) that can be portrayed as being somewhat complacent, bureaucratic, and unresponsive to customer needs. In contrast, Virgin presents itself as the underdog who cares, innovates, and delivers an attractive, viable alternative to customers. When British Airways attempted to prevent Virgin from gaining routes, Virgin painted British Airways as a bully standing in the way of an earnest youngster who offered better value and service. Virgin, personified by Branson, is the modern-day Robin Hood, the friend of the little guy.

The Virgin Personality

The Virgin brand has a strong, perhaps edgy personality largely reflecting its flamboyant service innovations and the values and actions of Richard Branson. Virgin as a person would be perceived as someone who:

- Flaunts the rules
- Has a sense of humor that can be outrageous at times
- Is an underdog, willing to attack the establishment
- Is competent, always does a good job, and has high standards

Interestingly, this personality spans several unrelated characteristics: rule-breaker, fun-loving, feisty, and competent. Many businesses would like to do the same but feel that they must choose between such personality extremes. The key is not only the personality of Branson himself but also the fact that Virgin has delivered on each facet of this personality.

Virgin is a remarkable example of how the right strategic position can allow a business to stretch far beyond what would be considered its acceptable scope of operations. Rather than restrict itself to records and entertainment, Virgin has used its strategic position to extend from record stores to airlines, colas, condoms, and dozens of other categories. The Virgin Group comprises some 100 companies in 22 countries, including a discount airline (Virgin Express), financial services (Virgin Direct), a cosmetics retail chain and direct sales operation (Virgin Vie), several media companies (Virgin Radio, Virgin TV), a rail service (Virgin Rail), soft drinks and other beverages (Virgin Cola, Virgin Energy, Virgin Vodka), a line of casual clothing (Virgin Clothing, Virgin Jeans), a new record label (V2 Records) and even a bridal store (Virgin Bride). In each business, the strategic position works to provide differentiation and advantage.

In fact, the decision to extend Virgin, a business then associated with rock music and youth, to an airline could have become a legendary blunder if it had failed. However, because the airline was successful and was able to deliver value with quality, flair, and innovation, the master Virgin brand developed associations that were not restricted to a single type of product. The elements of the Virgin strategic position— extraordinary service quality, value for money, the underdog personality, uniqueness— work over a large set of products and services. It has become a lifestyle brand with an attitude whose powerful relationship with customers is not solely based on functional benefits within a particular product category.

Virgin's success has been driven in part by pure visibility, largely based on publicity personally generated by Richard Branson. Realizing that Virgin Atlantic could not compete with British Airways in advertising expenditures, he used publicity stunts to create awareness and develop associations. When the first Virgin Atlantic Airlines flight took off in 1984 with friends, celebrities, and reporters on board, Branson appeared in the cockpit wearing a vintage World War I leather flight helmet. The on-board video (a pre-recorded tape of course) showed the "pilots"—Branson and two famous cricket players—greeting the passengers from the cockpit.[2]

Branson's publicity efforts have not by any means been limited to Virgin Atlantic. For the launching of Virgin Bride, a company that arranges weddings, he showed up in a wedding dress. At the 1996 opening of Virgin's first U.S. megastore in New York's Times Square, Branson (a balloonist holding several world records) was lowered on a huge silver ball from 100 feet above the store. These and other stunts have turned into windfalls of free publicity for Virgin, helping the brand in all contexts.

Branson has fully mastered his role. By employing British humor and the popular love of flouting the system, he has endeared himself to consumers. By never deviating from the core brand values of quality, value for money, being the underdog and having an edgy personality, he has gained their loyalty and confidence. Evidence of this high level of trust in Branson and Virgin abound. When BBC Radio asked 1,200 people who they thought would be most qualified to rewrite the Ten

Commandments, Branson came in fourth, after Mother Teresa, the Pope, and the Archbishop of Canterbury. When a British daily newspaper took a poll on who would be most qualified to become the next mayor of London, Branson won by a landslide.

The challenge for a business that is built on a track record of success and functional innovation like Virgin's is formidable. The next battle could always be its Waterloo and Virgin may indeed meet this fate with its Virgin Rail business. With nearly 30 million annual trips, the rail business is highly visible, and the ability to deliver high-quality performance is not entirely in Virgin's control. Passengers whose expectations were based on Virgin Atlantic Airways were disappointed with mediocre service and late or canceled trains. In retrospect, such a risky venture would have been better off under another name to provide some measure of protection to the Virgin brand.

The critical issue for Virgin, then, will be to manage the business as its consumers (and Branson) age and as it mushrooms into an ever-broader range of ventures. Can Virgin maintain its strategic position across all of its product categories and hold onto its energetic personality over time? A clear strategic position, and being able to implement it, will be the key to meeting that challenge.

IBM

Strategic positioning (or the lack thereof) has been an important element of IBM's fortunes over the years. In the 1950s, it changed from being a punch card processing business to being a computer manufacturer. In the 1960s, IBM evolved from a purveyor of hardware into a firm that delivered systems solutions reliably and competently. The adage that no one ever got fired for buying IBM reflected the incredible equity supporting that position. An antitrust settlement requiring the company to separate its service from its hardware systems undercut a central part of the IBM strategic position, however, and led to a difficult period.

In the middle to late 1980s, IBM lost its way. Its systems consulting business had atrophied, clones had undercut its PC position, and Microsoft (among others) had grasped the leadership role in software. IBM lacked a visible strategic position, and it was in crisis as a result.

When Lou Gerstner took over as CEO in the spring of 1993, one of his first initiatives was to create a strategic position.[3] A series of focus groups among executives in management of information systems (MIS) revealed that IBM was perceived as smart, innovative, a technological leader, and a producer of high-quality equipment. Nevertheless, these same executives would not buy IBM products. They were very emotional in claiming that IBM had betrayed their trust and support, disappointing the whole computer field by becoming too arrogant and turning away from customers. Further research revealed that MIS executives were looking for systems solutions, for firms that could integrate computer technology and apply it to their business problems with a systems perspective and scope (as opposed to a component orientation).

Gerstner took several steps to change the IBM culture, beginning with a program to have top managers (including himself) talk to customers on a regular basis.

He stopped internal consideration of breaking up the company, making clear that the IBM brand and the synergy of the organization would be a strategic point of advantage. Gerstner also identified the most promising initiatives in products and operations and made sure they were funded. All of these actions established a new strategic position that maintained IBM's image as the *global technology leader* while removing the appearance of being aloof and uncaring.

An advertising campaign developed by Ogilvy & Mather symbolically drove home this message. One ad showed two Czech nuns walking down a road, saying (in English subtitles) things like, "I can't wait to get my hands on OS/2." The tagline, "Solutions for a Small Planet," expressed the message of global leadership in a soft, understated way and it returned IBM to its roots as a customer- and solutions-oriented firm. This strategic position was credited with helping to bring IBM back from the brink of destruction.

Only a few years later, though, IBM faced a relevance problem. The Internet had progressed from buzz to reality, and IBM was seen as less connected to this new world than Cisco, Sun, and others, in part because of its product legacy and size. In response, an augmented and refocused strategic position around the e-business concept was developed to signal IBM's relevance to the Internet age and to represent its strategically important service business oriented toward creating systems solutions. From the introduction of the e-business label in late 1996, IBM ultimately spent over $5 billion communicating the concept. A host of products and programs (including a series of "e" subbrands, such as e-servers) provided substance and credibility for the new position.

As noted in Chapter 1, in 2003 Sam Palmisano became IBM's CEO and created a new business strategy and accompanying position based on the "on-demand" e-business concept. On-demand means that unused computer capacity could be accessed by those with a need for it through a managed network grid. Again, the IBM organization was mobilized from top to bottom in order to deliver on this new promise, with a host of on-demand products and services.

Products have had a large role in the strategic position of IBM over time. In the mid-1960s (when computers meant UNIVAC, not IBM), the company forged its dominance with the 360, a hugely successful mainframe computer that set the standard for years with a flow of upgrades and refinements. The 360 was the message and substance behind the strategic position of computer leadership.

Three small consumer products also played instrumental roles in shaping the IBM strategic position, even though each had only a minor portion of the company's sales. The first, in the early 1980s, was the original PC, which legitimized the personal computer world and IBM's place in it. This breakthrough reinforced the company's leader as a dominant leader in the field that could also be nimble and innovative.

The second was the PCjr, a strategically sound idea whose execution cost IBM most of the luster earned by the PC. The intent was to create a home computer related to the PC many customers used at work, but the product had an inadequate keyboard, no hard drive, and could not be hooked up to a printer. Even worse, the introductory ad campaign (with a humorous Charlie Chaplin character) became the focal point of ridicule. The PCjr thus revived the bureaucratic, out-of-touch perceptions of the IBM brand while dialing down the relevant, can-do elements.

The third product, the IBM ThinkPad, featured a striking design, innovative features (including the red TrackPoint), light weight, and solid performance. As it became a high-end leader in a very visible space, tracking studies showed customers' attitude toward IBM going up significantly, the company's only significant upward movement in a five-year time period.

Charles Schwab

Charles Schwab has reinvented itself several times since its inception in 1975. Because it extended rather than changed its strategic position in each case, however, it never had to undergo the difficult repositioning task that involves undoing past mistakes or overcoming the results of a failed program or policy.

In 1975, shortly after Schwab was founded, transaction commissions were deregulated by the SEC, and the firm became, a pure *discount broker.* Such companies were the alternative to a full service broker if you did not need or want to pay for advice (which at worst involved a conflict of interest, since the broker benefited from increasing the number of transactions, and at best was not worth the substantial cost, since the stock recommendations given were little better than random selection).

As its competitors merged, Schwab refined its strategic position. It presented itself as the best of the discount brokers, based on its state-of-the-art computer system, reliable execution, outstanding service, and excellent reporting tools. The competitors by necessity resorted to shouting price, rarely a healthy long-term strategic position.

In 1992, Schwab used its OneSource and free IRA accounts as vehicles to become an asset gatherer, a destination for portfolios in addition to being a discount broker. OneSource allowed Schwab customers to choose from a wide variety of mutual funds (aided by a comprehensive information system) with no transaction fee, removing the need to search for and analyze options from multiple firms. Increased support for mutual fund buyers—such as the Schwab Select List, which lists top mutual fund picks—has helped to enhance Schwab's strategic position over time.

Schwab's initial experiments with computer-based transaction, however, created confusion, frustration, and resentment among customers who had bad experiences or were left behind. Nevertheless, in 1997 Schwab made a commitment to the Internet and computer trading, risking much of the commission income that came from telephone orders. As one of the first *Internet securities companies,* Schwab offered a new differentiating service that further solidified its position as a leader in computer-based systems.

As it enters the new century, Schwab next added another dimension to its strategic position, that of a *money manager.* Many Schwab customers are relatively wealthy and want more advice than the firm has historically given. Schwab wanted to accommodate these clients, but using an approach that did not back away from its long-term position that full-service brokers are unnecessarily expensive. Thus,

Schwab responded with a number of cost-effective branded services using computer-aided systems.

These range from 400 independent Schwab Investment Advisors, offering fee-based services (invitation-only Signature Service advisors provide higher levels of advice) to "portfolio consultation" analyses in Schwab branches for a fixed charge. In addition, Schwab offers its customers branded software products such as the "Sell Analyzer," an online tool to evaluate the cost bases of the portfolio and the "Portfolio Tracer," which allows benchmarking against indexes.

The expansion of Schwab's strategic position was not planned at the outset, but indeed evolved over time. Each step was itself a product of an evolutionary process: the company offered mutual fund services before OneSource, computer trading before its commitment to the Internet, and financial advice (through a network of affiliated advisors) before providing full-scale money management. These initial dimensions of the strategic position were not eliminated or even dialed down but rather augmented, so that the business became richer and deeper instead of different. In short, Schwab improved while remaining true to its heritage.

The Schwab strategic position is really based on three brands, just as the Gap operates not only its own stores but Banana Republic for its high-end customers and Old Navy for the value end. While Schwab is the flagship brand, it has added scope by buying U.S. Trust (a firm whose flagship office on Park Avenue in Manhattan is complete with wood panel and gold-rimmed china) and Cybercorp (a firm that specializes in day-trading). These two acquisitions help Schwab to span the market without unduly stretching its namesake brand.[4]

STRATEGIC POSITION OPTIONS

There are as many strategic positioning avenues as there are products, markets, and business strategies. Successful positions can be based on the competitive strategy options discussed in the preceding three chapters:

- *The quality player with a defined product space.* For example, Gillette's Good News is the best of disposable razors, Saks Fifth Avenue aspires to be the best premium store, and Accenture hopes to be perceived as the best management consulting firm with an expanding scope of activities. To be successful with this strategic position, a firm must both deliver on the promise of being the best and manage the category definition that dictates the perceived set of competitors.

- *The value option.* Hyundai, Budget rental cars, Kmart, and eLoan.com are all positioned primarily as value players. Success in a value position generally requires a cost advantage, and again, it is important to carefully manage the perceived competitive set. Budget, for example, is only a value when compared against the leading rental firms, and Kmart similarly provides value among a well-defined set of competitors. When J. C. Penney attempted to upscale its offerings, it walked a fine line between enhancing value and changing its competitive set.

- **The innovator.** HP, 3M, Sony, GE, Shisheido, and Virgin Atlantic all present themselves as innovators. Creating this perception among customers is easiest when it is based on product or service innovations, as Sony and Virgin have shown. Perceived innovation can also be driven, however, by indicators of leadership and energy. Intel has built a reputation for being innovative by being so visible everywhere. And Virgin enhanced its innovative image with publicity stunts (often by Richard Branson, its CEO) that created enormous energy.

- **A *narrow product focus.*** The essence of Lets-go-fly-a-kite, Aamco, and Ferrari cars is their narrow product offering. As such, they are imbued with credibility that they know their product well. The challenge is to be disciplined about not expanding the product scope in a way that would dilute this credibility.

- **A *target segment focus.*** An on-line business with focus is Gold Violin, which provides products and services for the retired generation (whom it conceptualizes as modern-day heroes). Another is Bolt, an online brand focusing on 15 to 18 year-olds that is differentiated in large part by its relentless reliance on community. *Business 2.0* has become one of the leading new economy magazines by focusing on "transformers"—innovative people with the power and dollars to influence the direction of business. Positioning with respect to a target segment can help ensure that the organization keeps its eye on the ball by keeping the product experience responsive and relevant to that segment.

- **Being global.** Citigroup is a global financial institution. Visa is a global credit card. Toyota is a global car company. Being global provides functional benefits in that you can access the services of Citigroup or Visa anywhere. It also provides the prestige and assurance of knowing that the firm has the business capabilities to compete successfully in other countries. Awareness that Toyota is strong in the United States, for example, helps the firm in Europe, where customers might otherwise see it as a modest player.

There are, of course, a host of additional dimensions on which to base a strategic position as suggested by Figure 12.2. Some, but not all, are based on a strategic option. The following have proven their ability to drive success:

- product category
- product attributes and functional benefits
- breadth of product line
- organizational intangibles
- emotional self-expressive benefits

Strategic Positions	Firms
The best	Accenture, Saks
Value	Hyundai, eLoan
Innovator	HP, 3M, Sony
Product focus	Lets-go-fly-a-kite, Castrol
Target segment	Gerber, Gold Violin
Product categories	Gatorade, Oracle
Product attributes	Volvo, Crest
Product line scope	Amazon, Barnes & Noble
Organizational intangibles	HP, Kaiser Hospital
Emotional benefits	MTV, Hallmark
Self-expressive benefits	GAP, Mercedes
Experience	Nike, Nordstrom
Contemporary	Lane Bryant, Oprah
Personality	Harley-Davidson, Tiffany
Competitors	Visa, Avis

Figure 12.2   Strategic Positions

- experience
- being contemporary
- brand personality
- competitor position

As they are discussed and illustrated, it will become clear that many of these dimensions are interrelated. A purely one-dimensional strategy position is rare.

Product Category

The choice of a product category to which a business will associate itself can have enormous strategic as well as tactical implications. Schweppes positioned its tonic in Europe as an adult soft drink, and the popularity of new-age adult drinks has carried it to a dominant position. In the U.S., however, Schweppes (perhaps wanting to avoid the Coke/Pepsi juggernaut) positioned its entry as a mixed drink, which relegated it to being a minor player when the market changed. Energy bars became a big business by creating a category distinct from candy. Wasa Crispbread expanded its market by positioning itself as an alternative to bread rather than being in a category with rice cakes and Ry-Krisp.

Maintaining Relevance

As suggested in Chapter 5, the relevance concept can help with the difficult task of managing an evolving category with emerging and receding subcategories. Relevance is, in essence, being perceived as associated with the product category in which the customer is interested. In the Brand Asset Valuator, the product of Young & Rubicam's mammoth study of global brands, relevance was one of four key dimensions identified (along with differentiation, esteem, and knowledge). Although differentiation got top billing in the study's results, relevance may be as powerful in dynamic markets. After all, if a business loses relevance, differentiation may not matter.

The ability of a firm to maintain relevance varies along a spectrum, as shown in Figure 12.3. At one extreme are trend neglectors—firms that miss or misinterpret trends, or are so focused on a particular business model that they ignore them. Such firms are often characterized as having inadequate strategic analysis capability, organizational inflexibility, and/or a weak brand portfolio strategy; they eventually wake up in surprise to find that their products are no longer relevant. At the other end of the spectrum are trend drivers, the firms who actually propel the trends that define the category. In the middle are trend responders, who track closely the trends and the evolution of categories, making sure that their products stay current.

Virgin Atlantic Airlines, IBM, and Schwab all have been trend drivers. Virgin has created new subcategories by introducing and owning new services such as massage services in first class. IBM was able to define a category with its e-business and on-demand e-business services, supported by enormous brand-building resources. Schwab's OneSource defined a new subcategory of brokerage firms.

Trend responders—those firms that can recognize trends, evaluate them accurately, and then implement a response—can sustain success in dynamic markets. Some fashion brands, such as Tommy Hilfiger, have been nimble in staying abreast of fashion trends. Barbie has changed with the times, always keeping up with fresh concepts: an astronaut in 1965, a surgeon in 1973, a presidential candidate in 1992, the video "Barbie in The Nutcracker" in 2001, and Barbie couture in 2004. L.L. Bean's position has evolved from hunting, fishing, and camping to a broader outdoors image that is relevant to hikers, mountain bikers, cross-country skiers, and water-sports enthusiasts, the heart of its marketplace. Adapting quickly to the digital age, Fuji Film became a leader with its Super CCD high-quality image sensor for digital cameras (the fourth generation of which was introduced in 2003) and products such as digital photo printers.

Being a successful trend responder, however, is not easy. As suggested in Chapter 5, it can be difficult to identify and evaluate trends well enough to separate them from mere fads. It is also difficult to respond to emerging subcategories, especially if they start small and if the existing business and brand are established. Consider, for example, the difficulty that McDonald's, Burger King, KFC, and the other fast-food giants have had in responding to the healthy eating trend. They were simply not good at product development and delivery in that arena because it is not in their DNA; they lacked the people and culture to be successful. Further, their brands have become a liability as the firms attempt to change perceptions established over decades.

Figure 12.3 Staying Relevant

Product Attributes/Functional Benefits

When a business is blessed with a strong, sustainable product attribute or functional benefit that is valued by the market, that element should be a prominent part of the strategic position. Crest's strong association with cavity control, in part created by an endorsement by the American Dental Association, directly drove a leading market position in toothpaste that hovered around 40 percent for years. Only when Colgate came up with a broader position driven by its Colgate Total product, which combined decay prevention with whitening, was Crest's leadership finally challenged.

In some product classes, different brands will target different "benefit segments" and be positioned accordingly. For example, Volvo has stressed durability, showing commercials of "crash tests" and telling how long its cars last. Jaguar has emphasized its distinctive styling. BMW, in contrast, talks of performance, handling, and engineering efficiency, with the tag line "the ultimate driving machine." Mercedes stresses comfort and luxury. Each of these automakers has selected a different attribute/benefit on which to base its strategic position.

Attribute/benefit positioning is powerful because it often provides a reason to buy and thus resonates with customers. Finding an attribute that is important to a major segment that is not already occupied by a competitor, however, is often a challenge. One solution is to identify an unmet customer problem, as discussed in Chapter 3. Brands of paper towels had emphasized absorbency until Viva discovered customers were irritated with towels that disintegrated when wet. It introduced a more durable towel, with demonstrations supporting the claim that Viva "keeps on working."

Breadth of Product Line

A broad product offering signals substance, acceptance, leadership, and often the convenience of one-stop shopping. For example, the strategic position that drove Amazon's operations and marketing was never about selling books, even at the beginning. (It was no accident that the company was not called books.com.) Rather, the firm positioned itself as delivering a superior shopping/buying experience based on the "Earth's Biggest Selection"—an array of choices so wide that customers would have no reason to look anywhere else. This position allows Amazon to enter a variety of product markets, although it also puts pressure on the company to deliver in each venue.

Breadth also works well as a dimension for other firms, such as Chevrolet, Wal-Mart, and Black & Decker. As noted above, however, product and/or market focus is the key to competitive strength for most brands. Especially in the on-line world, businesses must resist enormous pressures to add functions and segments that appear to offer marginal revenue at almost no cost.

Why? On the one hand, product expansion exploits assets such as brand equity and distribution, creates synergies for the customer and the firm, and can develop associations of acceptance and leadership. On the other, a poorly handled expansion can degrade the brand asset, create inefficiencies, and divert needed resources. Sometimes the worst damage happens when the firm goes halfway—stepping away from a focused strategy, but not achieving worthwhile breadth.

Organizational Intangibles

Companies love to make product claims. They often engage in shouting matches attempting to convince customers that their offering is superior in some key dimension: Bayer is faster acting, and Texas Instruments has a faster chip. Lean Cuisine has fewer calories. Volvo has a longer life. Bran One has more fiber than other cereals. A server has more capacity. A plane has more range.

There are several problems with such specmanship. First, a position based upon some attribute is vulnerable to an innovation that gives your competitor more speed, more fiber, or greater range. In the words of Regis McKenna, the Silicon Valley marketing guru, "You can always get outspeced."

Second, when firms start a specification shouting match, they all eventually lose credibility. After a while, nobody believes that any aspirin is more effective or faster acting than another. There have been so many conflicting claims that all of them are discounted.

Third, people do not always make decisions based upon a particular specification, anyway. They may feel that small differences in some attribute are not important, or simply lack the motivation or ability to process information at such a detailed level.

In contrast to attribute positioning, intangible factors can differentiate a business more effectively and in a more enduring fashion. Organizational attributes, such as being global (Visa), innovative (3M), quality driven (Cadillac), customer driven (Nordstrom), or concerned about the environment (Toyota), are usually longer lasting and more resistant to competitive claims than product-attribute associations. Not only are they harder to copy (because they are based on the people, culture, values, and programs of the entire organization), it is difficult for a competitor to demonstrate that it has overcome a perceived intangible gap. It is easier to show that a competitor's printer is faster, for example, than to show that its organization is more innovative.

A laboratory study of cameras demonstrated the power of an intangible attribute. Customers were shown two camera brands, one of which was positioned as being more technically sophisticated, and the other as easier to use. Detailed specifications of each brand, which were also provided, clearly showed that the easier-to-use brand in fact had superior technology as well. When subjects were shown both brands together, the easy-to-use brand was rated superior on technology by 94 percent of the subjects. However, two days later (when the specifications were not fresh in their minds) only 36 percent of respondents felt that it had the best technology. Using technology as an abstract attribute dominated the actual specifications.

Emotional and Self-Expressive Benefits

Another way to move beyond attribute/functional claims is to create a position based on emotional or self-expressive benefits.

Emotional benefits relate to the ability of the offering to make the customer feel something during the purchase or use experience. The strongest identities often include emotional benefits. Thus, a buyer or user can feel:

- safe in a Volvo
- exhilarated in a BMW
- energized while watching MTV
- important when at Tiffany's
- healthy when drinking Evian
- warm when buying or reading a Hallmark card
- strong and rugged when driving a Ford Explorer

Snicker's is an example of a brand that extended its association from just another candy bar to a reward at the end of the day. Similarly, the "Miller Time" campaign was used to associate Miller's High Life beer with a well-deserved break after a day of hard work. Thus, the position of a product class (with all its associations of calories, sugar, and alcohol) is replaced with the emotional benefit of a reward for a job well done, which is linked to positive feelings and people.

Emotional benefits are all about the "I feel ____" statement: I feel energized, I feel warm, I feel elegant. To see if an emotional benefit can play a role in differentiating a brand, try the "I feel" question with customers. If the hard-core loyalists consistently come up with a particular emotional benefit, then it should be considered as part of the strategic position.

Self-expressive benefits reflect the ability of the purchase and use of an offering to provide a vehicle by which a person can express him or herself. To illustrate, a person might express a self-concept of being:

- adventurous or daring by owning Rosignol powder skis
- cool by buying fashions from Gap
- sophisticated by using Ralph Lauren
- successful, in control, and a leader by driving a BMW
- frugal and unpretentious by shopping at Kmart
- competent by using Microsoft Office
- a nurturing mother by preparing Quaker Oats hot cereal in the morning

Self-expressive benefits are all about the "I am ____" statement: I am successful, I am young, I am a great athlete. To see if a self-expressive benefit can play a role in differentiating a brand, try the "I am" question with loyal customers and see if any consistent self-expressive benefits emerge.

The Experience

The experience of using the brand could include emotional or self-expressive benefits without any functional advantage, but when an experience combines both, it is usually broader and more rewarding. The experience at Nordstrom includes a host of factors (such as the merchandise, the ambiance, and the service) that combine to provide a pleasant, satisfying time. The experience of using Nike combines functional, emotional, and self-expressive benefits to provide a depth of connection that competitor brands lack.

In addition to the breadth of its offering, Amazon is also positioned with respect to the experience it delivers. Its promise is to create a world-class shopping experience that is both efficient and enjoyable. The fast and easy selection, one-click ordering, special-occasion reminders, safe-shopping guarantee, and reliable deliveries lie behind the experience Amazon creates. The Amazon experience also provides emotional benefits by offering the excitement of the discovery of a book, CD, or gift that is just right (as enhanced by its personalized book recommendation). The Amazon River, representing the ultimate in discovery and adventure, provides an aspirational metaphor. One of the challenges for the Amazon brand is to make sure this emotional aspect is not submerged by the functional benefits the site provides.

Being Contemporary

Most established businesses face the problem of remaining or becoming contemporary. A business with a long heritage is given credit for being reliable, safe, a friend, and even innovative if that is part of its tradition. However, as noted earlier, it also can be perceived as "your father's (or even grandfather's) brand." The challenge is to have energy, vitality, and relevance in today's marketplace—to be part of the contemporary scene. The answer usually entails breaking out of the functional-benefit trap.

Lane Bryant, a retailer to plus-sized women, developed a dowdy, apologetic image that was holding it back. To break out, it developed a new, contemporary strategic position. It spread the message with new, even sexy fashions; a Lane Bryant fashion show in New York; revitalized stores; and a new spokesperson, rapper/actress Queen Latifah, in ads, on its Web site, and in a voter-registration program. Ironically, Lane Bryant's sister company, Victoria's Secret, had to reposition itself previously from an edgy (Frederick's of Hollywood) brand to a more mainstream one, albeit at the edge of the mainstream market.

Brand Personality

As with human beings, a business with a personality tends to be more memorable and better liked than one that is bland, nothing more than the sum of its attributes. And like people, brands can have a variety of personalities, such as being professional and competent (CNN and McKinsey), upscale and sophisticated (Jaguar and Tiffany's), trustworthy and genuine (Hallmark and John Deere), exciting and daring (Porsche and Benetton), or active and tough (Levi's and Nike). Certainly, Virgin is a brand whose strategic position includes a strong personality.

Harley-Davidson has a strong personality reflecting a macho, America-loving, freedom-seeking person who is willing to break out of confining social norms. The experience of riding a Harley (or even the association that comes from wearing Harley-Davidson clothing) helps some people to express a part of their personality, which results in intense loyalty. More than 250,000 of these people belong to one of the 800 chapters of the Harley Owners Group (HOG). Twice a year, believers from all over the country gather for a bonding experience. Harley is much more than a motorcycle; it is an experience, an attitude, a lifestyle, a vehicle to express "who I am."

Joie de Vivre is a San Francisco firm whose boutique hotels are each inspired by a theme that reflects a personality. The "Rolling Stone" Phoenix hotel attracts rock-and-roll and other entertainment personalities with its irreverent sense of cool and funky, adventurous decor. The "New Yorker" Rex hotel is clever and sophisticated, with a literary sensibility. The "1920s luxury liner" Commodore Hotel, with its Titanic Café, looks and feels like a party straight out of The Great Gatsby. The "movie palace" Hotel Bijou has a miniature movie theater in the lobby, accompanied by dramatic Hollywood portraits.

Competitor Position

Letting the competitor be the anchor of the strategic position can be effective, especially when the competitor already has an established position. Visa, for example, has continually and successfully fought for market share by offering both functional and self-expressive benefits that are superior to those offered by MasterCard. The strategic position, however, is against American Express, a less formidable competitor whose upscale associations Visa would like to share. One way this positioning is implemented is by noting prestigious Visa-sponsored venues that do not accept American Express.

The classic competitor position was staked out by Avis which was having trouble differentiating itself from two other major rental car agencies (Hertz and National) and several lesser players such as Budget. With Hertz capitalizing on being the leading firm, Avis brilliantly stepped forward with the slogan, "We're Number 2, we try harder." By proclaiming itself the logical alternative to Hertz, Avis deftly positioned National and others as also-rans. Further, it provided a point of differentiation along a dimension (effort, plus the spirit of an underdog) that resonated with customers.

Multiple Strategic Positions

Arbitrarily insisting that a strategic position should apply to all products or market segments can be self-defeating. Rather, consideration should be given to adapting the position to each context. A shared strategic position that is augmented with additional dimensions in each market will ensure that a consistent message is received, without the unnecessary limitations of a "one size fits all" philosophy.

For example, Honda is associated with youth and racing in Japan while being more family oriented in the United States, but both positions share a focus on quality and motor expertise. Liquid Wit is an Internet firm that provides marketing and communication companies with names, taglines, ad copy, and guerrilla marketing within a short time frame. By tapping freelance talent, ts offering is positioned as contemporary (real time, in the know, and continuously relevant), substantial (a solid organization that will be around), and eccentric (inventive, extraordinary, a wide range of interests). In addition, the position is augmented differently for potential buyers of the service and the members who do the work. To clients, LiquidWit means fresh ideas and leverage (using existing organizational processes as opposed to outsourcing). To members, it offers the stimulation of being challenged by different problems and the rewarding feeling of being paid based on your results rather than your resume.

Capturing the Essence of the Strategic Position

The strategic position, as in the case of Virgin Atlantic Airways, often requires three to six dimensions to be expressed. There are times, however, when a single conceptual phrase can represent the essence of the strategic position and the organization. For example, consider the following essence statements:

- **Cisco**—The network is the solution
- **BMW**—The ultimate driving machine
- **Lexus**—The passionate pursuit of perfection (formerly the relentless pursuit of perfection)
- **Banana Republic**—Casual luxury
- **American Express**—Do more
- **London Business School**—Transforming futures

An essence statement needs to communicate the strategic position both inside and outside the organization. Thus, it is not necessarily a tagline, which is designed to communicate to customers. It can be understated ("It simply works better") or aspirational ("The passionate pursuit of perfection"). In either case, a successful statement should capture the very soul of the organization, inspire those implementing the strategy, resonate with customers, and differentiate the company from its competitors.

DEVELOPING AND SELECTING A STRATEGIC POSITION

How should a business select the position(s) that will drive its strategy, both internally and externally, and create compelling and sustainable competitive advantages? As suggested in Figure 12.1, the process parallels the dimensions that should guide strategic decisions (set forth in Chapter 7). The strategic position should resonate with customers, differentiate the firm from its competitors, and reflect and be supported by the overall business strategy. It therefore follows that a position needs to be supported by analyses of the organization's customers and competitors, as well as its own strengths, initiatives, and strategies.

- **Resonate with the target market.** Ultimately the market dictates success, and thus the strategic position needs to create a point of difference that resonates with customers. Associations that create emotional or self-expressive benefits can add value beyond the usual, practical reasons to buy a product.

Certainly the act of opening a Tiffany's package is more intense than opening a Macy's package, and the wearer of a Tiffany's bracelet will usually feel more special than if the same bracelet had been purchased at a department store.

- **Differentiate from competitors.** Differentiation is often the key to winning. As noted earlier, the Brand Asset Valuator data from Young & Rubicam showed differentiation to be the single most important predictor of brand strength. The same research provided evidence to support the notion that up-and-coming brands lead with differentiation, and fading brands lose differentiation first.

- **Reflect the culture, strategy, and capabilities of the business.** Don't try to be something you are not. Creating a position that is different than what the brand delivers is not only wasteful, but strategically damaging—it will undermine the basic equity of the brand—by making customers skeptical about future claims.

Proof Points and Strategic Imperatives

A business needs to deliver on its promise. This goal involves proof points and often strategic imperatives as well.

Proof points are programs, initiatives, and assets already in place that provide substance to the strategic position, helping to communicate what it means. For L.L. Bean's position around outdoor enthusiasts, proof points include the brand's heritage of outdoor activities, a flagship store geared to the outdoors, and the expertise and professionalism of the customer contact staff. Nordstrom has a customer service position supported by the following proof points:

- An existing reputation for exceptional customer service
- Its policy of dedicating service personnel to individual customers rather than a product area
- A well-known and credible return policy
- A compensation program that makes positive customer experiences a priority
- The quality of the staff and the Nordstrom hiring program
- An empowerment policy that permits innovative responses to customer concerns

A gap between what the brand now delivers, even given the proof points, and the promise implied by the strategic position should lead to strategic imperatives. A *strategic imperative* is an investment in an asset or program that is essential if the promise to customers is to be delivered. What organizational assets and competencies are implied by the strategic position? What investments are needed in order to establish any of those assets and competencies that do not already exist?

If a regional bank aspires to deliver a relationship with customers, for instance, two strategic imperatives might be needed. First, a customer database might need to be created so that each customer contact person has access to all of a given customer's accounts. Second, a program to improve the interpersonal skills of these employees (including both training and measurement) might be needed.

KEY LEARNINGS

- A strategic position specifies how the business is to be perceived relative to its competitors and market by customers, employees, and partners. It should differentiate the company from its competitors, and resonate with customers. It should also drive strategic initiatives and the culture and values of the organization, as well as communication programs.

- Virgin Atlantic Airways is positioned with respect to extraordinary service quality, value for money, being the underdog, and a desire to flaunt the rules.

- IBM's strategic position evolved over the years as its market changed. A particularly defining moment was in the mid-1990s, when Gerstner arrived with the e-business position.

- Schwab has expanded its strategic position over time from being a discount broker to become as asset accumulator, an e-trader, and finally a money manager.

- Among the strategic positions described in the preceding two chapters are being the quality player, the focus business, the value option, the innovator, and the global player.

- Other options include positioning with respect to product category, product attributes, breadth of offering, organizational intangibles, emotional/self-expressive benefits, experience, being contemporary, brand personality, and being distinct from competitors.

- In coping with dynamic environments, trend drivers create new categories, trend responders adapt to emerging subcategories, and trend neglectors ignore them.

- A strategic position needs to reflect the culture and strategy of the business, to differentiate it from its competitors, and to resonate with the target market. Proof points and strategic initiatives are needed to make sure that the brand delivers on the aspirational promise.

FOR DISCUSSION

1. How is Virgin Atlantic Airlines positioned? Are the dimensions, particularly the high quality and high service, inconsistent with its personality? If so, how is that handled? How has the positioning been brought to

life? What are the proof points? Why don't more brands emulate Virgin's brand-building programs?

2. Trace the positions of IBM through the years. How has the firm evolved? How would you advise IBM to implement the new on-demand position? What are the keys to success? Why was the logic behind PCjr? Why did it fail? What was the long-term impact on IBM's image?

3. Charles Schwab has repositioned itself five times. Identify each repositioning. In each case, was the exiting image a liability with respect to the new position?

4. Pick out three brands from a particular industry. How are they positioned? Which is the best in your view? Does that brand's positioning provide any emotional or self-expressive benefits? How would you evaluate each brand's positioning strategy? Hypothesize proof points and strategic imperatives for each brand.

5. How would you adapt to the healthy eating trend if you were McDonald's or Burger King? What are the options? Discuss the problems in implementing each option. How would you deal with those problems?

6. Consider the Joie de Vivre hotel concept. Think of themes stimulated by magazines or movies, and discuss how you would design a hotel around each concept. For each theme, choose five words that reflect that theme.

NOTES

1. The complete brand identity also includes the extended identity (aspirational associations that are less important to customers than the core identity) and the brand essence (a single thought that captures much of the brand identity). In addition, the brand identity model suggests that the brand identity should create a value proposition involving functional, emotional, and/or self-expressive benefits and support a brand customer relationship. For more information, see David A. Aaker, *Building Strong Brands,* New York: The Free Press, 1996, and David A. Aaker and Erich Joachimsthaler, *Brand Leadership,* New York: The Free Press, 1999.

2. Pantea Denoyelle and Jean-Claude Larreche, Virgin Atlantic Airways, Case publication INSEAD, 595-023-1.

3. Louis V. Gerstner, Jr., *Who Says Elephants Can't Dance?* New York: Harper Business, 2002.

4. John Gorham, "Charles Schwab: Version 4.0," *Forbes,* January 8, 2001, pp. 88–96.

Strategic Repositioning: the Quality Option
HOBART CORPORATION

While Hobart Corporation, a manufacturer of equipment for the food service (restaurants and institutions) and retail (grocery and convenience stores) sectors for more than a century, had developed a solid reputation for high quality and extremely reliable products, it wasn't necessarily seen as an industry leader. It had credentials, however. In addition to being the largest firm in terms of sales, it also had broad coverage of the industry and its product categories and a respected service network, with some 200 locations and over 1,700 service vans. The better competitors excelled in a particular product category (refrigeration, for instance) or were well known in one of the industry sectors but lacked Hobart's breadth of offerings.

Hobart was concerned with less expensive competing products that were made overseas. Most customers were continuing to buy Hobart products, but the threat was growing. Further, it was hard to create advertising and trade show material that would break out of the clutter. Breakthrough products that would attract attention were not easily generated.

In response to these concerns, Hobart sought to establish a different customer-facing brand that would be the "thought leader" in the industry, not just the product leader. It wanted to be known for the best quality, "plus more." The driving idea was to offer solutions to everyday issues its customers faced in their businesses—things like finding, training, and retaining good workers; keeping food safe; providing enticing dining experiences; eliminating costs; reducing shrinkage; and enhancing same-store sales growth. The firm systematically marshaled a knowledge base in order to address these problems.

This driving idea of solving everyday concerns led to a powerful brand-building program around the tagline, "Sound Equipment, Sound Advice." A key element was a customer magazine called "Sage: Seasoned Advice for the Food Industry Professional" (also available via the Internet at Sage Online). Sage's in-depth, objective treatment of customer problems and issues made it feel more like a newsstand publication than a corporate promotional tool. At industry trade shows, the Hobart company booth had an "Idea Center" where people could approach industry experts for sound advice about the problems they faced in their businesses. Internally, the leadership message was reinforced at department and company-wide meetings and through internal newsletters.

Hobart also offered useful content about key issues on its website, hobartcorp.com. Visitors could find papers, question-and-answer sessions with industry experts, briefing documents, and other material updated on a weekly basis. The brand lived on the Web and in other places as well, thanks to the strategic placement of Hobart content on many other sites frequented by people in the industry. Select elements of this Web content were converted to printed pieces and disseminated broadly.

Hobart shared more sound advice through speeches at key industry shows, events like the Home Meal Replacement Summit, and articles for trade magazines (for example, "Cold War: Smart Refrigeration Arms Restaurateurs Against Food-Borne Illnesses" in *Hotel Magazine*). The goal of public relations became idea placement, rather than product placement. Hobart also changed its approach to new product releases to emphasize how each product helps the customer deal with key business issues. For instance, rather than emphasize specific features like the recessed nozzles on the Hobart TurboWash, the firm communicated how easy it made the task of scrubbing pots and pans, thereby creating happier restaurant and food service employees.

Print advertising, once the prime brand-building tool, played a lesser but still important role, focusing on key customer issues. For instance, one ad showed a sign at a bathroom sink reading, "Employees Must Wash Hands Before Returning to Work." The text underneath the picture asked, "Need a more comprehensive approach to food safety?" and then described the solutions recommended by Hobart.

FOR DISCUSSION

1. Why do chefs buy Hobart for their kitchens?
2. What was the strategic position before the "Solid Equipment, Sound Advice" program? How did it change?
3. What strategic options did Hobart pursue?
4. The new program soaked up resources, thereby reducing the effort to communicate new product innovations. Was that a wise decision? Which approach is likely to create better support toward a quality position?
5. How could competitors position themselves against Hobart's strategic position? What criteria would be useful in developing this strategic position?

Source: Adapted with the permission of the Free Press, a division of Simon & Schuster Adult Publishing Group from *Brand Leadership*, by David A. Aaker and Erich Joachimsthaler. Copyright © 2000 by David A. Aaker and Erich Joachimsthaler. All rights reserved.

Developing and countering SCAs, and the perils of success
XEROX: THE EARLY DAYS

When Chester Carlson invented xerography in the 1930s, he attempted to market his idea to a host of firms, including Kodak and General Electric. All viewed the rather crude invention as unnecessary in the face of carbon paper and the coated-paper copiers of the day. Finally, in the 1950s, a small firm took the gamble. The result was the Xerox 914, introduced in 1959, which truly revolutionized the copying industry. The first plain-paper copier, it was easy to use and operated at seven copies per minute. The 914 was responsible for the number of copies made in the United States increasing from 20 million to 9.5 billion in only ten years.

The Xerox business strategy through the 1970s involved several pillars. First, the machines were leased at $95 per month, including 2,000 free copies per month to firms who mistakenly felt that their use would never exceed that level. Second, an extensive direct sales and service operation was developed to market the 914 and more expensive models, all of which were relatively complex and needed informed salespeople and responsive service. Third, the R&D focused on the high end of the market, where the best margins were. The low end was virtually ceded to the Japanese, first with coated-paper machines and later with inexpensive plain-paper products. Fourth, international growth was based on a joint venture with Fuji.

The fifth pillar, a major strategic thrust for Xerox in the 1970s, was the "Office of the Future." This concept recognized that the copier was only one instrument of office productivity and business communication, and Xerox wanted to be a leader in the broader playing field. Clearly, the key to the strategy was a computer capability. To fill that gaping hole, Xerox in 1969 purchased Scientific Data Systems, a firm that targeted the scientific community, and changed its name to Xerox Data Systems (XDS). Despite pouring investment into XDS, the firm's products for the business data-processing market never had any success in the office, Xerox's territory. Further, the Xerox organization had too many layers of bureaucracy in too many locations to encourage the integration of computer and copier products. In 1975, after six years of losses, Xerox closed XDS, judging that the computer mainframe market was not part of its core business after all.

Competitors: Savin, Canon, IBM, and Kodak

Savin was a small company obsessed with participating in the copier market and frustrated by the patent chokehold of Xerox. Finally, with the help of an Australian inventor and a consortium of firms from the United States, Germany, and Japan, Savin developed a liquid-toner approach that avoided Xerox patents. Its breakthrough became the Savin 750, manufactured by Ricoh in Japan and introduced in 1975 at $4,999, less than the (then) annual lease price of a Xerox machine. Instead of a direct sales force, Savin sold through dealers who would contact Xerox customers with an attractive alternative when their contracts expired. Dealer service was feasible because the machine was relatively small and reliable; the Savin 750 averaged 17,000 copies between failures. It made twenty copies per minute, the first in less than five seconds, a pace far superior to Xerox efforts at the low end. By 1977, Savin placed more copiers in the United States than Xerox. Meanwhile, Ricoh captured the top market share in Japan, as measured in units.

Canon also avoided the Xerox patents by developing an alternative technology that was licensed to other Japanese firms. Rather than using joint ventures, Canon deliberately decided to market its copiers throughout the world under its own name, even though that would mean relatively slow market penetration in a fast-moving industry. In the long run, keeping control of the brand and operations became a strength. Canon struggled in the United States until 1978, when its NP-80 combined with an aggressive advertising campaign, succeeded in the mid-volume market. By 1979, Canon became a leader among the Japanese copier firms. In 1982, it introduced its Personal Copier, which sold for under $1,000 and had a $65 disposable cartridge. The slower copying speed was unimportant to the target customers, who wanted a small, inexpensive, worry-free machine for the home or office. In 1985, with Savin fading, Canon became the world leader in low-end machines and the second overall company behind Xerox.

IBM attempted through the 1970s to participate in the copier market with a series of products. It was generally unsuccessful, despite its famous name and a large sales force, in part because it was technologically behind and its products were unreliable.

Kodak entered the market in 1975 with its Ektaprint 100, a plain-paper copier that soon became the industry standard for reliability in the mid-volume market. The firm then developed a series of high-end machines that were by many measures the best in the industry. Kodak moved slowly, however, making sure the products were reliable, carefully building a strong service and marketing organization, and avoiding building capacity too quickly. Kodak was still able to move into fourth place in copier sales by 1985 because of its technology, reputation, and resources—and because Xerox was not successful in developing comparable products. A Xerox executive opined that if IBM, with its size and superior marketing skills, had the Kodak machine it would have aggressively captured market share at the middle and high ends, and Xerox would have been severely damaged.

Problems at Xerox

After many years of dramatic success, Xerox faced significant threats in 1980. The firm managed to hold onto its dominance in medium- and high-speed machines, still controlling 60 percent of the market for machines over $40,000 in 1981. Performance at the lower end was much worse, however, and as a result Xerox's share of U.S. copier revenues declined dramatically, from 96 percent in 1970 to 46 percent in 1980. Between 1976 and 1982, Xerox's share of worldwide copier revenues dropped from 82 percent to 41 percent. Why? How did this happen?

One problem was the development of an unwieldy bureaucracy. In 1966, an executive from Ford was brought in to control an undisciplined organization that was expanding at an unmanageable rate. The result was a divisional structure that looked too much like an auto firm, with a painfully complex and slow process of getting a product from design to manufacturing to marketing. Throughout this marathon, the product would be subjected to a system (adopted from NASA) of staged program management, which entailed constant review and criticism.

In part because of this organizational paralysis, Xerox was not able to respond to the Kodak threat at the high end of the market. Xerox had long prided itself on its superior technology, but it actually lagged behind in product development. In the 1970s, it only introduced three completely new machines, only one of which was a success—and that one cost more that $300 million to develop. For Xerox to have grown as it did during this decade was more a tribute to its sales force than to the quality of its products.

One of Xerox's major problems in the 1970s was its focus on making the largest, fastest, and fanciest machines. It paid far less attention to reliability, and therefore it was not prepared to compete with machines made by Kodak. Rather than being lean and trim, it became bloated and failed to locate low-cost outsourcing opportunities. When machines like the Savin 750 were introduced, Xerox could not compete in either price or quality.

Despite its large staff, Xerox was weak in customer and market research, even as it transitioned from being a virtual monopoly to a participant in a competitive market. In particular, Xerox gave no thought to the fact that its customers might be willing to trade speed for price and reliability, or that they might prefer to have more smaller, slower machines rather than a few large, faster ones.

Xerox USA ignored the Japanese threat, allowing those firms to get a foothold at the low end of the market that they exploited by moving up. One rationale was that the early Japanese machines were of low quality and priced too high; the Savin 750 was a shock. A second rationale was that the margins at the higher end were much more attractive than those at the low end. Xerox USA, however, failed to recognize that the Japanese firms would use their advantage further down to climb the market ladder. There was also a strong "not invented here" syndrome. After introducing its 2200 model in Japan in 1973, Fuji Xerox offered to export it to the United States, but Xerox USA refused, unable to believe that a Japanese product would be up to Xerox USA standards. It was not until 1979 that Xerox USA finally accepted a Fuji Xerox machine for the American market.

FOR DISCUSSION

1. Identify and evaluate Xerox's strategy in the 1960s. What entry barriers did Xerox create in that decade?

2. Identify and evaluate the strategies of Savin, Canon, IBM, and Kodak. How did each overcome Xerox's entry barriers? Kodak did not aggressively invest behind its equipment at a time when it held a significant technological edge. Why?

3. Why did Xerox lose position in the 1970s? How could that happen? How could a large successful, admired company be so clueless?

4. What were the strengths and weaknesses of Xerox in the 1980s? What were its strategic imperatives?

5. Xerox had a research think tank in Palo Alto that essentially developed what became the Apple computer. When the Xerox organization was not interested, Steve Jobs and others accessed the concept and started Apple. Why do you think such a blunder happened?

Source: Drawn in part from John Hillkirk and Gary Jacobson, *Xerox: American Samurai,* New York: Macmillan, 1986, pp. 55–57.

GROWTH STRATEGIES

Growth Strategies: Penetration, Product-Market Expansion, Vertical Integration, and the Big Idea

Marketing should focus on market creation, not market sharing
  Regis McKenna

Results are gained by exploiting opportunities, not by solving problems.
—*Peter Drucker*

Only the paranoid survive.
—*Andrew Grove, former CEO, Intel*

Many firms have focused on improving performance by downsizing, restructuring, redeploying assets, and reducing costs. Most have, or will soon, come to the point of diminishing returns; there is a limit to how much you can improve profits with efficiency programs. Only so many people and offices can be eliminated. Further, downsizing can eventually be debilitating to the organization. Muscle needed to create and support growth opportunities is lost along with the fat. Employees and partners will lose motivation when they see that productivity innovations will cost them roles and jobs.

There is thus an increasing realization that the road to improved performance must involve a renewed emphasis on growth. Growth not only provides the potential for enhanced profitability, but it also introduces vitality to an organization by providing challenges and rewards. It is simply more fun and stimulating to create growth than to improve productivity by downsizing. A renewed focus on growth does not mean that operational efficiency is ignored, only that it is not dominant. Both are needed for a successful long-term strategy.

Achieving profitable growth involves some fundamentals of sound strategic management, such as the following:

- Excel at the base business. Growth options may be tempting, but they can also distract from the core business, which has growth potential and ultimately funds growth in other growth directions.

- Withdraw resources from areas that lack future growth prospects, or do not fit strategically with the firm. Resources to fund growth cannot be squandered on futile attempts to turn around problem business areas.

- Develop skills in strategic analysis, especially the ability to detect emerging trends and subcategories.

- Develop options for future offerings. Growth options can be created internally by understanding and applying creative thinking methods. They also can be sourced externally through a network of partners that can supply products (or assets and competencies) that will fuel or enable growth.

- Develop and leverage core assets and competencies. Growth arenas will require these, and success probabilities go up when they are already in place.

Figure 13.1 shows a way to structure alternative growth strategies based, in part, on the product-market matrix introduced in Chapter 2. The first set of growth strategies involves existing product markets. The next two concern product development and market development. The fourth concerns vertical integration strategies, and the fifth, diversification strategies, which will be covered in Chapter 13. The distinctions between some of these categories may be blurred, but the structure is still helpful in generating strategic options.

GROWTH IN EXISTING PRODUCT MARKETS

Existing product markets are often attractive growth avenues. An established firm has a base on which to build and momentum that can be exploited. Furthermore, the firm may have experience, knowledge, and resources (including human resources) already in place. Growth can be achieved in existing product markets by increasing share through capturing sales held by competitors. Alternatively, product usage among existing customers can be increased.

Increasing Market Share

Perhaps the most obvious way to grow is to improve market share. A program based on tactical actions (such as advertising, promotion, or price reductions) can be expensive and unprofitable, however, resulting in transitory share gains from attracting price-sensitive customers. Firms can generate a more permanent share gain by delivering solid value and thereby creating customer satisfaction and loyalty. Developing

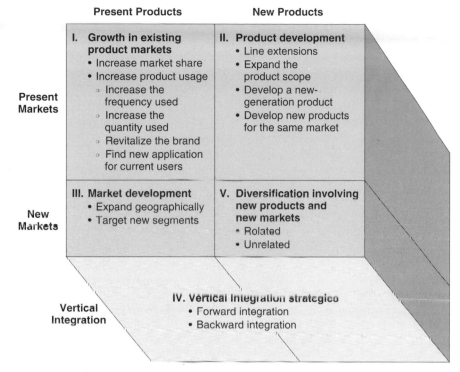

Figure 13.1   Alternative Growth Strategies

the assets and competences that lead to this result, though, often involves more heavy lifting than designing a price promotion.

Another expensive and risky approach is to pursue increased market share by focusing on competitors and their customers. The worst-case scenario of this strategy was played out in the long-distance telephone battles, where people were rewarded for being disloyal. In contrast, increasing the loyalty of existing customers is not only much easier but also more rewarding. When existing customers are made to feel like winners, new customers—and a market share gain—will usually follow.

Increasing Product Usage

Attempts to increase market share will very likely affect competitors directly and therefore precipitate competitor responses. The alternative of attempting to increase usage among current customers is usually less threatening to competitors.

When developing programs to increase usage, it is useful to begin by asking some fundamental questions about the user and the consumption system in which the product is embedded. Why isn't the product or service used more? What are the barriers to increased use? Who are the light users, and can they be influenced to use more? What about the heavy users?

CREATIVE THINKING METHODS

Not all growth strategies are obvious. In fact, the obvious ones are likely to be marginal in terms of likely success and impact, so it is useful to look for breakthrough ideas. Methods and concepts of creative thinking, as described in books by Edward de Bono and others, can help in this process. Among the guidelines suggested most often are the following:

- Pursue creative thinking in groups, as multiple perspectives and backgrounds can stimulate useful alternatives.
- Begin with warm-up exercises that break down inhibitions. To make whimsy acceptable, for example, ask individuals to identify what animal expresses their personality and to imitate the sound made by that animal. To stretch minds, ask someone to start a story based on two random words (e.g., *blue* and *sail*), then ask the group to create a position for a brand based on that story.[1]
- Focus on a particular task, such as how to exploit an asset (a brand name, for example), or a competence (such as the ability to design colorful plastic items).
- Develop options without judging them. Discipline in avoiding evaluation while generating alternatives is a key to creative thinking.
- Engage in lateral thinking to change the perspective of the problem. Challenge an obvious assumption ("What if we had two telephones in a booth?"), or simply pick a random word or object (such as *tiger,* or the Rockefeller Center) to stimulate a new line of thought.
- Evaluate the options based on potential impact without regard to how feasible they are.
- Engage in a second stage of creative thinking aimed at improving the success chances of an attractive option—possibly one with high potential impact that seems too expensive or too difficult to implement.
- Evaluate the final choices not just rationally ("What do the facts say?") but emotionally ("What does your gut say?").
- Create an action plan to go forward.

Heavy users are usually the most fruitful target. It is often easier to get a holder of two season football tickets to buy four or six than it is to get an occasional attendee of games to buy two. It is helpful to look at the extra-heavy user subsegment—special treatment might solidify and expand usage by a substantial amount. Consider Schwab's Gold Signature Services, the special dinner parties and courier service offered by Chase Manhattan to its biggest accounts, or the first-class treatment provided to high rollers by Las Vegas casinos.

Light users should not be ignored, because there may be a way to unlock their potential. Who are the light users and why don't they use more? Hillside Coffee noted that people in their early twenties were light coffee users. Exploiting a sweet tooth in this segment, the company successfully introduced flavored coffees, such as vanilla nut and Swiss chocolate almond.

Greater usage can be precipitated in two ways, by increasing either the frequency of use or the quantity used. In either case, there are several approaches that can be effective as Figure 13.2 suggests.

Provide Reminder Communications

For some use contexts, awareness, or recall of a brand, is the driving force. People who know about a brand and its use may not think to use it on particular occasions without reminders.

Reminder communication may be necessary. An e-mail program to remind Red Envelope customers about an upcoming birthday may ensure that they buy a present. Several brands, including Jell-O, have conducted advertising campaigns aimed at getting their product out of the cupboard and onto the table. It is not enough for people to have recipes if they never get around to using them.

Routine maintenance functions such as dental checkups or car lubrication are easily forgotten and reminders can make a difference. Some car dealers provide free oil changes in order to provide a strong link to their customers who will be accessing their maintenance and repair business.

Position for Regular or Frequent Use

Provide a reason for more frequent use. On Web sites, what works is to have information that is frequently updated. People go to MyYahoo to see the latest headlines or learn how their stocks are doing, as often as every few minutes when important things are happening. Other incentives might include a new cartoon each day at a teen Web site, or a best-practices bulletin board at a brand consulting site.

The image of a product can change from that of occasional to frequent usage by a repositioning campaign. For example, the advertising campaigns for Clinique's "twice-a-day" moisturizer and "three glasses of milk per day" both represent efforts to change the perception of the products involved. The use of programs such as the Book-of-the-Month Club, CD clubs, DVD clubs, and flower-of-the-month or fruit-of-the-month delivery can turn infrequent purchasers into once-a-monthers.

Make the Use Easier

Asking why customers do not use a product or service more often can lead to approaches that make the product easier to use. For example, a Dixie-cup or

Strategy	Examples
Provide reminder communications	Send e-mail about upcoming birthday
Position for frequent use	Checking stocks on Yahoo!
Position for regular use	Flossing after meals
Make use easier	Microwaveable containers
Provide incentives	Frequent-flyer miles
Reduce undesirable consequences	Gentle shampoo for frequent use
Revitalize the brand	New VW Beetle
Find new applications	Jell-O salads

Figure 13.2   Increasing Usage in Existing Product Markets

paper-towel dispenser encourages use by reducing the usage effort. Packages that can be placed directly in a microwave make usage more convenient. A reservation service can help those who must select a hotel or similar service. Frozen waffles and Stove Top stuffing are examples of product modifications that increased consumption by making usage more convenient.

Provide Incentives

Incentives can be provided to increase consumption frequency. Promotions such as double mileage trips offered by airlines with frequent-flyer plans can increase usage. A fast-food restaurant might offer a large drink at a discounted price if it is purchased with a meal. A challenge is to structure the incentive so that usage is increased without creating a vehicle for debilitating price competition. Price incentives, such as two for the price of one, can be effective, but they also may stimulate price retaliation.

Reduce Undesirable Consequences of Frequent Use

Sometimes there are good reasons why a customer is inhibited from using a product more frequently. If such reasons can be addressed, usage may increase. For example, some people might believe that frequent hair washing may not be healthy. A product that is designed to be gentle enough for daily use might alleviate this worry and thereby stimulate increased usage. A low-calorie, low-sodium, or low-fat version of a food product may sharply increase the market. The brand that becomes associated with a product change will be in the best position to capitalize on the increased market.

Revitalize the Brand

Especially for a leading brand, it is easy to become stale over time. Customers may perceive it to be of excellent quality, but something their parents (or worse, grandparents) would buy. The challenge is to revitalize the brand, to introduce some energy, vitality, and buzz into it. In Chapter 15, approaches to revitalization involving new products, new markets, and new applications are discussed. However, revitalization can occur often by simply acting young again within the same product-market-application space.

Abercrombie and Fitch was a retailer where an English gentleman might go to get his hunting clothes, until one of the most remarkable transformations in retail history made it a trendy place for young adults to shop. The stores (including the walls) were entirely redesigned, young salespeople were employed, trendy clothes were displayed in an interesting way, and energetic contemporary music set a new, vibrant tone. London's once-stuffy Selfridge's broke out of a stagnant sales pattern by a similar infusion of energy that involved fashion shows and celebrity visits.

The best firms continuously inject excitement and news into their operations with specific programs. Disneyland, for example, adds and updates rides so often that it is worth going twice a year just to see what is new. Virgin has a continuous flow of publicity stunts that keep customers wondering what they will do next.

New Applications for Existing Product Users

The detection and exploitation of a new functional use for a brand can rejuvenate a business that has been considered a has-been for years. A classic example is Jell-O, which began strictly as a dessert product but found major sources of new sales in applications such as Jell-O salads. Another classic story is that of Arm & Hammer baking soda, which saw annual sales grow tenfold by persuading people to use its product as a refrigerator deodorizer. An initial 14-month advertising campaign boosted the use of Arm & Hammer as a deodorizer from 1 to 57 percent. The brand subsequently was extended into other deodorizer products, dentifrices, and laundry detergent. A chemical process used in oil fields to separate waste from oil found a new application when it was applied to water plants to eliminate unwanted oil.

New uses can best be identified by conducting market research to determine exactly how customers use a brand. From the set of uses that emerge, several can be selected to pursue. For example, users of external analgesics were asked to keep a diary of their uses.[2] A surprising finding was that about one-third of BenGay's usage and more than one half of its volume was for arthritis relief instead of muscle aches. A separate marketing strategy was developed for this use, and the brand caught a wave of growth.

Another tactic is to look at the applications of competing products. The widespread use of raisins prompted Ocean Spray to create dried cranberries, which can be found in cookies and in cereal such as Muesli with a "made with real Ocean Spray cranberries" seal on the package. They are also being sold as a snack food called Ocean Spray Craisins.

Sometimes a large payoff will result for a firm that can provide applications not currently in general use. Thus, surveys of current applications may be inadequate. Firms such as General Mills have sponsored recipe contests, one objective of which has been to create new uses for a product by discovering a new "recipe classic." For a product, such as stick-on labels, that can be used in many ways, it might be worthwhile to conduct formal brainstorming sessions or other creative exercises.

PRODUCT DEVELOPMENT FOR THE EXISTING MARKET

As reflected in Figure 13.1, product development can occur in a variety of ways, and it is helpful to distinguish among them. They include the addition of product features, the development of new-generation products, and the development of new products for an existing market.

Line Extensions

One type of product development is the addition of features to a firm's current product. The right feature can dramatically change the competitive dynamics. For instance, General Mills' Yoplait overtook longtime category leader Dannon with Go-Gurt, the yogurt in a tube that kids slurp up. This "lose the spoon" yogurt redefined the category for this important segment. To maintain balance, Yoplait followed this success with the adult flavors of Yoplait Expressé. An automobile firm could add a transmission or sun-roof option that would improve its penetration of an existing market. For some candy firms, the creation of novel packages provides a key to sales. Adding product features involves almost total commonality of marketing, operations, and management. Because additional features represent such visible growth opportunities and are accomplished relatively easily, they can be very enticing. They still absorb resources, however, and should be resisted if the prospective ROI is unsatisfactory.

Product modifications can also occur when high-tech or industrial firms are asked by a customer to produce a special-purpose version of a product. Such development work can lead to substantial sales and even to new products, but the attraction of a visible customer need can be overly enticing. If this type of activity is permitted to preempt more ambitious development programs, the long-term health of an organization can suffer.

Developing New-Generation Products

Growth can also be obtained in an existing market by creating new-generation products. FedEx, for example, is under attack from companies that are developing supply chain management systems designed to eliminate much of the unpredictability in their process (and thus the need for overnight shipments). In response, FedEx has bought Kinko's and developed a management system that can provide a company with information exchanges that supplant a company's inefficient stream of faxes and phone calls. The concept is to make FedEx the system rather than a component of it.

Yamaha revitalized a declining piano market by developing the Disklavier, whose electronic control system allowed a performance to be recorded and stored in memory, thus creating a modern version of the old player piano. The technology could be used by a student, a professional player, or a composer, in addition to those who wanted the feeling of having a great pianist play in their home.

While the outsider has nothing to lose and much to gain from pursuing an innovation that will disrupt the marketplace, the established market participant faces the "incumbent's curse," two forces that inhibit innovation. First, even if the new technology is successful, often the best result is that a significant investment will be required just to maintain the same level of sales and profits. And the new technology could present problems that add time and expense and reduce customer acceptance—hardly an attractive incentive. Second, the existing market participants need to focus on improving costs, quality, and service for the existing offering, which leaves little time and effort to explore a totally new technology.

Although new technologies, such as satellite TV channels, can disrupt an established business, they can also create profitable growth opportunities. Existing market participants should be aware of their biases against detecting and exploiting such opportunities. If the biases are visible, the chances that they will inhibit the organization from participating in a new technology will be reduced.

Expand the Product Scope

Existing customers might be served further by broadening the use context. Thus, instead of being in the orange juice business, a firm might choose to be in the breakfast business. Instead of selling only basketballs, it might consider making baskets and courts. GE's Jack Welch has said that dominant companies in slow-growing businesses in particular should redefine their markets, looking for a broader scope that will have more opportunities.

The manager and originator of Microsoft Office, Jeffrey Raikes, was inspired by Welch's concept. As a result, he decided to develop products not just for office workers but for anyone who uses information, including pilots, nurses, factory workers, and truck drivers.[3] Toward that end, Microsoft has researched customer needs and tested innovations in prototypical workplaces of the future.

Slywotsky and Wise make a similar suggestion in their book How to Grow When Markets Don't.[4] They recommend identifying and serving the customer needs that emanate from the use of existing products. Cardinal Health, for example, moved beyond distributing drugs to pharmacies to managing the dispensing of drugs and related record-keeping for hospitals, as well as creating medical-supply kits for surgeons. Clarke American Checks went from check printing to managing customer relations for banks, including running call centers and helping banks come up with incentives to increase customer retention. John Deere, the equipment manufacturer, decided to offer a one-stop shop for landscaping.

New Products for Existing Markets

A classic growth pattern is to exploit a marketing or distribution strength by adding compatible products that share customers with but are different from existing products. Synergy is usually obtained at least in part by the commonality in distribution, marketing, and brand-name recognition and identity. Lenox, a maker of fine china, exploited its traditional, high-quality image and its distribution system by expanding into the areas of jewelry and giftware. H&R Block added legal services to its chain of income tax services, hoping to gain synergy by sharing office space and operations. A ski boot manufacturer added skis and then ski clothing.

Leveraging brand equity into other product categories is a route to product extension that will be explored in Chapter 14. Examples of this would include Duracell's Durabeam flashlights, Gerber baby clothes, Starbucks ice cream, Pierre Cardin wallets, Benihana frozen entrées, Oracle Discoverer, and Arm & Hammer oven cleaner, which capitalizes on Arm & Hammer's 97 percent name recognition. Each has strong name identification and associations that can drive success in the new category. Managers must make sure that the extension fits the brand, that it provides helpful associations, and that it does not damage or dilute associations of the brand.

A rationale for product additions is to achieve synergies. Sometimes, however, synergies are simply illusory. A packaged food firm had little in common with a fast-food restaurant chain that it acquired, even though both involved food. More often, synergy exists, but its benefit is modest and does not overcome the costs and problems associated with the new area. The effort to combine United Airlines, Westin Hotel and Resorts, and Hertz into one organization was aborted, in part because the potential synergies, mostly involving a common reservation system and cross-selling, had substantial implementation problems and were not valued by the stock market.

There is significant risk to any new product venture, especially with respect to customer acceptance. Clairol failed with Small Miracle hair conditioner, which could be used through several shampoos, in part because customers could not be convinced that the product would not build up on their hair if it were not washed off with each use. Even the use of an established brand cannot guarantee success. The concept of a colorless cola, Crystal Pepsi, did not achieve acceptance. Rice-a-Roni's Savory Classics did not fit the consumer's notion of the role of Rice-a-Roni in the kitchen. The Arm & Hammer name also spawned two failures, a spray underarm deodorant, for which the Arm & Hammer name may have had the wrong connotations, and a spray disinfectant.

Product-line expansion will be based on many factors, of course, but will often involve consideration of the following questions:

- *Will customers benefit from a systems capability or service convenience made possible by a broad product line?* The inclusion of a software line and printers with a line of computers provides the potential of offering a more complete system. However, customers may want not only systems design but also systems support.

- *Do potential manufacturing, marketing, or distribution cost efficiencies exist from an expanded product line?* To the extent that there are shared costs, the experience and scale effects on costs will be enhanced. The question is whether, even with this cost advantage, the proposed product-line expansion will have a satisfactory ROI. So when Schwinn went into exercise bicycles, for example, it could draw upon product design, manufacturing, and distribution efficiencies. Avon leveraged its home sales organization by offering clothing and nutritional supplements and vitamins as well as cosmetics and jewelry.

- *Can assets or competencies be applied to a product-line expansion?* The most prominent asset is often the brand name itself. The Schwinn brand name in bicycles has given its Johnny G. Spinner bike an edge with its endorsement. In the next chapter, brand extensions will be treated in more detail. Do not automatically assume, though, that assets and competences can work in new contexts. The marketing and distribution competences of Gatorade, for instance, are not guaranteed to work with Snapple—in fact, trying to force the Gatorade system onto Snapple was one reason (among several) that the Snapple acquisition by Gatorade's parent firm, Quaker, was a failure.

- *Does a firm have the needed competencies and resources in R&D, manufacturing, and marketing to add the various products proposed?* Sometimes an apparently simple line extension, such as adding wood stains to a line of paints, can involve a totally new manufacturing effort, raw materials technology, or marketing effort and thus may not fit the capabilities of the firm.

MARKET DEVELOPMENT USING EXISTING PRODUCTS

A logical avenue of growth is to develop new markets by duplicating the business operation, perhaps with minor adaptive changes. With market expansion, the same expertise and technology and sometimes even the same plant and operations facility can be used. Thus, there is potential for synergy and resulting reductions in investment and operating costs. Of course, market development is based on the premise that the business is operating successfully. There is no point in exporting failure or mediocrity.

Expanding Geographically

Geographic expansion may involve changing from a regional operation to a national operation, moving into another region, or expanding to another country. KFC, McDonald's, GE, IBM, and Visa have successfully exported their operations to other countries. Most of these companies and many others are counting on countries such as China, India, and Russia to fuel much of their growth in the coming decades. They realize that success will involve significant investment in logistics, distribution infrastructures, and organization building and adaptation.

Moving from local to regional to national is another option. Samuel Adams and other microbreweries have generated growth by geographic expansion. Often, however, this expansion is best implemented by connecting, through an alliance or merger, to a partner that already has the capability to market more broadly.

Expanding into New Market Segments

A firm can also grow by reaching into new market segments. There are a variety of ways to define target segments and therefore growth directions:

- *Usage.* The nonuser can be an attractive target. An audio electronics firm could target those who don't own an audio system.

- *Distribution channel.* A firm can reach new segments by opening up a second or third channel of distribution. A retail sporting goods store could market to schools via a direct sales force. A direct marketer such as Avon could introduce its products into department stores under another brand name.

- *Age.* Johnson & Johnson's baby shampoo was languishing until the company looked toward adults who wash their hair frequently.

- *Attribute preference.* An instrumentation firm might extend its line to include more precise equipment to serve a segment that requires greater accuracy.

- *Application-defined market.* American Airlines offered a door-to-door, same-day package delivery service in conjunction with a shipping service, NextJet. A customer places an order on a Web site, a courier picks it up, and delivers it to an American flight, and another courier then delivers it to the recipient.

A key to detecting new markets is to consider a wide variety of segmentation variables. Sometimes looking at markets in a different way will uncover a useful segment. It is especially helpful to identify segments that are not being served well, such as the women's calculator market or the fashion needs of older people. In general, segments should be sought for which the brand can provide value. Entering a new market without providing any incremental customer value is very risky.

Evaluating Market Expansion Alternatives

Although synergy can potentially be high, several other considerations are involved in a market expansion:

- *Is the market attractive?* Will customers value the product or service? Does it really offer meaningful and distinctive value? How formidable and committed are competitors? Can their assets and competencies be neutralized by the right strategy? Are market and environmental trends supportive?

- *Do the resources and will exist to make the necessary commitment in the face of uncertainties?* Does the move make strategic sense? Compaq bailed out of the printer business despite having a superior product because the prospects of catching HP and the other leaders were too formidable. The commitment was lacking.

- *Can the business be adapted to the new market?* To the extent that conditions differ, is there a convincing plan to adapt the business? For example, Rheingold Brewery, a New York company, failed in an attempt to enter the California market, in part because it tried to use a distribution channel unsuitable for California and in part because a promotion that was effective in New York fell flat in California.

- *Can the assets and competencies that are at the heart of business success be transferred into the new business environment?* Procter & Gamble was unable to capitalize on its marketing and distribution assets in efforts to market soft drinks, and it struggled in cosmetics and fragrances as well until it acquired brands with established distribution.

The experience of FedEx when it attempted to duplicate its concept in Europe illustrates the last two issues.[5] Setting up a hub-and-spoke system in Europe was inhibited by regulatory roadblocks at every turn. Attempts to short-circuit regulations by acquiring firms with related abilities resulted in something of a hodgepodge—FedEx now owns a barge company, for example. The firm also lacked a first-mover advantage in Europe because DHL and others had employed the FedEx concept years earlier. A reliance on the English language and a decision to impose a pickup deadline of five o'clock in Spain (where people work until eight) caused additional implementation problems.

VERTICAL INTEGRATION STRATEGIES

Vertical integration represents another potential growth direction. Forward integration occurs when a firm moves downstream with respect to product flow, such as a manufacturer buying a retail chain. Backward integration is moving upstream such as when a manufacturer invests in a raw material source. A good way to understand when vertical integration should be considered and how it should be evaluated is to look at the possible benefits and costs of a vertical integration strategy. Vertical integration potentially provides:

- Access to supply or demand
- Control of the quality of the product or service
- Entry into an attractive business area

But introduces:

- The risks of managing a very different business
- A reduction in strategy flexibility

Access to Supply or Demand

Access to Supply

In some contexts, a key success factor is access to a supply of raw material, a part, or another input factor; backward integration can reduce the availability risk. A forest products firm may thus acquire timberland. Hewlett-Packard lost a crucial six months getting a workstation to the market when a key supplier of chips was six months late, whereas IBM, with internal sources, did not have that problem. Sometimes suppliers are not capable of or interested in providing the needed component. For example, when refrigerated boxcars and warehouses were first needed by meat packers, they had to develop them because there was no source.

Access to Demand

Similarly, forward integration could be motivated by a concern about product outlets. Thus, an insurance firm could buy regional insurance agencies to provide sales outlets. A motivation to gain access to major buyers was behind the large automakers' investment in car rental firms—Ford invested in Hertz and Budget, General Motors in Avis and National, and Chrysler in Thrifty and Snappy. These vertical relationships provide not only sales, but also important exposure of new models to prospective customers.

Control of the Product System

It may become necessary to integrate vertically in order to gain sufficient control over a product or service to maintain the integrity of a differentiation strategy. For example, a vital component may need to be made with precision, and outside contractors may be unable to provide it or unwilling to make an investment in the specialized assets required. Vertical integration may be the only way to ensure that the desired quality is achieved.

Samsung has made a dramatic transformation since the mid-1990s. Once a manufacturer of low-priced consumer electronic equipment with adequate quality distributed through value retailers, the Korean firm now sells its high-priced, top-quality wares through premium channels. One reason behind this turnaround was Samsung's emergence as a product leader in mobile phones and flat-screen television sets and computer monitors. The company attributes its ability to make these product advances—and get the resulting buzz—to its backward integration into microprocessors and memory chips. By inventing, manufacturing, and owning its advances, Samsung can get (and stay) ahead of competition that must rely on an outside supplier.

Sony has lived with the memory of its superior Beta format being overrun by the consortium of VHS firms. The final nail was hammered in when the movie studios stopped producing films in the Beta format. Sony has since become a one-stop shop for entertainment so that in the future it can guarantee a supply of software for its hardware products. By buying Columbia Pictures, Tri-Star Pictures, Columbia Pictures Television, and CBS Records, Sony has substantial control over supplier decisions.

Entry into a Profitable Business Area

Many manufacturers have struggled because of margin pressures. Those that have prospered have often vertically integrated downward to the customer, because that is where the money is. From automobiles to railroad equipment to computers, the size of the installed base is much larger than the new unit sales. In corporate computing, for example, the average company specs only about one-fifth of its annual personal-computer budget on buying boxes—the rest goes to technical support. Four different downstream business models can be considered:

Comprehensive Services

Suites of services are packaged along with the product. Boeing combines financing, local parts supply, ground maintenance, logistics management, and pilot training into a thriving service business. IBM and GE have seen much of their growth and profits come from services that augment their products. In many cases, the product is the tail that wags the dog.

Distributor/Retailer

When a distributor or retailer is used they will command a substantial margin. By going direct to customers as Avon and Dell do with a direct model and Apple and Krispy Kreme do with their retail sites, the potential for a profitable business may exist.

Embedded Services

With digital technology, services that once were external to the product can be built in. John Deere's GreenStart machinery has computer-enhanced yield management and precision farming capability. Stryker makes surgical equipment that can be controlled through voice recognition. Each of these augmentations extends the product's value.

Integrated Solutions

Nokia illustrates how a firm can combine products and services into a seamless offering that addresses a customer need. When it recognized that telephone carriers (its customer) were struggling with the conversion from analog to digital and a massive growth in demand, Nokia broke into a leadership position by creating an array of cellular products, including handsets, transmission equipment, and switches. In addition to deploying these products with a range of services, the company helped the carriers plan and manage their networks.

Two sets of questions will help guide any downstream option. First, can it be successfully implemented by your organization? Can the needed assets and competencies be developed? Second, is the opportunity attractive in terms of profitability? Will the demand support the business? Will the competitive landscape allow health margins?

Risks of Managing a Different Business

Vertical integration involves adding an operation whose required organizational assets and competences may differ markedly from those of the firm's other business areas. Dell, for example, would require a very different type of organization if it attempted to manufacture disk drives or microprocessors, than the one it has developed for selling finished computers. The difference between managing packaged goods like Pepsi or Frito-Lay chips and restaurants such as KFC, Taco Bell, and Pizza Hut helped PepsiCo decide to get out of the restaurant business. Another influence on the decision was the problem with being a competitor to large customers (Round Table Pizza was reluctant to offer Pepsi in its locations, given that PepsiCo owned its rival Pizza Hut). And running an integrated organization introduces added complexities.

Reduction in Strategic Flexibility

The increased commitment to a business and its market reflected by vertical integration reduces strategic flexibility. If that market is healthy, then integration may enhance products. On the other hand, if the market turns down, integration may cause a larger drop in profits. Integration also raises exit barriers. If the business becomes weak, the additional investment and commitment created by integration will inhibit consideration of an exit alternative. Furthermore, if one operation becomes dependent on the other, an exit strategy may be inhibited.

Alternatives to Integration

Several alternatives to integration exist, such as long-term contracts, exclusive dealing agreements, asset ownership, joint ventures, strategic alliances, technology licenses, and franchising. For example, a winery can have a long-term contract with vineyards that protects both. Exclusive dealing agreements that link a manufacturer and a retail chain or distributor can provide the needed information transfer, strategy coordination, and transaction and distribution efficiency. Automobile firms that own the special tooling used by their suppliers provide a technological and financial link that helps insure reliable supply. Most of these alternatives involve difficulties, especially as circumstances and power relationships change over time, but they also provide many of the advantages of integration with fewer disadvantages. They should usually be considered before commitments to integration are pursued.

Although net profit as a percent of sales does increase with vertical integration, the return on investment (ROI) may not because of the increase in investment. One study of 1,650 businesses suggested that the most profitable businesses are at the extremes of the vertical integration spectrum.[6] A V-shaped relationship between vertical integration and profitability was found. Thus, manufacturers should be wary of taking a middle course. The business that puts together systems and farms out component production will tend to minimize investment, seek out low prices, and have maximum flexibility. The heavily integrated firm will maximize the benefits of vertical integration.

THE BIG IDEA

The foregoing has introduced five paths to growth. Each path comprises a spectrum of strategies that range from the incremental to really big ideas, as Figure 13.3 suggests.

Although incremental growth strategies can and should be the foundation for growth, some significant growth initiatives and big ideas ought to be on the table as well. If no big ideas are ever considered, there is virtually no chance to create breakthrough strategy—so expand your horizon and look for the Disneyland and Niketown type of ideas.

Creativity and innovation comes from a diversity of ideas and idea sources. Get multiple sources and perspectives involved, then test the best ideas. Since it is hard to predict what will be a significant growth initiative or a big idea, don't be afraid to take five lesser ideas and see which one surprises you.

Strategy as Revolution

Gary Hamel has put forward the thesis that the real payoff results from development of revolutionary strategies that break out of industry norms or operations. Dell Computer, for example, sold computers by mail when that was just a

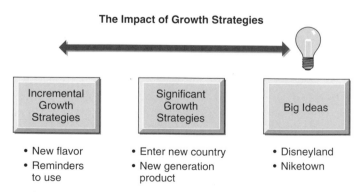

Figure 13.3 The Impact of Growth Strategies

hypothetical idea. Southwest Airlines offered point-to-point service without seat assignments, meals, or other amenities when a hub-and-spoke system was regarded as a key success factor in the industry. Federal Express pioneered a completely different way to deliver packages. Revolutionary strategies, when successful, can lead to strategic advantage and avoid the difficult task of improving on the same strategies used by competitors.

How can revolutionary strategies be developed, especially within an organization committed to the accepted ways of operation? The answer involves some creative thinking. Use the guidelines suggested on page 246. During external and internal analysis look for revolutionary ideas. Hamel suggests some additional guidelines.[7]

- List the fundamental beliefs that incumbents in your industry share. What new opportunities would exist if one or more of these were relaxed? What if hotels operated similarly to rental-car agencies, selling rooms on a 24-hour basis instead of using a rigid check-in system?
- Look at the functional benefits received by the customer and consider different ways of supplying those benefits.
- Consider how assets or competencies could be exploited in different settings or in different ways.
- Look at the discontinuities in the industry and let them lead to unconventional strategy options.
- Consider offering a scaled-down version of the product or service, such as bed-and-breakfast inns or microbreweries. Or, think about an expanded version, from local to global, perhaps.
- Push the boundaries of universality. For example, make disposable cameras that children can use.
- Add excitement or fun to the product or service, thereby redefining the offering. For example, a supermarket added a children's playland, a minor league baseball team added a jazz band and gourmet picnic food, and Trader Joe's added fashion to food retailing.
- The most fruitful growth area is often to increase product usage within the existing product market by increasing the frequency or quantity used, by finding new applications or revitalizing the brand.

KEY LEARNINGS

- The most fruitful growth area is often to increase product usage within the existing product market, where assets and competences are in place and only need to be leveraged. Growth within a product market can involve adding product features, new-generation products, expansion of the product scope, or new products.

- Developing new products, a second route to growth, can involve line extensions, expanded product scope, or new generation products.

- A third growth route, market development, involves expanding the market either geographically or by targeting new market segments.

- A key consideration of any growth strategy is how to achieve synergy by leveraging current assets and competences.

- Vertical integration, another growth direction, can provide access to supply or demand, control of the quality of the product or service, and entry into an attractive business area. It also, however, introduces the risks of managing a very different business and reducing strategy flexibility.

- Outsourcing rather than vertical integration makes it easier to change strategic direction in response to threats and pressures for the market.

- Growth can be achieved with incremental growth strategies, significant growth initiatives, or big ideas. All businesses should strive to uncover and implement big ideas, because they are usually the source of breakthrough strategies.

FOR DISCUSSION

1. Pick an industry and a product or service. Engage in a creative thinking process (as outlined in the insert in the chapter) to generate an improved offering. Do the same to create an entirely new offering that uses one or more of the assets and competencies of the firm.

2. Pick a firm and business and use the eight suggestions proposed by Gary Hamel to come up with a big idea.

3. How would you increase the usage of products if you were the manager of:
   a. Doritos
   b. Charles Schwab
   c. Gap

4. Starbucks Coffee is now being offered by United Airlines in flight service and Starbucks Ice Cream is distributed by Dreyer's. Evaluate these two growth initiatives. In each case, what is the asset or competency that is being leveraged? Was it as wise decision?

5. Recall the Dell case in Chapter 10. Dell is planning to expand its service business, as it has higher margins and is a growth area. What must Dell do to be successful in this arena? What suggestions would you make as to the business model that will allow Dell to compete with HP and IBM?

NOTES

1. Suggestions with respect to this second bullet, as well as the seventh bullet following, come from Alexander Biel, an active and successful creative thinking innovator and facilitator.

2. Linden A. Davis, Jr., "Market Positioning Considerations," *Product-Line Strategies*, New York: The Conference Board, 1991, pp. 37–39.

3. Jay Greene, "Beyond the Office," *Business Week*, September 16, 2002, pp. 54–56.

4. Adrian Slywotsky and Richard Wise, *How to Grow When Markets Don't*, New York: Warner Business Books, 2003.

5. Daniel Pearl, "Federal Express Finds Its Pioneering Formula Falls Flat Overseas," *Wall Street Journal*, April 15, 1991, pp. A1–A6.

6. Robert D. Buzzell, "Is Vertical Integration Profitable?" *Harvard Business Review*, January–February 1983, pp. 92–102.

7. Gary Hamel, "Strategy As Revolution" *Harvard Business Review*, July–August 1996, pp. 69–81.

CHAPTER FOURTEEN

Diversification

'Tis the part of a wiseman to keep himself today for tomorrow, and not venture all his eggs in one basket.
—*Miguel de Cervantes*

Put all your eggs in one basket and—WATCH THAT BASKET.
—*Mark Twain*

A tobacco firm buys a frozen-food company, a cola firm enters the wine business, a chemical company goes into swimming pool supplies, or an aerospace firm starts making automobile parts. Such diversification moves represent both the opportunity for growth and revitalization and the substantial risk of operating an unfamiliar business in a new context.

Diversification is the strategy of entering product markets different from those in which a firm is currently engaged. Two growth strategies discussed in Chapter 13, product expansion and market expansion, usually involve entry into new product markets, thus representing diversification. However, diversification can also involve both new products and new markets. A diversification strategy can be implemented by either an acquisition (or merger) or a new business venture.

It is helpful to categorize diversification as related and unrelated. In a related diversification, the new business area has meaningful commonalities with the core business. Meaningful commonalities provide the potential to generate economies of scale or synergies based on an exchange of assets or competencies. The resulting combined business should be able to achieve improved ROI because of increased revenues, decreased costs, or reduced investment. As noted in Chapter 8, meaningful commonalities can involve sharing of:

- Customers and sometimes customer applications (potentially creating a systems solution)

- A sales force or channel of distribution
- A brand name and its image
- Facilities used for manufacturing, offices, or warehousing
- R&D efforts
- Staff and operating systems
- Marketing and marketing research

The product expansion growth strategy normally involves the same market and distribution system, so it would qualify as a related diversification. The market expansion growth strategy is usually also a related diversification because it applies the same production technology and often involves a similar market and distribution system. Vertical integration is usually an unrelated diversification, however, because it typically lacks an area of commonality.

An important issue to consider in any diversification decision is whether, in fact, there is a real and meaningful area of commonality that will affect the ultimate ROI. An unrelated diversification (a diversification lacking meaningful commonalities) may still be justifiable, but a different rationale would be needed. Thus, the concept of related diversification is more than an issue of definition. In the following section we consider the rationale and risks of related diversification and then those of unrelated diversification.

RELATED DIVERSIFICATION

Exporting or Exchanging Assets and Competencies

Related diversification provides the potential to attain synergies by sharing assets or competencies across businesses (see Figure 14.1). When related diversification is accomplished by internal expansion, the goal is to export assets or competencies. When acquisition of or merger with another business is the vehicle, the goal is to combine two sets of complementary assets and competencies, with each party contributing what the other lacks. In either case, a business exploring related diversification should consider three steps.

The first step is to inventory assets and competencies in order to identify real strengths that are exportable to another business area. Recall the discussion in Chapter 4 on identifying assets and competencies. Among exportable assets and competencies are brand names, marketing skills, sales and distribution capacity, manufacturing skills, and R&D capabilities.

Figure 14.1   Leveraging Assets and Competencies

The second step toward related diversification is to find a business area where the assets and competencies can be applied to generate an advantage. A line of greeting cards sold through drugstores might be able to use the distribution assets and competencies of an over-the-counter drug marketer.

One fruitful exercise is to examine each asset for excess capacity. Are some assets underutilized? A tax firm that considered this question took advantage of excess office space to offer legal services. A supermarket chain with obsolete sites went into the discount liquor business. A cookie plant began making muffins. The advent of multi-screen cinemas exploited the excess capacity of the staff. If a diversification can use excess capacity, a substantial, sustainable cost advantage could result.

An example of synergy based, in part, on exploiting excess capacity is the Los Angeles sports empire of Jerry Buss. Buss owns four sports teams, including the Lakers basketball team and the Kings hockey team, all of which play in his 17,500-seat Forum and appear on his Prime Ticket regional cable channel, which reaches nearly 1.6 million homes. The teams provide a product for the Forum and the cable channel, both of which have excess capacity. Furthermore, the cable channel helps generate interest in the teams and other Forum events, such as rock concerts.

Finally, implementation problems need to be addressed. Assets and competencies may require adaptations when applied to a different business. Further, new capabilities may have to be found or developed. When acquisitions are involved, two organizations with different systems, people, and cultures will have to be merged. Many efforts at achieving synergy falter because of implementation difficulties.

Brand Name

One common exportable resource is a strong, established brand name—a name with visibility, associations, perceived quality, and loyalty among a customer group. The challenge is to take this brand asset and use it to enter new product-markets. The name can make the task of establishing a new product more feasible and efficient, because it makes developing awareness, trust, and interest all easier.

Many firms have built large, diverse businesses around a strong brand, including Sony, HP, IBM, Mitsubishi, Seimens, GE, Schwab, Virgin, and Disney. More than 300 businesses carry the Virgin name, and all gain from the public-relations flair of Richard Branson, its owner. Mitsubishi has its name on thousands of products, each of which benefits from the name exposure and from the cumulative new-product vitality.

Disney, founded in 1920 as a cartoon company with Mickey Mouse (then known as Steamboat Willie) as its initial asset, might be the most successful firm ever at leveraging its brand. In the 1950s, the company built Disneyland and launched a TV show linked to the theme park, dramatically changing the brand by making it much richer and deeper than before. Particularly after extending Disneyland to Florida, Paris, and Japan, and establishing its own retail stores, resorts, and a cruise ship, Disney can deliver an experience that goes far beyond watching cartoons. As a result of this brand power, the Disney Channel is arguably one of the strongest TV channels available, an incredible achievement if you consider what others have put into that space.

It is instructive to see why Disney has done so well with an aggressive brand-extension strategy. First, from the beginning the company has known what it stands for—magical family entertainment, executed with consistent excellence. Everything Disney does reinforces that brand identity; when it went into films for mature audiences, it did so under the name Touchstone rather than Disney. Second, Disney has relentless, uncompromising drive for operational excellence that started with Walt Disney's fanatical concern for detail in the earliest cartoons and theme parks. The parks are run so well that Disney holds schools for other firms seeking to learn how to maintain energy and consistency. The cruise ship was delayed, despite ballooning costs, until everything was judged perfect. Third, the organization actively manages a host of subbrands that have their own identities, including Mickey Mouse, Donald Duck, a mountain (the Matterhorn), a song ("It's a Small World"), film characters like Mary Poppins or the Lion King, and on and on. Fourth, Disney understands synergy across products. The Lion King is not only a film but supports video/DVD sales, the Disney store, an exhaustive set of promotions, and a musical.

The brand-extension decision is largely based on three questions. Each must be answered in the affirmative for the extension to be viable.[1]

1. ***Does the brand fit the new product context?*** If the customer is uncomfortable and senses a lack of fit, acceptance will not come easily. The brand may not be seen as having the needed credibility or expertise, or it may have the wrong associations for the context. In general, a brand that has strong ties to a product class and attributes (for example, Boeing, Books.com, or Kleenex) will have a more difficult time stretching than a brand that is associated with intangibles such as fashion, value, German engineering, or active lifestyles. Certainly, all of the Disney extensions fit because they were supporting or part of the "magical family entertainment" brand identity. The Disney store, for example, fits because it is full of Disney characters, videos, and spirit.

2. ***Does the brand add value to the offering in the new product class?*** A customer should be able to express why the brand would be preferred in its new context. Despite the fact that cruise ships are difficult to tell apart, nearly anyone could verbalize rather clearly how a Disney Cruise ship would be different from others—it would have Disney characters aboard, contain more kids and families, and provide magical family entertainment.

   If the brand name does not add value in the eyes of the customer, the extension will be vulnerable to competition. For example, Pillsbury Microwave Popcorn initially benefited from the Pillsbury name but was vulnerable to the entry of an established popcorn name. Thus, although Orville Redenbacher entered the microwave category late, it still won with a name that meant quality and authenticity in popcorn.

A concept test can help determine what value is added by the brand. Prospective customers can be given only the brand name, then asked whether they would be attracted to the product and why. If they cannot articulate a specific reason why the offering would be attractive to them, it is unlikely that the brand name will add significant value.

3. Will the extension enhance the brand name and image? The ideal is to have an extension that will provide visibility, energy, and associations that support the brand. Coach was a successful, but somewhat stodgy maker of leather bags until it hired a new designer and extended its brand to hats, shoes, sunglasses, coats, watches, and even straw beach hats, all with the signature "C" in leather. The extensions provided energy to the brand and helped attract younger customers, boosting the firm's long-term future. Sunkist's associations with oranges, health, and vitality are reinforced by the promotion of Sunkist juice-based drinks and vitamin C tablets, while Sunkist fruit rolls may be a risk. The Disney extensions into theme parks, cruise ships, and retail stores all reinforced the brand.

If an extension will damage the brand, another branding option needs to be found. When Gap introduced a value chain and called it Gap Warehouse, the primary namesake brand was in danger of being confused and tarnished. The firm quickly reconsidered and protected the Gap brand by changing the name of the new chain to Old Navy.

Subbrands and Endorsed Brands

Two unfortunate realities can interfere with brand extensions. First, a new brand may not be feasible because the space is too cluttered and the organization does not have the size or resources to build a new brand in that context. Second, the existing brand may have the wrong associations or risk being damaged by the extension, perhaps because the latter's perceived quality or personality is incompatible with the brand.

In these cases, the answer may lie in the use of subbrands or endorsed brands. The GE Profile subbrand allowed General Electric to stretch into a premium segment with it's product energy and high margins. Similarly, the Pentium Zeon subbrand allowed Intel to offer a high-end server microprocessor. A subbrand lets the offering separate itself somewhat from the parent brand, and it offers the parent brand some degree of insulation.

An endorsed brand offers even more separation. For example, Marriott needed to enter the business hotel arena because it was huge and growing. Because it would have been extremely expensive to create a stand-alone brand in that area and the existing brands were all too messy to buy, the company created Courtyard by Marriott. The endorsement indicated that Marriott as an organization stood behind the Courtyard brand, so visitors could be confident that the chain would deliver a reliable experience. Leveraging a brand by using it to endorse other brands, often provides a trust umbrella.

Marketing Skills

A firm will often either possess or lack strong marketing skills for a particular market. Thus, a frequent motive for diversification is to export or import marketing skills.

Black & Decker had developed and exploited an aggressive new-products program (e.g., cordless screwdrivers and HandyChopper), effective consumer marketing (for names such as Spacemaker, Dustbuster, and ThunderVolt cordless tools), and intensive customer service and dealer relations.[2] The acquisition of Ernhart, with its branded door locks, decorative faucets, outdoor lighting, and racks, provided Black & Decker with an opportunity to apply its marketing skills and distribution clout to a firm that lacked a marketing culture.

Applying marketing skills is not always as easy as it appears. Philip Morris, a successful marketer of Miller Lite and other brands, failed with 7 UP, which it attempted to position as a caffeine-free soft drink in response to health interests of consumers. After a seven-year battle, Philip Morris gave up and sold the line to Pepsi-Cola. The problems that beset Philip Morris included the reaction of competitors who rushed caffeine-free drinks to the market, the power of existing bottlers and distributors, and the limited appeal of lemon-lime drinks.

Capacity in Sales or Distribution

A firm with a strong distribution capability may add products or services that could exploit that capability. Thus, Black & Decker's distribution strength helped provide a boost to the Ernhart lines. A joint venture between Nestlé and Coca-Cola in the canned tea business combined Coke's distribution strength with the product knowledge and name of Nestlé.

E-commerce firms usually have operations that can add capacity just by adding a button to access another product group. The result can be additional sales and margins to off-set the fixed costs of the operation.

Manufacturing Skills

Manufacturing or processing ability can be the basis for entry into a new business area. The ability to design and make small motors helped Honda succeed in the motorcycle business and led to its entry into lawn-care equipment, outboard motors, and a host of other products. The ability to make small products has been a key for Sony as it has moved from product to product in consumer electronics.

R&D Skills

Expertise in a certain technology can lead to a new business based on that technology. GE's early research has spawned very successful businesses. For example, its research on turbines for electricity generation provided the basis for its aircraft engine business, and its light bulb research provided the foundation for what became the medical instrumentation business. The challenge is to be open to channel R&D toward new business areas. Too often there is a tendency to focus exclusively on evolving the existing business.

Achieving Economies of Scale

Related diversification can sometimes provide economies of scale. Two smaller consumer products firms, for example, may not each be able to afford an effective sales force, new product development or testing programs, or warehousing and logistics systems. However, the combination of these firms may be able to operate at an efficient level. Similarly, two firms, when combined, may be able to justify an expensive piece of automated production equipment.

Sometimes a critical mass is needed in order to be effective. For example, a specialized electronics firm may need an R&D effort, but R&D productivity may be low if it is not feasible to have several researchers who can interact.

THE MIRAGE OF SYNERGY

Synergy, as suggested in Chapter 8, is an important source of competitive advantage. However, synergy is often more mirage than reality. Synergy is often assumed when, in fact, it does not exist, cannot be realized because of implementation problems, or is vastly overextended.

Potential synergy does not exist. Strategists often manipulate semantics to delude themselves that a synergistic justification exists. But when packaged-goods manufacturer General Foods bought Burger Chef, a chain of 700 fast-food restaurants, the fact that both entities were technically in the food business was of little consequence. Because General Foods never could master the skills needed to run restaurants, there was considerable negative organizational synergy. The apparent synergy of one-stop financial shopping turned out to be illusory as well, in part because customers simply did not value its purported convenience.

Potential synergy exists, but implementation barriers make it unattainable. This happens when a diversification move integrates two organizations that have fundamental differences. The Daimler-Benz and Chrysler merger seemed to have a host of paper synergies, but the burden of combining two very different organizational structures, systems, and cultures in part not only inhibited these synergies but added an array of new problems. As a result, the market value of the merged entity quickly fell far more than the $36 billion Daimler-Benz had paid for Chrysler.

Synergy is about resources more than products. One firm making industrial thermostats decided to leverage its technology by capitalizing on a growth market for household thermostats. Three years later, the effort was written off as an expensive failure because of the company's lack of expertise in design, packaging, mass production, and distribution to marketers and contractors.[3] The ultimate integration challenge is when a group of entities are combined to provide an integrated customer solution. Lou Gerstner indicated that integrating the country, product, and service silos at IBM was his most significant legacy.[4] He also noted, though, that it took five years to accomplish the progress that was made. Citing the failures of many firms to create true financial supermarkets, multi-service telecommunication companies, and fully integrated entertainment companies, he opined that integrating decentralized operations is a struggle at which few have been successful.

Potential synergy is overvalued. One risk of buying a business in another area, even a related one, is that the potential synergy may seem more enticing than it really is. Perhaps carried away by its success with Gatorade, Quaker Oats, purchased the Snapple business in 1994 for $1.7 billion, only to sell it two years later for a mere $300 million. Quaker had difficulties in distribution and was inept at taking

THE ELUSIVE SEARCH FOR SYNERGY

The concept of a total communications firm that comprises advertising, direct marketing, marketing research, public relations, design, sales promotions, and now Internet communications has been a dream of many organizations for two decades. The concept has been that synergy will be created by providing clients with more consistent, coordinated communication efforts and by cross-selling services. Thus, Young & Rubicam had the "whole egg" and Ogilvy & Mather talked about "Ogilvy orchestrations."

Despite the compelling logic and considerable efforts, such synergy has been elusive. Because each communication discipline involved different people, paradigms, cultures, standards, and processes, the disparate groups had difficulty not only working together but even doing simple things like sharing strategies and visuals. A related problem was a reluctance to refer clients to sister units who were suspected to deliver inferior results, which created client relationship ownership issues.

Young & Rubicam has been perhaps the most successful, in large part because it merged its direct marketing, public relations, Internet communications, and advertising firms into one organization, with shared locations and client-relations leadership. Each major account has a director and dedicated space. With these four units together already, it became easier to include a design firm such as Landor in client engagements. DDB Needham has had success with virtual client teams drawn from its family of communication companies. These cross-discipline teams create their own culture and processes that allow them to provide the coordinated communication that clients need.

The lesson here is that synergy does not just happen, despite logic and motivation. It can require real innovation in implementation—not just trying harder.

a quirky personality brand into the mainstream beverage market (its program was based on pedestrian advertising and a giant sampling giveaway). Moreover, the fact that Quaker paid several times more than Snapple was worth was a fatal handicap.

The acquisition of The Learning Company—a popular children's software publisher with titles like Reader Rabbit, Learn to Speak, and Oregon Trail—seemed like a logical move by Mattel, the powerful toy company with Barbie among its properties. Yet less than a year and a half after paying $3.5 billion for it, Mattel basically gave The Learning Company away to get out from under mounting losses.

One study of seventy-five people from forty companies that were experienced at acquisition led to several conclusions. First, few companies do a rigorous risk analysis looking at the least and most favorable outcome. With optimistic vibes abounding, it is particularly wise to look at the downside: What can go wrong? Second, it is useful to set a price over which you will not pay. Avoid getting so exuberant about the synergistic potential that you ultimately pay more than you will ever be able to recoup.[5]

One-Stop Shopping for Financial Services

During the 1980s, several conglomerates were created to provide one-stop financial services to customers and to take advantage of operational synergies. One of these was formed when Sears brought the real estate company Coldwell Banker and the brokerage house Dean Witter into a firm that already had Allstate Insurance, Allstate Savings and Loan, and 25 million active Sears charge-card users. To exploit the perceived synergy represented by this array of services, Sears opened more than 300 financial boutiques in its larger stores with various combinations of Allstate salespeople, Dean Witter brokers, and Coldwell Banker agents. In addition, it introduced the Discover card.

The hoped-for synergy, though, did not happen. The Sears name and culture, which meant value and trust in tires and tools, was not an asset in securities; the merger also contributed to the departure of key Dean Witter mortgage banking people. Nor was the Sears customer base a source of profitable brokerage customers. Most importantly, the basic assumption that customers would value one-stop shopping in financial services was simply wrong. They wanted the least expensive mortgages, the best brokerage advice, the most convenient banking, and so on. Having these services under one roof did not add value. In addition, the implementation of cross-selling was disappointing because it was difficult to motivate the financial service units to recommend each other. Sears ultimately gave up on the concept, and the financial units—including Allstate, Discover, Dean Witter, and Coldwell Banker—were spun off to again operate independently.

More recently, one-stop financial shopping has reemerged with better prospects of achieving synergy, although the verdict is still in doubt. One positive difference is the maturity of Internet sites as devices to expose customers to services and to provide reporting that can span products. Another is the more forceful and effective use of cross-selling by Wells Fargo and others using targeted marketing efforts, customer incentives, and performance measures. Still another is the realization of cost savings by combining organizations. One lesson is that capturing synergy can require real effort, the right product mix, an effective brand portfolio strategy, and timing.

UNRELATED DIVERSIFICATION

Unrelated diversification lacks enough commonality in brands, marketing, distribution, channels, manufacturing, or R&D thrust to provide the opportunity for synergy through the exchange or sharing of assets or competencies. The objectives are therefore mainly financial, to generate profit streams that are either larger, less uncertain, or more stable than they would otherwise be. Figure 14.2 summarizes the motivations for both unrelated and related diversification.

Managing and Allocating Cash Flow

Unrelated diversification can balance the cash flows of business units. A firm with businesses that merit investment might buy or merge with a cash cow (a business with a substantial cash flow) to provide a source of financial resources. Conversely, a firm with a cash cow may enter new markets seeking growth opportunities. The tobacco firms, for example, have used their enormous cash flows to buy a host of firms, including General Foods, Nabisco, and Del Monte.

Related Diversification	Unrelated Diversification

• Exchange or share assets or competencies, thereby exploiting a
  ○ Brand name
  ○ Marketing skills
  ○ Sales and distribution capacity
  ○ Manufacturing skills
  ○ R&D and new product capability
• Economies of scale
	• Manage and allocate cash flow
	• Obtain high ROI
	• Obtain a bargain price
	• Refocus a firm
	• Reduce risk by operating in multiple product markets
	• Tax benefits
	• Obtain liquid assets
	• Vertical integration
	• Defend against a takeover
	• Provide executive interest

Figure 14.2   Motivations for Diversification

Entering Business Areas with High ROI Prospects

One basic motivation for diversifying is to improve ROI by moving into business areas with high growth prospects. Heinz bought Weight Watchers in the late 1970s for this reason. A decade later, it had extended the Weight Watchers brand into some 200 products and was earning close to its acquisition cost each year. Fuji Film and Kodak, both looking at the decline in film processing and film-based cameras, have aggressively moved into digital cameras and their accessories.

Many disastrous mergers or acquisitions have been motivated by the enticement of ROI prospects. In some cases, the catastrophe was caused in part by an inability to manage the resulting organization, as well as a mistaken promise of synergy. Other times, however, it was caused by an overestimation of the ROI prospects by a firm unfamiliar with the industry. Avon, for example, lost a fortune buying Tiffany & Co. and perfumer Giorgio Beverly Hills, in part because it overpaid for those businesses. The same can be said about Quaker's acquisition of Snapple, Daimler-Benz's acquisition of Chrysler, and many more.

Obtaining a Bargain Price for a Business

There are certainly bargains for the astute buyer. Bargains are most likely when there has been a crash. In real estate, one truism is that the second (or third) buyer—after the first has gone bankrupt—will be successful. This can happen in other sectors. After the dot-com crash, many viable firms were available for reasonable prices for those who could identify the businesses with real assets.

On average, instead of getting bargains, acquiring firms fail to realize value because they misread market prospects and threats, fail to capture hoped-for synergy, mismanage the integration of firms (often because cutting costs takes precedence over delivering customer satisfaction), and are unable to combine cultures and operate the acquired business. Numerous studies have explored the stock-return payoff when an acquisition is made. One review of some forty-one such studies concludes that the acquired stock was purchased at a premium of around 22 percent.[6] Another study of acquisitions over time showed that around 60 percent of them resulted in the total market-adjusted return of the acquiring company going down upon the announcement and, in most cases, staying down for the next year.[7]

The business model for too many firms is to acquire a business with a low price–earnings multiplier, which will create "earnings growth" when combined with the acquiring company. The result is apparent financial success as long the bargains persist, acquisitions continue, and investors remained convinced that the earnings growth is real. The problem is that eventually the absence of a real strategy and operational excellence will show through, and the house of cards will collapse.

The Potential to Refocus a Firm

An acquisition can provide the basis for a refocus of the acquired firm, the acquiring firm, or both. The objective would be to change the thrust of a firm from one set of industries to another. For example, Esmark dramatically refocused by selling its oil and gas businesses and its Swift operation and concentrating the resulting assets on its consumer products businesses. Not incidentally, the thrust change may result in investors' perceiving a firm to be in more attractive industries, thus causing its stock price to rise.

The key is to identify firms that are undervalued with respect to their potential after a refocus. One approach suggested by Booz Allen acquisition specialists is to group a firm's businesses into four categories:[8]

1. ***Core businesses.*** A core business might represent 25 to 60 percent of sales. Strategically, the core business should be strong and have some sustainable competitive advantages on which to build.

2. ***Successful diversifications.*** These would be the firm's stars with strong positions in attractive markets.

3. ***Unsuccessful diversifications.*** An undervalued firm typically has a substantial proportion of sales in unsuccessful diversifications, which is a major drag on performance.

4. ***Nonoperating investments.*** These could be stock investments or physical assets carried below market value.

Unsuccessful diversifications and their effect on performance may generate associations and perceived risks that cause a firm to be undervalued. The core business, successful diversifications, and nonoperating investments may be worth much more than the current firm as a whole. Liquidating or divesting the unsuccessful diversifications would be one way to realize that value. Another possibility would be to spin off the core business, which by itself may be valued relatively highly, and thereby use the successful diversifications as a base to generate a new core business. If the original core business is in an industry not highly regarded by the stock market, the revised core could be valued higher.

Reducing Risk

The reduction of risk can be another motivation for unrelated diversification. Heavy reliance on a single product line can stimulate a diversification move. Hershey was almost totally dependent on its candy and confectionery business, a business that was vulnerable to an increased interest in health and health foods. Hershey purchased Friendly Ice Cream, a chain of family restaurants based in Massachusetts, and the Skinner Macaroni Company with the goal of making non-confection revenues a significant percentage of sales.

Stockholder Risk versus Management Risk

Diversification may reduce the market risk facing a firm and thus protect the firm's employees, customers, and managers. Managers, in particular, face the loss of job and reputation from a business downturn over which they may have no control, and thus they may be motivated to diversify. However, risk reduction obtained from unrelated diversification is of no value to stockholders, who are free to diversify by holding a portfolio of stocks. Based on the premise that stockholders are the only relevant stakeholders of a business, it can be argued that the reduction of risk is not a legitimate objective.

Even stockholders cannot diversify from systematic risk, that portion of variation of the stock return correlated with general economic conditions. Thus, a diversification that would reduce a firm's systematic risk would be of value to stockholders. For example, an upscale chain of restaurants might acquire a set of Taco Bell outlets, which would do well when the economy is down.

Tax Implications

Tax considerations can stimulate mergers or acquisitions of unrelated firms. Firms can accumulate large tax-loss carryovers, which they can exploit. Thus, a firm with a large series of losses from its automatic teller machines purchased a profitable sweater manufacturer, which could utilize the losses to reduce taxes. Mergers have also been motivated by firms that have underutilized tax incentives to make capital investments.

Obtaining Liquid Assets

A firm can become an attractive acquisition candidate because of substantial liquid assets that can be readily deployed or because of a low debt-to-equity ratio that provides the potential to support debt financing. Banks and insurance companies can be attractive acquisition targets because they provide access to money.

Vertical Integration Motivations

A vertical integration is usually an unrelated diversification. In Chapter 13, some of the motivations for vertical integration were discussed, such as gaining access to supply or demand, controlling quality, and gaining entry into attractive business areas.

Defending against a Takeover

The threat of an unfriendly takeover can lead to an acquisition. One firm bought a small banana company to generate an antitrust obstacle to a takeover by United Fruit. Martin Marietta responded to a takeover move by Bendix by attempting to buy Bendix with the help of a third firm, United Technologies. The complex and expensive maneuvering ended with a fourth company, Allied Corporation, buying Bendix, while Martin Marietta remained independent.

Providing Executive Interest

For the executives making the decision, diversification can be stimulating. It can also lead to the prestige of a larger organization. A study in which fourteen merger experts were queried as to the motivations involved found that enhancement of personal power as measured by the sales volume controlled by a chief executive may be a moderately important motivation in merger decisions.[9] Another related conclusion was that the merger decisions were ultimately made by one person, the CEO.

Risks of Unrelated Diversification

The very concept of unrelated diversification suggests risk and difficulty because, by definition, there is no possibility of synergy. Many knowledgeable people have made blanket statements warning against unrelated diversification. Peter Drucker claims that all successful diversification requires a common core or unity represented by common markets, technology, or production processes.[10] He states that without such unity, diversification never works; financial ties alone are insufficient. Among the major risks:

- Attention may be diverted from the core business.
- Managing the new business may be difficult.
- The new business may be overvalued.

Unrelated diversification, if unsuccessful, may actually damage the original core business by diverting attention and resources from it. Quaker Oats embarked on an aggressive acquisition program in the early 1970s, going into toys and theme restaurants. In the process, however, the company allowed its core business areas to deteriorate. The new product effort suffered, and the market share and shelf facings fell as a result.

The potential for difficulties in managing a diversification is magnified when an unrelated business is acquired. The new business may require assets, competencies, and an organizational culture that differ from those of the core business. Furthermore, a skilled, valued management team in the acquired company might leave and be difficult to replace.

A new business area might be incorrectly evaluated. For example, environmental threats may be overlooked or misjudged. If an acquisition is involved, its strategic liabilities, weaknesses, and problems may be undiscovered or miscalculated. General Host, a food store and baked-goods firm, acquired Cudahy, the meat-packing firm, just before its plant and methods were made virtually obsolete by new packers with highly automated plants. National Intergroup, with steel and oil as its core businesses, bought a drug wholesaler, only to find that a price war was starting and that a project to sell computer services to druggists was a disaster.

Performance of Diversified Firms

A case can be made for a focused strategy—keep your eye on the ball, stick to your knitting, and so forth. Although of little value to a shareholder, however, diversification can provide a firm with strategic flexibility and a cushion against bad events (the operative cliché in this case being not to put all of your eggs in one basket). One research study by a McKinsey group suggests a middle ground, noting that moderate diversification may, on average, be better than either extreme.[11]

In the study, a total of 412 of the S&P 500 companies were classified as focused (deriving at least 67 percent of revenues coming from one business), moderately diversified (with at least 67 percent of revenues from two segments), or diversified (with less than 67 percent of revenues from two segments). Total return to shareholders between 1990 and 2000 for the moderately diversified firms was 13 percent more than for their industry peers, as compared to 8 percent for the focused companies and 4 percent for the diversified firms.

Why might moderately diversified firms perform better? More diversified firms tend to suffer from spreading their resources and culture too broadly, resulting in a reduced ability to gain efficiencies and market leadership. More focused firms, conversely, may find it difficult to manage market dynamics because of what is termed "strategic stubbornness" in Chapter 8. In an example of moderate diversification, though, Cincinnati Bell leveraged its local telephone-related capabilities during the 1980s to create a significant business by providing call-center and back-office services to other companies.[12] As a result, the company (eventually renamed Broadwing) was in a much better position to deal with the deregulated markets of the 1990s.

ENTRY STRATEGIES

When the decision is made to enter a new product market, the entry strategy becomes critical.[13] Figure 14.3 summarizes eight alternative strategies with their advantages and disadvantages.

The most common entry routes are internal development and acquisition. Developing a new business internally means that a concept, strategy, and team can be created without the limitations, liabilities, or acquisition costs represented by acquiring an existing business. An internal venture is a variant in which a separate entity within the existing firm is established, so that the new business will not be constrained by existing organizational culture, systems, and structure. For example, the IBM PC was developed and marketed by a separate organizational entity in a remarkably short time.

The acquisition route saves calendar time. An acquisition can mean that a firm becomes an established player in a matter of weeks instead of years. Perhaps more important, it means that substantial entry barriers such as distribution or brandname

Entry Strategy	Major Advantages	Major Disadvantages
Internal Development	• Uses existing resources • Avoids acquisition cost especially if unfamiliar with product/market	• Time lag • Uncertain prospects
Internal Venture	• Uses existing resources • May keep talented entrepreneurs	• Mixed success record • Can create internal stresses
Acquisition	• Saves calendar time • Overcomes entry barriers	• Costly—usually buy redundant assets • Problem of integrating two organizations
Joint Venture or Alliance	• Technological/marketing unions can exploit small/large firm synergies • Distributes risk	• Potential for conflict in operations between firms • Value of one firm may be reduced over time
Licensing from Others	• Rapid access to technology • Reduced financial risk	• Will lack proprietary technology and technological skills • Will be dependent on licensor
Educational Acquisition	• Provides window and initial staff	• Risk of departure of entrepreneurs
Venture Capital and Nurturing	• Can provide window on new technology or market	• Unlikely alone to be a major stimulus of firm growth
Licensing to Others	• Rapid access to a market • Low cost/risk	• Will lack knowledge/control of market • Will be dependent on licensee

Figure 14.3 Entry Strategies

Source: Adapted from Edward B. Roberts and Charles A. Berry, "Entering New Businesses: Selecting Strategies for Success," *Sloan Management Review,* Spring 1985, pp. 3–17.

recognition are overcome. A variant is an educational acquisition in which a small firm that is not established as a major force is acquired in order to obtain a window into a technology or market, as well as knowledge, experience, and a base from which to grow.

The other options shown in Figure 14.3 represent reduced risk and commitment, as well as a reduced chance that the route will lead to an established business supported by SCAs. A joint venture will share the risk with others and provide one or more missing and needed assets and competencies. For example, a small firm that possesses a new technology could enter into a joint venture with a larger firm that has financial resources and access to distribution. Licensing a technology from others provides a fast way to overcome one entry barrier, but makes it difficult to gain control of that same technology in the future. Both entry options are important in international business contexts and are discussed in detail in Chapter 11. An alternative to a joint venture is an alliance in which the parties share assets to attack a market. For example, Sony's cooperative technology-sharing arrangements with a host of small high-tech firms serve to keep Sony on the cutting edge of technology and also provide the small firms with access to Sony's production, engineering, and marketing assets.

The lowest involvement options are licensing others to use and market a technology or entering into a business as a venture capital investor. General Electric and Union Carbide are among firms that have made minority investments in young and growing high-tech enterprises in order to secure some relationship to a new technology. Both licensing and becoming a venture capital investor offer the potential to increase involvement over time, if the business does well, and to control any risk.

Selecting the Right Entry Strategy

Roberts and Berry suggest that the selection of the right entry strategy depends on the level of a firm's familiarity with the product market to be entered.[14] They define familiarity along two dimensions: (1) market and (2) technology or service embodied in the product.

With respect to market factors, three levels of familiarity are defined:

- *Base.* Existing products are sold within this market.
- *New/familiar.* The company is familiar with the market because of extensive research, experienced staff, or links with the market as a customer.
- *New/unfamiliar.* Knowledge of and experience with the market are lacking.

An analogous set of three levels of familiarity with the technologies or services embodied in the product is set forth:

- *Base.* The technology or service is embodied within existing products.
- *New/familiar.* The company is familiar with the technology because of work in related technologies, an established R&D effort in the technology, or extensive focused research in the technology.
- *New/unfamiliar.* Knowledge of and experience with the technology are lacking.

The basic suggestion is that as the level of familiarity on these two dimensions declines, the commitment level should be reduced. Figure 14.4 shows the baseline entry strategy recommendations that follow from a familiarity assessment. Of course, there will be contexts in which a high-commitment approach in the new/unfamiliar cell will make sense. However, Roberts and Berry suggest, on the basis of experience and theory, that substantial risk is associated with such an approach and the option of gaining familiarity should be seriously considered.

Technologies or Services Embodied in the Product

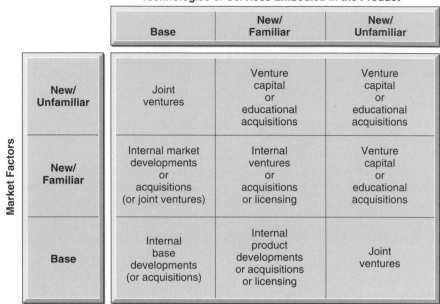

	Base	New/ Familiar	New/ Unfamiliar
New/ Unfamiliar	Joint ventures	Venture capital or educational acquisitions	Venture capital or educational acquisitions
New/ Familiar	Internal market developments or acquisitions (or joint ventures)	Internal ventures or acquisitions or licensing	Venture capital or educational acquisitions
Base	Internal base developments (or acquisitions)	Internal product developments or acquisitions or licensing	Joint ventures

(Market Factors — row axis label)

Figure 14.4   Optimal Entry Strategies

Source: Adapted from Edward B. Roberts and Charles A. Berry, "Entering New Businesses: Selecting Strategies for Success," *Sloan Management Review,* Spring 1985, pp. 3–17.

KEY LEARNINGS

- Related diversification involves the potential to attain synergies by exporting or exchanging assets or competences.

- The brand is one asset that often can be leveraged. Disney and Sony are examples of brands that have provided the basis for a broad array of businesses.

- A brand should fit a proposed new product market and add value. And, importantly, the new product market context should enhance and reinforce the brand (and certainly should not damage it).

- Synergy can be illusory, being perceived when in fact it does not exist, implementation barriers make it unachievable, or it is overvalued.

- There are eleven motivations for unrelated diversification, including to manage cash flow, to obtain attractive businesses, to refocus a firm, and to reduce risk.

- Figure 14.3 illustrates eight approaches to market entry based on how new the technology or market is to the organization.

FOR DISCUSSION

1. What is the difference between related and unrelated diversification? Are the following related or unrelated? Why?

   a. Dell selling TV sets

   b. Bank of America owning theme parks

   c. Crest purchasing a chain of dental offices

   d. Caterpillar manufacturing automobiles

   e. Snackwells owning exercise clubs

2. Pick a branded offering, such as Southwest Airlines. Come up with twenty products or services that are alternative extension options. Include some that would be a stretch. Evaluate each of the extension options using the three criteria listed in the chapter.

3. Consider the following mergers or acquisitions. In which cases would synergy be logically possible? What would inhibit this synergy? Consider operations, culture, and brand equities.

   a. Citicorp acquires Providian (a credit card firm serving low-income segments)

   b. Pepsi (the owners of Frito-Lay) acquires Quaker Oats and Gatorade

   c. Daimler-Benz acquires Chrysler

4. Consider the alliance of Starbucks and Barnes & Noble, initiated in 1993, in which Starbucks cafés were opened inside the bookstores. Evaluate this alliance from both sides. When Barnes & Noble opened stores in areas of the Midwest where Starbuck's had no presence, the cafés were branded Barnes & Noble but sold Starbucks coffee. Would you accept this arrangement if you were Starbucks? (Eventually, it was applied to nearly all of the cafés.) Again, comment from both sides.

NOTES

1. David A. Aaker, *Managing Brand Equity*, New York: The Free Press, 1991, Chapter 9 and David A. Aaker and Erich Joachimsthaler, *Brand Leadership*, New York: The Free Press, 2000, chapter 5.

2. Michael J. McDermott, "The House That Nolan's Building," *Adweek's Marketing Week*, August 14, 1989, pp. 20–22.

3. David J. Collis and Cynthia A. Montgomery, "Creating Corporate Advantage," *Harvard Business Review*, May–June 1998, pp. 71–83.

4. Louis V. Gerstner, Jr., *Who Says Elephants Can't Dance*, New York: Harper Business, 2002, pp. 251–252.

5. Robert G. Eccles, Kersten L. Lanes, and Thomas C. Wilson, "Are You Paying Too Much for That Acquisition?," *Harvard Business Review*, July–August 1999, pp. 136–143.

6. Deepak K. Datta, George E. Pinches, and V. K. Narayanan, "Factors Influencing Wealth Creation from Mergers and Acquisitions: A Meta-Analysis," *Strategic Management Journal* 13, 1992, pp. 67–84.

7. Op. Cit. Eccles et. al. pp. 126–142.

8. Michael G. Allen, Alexander R. Oliver, and Edward H. Schwallie, "The Key to Successful Acquisitions," *Journal of Business Strategy,* Fall 1981, pp. 14–24.

9. Wayne I. Boucher, "The Process of Conglomerate Merger," prepared for the Bureau of Competition, Federal Trade Commission, June 1980.

10. Peter Drucker, "The Five Rules of Successful Acquisition," *Wall Street Journal,* October 15, 1981, p. 16.

11. Neil W. C. Harper and S. Patrick Viguerie, "Are You Too Focused?" *McKinsey Quarterly,* 2002, No. 2, pp. 28–37.

12. Ibid., p. 32.

13. Edward B. Roberts and Charles A. Berry, "Entering New Businesses: Selecting Strategies for Success," *Sloan Management Review,* Spring 1985, pp. 3–17.

14. Ibid.

CHAPTER FIFTEEN

Strategies in Declining and Hostile Markets

Anyone can hold the helm when the sea is calm.
—*Publilius Syrus*

Where there is no wind, row.
—*Portuguese proverb*

There is nothing so useless as doing efficiently that which should not be done at all.
—*Peter Drucker*

S trategic planning is often associated with a search for healthy, growing markets and the development of strategies to penetrate those markets. However, as the discussion in Chapter 5 makes clear, there are a variety of risks in high-growth contexts, including the possibility that a market can be crowded with competitors, each trying to find a niche. On the other hand, declining markets as well as mature markets can represent real opportunities for a business following the right strategy, in part because they are not as attractive to competitors. Thus, declining markets are not always to be avoided.

A declining market involves a fall in demand, often caused by an external event such as the creation of a competing technology, a change in customer needs or tastes, or a shift in government policy. Of course, a participant in a declining market will attempt to obtain sustainable competitive advantages (SCAs) and compete successfully. In a market characterized by zero or negative growth, however, the options of milking and even exiting should be considered, as suggested by the portfolio models. Thus, it is important to understand these options as well.

In this chapter several strategic alternatives especially relevant to declining markets are considered:

1. Create a growth context by revitalizing the industry so that it becomes a growth industry or by focusing on a growth submarket.
2. Be the profitable survivor in the industry by dominating the market, thus encouraging others to exit.
3. Milk or harvest. Withdraw resources so that they can be invested elsewhere.
4. Exit or liquidate. Salvage existing assets.

Hostile markets are those with overcapacity, low margins, intense competition, and management in turmoil. Hostility has two primary causes. The first is a decline in demand. The second and most important cause of hostility is competitive expansion. Certainly one reason for the collapse of many sectors of e-commerce was the explosion of well-funded competitors, especially on-line. Thus, even a growing market can be hostile.

Hostile markets are all too common. Of thousands of executives in this author's executive programs, only one has admitted to competing in a market that was not hostile, and that person was the manager of the Panama Canal! It is thus important to understand the dynamics of hostile markets and why some competitors do better than others in such environments. In the final section of this chapter, the life cycle of a hostile market will be described and the strategies of above-average performers will be discussed.

CREATING GROWTH IN DECLINING INDUSTRIES

It is usually assumed that existing participants have already fully exploited the market potential of a stagnant or declining industry. If that assumption is untrue, a dramatic opportunity exists for a business to participate in revitalizing the industry and achieve a commanding position in the new growth context. As suggested by Figure 15.1, there are at least seven routes to revitalizing a stagnant market.

New Markets

An obvious way to generate growth is to move into neglected or ignored market segments that have the potential for new growth. Consumer electronics companies could focus on women or the elderly, both of which are underserved markets. Some industries have seen international expansion fuel growth. The Barbie doll, for example, found new market viability in Europe and Japan.

New Products

Sometimes a dormant industry can be revitalized by a product that makes existing products obsolete and accelerates the replacement cycle. The consumer electronics market has seen color television, CDs, big screen television, and other technological

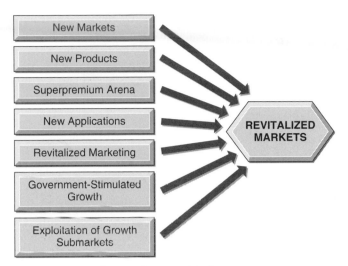

Figure 15.1   Routes to Revitalizing a Stagnant Market

advances create vitality in declining markets. A new product variant can add interest, such as the introduction of gourmet coffees or Internet-enabled phones.

The Superpremium Arena

In many hostile market environments, from beer to water to cars to banking, there is a superpremium category that has healthy margins and product vitality. For example, despite the difficult nature of the heavy appliance market, Whirlpool introduced its Duet washer/dryer set with rounded styling, room for nearly two dozen bath towels, and a computer that optimizes the process to save time, save energy, protect fabrics, and improve cleaning.[1] Despite being priced at a breathtaking three times as much as the average Whirlpool washer/dryer set, it became a hot product for middle-class customers as well as the wealthy.

New Applications

A new application for a product can stimulate industry growth. In Chapter 13, the graphic example of baking soda and its use as a deodorizer was given. The cranberry industry has created new growth by finding new recipes for its product and encouraging cranberry use other than for holiday meals. The maker of Lysol Disinfectant Spray gave its product a new scent and targeted day-care centers. The small refrigerator opened up new sources of sales in offices and student dormitories. A prime way to find promising applications is to learn how existing customers are using the product or service.

Revitalized Marketing

A product class may be revived by a fresh marketing approach, such as changing the distribution channel by using new types of stores or direct selling, selling the product to firms to use as giveaway promotion items, changing the pricing structure, or perhaps changing the advertising. A dormant headache product was rejuvenated by linking it to its rural southeastern roots. The original packaging and bitter taste were restored, advertisements were run featuring southern spokespersons, and associations were developed with events such as bass-fishing tournaments and minor league baseball.

Government-Stimulated Growth

There is an old adage, "If all else fails, change the rules of the game." Strategically, the idea is to change the environment so that industry sales will be enhanced. A governmental body can provide incentives for change, such as tax incentives for installing home insulation or refurbishing low-income housing. Or a government might dictate that air bags be installed in cars, thus stimulating a new industry.

Exploitation of Growth Submarkets

Some firms have been successful in declining or mature industries because they have been able to focus on growth subareas, pockets of demand that are healthy and perhaps even growing nicely. The superdry, nonalcoholic, and microbrewery brands are all growing in the mature beer market. Convertibles are again a growth segment in the automobile industry.

Sometimes a growth submarket has the same visibility and risk as another growth market, but it is neglected because its parent industry is unattractive. As a result, it is likely to receive less competitive attention.

BE THE PROFITABLE SURVIVOR

The conventional advice is to avoid investing in declining markets and to milk or exit businesses that are trapped in a declining situation.[2] However, an aggressive alternative is to invest in order to obtain or strengthen a leadership position. A strong survivor may be profitable, in part because there may be little competition and in part because the investment might be relatively low. The cornerstone of this strategy is to encourage competitors to exit. Toward that end a firm can:

- Be visible about its commitment to be the surviving leader in the industry.
- Raise the costs of competing by price reductions or increased promotion.
- Introduce new products and cover new segments, thereby making it more difficult for a competitor to find a profitable niche.
- Reduce competitors' exit barriers by assuming their long-term contracts, supplying spare parts and servicing their products in the field, or supplying them with products. For example, a regional bakery could supply private-label products to a local retailer, thus enabling the retailer to exit from doing its own baking.
- Create a national, dominant brand in a declining industry that is fragmented. Chesebrough-Ponds, for example, bought Ragu Packing, a regional

spaghetti sauce maker, and created a major national brand, thereby generating economies of scale in both marketing and manufacturing.

- Purchase a competitor's market share and/or its production capacity. This is the ultimate removal of a competitor's exit barriers and ensures that a tired competitor won't be taken over by a more vigorous organization. In the late 1980s, Kunz, which made passbooks for financial institutions, was able to buy competitor assets so far under book value that the payback period was measured in months. As a result, Kunz had record years in a business area others had written off as all but dead decades earlier.

MILK OR HARVEST

A milk or harvest strategy aims to generate cash flow by reducing investment and operating expenses, even if that causes a reduction in sales and market share. The underlying assumptions are that the firm has better uses for the funds, that the involved business is not crucial to the firm either financially or synergistically, and that milking is feasible because sales will decline in an orderly way.

A milking strategy can be precipitated by a new entrant that turns a market hostile. Chase & Sanborn was once a leading coffee; the "Chase & Sanborn Hour," starring Edgar Bergen, was one of the most popular radio shows of its time. After World War II, though, Chase & Sanborn decided to retreat to a milking strategy rather than fight an expensive market retention battle against the rising popularity of instant coffee and the appearance of General Foods' heavily advertised Maxwell House brand.

There are variants of milking strategies. A *slow milking* strategy would sharply reduce long-term investment but continue to support operating areas such as marketing and service. A *fast milking* strategy would be disciplined about minimizing the expenditures toward the brand and maximizing the short-term cash flow, accepting the risk of a fast exit.

Conditions Favoring a Milking Strategy

Several conditions support a milking strategy rather than a hold or exit strategy:

- The decline rate is pronounced and unlikely to change but not excessively steep, and pockets of enduring demand ensure that the decline rate will not suddenly become precipitous.
- The price structure is stable at a level that is profitable for efficient firms.
- The business position is weak but there is enough customer loyalty, perhaps in a limited part of the market, to generate sales and profits in a milking mode. The risk of losing relative position with a milking strategy is low.
- The business is not central to the current strategic direction of the firm.
- A milking strategy can be successfully managed.

Implementation Problems

Implementation of a milking strategy can be difficult. One of the most serious problems is that if employees and customers suspect that a milking strategy is being employed, the resulting lack of trust may upset the whole strategy. As the line between a milking strategy and abandonment is sometimes very thin, customers may lose confidence in the firm's product and employee morale may suffer. Competitors may attack more vigorously. All these possibilities can create a sharper-than-anticipated decline. To minimize such effects, it is helpful to keep a milking strategy as inconspicuous as possible.

Another serious problem is the difficulty of placing and motivating a manager in a milking situation. Most business managers do not have the orientation, background, or skills to engage in a successful milking strategy. Adjusting performance measures and rewards appropriately can be difficult for both the organization and the managers involved. It might seem reasonable to use a manager who specializes in milking strategies, but that is often not feasible simply because such specialization is rare. Most firms rotate managers through different types of situations, and career paths simply are not geared to creating milking specialists.

When the Premises Are Wrong

One advantage of milking rather than divesting is that a milking strategy can often be reversed if it turns out to be based on incorrect premises regarding market prospects, competitor moves, cost projections, or other relevant factors. A resurgence in product classes that were seemingly dead or in terminal decline gives pause. Oatmeal, for example, has experienced a sharp increase in sales because of its low cost and associations with nutrition and health. In men's apparel, suspenders and pocket watches have shown signs of growth. Fountain pens, invented in 1884, were virtually killed by the appearance in 1939 of the ballpoint. However, the combination of nostalgia and a desire for prestige has provided a major comeback for the luxury fountain pen. As a result, the industry has seen years in which sales doubled.

Forecasting and Managing the Flow of Funds from Milking

The flow of funds from a milking strategy needs to be both forecasted and managed properly. AT&T planned to use funds from its long-distance business to invest in creating millions of broadband-cable households who would be sold local as well as long-distance services. Because the value of the long-distance cash cow fell much faster than planned, however, the aggressive investment in cable could not be supported. The lesson is to make sure that the cash flow actually exists before it is spent.

The Hold Strategy

A variant of the milking strategy is the hold strategy, in which growth-motivated investment is avoided, but an adequate level of investment is employed to maintain product quality, production facilities, and customer loyalty. A hold strategy is appropriate when an industry is declining in an orderly way, pockets of enduring demand exist, price pressures are not extreme, a firm has exploitable assets or competencies, and a business contributes by its presence to other business units in the firm. A hold strategy would be preferable to an invest strategy when an industry lacks growth opportunities and a strategy of increasing share would risk triggering competitive retaliation. The hold strategy can be a long-term strategy to manage a cash cow or an interim strategy employed until the uncertainties of an industry are resolved.

A problem with the hold strategy is that if conditions change, reluctance or slowness to reinvest may result in lost market share. The two largest can manufacturers, American and Continental, failed to invest in the two-piece can process when it was developed because they were engaged in diversification efforts and were attempting to avoid investments in their cash cow. As a result, they lost substantial market share.

DIVESTMENT OR LIQUIDATION

As Figure 15.2 suggests, when a business environment and business position are both unfavorable, then the final alternative, divestment or liquidation, is precipitated. Among the conditions that would suggest an exit decision rather than a milking decision are the following:

- The decline rate is rapid and accelerating, and no pockets of enduring demand are accessible to the business.
- The price pressures are expected to be extreme, caused by determined competitors with high exit barriers and by a lack of brand loyalty and product differentiation. Thus, a milking strategy is unlikely to be profitable for anyone.
- The business position is weak; one or more dominant competitors have achieved irreversible advantage. The business is now losing money, and future prospects are dim.
- The firm's strategic direction has changed, and the role of the business has become superfluous or even unwanted.
- Exit barriers can be overcome.

Figure 15.2 Strategies for Declining or Stagnant Industries

A set of exit barriers can inhibit an exit decision. In particular:

- Specialized assets such as plant and equipment may have little value to others.
- Long-term contracts with suppliers and with labor groups may be expensive to break.
- The business may have commitments to provide spare parts and service backup to retailers and customers. For example, in the 1960s, many vacuum-tube manufacturers, such as RCA, also made TV sets that used specialized tubes. The customers' assumption that RCA would supply parts provided a substantial exit barrier for the RCA vacuum-tube business.
- Firms' financial and management resources are being absorbed when they could be employed more effectively elsewhere.
- An exit decision may affect the reputation and operation of other company businesses. Thus, GE was concerned about the impact its decision to discontinue small appliances would have on its lamp and large-appliance business retailers and consumers.
- Government restrictions can effectively prohibit an exit decision. Rail service, for example, cannot simply be terminated.

Managerial pride may also be a factor. Professional managers often view themselves as problem solvers and are reluctant to admit defeat. Several anecdotes describe firms that have had to send a series of executives to close down a subsidiary, because each executive convinced him- or herself after arriving that a turnaround was possible, only subsequently to fail at the effort. Furthermore, there may be an emotional attachment to a business that has been in the "family" for many years or that was even the original business on which the rest of the firm was based. It is difficult to turn your back on such a valued friend.

Many firms avoid divestiture decisions until they become obvious or are forced on the firms by external forces. The better-managed—and, according to one study, more profitable—organizations will actively manage these decisions by systematically evaluating the strategic fit and future prospects of each business, then regularly making divestiture decisions or placing business units on a probationary status.[3] Jack Welch, during his first four years as GE's CEO, divested 117 business units accounting for 20 percent of the corporation's assets. Such divestitures can generate cash at a fair (as opposed to a forced sale) price, liberate management talent, help reposition the firm to match its strategic vision, and add vitality. The divested businesses will often benefit as well, as they will likely move to environments that will be more supportive in terms of not only assets and competencies but also the commitment to succeed.

SELECTING THE RIGHT STRATEGY FOR THE DECLINING ENVIRONMENT

The spectrum of investment alternatives ranges from invest to hold to milk to exit. In order to determine the optimal alternative in a declining environment, a firm needs to consider strategic uncertainties in the five areas summarized in Figure 15.3 and discussed next.

Market Prospects

A basic consideration is the rate and pattern of decline. A precipitous decline should be distinguished from a slow, steady decline. One determining factor is the existence of pockets of enduring demand, segments that are capable of supporting a core demand level. The vacuum-tube industry had replacement demand even after vacuum tubes had all but disappeared from new products. In the leather industry, leather upholstery is still a healthy market.

Another factor affecting the decline rate, particularly in dynamic industries, is product obsolescence. When disposable diapers were introduced, the sale of rubber panties for babies dramatically declined.

A related issue is the predictability of the pattern. If the pattern is based on demographics, such as the size of the teen population, then it may be predictable. In contrast, fashion and technology can change quickly, and therefore predictions based on

---

SOME STRATEGIC UNCERTAINTIES

Market Prospects
1. Is the rate of decline orderly and predictable?
2. Are there pockets of enduring demand?
3. What are the reasons for the decline—is it temporary?

Competitive Intensity
4. Are there dominant competitors with unique skills or competencies?
5. Are there many competitors unwilling to exit or contract gracefully?
6. Are customers brand loyal? Is there product differentiation?
7. Are there price pressures?

Performance/Strengths
8. Is the business profitable? What are its future prospects?
9. What is the market-share position and trend?
10. Does the business have some SCAs with respect to key segments?
11. Can the business manage costs in the face of declining sales?

Interrelationships with Other Businesses
12. Is there synergy with other businesses?
13. Is the business compatible with the firm's current strategic thrust?
14. Can the firm support the cash needs of the business?

Implementation Barriers
15. What are the exit barriers?
16. Can the organization manage all the investment options?

Figure 15.3   The Investment Decision in a Declining Industry

them are riskier. A slow decline may accelerate, or a declining market may suddenly be revived. For example, the natural food trend has revived oatmeal, and an inflation-stimulated price sensitivity at one point gave Kool-Aid a resurgence.

Competitive Intensity

Another consideration is the level of competitive intensity by the industry structure. Are there dominant competitors that have substantial shares and a set of unique assets and competencies that form formidable sustainable competitive advantages? Is there a relatively large set of competitors that is not disposed either to exit or to contract gracefully? If the answer to either of these questions is yes, the profit prospects for others may be dismal.

Another perspective comes from customers. A key to making a profit in a declining industry is price stability. Are customers relatively price insensitive, as are buyers of savings pass-books? Is there a relatively high level of product differentiation and brand loyalty? Or has the product become a commodity? Are costs involved in switching from one brand to another?

Performance/Strengths

A business position appraisal should focus on business strengths and capabilities, as well as on current performance. Sources of strength in a declining environment are usually quite different from those in other contexts. The strengths must reflect the reality that there are fewer products to make and fewer customers to serve. Thus, such sources of strength as economies of scale, vertical integration, and technological leadership may not be needed or may even be liabilities. Helpful strengths in a declining industry are:

- Strong established relationships with profitable customers, especially those in pockets of enduring demand.
- A strong brand name. At this stage it will be difficult for competitors to alter their images significantly. Thus, the nature of an established image can be most important.
- The ability to operate profitably with underutilized assets.
- The ability to reduce costs as business shrinks; flexibility in applying assets and resources.
- A large market share if economies of scale are present.

An analysis of current profitability is important to the assessment of future position, but care is needed, especially if an exit decision is involved. Book assets, for example, may be overstated, because their market value may be small or even negative if they have associated obligations. Some overhead items that would have to be shifted to other businesses under an exit alternative might be properly omitted from some analyses.

Interrelationships with Other Businesses

Interrelationships among businesses should be considered in a firm's investment decision. A business may support other businesses within the firm by providing part of a system, by supporting a distribution channel, or by using excess plant capacity or a by-product of another production process. If the firm is vertically integrated, a decision to leave a particular business may affect the other components.

Visibly closing down a business may generate a credibility problem for the parent corporation, especially if a large write-off is involved. Closing down could affect access to financial markets and influence the opinion of dealers, suppliers, and customers about the firm's other operations. When General Motors closed its Oldsmobile Division shock waves were felt among customers, suppliers, and other stakeholders.

Implementation Barriers

Finally, the possible implementation problems associated with each option must be considered. Exit barriers affect the exit option. The milk option presents difficult management problems in that both the managers and customers involved will have to accept a disinvest context. The hold option is also a delicate issue, because a passive investment strategy can inadvertently lead to a loss of position.

HOSTILE MARKETS

Declining markets can create hostile markets, markets usually associated with over-capacity, low margins, intense competition, and management in turmoil. However, hostile markets can also occur in growth contexts if there is overcapacity caused by too many competitors. It is not an exaggeration to say that most industries are either hostile or in danger of becoming hostile. It is thus useful to take a close look at hostility. Fortunately, a major study is available to provide insights.

Windemere Associates, a management consulting firm, has systematically studied more than forty hostile industries. Its findings are reported in two articles by Don Potter.[4] These reports suggest that hostility can be precipitated by competitors who are attracted to—and who tend to minimize the risks of— growth contexts in which margins and profits are high. Therefore, high prices and profits should be a cause for concern as well as celebration, and it might be worthwhile in the long run to forgo them or to build other barriers to discourage competitors from entering the market.

A Hostile Industry—Six Phases

The Windemere study identified six phases of hostile markets (shown in Figure 15.4) that could span decades. Although they don't always occur in the order set forth, most do occur. An understanding of this six-phase life cycle can help firms prevent or manage hostile environments.

Phase 1—Margin pressure
Phase 2—Share shifts
Phase 3—Product proliferation
Phase 4—Self-defeating cost reduction
Phase 5—Consolidation and shakeout
Phase 6—Rescue

Figure 15.4   Six Phases of Hostility

Phase 1—Margin Pressure

Predatory pricing to gain share, stimulated in part by overcapacity, leads to margin erosion; the prime beneficiaries are large customers. As a result, competitors attempt to create or find protected niches. However, others eventually will encroach on attractive niches. Note that efforts to isolate Japanese companies in the low end of copiers, cars, motorcycles, and semiconductors failed, as they eventually moved their product lines up, attacking the high-margin niche markets.

Phase 2—Share Shifts

Each year, 1 to 5 percent of the share in a hostile market will shift from one group of companies to another. One cause is the leader's trap, when a leading company, often the biggest and best firm, will not match discounting in its market, believing that a superior product and customer loyalty will support a large price premium. This strategy rarely works. The leader's prices eventually fall, but only after market share (which is difficult to regain) is lost and customers have become convinced that the leader's prices before the adjustment were excessive. The experience of PC brands that clung to high prices long after competitors such as Dell had established lower price points, is illustrative. Another cause of share shift is a flight to quality, when a company, such as FedEx, simply delivers more reliability or has more accessible distribution. A third cause is acquisitions, which occur when competitors become desperate to achieve economies of scale.

Phase 3—Product Proliferation

Competitors compete for market share by attempting to generate value for the customer through product proliferation. The product might be upgraded by bundling additional features or functions, such as a suite hotel room, color-tinted cement, or not-from-concentrate orange juice. A soup company might add new lines, such as low-sodium soups or new recipes. A bank might add new checking accounts with service variants. Product proliferation rarely results in winners, but raises the ante for all. Further, other firms such as Marriott's Fairfield Inn might offer versions of the product that delete features and services.

Phase 4—Self-Defeating Cost Reduction

A pressure to maintain margins leads to self-defeating cost reductions. A company intent on limiting investments may fail to match product and quality improvements of competitors, which can be costly in terms of share. For example, some manufacturers of organic-felt shingles for roofing were slow to invest in improved glass-fiber shingles until a major share shift occurred. Even more serious is the failure to keep pace with rising industry quality standards. As General Motors, Schlitz, and many others have learned, it is hard to recover from a damaged reputation. Attempting to squeeze margins out of the distribution channel or sales force may provide illusory short-term savings at the expense of market position.

Phase 5—Consolidation and Shakeout

Consolidation, generally geared to reducing overhead, occurs in three waves. The first is internal and involves reducing the workforce, closing facilities, and pruning businesses. The second involves mergers and acquisitions, with stronger firms buying weaker ones, in part to reduce overhead. The third is global in scope, with combinations of international players being formed, such as when Bridgestone bought Firestone Tires.

Phase 6—Rescue

Industries can emerge from hostility, some in as few as five years, but most after a decade or longer. One route is consolidation, when three or four key players control more than 80 percent of the market and all players have given up trying to win share through price competition. Procter & Gamble and Kimberly-Clark have achieved such a consolidation in the disposable diaper market. However, it can take fifteen to twenty years (as it did in appliances) for consolidation to play out. Industries may emerge from hostility more quickly if demand grows enough to soak up overcapacity. The necessary growth in demand may be fueled by expanded customer markets or shifts in the value of international currencies that stimulate export demand.

Strategies That Win in Hostile Markets

The Windemere study identifies two types of firms that have achieved above-average sales growth and profitability within the hostile industries. The first type, termed Gold competitors, holds the number one or two position and includes such firms as FedEx, American Airlines, Alcoa Aluminum, Canon Copiers, Owens Corning Fiberglas roofing, Yellow Freight trucking, and Paccar trucks. The second, termed Silver competitors, includes firms such as Airborne Express, Alaska Airlines, Pitney Bowes copiers, Tamko roofing, and Freightline trucks. Silver competitors are smaller and occupy number three slots, or lower, in sales.

An examination of how these two types of firms have succeeded in hostile conditions is illuminating. Their recipe for success has five basic ingredients.

Focus on Large Customers

Volume, which is crucial because it drives the cost structure, comes from a relatively small subset of customers. Gold competitors are the prime suppliers to the industry's largest customers, although they serve others as well. Their weapons are a strong brand identity with end users and close relationships with the large-volume distribution channels. They adapt well to channel shifts. Owens Corning Fiberglas, for example, added a strong retail marketing program to its wholesale distribution when retail channels became important. In industries without channels of distribution, Gold companies will attempt to create a large customer out of medium-sized firms. FedEx, for example, created a parts bank program that maintained an inventory of parts for firms in order to expedite shipment.

Because Silver companies rarely possess the infrastructure to serve the largest customers as effectively as their Gold competitors, they focus instead on developing strong relationships with medium-sized customers. Freightline focuses on selling its trucks to small fleet owners, for example. These second-tier customers tend to emphasize good service and reasonable prices to their own end-user customers. Silvers can thus service their customers without sacrificing margins. To attract these customers, Silvers often adopt industry specialties. Ball, for example, has become the major supplier of wide-mouth jars to the food industry.

Differentiate on Reliability

The top firms tend to differentiate on intangibles such as reliability and a relationship of trust and confidence rather than on product features and attributes, which are easier to copy. The focus is on providing the end user with a product or service that works consistently and the channel member with efficient and reliable delivery.

Gold companies use widespread physical presence and advertising to create a large share of mind and a strong brand identity with end users. With channel customers, Golds reduce costs by investing in information technology.

Silvers offer service levels that are higher and more consistent than those of their rivals. Pitney Bowes guarantees a four-hour response time on a copier service call, for example. Silvers tend to have strong channels and often offer exclusivity of territories to protect them.

Cover Broad Spectrum of Price Points

Golds will offer a broad array of products covering the high, medium, and low ends of the market. They avoid leaving niches available to others and end up with a product mix that mirrors the market. Silvers will usually participate in the high-end market but will not feel constrained by a niche segment. Rather, they will introduce products that are responsive to their largest customers.

Turn Price into a Commodity

In the early stages of hostility, price differences can be as large as 10 to 15 percent. However, price differentials eventually converge to within 5 percent and become less important. Golds, such as FedEx in air express, Roadway in less-than-truckload trucking, and IBM in personal computers, drop their price umbrella so that smaller competitors can grow and price at the market. They basically match the price of peers, thereby removing price from the customers' buying criteria. Their superior performance is rewarded by customer loyalty. Silvers gain share initially by discounting, but eventually their discount level is reduced and their focus shifts to delivering superior performance for key customers.

Have an Effective Cost Structure

The most successful companies in hostile markets have an effective cost structure. Golds such as Gallo in table wine and John Deere in farm equipment achieve high productivity not only by exploiting economies of scale but also by investing in automation and information systems to reduce costs. Silvers target the high end of the market where returns are better and focus intently on key customers. They are also customer focused in their R&D, and they stretch their marketing budgets by concentrating on existing customers and avoiding advertising directed at gaining new customers.

In summary, the companies that outperform others in hostile industries tend to focus attention on large customers, differentiate on reliability, cover a wide spectrum of price points, turn price into a commodity, and have effective cost structures. However, the Golds compete very differently from the Silvers. Golds enjoy significant economies of scale, have a broad presence in share of shelf and share of mind, and offer efficiencies to channel partners. Silver firms are smaller, offer above-standard service, compete at higher price points, protect the margins of their channel partners, and focus on low unit cost with key customers.

KEY LEARNINGS

- One strategic option in a declining or stagnant industry is to create a growth context, revitalizing the industry by seeking new markets, technologies, applications-marketing tactics, government-stimulated demand, and growth submarkets.

- Another option is to be the profitable survivor by strengthening a leadership position and encouraging others to exit, perhaps by buying their assets.

- A milking or harvest strategy (generating cash flow by reducing investment and operation expenses) works when the involved business is not crucial to the firm financially or synergistically. For milking to be feasible, though, sales must decline in an orderly way.

- The exit decision can be optimal, even though it is psychologically and professionally painful and usually must face organizational barriers. A proactive divestiture policy will be better than waiting until the situation deteriorates to the point that the decision is obvious.

- The investment decision in declining markets should rely on an analysis of market prospects, competitive intensity, business strengths, interrelationships with other businesses in the firm, and implementation barriers.

- Hostile markets, caused by too many competitors as well as declining demand, typically go through phases: margin pressures, share shifts, product proliferation, self-defeating cost reductions, consolidation, and rescue.

- Two strategies to gain above-average returns in hostile markets are represented by Golds (number one or two firms with economies of scale and substantial presence) and Silvers (number three or lower firms that focus on a smaller segment, usually at the high end of the market).

FOR DISCUSSION

1. Identify examples of brands that have created growth in stagnant or declining industries. What revitalization routes were taken?
2. Identify profitable survivors in declining markets. Why was Kunz so profitable over time? Why did others leave the marketplace?
3. Identify brands that are employing a milking strategy. What are the risks?
4. Consider a divestment strategy. Why is it hard to divest a business? Jack Welch divested hundreds of businesses during his tenure. What are some of the motivations that led to these divestitures?
5. Summarize the hostile market theory. What are the key assumptions? Evaluate the theory. How would you test it?

NOTES

1. Gregory L. White and Shirley Leung, "Middle Market Shrinks As Americans Migrate Toward the High End," *Wall Street Journal*, March 29, 2002, p. 1.
2. Some excellent research has been done on strategy development in declining industries, on which the balance of this chapter draws. It has been reported in Michael E. Porter, *Competitive Strategy*, New York: The Free Press, 1980, chapter 8; Kathryn Rudie Harrigan, *Strategies for Declining Businesses*, Lexington, Mass.: Lexington Books, 1980; and Kathryn Rudie Harrigan and Michael E. Porter, "End-Game Strategies for Declining Industries," *Harvard Business Review*, July–August 1983, pp. 111–120.
3. Lee Dranikoff, Tim Koller, and Antoon Schneider, "Divestiture: Strategy's Missing Link," *Harvard Business Review*, May 2002, pp. 75–83.
4. Donald V. Potter, "Success Under Fire: Policies to Prosper in Hostile Times," *California Management Review*, Winter 1991, pp. 24–38, and "Strategies That Win in Hostile Markets," *California Management Review*, Fall 1994.

Leveraging a Brand Asset

DOVE

In 1955, Unilever (then Lever Brothers) introduced Dove, which contained a patented, mild cleansing ingredient, into the soap category. It was positioned—then and now—as a "beauty bar" with one-fourth cleansing cream that moisturizes skin while washing (as opposed to the drying effect of regular soap). Advertisements reinforced the message by showing the cream being poured into the beauty bar. In 1979, the phrase "cleansing cream" was replaced with "moisturizer cream."

Also in 1979, a University of Pennsylvania dermatologist showed that Dove dried and irritated skin significantly less than ordinary soaps. Based on this study, Unilever began aggressively marketing Dove to doctors. Soon about 25 percent of Dove users said they bought the brand because a doctor recommended it, greatly enhancing the bar's credibility as a moisturizer. By the mid-1980s, Dove had become the best-selling soap brand and commanded a price premium. By 2003, Unilever was selling $330 million of Dove bar soap, occupying more than 24 percent of the market, far ahead of its nearest competitor.

The first effort to extend the Dove brand occurred in 1965. The extension, into dishwashing detergent, survives but has to be regarded as disappointing. Because the leading competitor at the time, Palmolive, promised to "soften hands while you do dishes," the hope was that the Dove cleansing-cream message would translate into a competitive benefit. Instead, customers felt no reason to change from the well-positioned Palmolive, and since Dove's reputation for moisturizing and beauty did not imply clean dishes, there was simply no perceived benefit. After receiving weak market acceptance for the extension, Dove lowered the price, creating another source of strain on the brand. Fifteen years after its launch, the brand languished at a rather poor seventh in the U.S. market, with a share of around 3 percent. The dishwashing detergent not only failed to enhance the Dove brand, it also undoubtedly inhibited Dove from extending its franchise further for decades.

In 1990 the Dove soap patent ran out, and arch-competitor P&G was soon testing an Olay beauty bar with moisturizing properties, a product that rolled out in 1993. One year later, Olay body wash appeared and soon garnered over 25 percent of a high-margin product category. Blindsided, the Dove brand team belatedly recognized that theirs was the natural brand to own the moisturizer body wash position. The firm had apparently missed the chance to be a leader in this new subcategory.

In response to Olay, the firm rushed Dove Moisturizing Body wash into stores. The product did not live up to the Dove promise, however, and a reformulation in 1996 was only a partial improvement. In 1999, though, Dove finally got it right with the innovative Nutrium line, based on a technology that deposited lipids, Vitamin E, and other ingredients onto the skin. The advanced skin-nourishing properties provided enough of a lift to allow Dove to charge a 50 percent premium over its regular body wash. Later,

Dove introduced a version of Nutrium with antioxidants (which have been linked to reduced signs of aging), which helped Dove to pull even with Olay in the body wash category. By leveraging strong brand equity, pursuing innovative technology, and being persistent, Dove was able to overcome a late entry into the market.

The Dove body wash efforts influenced the brand's soap business, which was flat until the mid-1990s (and, in fact, declined in 1996). The introduction of the body wash corresponded to a 30 percent growth surge in Dove soap from the mid-1990s to 2001, evidence that the energy and exposure of the Dove brand helped even though the product was somewhat wanting during much of that period. In addition, the Nutrium subbrand, established in the body wash category, was employed to help the soap business. In 2001, Unilever introduced a Dove Nutrium soap (positioned as replenishing skin nutrients) that was priced about 30 percent higher than regular Dove.

Another battlefield, entered in 2000, was the rather mature category of deodorants—even though dryness, the key benefit, seemed contradictory to the Dove promise of moisturizing, and the target segment was younger than the typical Dove customer. Despite these apparent risks, Dove introduced a deodorant line with uncharacteristically bold advertising (for example, one tag line was "Next stop, armpit heaven"). As it turned out, the deodorants were named as one of the top ten non-food new products in 2001, garnering over $70 million in sales with close to 5 percent of the market, making Dove the number two brand among female deodorants. The "one-quarter moisturizing lotion" positioning, effectively communicated as protecting sensitive underarm skin, generated a Dove spin on dryness that differentiated the product line.

In spite of this win, P&G's Olay again beat Dove to a new market in the summer of 2000, this time with disposable face cloths infused with moisturizers. It took Dove about a year to respond with its Dove Daily Hydrating Cleansing Cloths. With the body wash success behind it, however, the Dove brand was well suited to compete in this category, and initial results have been promising.

The next product extension was Dove Hair Care, whose moisturizing qualities were directly responsive to one of the top two unmet needs in the category. The product's branded differentiator, Weightless Moisturizers, is a set of fifteen ingredients designed to make the hair softer, smoother, and more vibrant without adding any extra weight. After achieving top-selling status in Japan and Taiwan, Dove Hair Care entered the U.S. market in early 2003 with a massive introduction campaign, joining a product family used by nearly one-third of American families.

With these extension successes, Dove in 2003 became a $2 billion dollar brand, over ten times as lucrative as it was in 1990.

FOR DISCUSSION

1. Why was Dove dormant for so long?
2. What were the keys to the success that Dove achieved in building its brand into a $2 billion business? What was the role of success momentum? The subbrand?

3. What was the role of a vigorous competitor? Would Dove have gotten there without P&G pushing (or, more accurately, pulling) the brand?

4. Why were Dove soap sales affected by the other Dove successes?

5. What does this case tell you about first-mover advantage?

Source: Adapted with the permission of the Free Press, a division of Simon & Schuster Adult Publishing Group from *Brand Portfolio Strategy: Creating Relevance, Differentiation, Energy, Leverage, and Clarity,* by David A. Aaker. Copyright © 2004 by David A. Aaker. All rights reserved.

Creating brand assets to support a growth strategy

INTEL

During the 1990s, Intel achieved remarkable success in terms of increased sales, stock return, and market capitalization. Sales of its microprocessors went from $1.2 billion in 1989 to over $33 billion in 2000. The firm's market capitalization grew to over $400 billion in just over three decades. Intel's ability and willingness to reinvent its product line again and again, making obsolete business areas in which it had big investments, certainly played a key role in its success. Its operational excellence in creating complex new products with breathtaking speed and operating microprocessor fabrication plants efficiently and effectively was also critical.

Intel's sustained rise would not have happened without the firm's ability to create and manage a brand portfolio that included a complex set of endorser brands and subbrands. The brand story really starts in 1978 when Intel created the microprocessor chip, the 8086, which won IBM's approval to power its first PC. The Intel chip and its subsequent generations—the 286 in 1982, the 386 in 1985, and the 486 in 1989—defined the industry standard and made Intel the dominant brand.

In early 1991, though, Intel was facing competitive pressures from competitors who were making clones of the 386 and exploiting the fact that Intel failed to obtain trademark protection on the X86 series. Calling their products names like the AMD386, these firms created confusion by implying that a AMD386 was as effective as any other 386.

To respond to this business challenge, in the spring of 1991 Intel began a remarkable ingredient branding program, establishing the "Intel Inside" brand with an initial budget of around $100 million. (The logo—which has a light, personal touch, as if it was written on an informal note—was a sharp departure from Intel's corporate "dropped-e" logo.) Under the branding program, computer manufacturers who properly displayed the Intel Inside logo received a 6 percent allowance on their purchases of Intel microprocessors, which could be used to pay for up to 50 percent of the partner's advertising. Partners also were required to create subbrands for products using a competing microprocessor, so that buyers would realize that they were buying a computer without Intel Inside.

This decision was very controversial within Intel. many people argued that brand building was irrelevant for a firm that only sold to a handful of computer manufacturers; the money could be used for R&D instead. Within a relatively short time, however, the Intel Inside logo became ubiquitous, and the program was an incredible success. Even as the budget grew to well over $1 billion per year, the brand-building effort was perceived to generate such loyalty that it more than paid for itself.

For many years, a computer with an Intel Inside logo could be sold at around a 10 percent premium (for the whole computer, not just the Intel microprocessor). Because of the logo's wide exposure, Intel was given credit for creating reliable and innovative products and for being an organization of substance and leadership—even though most computer buyers had no idea what a microprocessor was, or why Intel's were better.

In the fall of 1992, though, when Intel was ready to announce the successor to the 486 chip, it faced increasing competitor confusion despite the Intel Inside campaign. A huge decision loomed. Calling the successor the Intel 586 would leverage the Intel Inside brand and provide familiarity to customers who had become accustomed to the X86 progression. Even so, Intel elected to give the chip a new name: Pentium.

Four key issues guided the decision to adapt the Pentium brand. First, it would avoid confusion with competitors who might also use the 586 name. Second, the cost of creating a new brand and transitioning customers to it, although huge, was within the capacity and will of Intel. Third, the Intel Inside equity and program could be leveraged by adding "Intel Inside" on the new Pentium logo, in essence making the former brand an endorser for the latter. Finally, a new name would signal that the product was a significant enough advance to support demand at a premium price, which was necessary to pay for a costly new fabrication plant.

A few years later, Intel developed an improved Pentium with superior graphic capability. Rather than change the brand name itself, the firm added a branded technology, MMX, to the Pentium. This decision gave the Pentium brand more time to repay its investment, and it reserved the impact of announcing a new-generation chip for a more substantial technological leap. Subsequent generations did emerge and leveraged the Pentium name and equity with names like Pentium Pro (1995), Pentium II (1997), Pentium III (1999), and Pentium 4 (2000).

In 1998, Intel decided to extend its reach to mid-range and higher-end servers and workstations. To address this market, it developed features that allowed four or eight processors to be linked to supply the necessary computing power. This progress, however, raised a branding issue. On one hand. because the Pentium brand was associated with the lower-end personal computer market, it would not be regarded as suitable for servers and workstations. On the other hand, the market would not support developing yet another stand-alone brand alongside Intel Inside and Pentium. The solution was to introduce a subbrand, the Pentium II Xeon, in 1998. The subbrand distanced the new microprocessor enough from Pentium to make it palatable for the higher-end users. It also had the secondary advantage of enhancing the Pentium brand because it associated Pentium with a more advanced product.

In 2001, the Xeon subbrand stepped out from behind the Pentium name. Technological advances (in particular, the branded NetBurst architecture) had dramatically improved the chip's processing power. The Xeon brand had also become established, making it easier to support as a stand-alone brand, and initial trademark issues over the Xeon name had been resolved. Finally, because the target market had become even more important to Intel, having a brand devoted to it was now a strategic imperative.

In 1999, another problem or opportunity emerged. As the PC market matured, a value segment emerged, led by some competitors eager to find a niche and willing to undercut the Intel price points. Intel needed to compete in this market, if only defensively, but using the Pentium brand (even with a subbrand) would have been extremely risky. The solution was a stand-alone brand, Celeron. The brand-building budget, like that for many value brands, was minimal—the target market found the brand, rather than the other way around.

The decision was made to link the Celeron to Intel Inside, so there was an indirect link to Pentium. The trade-off was the credibility that the Intel endorsement would provide to Celeron versus the need to protect the Pentium brand from cannibalization and a tarnished image through association with a lower-end entry.

In 2001, Intel introduced the Itanium processor as a new-generation successor to the Pentium series. Why not call it the Pentium 5? The processor was built from the ground up with an entirely new architecture, based on a branded design termed Explicitly Parallel Instruction Computing (EPIC), and it had 64-bit computing power as opposed to the 32-bit Pentiums. Capable of delivering a new level of performance for high-end enterprise-class servers, the processor needed a new name to signal that it was qualitatively different than the Pentium.

In 2003, Intel introduced its Centrino mobile technology. The new processor provided laptop computers with enhanced performance, extended battery life, integrated wireless connectivity, and thinner, lighter designs. These groundbreaking advances promised to fundamentally affect personal lifestyles and business productivity by enabling people to "unconnect" (the Centrino advertising tag line is "Unwire Your Life"). The new Centrino logo reflects the Intel vision of the convergence of communication and computing, as well as a new approach to product development. Rather than simply pushing the performance envelope, this product responded to real customer needs as determined by market research.

The most dramatic element of the Centrino logo is its shape, a sharp departure from the rectangular design family that preceded it. The two wings suggest a merger of technology and lifestyle, a forward-looking perspective, and the freedom to go where you will. The magenta color used for the Centrino wing balances the Intel blue and visually connotes youth and excitement while suggesting a connection between technology and passion, logic and emotions. The Intel Inside logo has also evolved. More precise, sophisticated, and confident, it now provides a link to the classic dropped-E Intel corporate logo and reflects a world in which the positives of the corporate connection and the loyalty program can be linked.

FOR DISCUSSION

1. The Intel Inside campaign started in the spring of 1991, and $100 million was budgeted for it in 1992. Was that worthwhile? Why would Compaq participate in the program? What about Dell? How would you evaluate the program? What alternatives does a competitor such as AMD have to combat the Intel Inside branding strategy?

2. In the fall of 1992, when the "586" chip was ready, would you have called it Intel 586 or i586, or would you have started over with a new name? What are the pros and cons of each alternative?

3. What effects did changing the brand name from X86 to Pentium and others have on Intel's ability to manage the product life cycle of the newly branded products?

4. When would a new product require a new name (such as Pentium) versus a new subbrand (such as Xeon)?

5. Evaluate the Centrino brand strategy. Will it help Intel be relevant to the mobile computing world?

IMPLEMENTATION

CHAPTER SIXTEEN

Organizational Issues

All progress is initiated by challenging current conceptions and executed by supplanting existing institutions.
—*George Bernard Shaw*

Structure follows strategy.
—*Alfred Chandler, Jr.*

Those that implement the plans must make the plans.
—*Patrick Hagerty, Texas Instruments*

Korvette's started as a luggage and appliance discounter selling name brands for $5 from a second-floor loft in Manhattan. By 1962, it had become a profitable discount chain with a dozen stores, and its founder was named as one of the most influential retailers of the century by a Harvard retailing guru.[1] Its initial success prompted an aggressive growth strategy, which turned out to be a disaster. The firm dramatically expanded both the number of stores and the number of cities served, expanded its product line by adding fashion goods, furniture, and grocery products, and added more store amenities.

This was a defensible growth strategy, similar to that of other successful discounters, such as Kmart. The problem was its implementation. The strategy was not supported by the right people, structure, systems, or culture. Korvette's personnel lacked the depth to staff the new stores and the expertise to handle the new product areas. The centralized structure did not adapt well to multiple cities and product lines. The management systems were not sophisticated enough to handle the added complexity. The culture of casual management with low prices as the driving force was not replaced with another strong culture that would be appropriate to the new business areas. As a result, by 1966 the firm was near death, and it never recovered.

The Korvette story graphically illustrates the importance of strategy implementation. The assessment of any strategy should include a careful analysis of organizational risks and a judgment about the nature of any required organizational changes and their associated costs and feasibility. Toward that end, this chapter first develops a conceptual framework that will help in analyzing an organization.

A CONCEPTUAL FRAMEWORK

The conceptual framework shown in Figure 16.1 can be used to identify and position organizational components and their interactions. The heart of the framework is a set of four key constructs that describe the organization: structure, systems, people, and culture. The figure includes strategy, which must successfully interact with the four organizational components, and organizational performance. It also includes external analysis and internal analysis, which provide a link to Figure 2.1 and the strategy-development process. Recall that a strategy involves the product-market investment decision, the value proposition, the selection of functional area strategies, and the identification of bases for sustainable competitive advantage.

Consideration of organizational components can help a business identify actual and potential implementation problems, as well as determine how its organization would adapt to a new strategy. The first section of this chapter discusses each central component and its link to strategy. The need for achieving a fit or congruence among these four organizational components and strategy is then considered. Finally, ways by which an organization can become more innovative and responsive to change are suggested.

STRUCTURE

Organizational structure defines lines of authority and communication and specifies the mechanism by which organizational tasks and programs are accomplished.

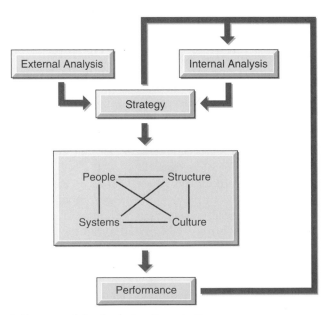

Figure 16.1   A Framework for Analyzing Organizations

Decentralization versus Centralization

Nearly every organization, from Stanford University to P&G, GE, HP, and BofA, prides itself on being decentralized. And with good reasons.

Autonomous groups running distinct businesses have enormous inherent advantages. The managers are close to the market and can therefore understand customer needs. They are also intimate with the product technology and thus can chart the direction of product offerings. Being empowered to act quickly in an environment means no delays in making and implementing strategic decisions, a difference that is vital in dynamic markets. Also, because distinct business units can be held accountable for investments and results, business performance will be known in a timelier and less ambiguous manner. The most impressive feature of decentralization, however, is that it fosters incredible energy and vitality. Managers are empowered and motivated to innovate, to gain competitive advantage by providing superior value propositions to the customers. Nevertheless, there are challenges as well.

One challenge facing a decentralized organization is creating cross-business synergy. Potential synergy is often unrealized because having a host of silos can involve duplication, inefficiencies, and lost opportunities to create value for customers. In addition, it may be hard for a business to support a world-class marketing, IT, or sales function unless it finds a way to combine resources with other units. The failure to achieve synergies can be debilitating when competition for customers is intense and margins are under pressure.

A second challenge is to respond strategically at the firm level to market dynamics. What is strategically optimal for a business unit may not be the best for the firm as a whole. Brand portfolio strategy, for example, is easily undermined if a brand is shared across business units, with each using the brand to its local advantage. Conversely, a technology R&D project that could result in advantage for several business units might not be justified when evaluated at the business level.

One way to address these problems is with centralized control, the polar opposite of decentralization. In this model, a centralized team makes all the strategic and tactical decisions and has a strong functional capability to implement them (or at least manage their implementation). Such a group will create business strategy from a firmwide perspective, and it can make sure that synergy opportunities are detected and exploited. To succeed, the central team needs to have credible knowledge of the products and the markets, the necessary resources, and the authority and stature to get things done. It will work best when the business scope is limited or there is a seasoned, knowledgeable CEO who has earned respect throughout the organization.

A central management team can influence decentralized business units even without controlling them by utilizing the approaches described in Chapter 11—namely, playing the role of a service provider, consultant, or facilitator. In the service provider role, the central team will manage a variety of support functions, such as sponsorship, marketing research, IT, advertising, and performance tracking. Business units would buy services from the central team. In the consultative role, the central team will develop insights and recommend strategies. As a facilitator of strategy development, the central team would be less aggressive in suggesting strategies but would support and facilitate them, using the resources and processes of the organization.

Whatever management style used by the central team—controlling, service provider, consultative, or facilitative—needs to match the organizational heritage and culture. If it is too disparate, it may be rejected like an incompatible transplanted organ in a human body. Sometimes a change agent is needed, though, and some organizational stress may be healthy. Whatever style is used, the central team will be most effective when it has resources, market knowledge, product knowledge, and respect. If it lacks any of these, it will be marginalized.

Matrix Organization

A matrix organization allows a person to have two or more reporting links. Several business units could share a sales force by having the salespeople report to a business unit as well as to the sales manager. An R&D group could have a research team that reports both to the business unit and to the R&D manager. As a result, the salespeople and the research team in these examples are each supported by a critical mass of employees and infrastructure that allows them to excel while still being a part of the business unit. A person might also be attached to a task force (assigned, for instance, to explore a new market opportunity). That person would report to both the task force manager and his or her business unit. The concept of dual reporting requires coordination and communication that can be stressful and costly, but it also provides the flexibility needed to deal with a fast-moving market.

The Virtual Corporation

The virtual corporation is a team of people and organizations specifically designed for a particular client or job. The organizations brought together may be suppliers, customers, and competitors. The people can be drawn from a variety of sources and might include contract workers who are hired only for the project at hand. The virtual corporation can sometimes be formed or modified in a matter of days, which means it is the ultimate response in a fast-moving environment.

Communication firms, for example, are now forming teams tailored to the needs of particular clients. Some members of the team will come from subsidiary firms specializing in corporate design, packaging, direct marketing, and promotions. Others may come from firms that specialize in brochures and the media. The core of the team is likely to be located in a single building, but some team members will be connected via computer workstations that share visual images and in-process advertising. Thus, clients do not have to wait for an agency with the optimal set of characteristics to evolve; it can be formed almost overnight. WPP, the world's largest communication firm, has formed an ongoing virtual firm around health-care marketing services that has become a dominant force in its market, with the virtual firm's CEO as the only employee.[2]

Alliance Networks

In the global environment, markets and competitors can change significantly, and it is important to be able to respond quickly. There may not be time to develop needed assets and competencies, and responses that require large commitments to new technologies or distribution channels may be risky, especially for a firm with little relevant background. One way to be able to go on-line immediately with necessary business changes is to form a network of alliances and joint ventures with suppliers, customers, distributors, and even competitors. With such a network, needed assets can be made available instantly, the firm can focus on what it does best, the risk of failure is shared, and many more opportunities can be funded.

The use of strategic alliances, their motivations, and how to make them work are discussed in detail in Chapter 11. These alliances play an especially important role in global strategy development.

SYSTEMS

Several management systems are strategically relevant. Among them are the budgeting/accounting, information, measurement and reward, and planning systems.

Accounting and Budgeting System

Accounting and budgeting are key elements in any management system. The risk that these systems cannot be adapted to the needs of a new strategy can be very real. An accounting and budgeting system that is well conceived and contains valuable historical data may not fit the reorganized structure required by the new strategy. Or a system that worked well for an electronic instruments firm may not work when applied to a new service business. Another concern is the system's influence on investment decisions, especially when a new strategy is proposed that does not fit a familiar pattern.

Information System

The information system and the technology, databases, models, and expert systems on which it is based can fundamentally affect strategy. The link between manufacturers and retailers, for example, is increasingly being forged by information technology.

EASY STEPS TO DESTROYING REAL VALUE
by Henry Mintzberg[3]

1. Manage the bottom line (as if companies make money by managing money).
2. Make a plan for every action. (No spontaneity please, definitely no learning.)
3. Move managers around to be certain they never get to know anything but management well, and let the boss kick himself upstairs so that he can manage a portfolio instead of a real business.
4. When in trouble, rationalize, fire, and divest; when out of trouble, expand, acquire, and still fire (it keeps employees on their toes); above all, never create or invent anything (it takes too long).

New systems control inventory and handle ordering, pricing, and promotions. The ability to control the information generated by retail scanners can be key to strategies of manufacturers and retailers. The creation, organization, and use of knowledge banks can be a significant strategic asset. Thus, understanding the current capability and future direction of an organization's information system is a key dimension of strategy development.

Measurement and Reward System

Measurement can drive behavior and thus directly affect strategy implementation. The key to strategy is often the ability to introduce appropriate performance measures that are linked to the reward structure.

One concern is to motivate employees to cooperate, communicate, and create synergy. Rewards that are based too closely on a business unit's performance can work against this motivational goal. As a result, many companies deliberately base a portion of their bonuses or evaluations on the results of a larger unit. Prophet, a brand strategy consulting firm with seven offices, encourages cross-office support by making its bonuses conditional on firmwide performance. Another business may focus on divisional performance because synergy across divisions is not realistic.

Another prerequisite is to create measures reflecting a long-term perspective in order to balance short-term financial results. Thus, measures such as customer satisfaction, customer loyalty, quality indicators, new products brought to market, or training program productivity may be useful to gauge the progress of strategic initiatives.

Planning System

An annual strategic planning process is almost always useful because it forces managers to take time out to consider strategic uncertainties. Without that impetus, routine tasks will generally absorb management's available time. Workshops and retreats are often crucial elements in dedicating quality time to planning.

Creative, out-of-the-box thinking (perhaps aided by formal creative-thinking exercises) is a vital part of any planning system. Too often, strategic planning is nothing but an extrapolation of past strategies, with a financial spreadsheet as the dominant tool. There are two problems with this approach. First, it will not lead to the breakthrough strategies that can reinvent a business when needed. Second, it will not provide the consideration of strategic options that provides the basis for adapting to new events or trends. When Eisenhower said, "Plans are nothing, planning is everything" in part he meant that the process of examining a variety of strategic options makes the manager more capable of adapting or changing when necessary.

Planning should not be separated from the values, culture, and energy of the organization. According to Mintzberg, successful planning is often based on a committing, rather than a calculating style of management: "Managers with a committing style engage people in a journey. They lead in such a way that everyone on the journey helps shape its course. As a result, enthusiasm inevitably builds along the way." Mintzberg paraphrases the sociologist Philip Selznick when he says that "strategies only take on value as committed people infuse them with energy." The output of strategic planning should have soul as well as logic.[4]

PEOPLE

A strategy is generally based on an organizational competency that, in turn, is based on people. Thus, strategies require certain types of people. For each strategy, it is important to know how many people, with what experience, depth, and skills, are needed for:

- Functional areas, such as marketing, manufacturing, assembly, and finance
- Product or market areas
- New product programs
- Management of particular types of people
- Management of a particular type of operation
- Management of growth and change

Make, Buy, or Convert

If a strategy requires capabilities not already available in the business, it will be necessary to obtain them. The make approach, developing a broad managerial or technical

---

STRATEGY AND PEOPLE DEVELOPMENT AT GE

Jack Welch, the legendary former GE CEO, created a system and culture to develop both strategy and people throughout his twenty-year tenure. Five elements were involved:[5]

- Each January, the top 5,000 GE executives gathered in Boca Raton to share best practices and set major business priorities. (In 2000, the priorities were e-commerce, globalization, and six-sigma quality.) Webcasts of the event were available to the whole organization.
- Each quarter, top executives met in two-day retreats facilitated by Welch and focused on initiatives related to the agenda set in Boca Raton. This was a key place for future leaders to emerge, earn respect, and demonstrate growth.
- Twice a year, Welch and others focused on personnel needs for each business, such as how to handle each unit's top 20 percent and bottom 10 percent of employees.
- Similar biannual sessions (one in the spring and one in the fall) looked at each business over a three-year horizon.
- The entire effort was supported by the GE social architecture of informality, candor, substantive dialogue, boundaryless behavior, emphasis on follow-through, and making judgments on qualitative business dimensions.

base by hiring and grooming workers, ensures that people will fit the organization, but it can take years.

The convert approach, converting the existing workforce to the new strategy, takes less time. AT&T is an example of a firm that attempted to change its orientation from that of service to marketing, largely by retraining existing staff. A host of strategies, particularly those precipitated by acquisitions, have failed because of the faulty assumption that an old staff could adapt to a new context. A supermarket buying team, for example, could not be adapted to the needs of a discount drugstore, mainly because a discount orientation and background were missing.

The buy approach, bringing in experienced people from the outside, is the immediate solution when a dramatic change in strategy needs to be implemented quickly, but it involves the risk of bringing in people who are accustomed to different systems and cultures.

Motivation

In addition to the type and quality of people, the motivation level can affect strategy implementation. There are, of course, a variety of ways to motivate people, including the fear of losing a job, financial incentives, self-fulfillment goals, and the development of goals for the organization or groups within the organization, such as teams or quality circles.

Motivation usually is enhanced if employees are empowered to accomplish their goals even when a departure from the routine response is required. People who are inhibited from using their initiative will eventually lose interest and become cynical. Motivation also is enhanced when employees are linked to the corporate culture and objectives. Companies can accomplish these links in part simply by providing titles, such as "host" (Disney), "crew member" (McDonald's), and "associate" (J. C. Penney).

CULTURE

As suggested by Figure 16.2, an organizational culture involves three elements:

- A set of shared values or dominant beliefs that define an organization's priorities.
- A set of norms of behavior.
- Symbols and symbolic activities used to develop and nurture those shared values and norms.

Shared Values

Shared values or dominant beliefs underlie a culture by specifying what is important. In a strong culture, the values will be widely accepted, and virtually everyone will be able to identify them and describe their rationale.

Shared values can have a variety of foci. They can involve, for example:

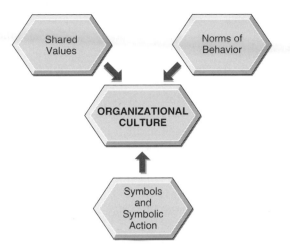

Figure 16.2   Organizational Culture

- A key asset or competency that is the essence of a firm's competitive advantage: We will be the most creative advertising agency.
- An operational focus: SAS focused on on-time performance.
- An organizational output: We will deliver zero defects or 100 percent customer satisfaction.
- An emphasis on a functional area: Black & Decker transformed itself from a firm with a manufacturing focus to one with a market-driven approach.
- A management style: This is an informal, flat organization that fosters communication and encourages unconventional thinking.
- A belief in the importance of people as individuals.
- A general objective, such as a belief in being the best or comparable to the best: Komatsu set out to beat Caterpillar; Samsung strove to be a major player in microwave ovens; Sharp wants to be one of the most innovative in any area in which it competes.

Norms

To make a real difference, the culture must be strong enough to develop norms of behavior—informal rules that influence decisions and actions throughout an organization by suggesting what is appropriate and what is not. Charles O'Reilly of Stanford University talks of culture as a social control system with norms as behavior guides.[6] The fact is that strong norms can generate much more effective control over what is actually done or not done in an organization than a very specific set of objectives, measures, and sanctions. People can always get around rules. The concept of norms is that people will not attempt to avoid them because they will be accompanied by a commitment to shared values.

O'Reilly suggests that norms can vary on two dimensions: the intensity or amount of approval/disapproval attached to an expectation and the degree of consensus or consistency with which a norm is shared.[7] It is only when both intensity and consensus exist that strong cultures emerge.

Norms encourage behavior consistent with shared values. Thus, in a quality service culture, an extraordinary effort by an employee, such as renting a helicopter to fix a communication component (a FedEx legend), would not seem out of line and risky; instead, it would be something that most in that culture would do under similar circumstances. Furthermore, sloppy work affecting quality would be informally policed by fellow workers, without reliance on a formal system. One production firm uses no quality-control inspectors or janitors. Each production-line person is responsible for the quality of his or her output and for keeping the work area clean. Such a policy would not work without support from a strong culture.

Symbols and Symbolic Action

Corporate cultures are largely developed and maintained by the use of consistent, visible symbols and symbolic action. In fact, the more obvious methods of affecting behavior, such as changing systems or structure, are often much less effective than seemingly trivial symbolic actions.

A host of symbols and symbolic actions are available. A few of the more useful are discussed next.

The Founder and Original Mission

A corporation's unique roots, including the personal style and experience of its founder, can provide extremely potent symbols. The strong culture of the Shaklee Corporation is due largely to its founder's involvement in holistic medicine, his contributions to vitamin development and use, and his ability to arouse enthusiasm in groups. The concept of entertainment developed by Walt Disney, the customer-oriented philosophy of J. C. Penney, and the product and advertising traditions started by the founders of Procter & Gamble continue to influence the cultures of their firms generations later.

Modern Role Models

Modern heroes and role models help communicate, personalize, and legitimize values and norms. Lou Gerstner became a symbol of the new marketing-focused culture at IBM. Other examples are the managers at 3M who tenaciously pursued ideas despite setbacks until they succeeded in building major divisions such as the Post-it Notes division, and the Frito-Lay workers who maintained customer service in the face of natural disasters.

Activities

An executive's use of time can be a symbolic action affecting the culture. An airline executive who spends two weeks a month obtaining a firsthand look at customer service sends a strong signal to the organization. Patterns of consistent

REPRESENTING CULTURE AND STRATEGY WITH STORIES, NOT BULLETS

Research has shown that stories are more likely than lists to be read and remembered. Nevertheless, most business strategists rely on bullet points to communicate both culture and strategy. 3M is one firm that has based its culture on classic stories—how initial failures of abrasive products led to product breakthroughs; how masking tape was invented; how a scientist conceived of Post-it Notes when his bookmarks fell out of a hymnal, and how the Post-it-Notes team, instead of giving up in the face of low initial sales, got people hooked on the product by flooding a city with samples. These stories communicate how innovation occurs at 3M and how its entrepreneurial culture operates.

At 3M, business strategy is also communicated via stories rather than the conventional bullets, which tend to be generic (the goal of increased market share applies to any business), skip over critical assumptions about how the business works (will increased market share fund new products, or result from new products?), and leave causal relationship, unspecified (if A is done, B becomes effective). A strategic story will involves several phases—setting the stage by describing the current situation, introducing the dramatic conflict in the form of challenges and critical issues, and reaching resolution with convincing stories about how the company can overcome obstacles and win. Presenting a narrative motivates the audience, adds richness and detail, and provides a glimpse into the logic of the strategist.[8]

reinforcement can represent another important symbolic activity. For example, a firm that regularly recognizes cost-saving accomplishments in a meaningful way with the visible support of top management can, over time, affect the culture.

Questions Asked

An executive of a major bank reportedly shifted concern from revenue to profit by continually asking about profit implications. When a type of question is continually asked by top executives and made a central part of meeting agendas and report formats, it will eventually influence the shared values of an organization.

Rituals

Rituals of work life, from hiring to eating lunch to retirement dinners, help define a culture. One of the early success stories in Silicon Valley was a firm with a culture that was based in part on a requirement that a person commit before knowing his or her salary and considerable pride in a Friday afternoon beer bust ritual.

OBTAINING STRATEGIC CONGRUENCE

Figure 16.3 lists a set of questions that provide a basis for analyzing an organization and its relationship to a proposed strategy. As discussed earlier, a strategy must match

STRUCTURE

- What is the organization's structure? How decentralized is it?
- What are the lines of authority and communication?
- What are the roles of task forces, committees, or similar mechanisms?

SYSTEMS

- How are budgets set?
- What is the nature of the planning system?
- What are the key measures used to evaluate performance?
- How does the accounting system work?
- How do product and information flow?

PEOPLE

- What are the skills, knowledge, and experience of the firm's employees?
- What is their depth and quality?
- What are the employees' expectations?
- What are their attitudes toward the firm and their jobs?

CULTURE

- Are there shared values that are visible and accepted?
- What are these shared values and how are they communicated?
- What are the norms of behavior?
- What are the significant symbols and symbolic activities?
- What is the dominant management style?
- How is conflict resolved?

STRATEGY

- Where would the new strategy fit into the organization?
- Would the new strategy fit into the strategic plan and be adequately funded?
- Would the systems and culture support the new strategy?
- What organizational changes would be required for the new strategy to succeed?
- What impact would these changes have? Are they feasible?

Figure 16.3 Obtaining Information about Organizational Components

the structure, systems, people, and culture of the organization. In addition, each organizational component needs to fit with the others. If an inconsistency exists, it is likely that implementation of the strategy will be affected.

The concept of organizational congruence suggests that interactions between organizational components should be considered, such as:

- ***Do the systems fit the structure?*** Does the compensation system emphasize teamwork rather than individual performance when teamwork and cooperation are required?

THE E-ORGANIZATION

E-organizations use the Internet to transform their business by fundamentally changing the way they interact and conduct business with suppliers, partners, and customers. These firms, such as Cisco, have developed very new organizational forms. In particular:

- **Structure**—Rather than hierarchical structures, flat, flexible, decentralized team- and alliance-based organizations are needed to allow fast and focused responses to strategic opportunities and problems around the world. Alliance partners have become an integral part of the firm at Dell and Cisco. Business units and teams are more likely to be organized around customers.
- **Systems**—At firms like Dell, suppliers, partners, and customers are integrated into virtually all systems. The latest information systems are required in order to improve customer service and increase personalization. Intranets become a key instrument in communicating experiences and managing initiatives.
- **People**—Leadership is now the province of the many rather than the few. An army of people is empowered to achieve change and support others in responding to emerging opportunities and threats. British Telecom, for example, created a team of evangelistic visionaries and mavericks who could quickly find markets for the firm's cutting-edge research.
- **Culture**—The culture tends to emphasize the customer, change, and innovation. Customer focus is a driving force at Cisco and IBM, for example, where customer-obsessed CEOs lead the way. Change, even fundamental business-model change, is supported by the culture. Innovation is the norm for e-organizations and acceptance of failure is often a visible value.[9]

- ***Do the people fit the structure?*** Can they operate within the organizational groups and integrate mechanisms to complete the task? For example, creative or entrepreneurial managers may be uncomfortable in a highly structured organization.
- ***Does the structure fit the culture?*** Does the structure complement the values or norms of the organization? For example, a top management group accustomed to controlling dedicated resources may be less effective in a matrix organization, in which persuasion and coordination are more important.

Corporate Culture and Strategy

Organizational culture provides the key to strategy implementation because it is such a powerful force for providing focus, motivation, and norms. Many strategies concentrate on an organizational asset or competency, such as the product quality level, service system, or customer support, or on a functional area, such as manufacturing or sales. A culture can provide support if it is congruent with the new structures, systems, and people required by a new strategy. If it is not congruent, however, the culture's motivations and norms could cripple the strategy.

A new strategy's fit with an organization's culture is of greater concern than the strategy's fit with the other organizational components because culture is so difficult to change. An oil company CEO developed elaborate diversification plans that failed because they were incompatible with the firm's oil business culture. The problems experienced by AT&T in its efforts to change from what was a service/production/internal focus to a marketing/external orientation illustrate how powerful and resistant to change a culture can be. AT&T very visibly changed its strategy and even the associated structure and systems (introducing product/market organizations and sales incentives), but was inhibited by the culture. When AT&T hired different types of personnel—MBAs and marketing people—it found inconsistencies between the new people and the change-resistant culture.

When a new strategy is proposed, it is important to understand the relationship of that strategy to the shared values and norms of the organization. Is it compatible? Will the culture have to be modified? If so, what impact will that have on the organization? Often the worst case develops when a strong positive culture is sacrificed to accommodate a new strategy, and the result is an absence of any positive culture. The Korvette case discussed at the beginning of this chapter illustrates this point.

Hit-Industry Topology

The need for congruence between strategy and organizational components can be illustrated by the three very different types of firms that compete in hit industries.[10] A hit industry is one in which the goal is to obtain, produce, and exploit a product that will have a relatively short life cycle. Examples of such industries include movies, records, fashion, publishing, video games, computer software, venture capital (especially in high-tech areas), and oil. Industries with short life cycles are interesting because many of their organizational problems are more intense and graphic.

The model in Figure 16.4 divides a hit industry into three functions, which are shown as being performed by different organizations, although often two or more will coexist within the same organization. An oil industry analogy provides the conceptual framework.

The first organizational type is termed drillers. They are the wildcatters who find oil fields and drill wells, the talent scouts and artists of the record industry the producers and writers in the movie industry, and the editors and authors in the publishing industry. A key success factor is to locate or create the new wells, properties, or projects. An ultimate goal in the record business, for example, would be to get a lock on performing talent and keep the artists so happy that they would not consider leaving the company. Key people tend to be creative, high-energy, decisive risk takers. They thrive in a flat organization with little structure and high bottom-line incentives.

The second organizational type is termed pumpers. They are the well operators and refiners of the oil business, the DVD pressers, the movie directors, and the printers in publishing. The key success factors in a pumping organization are operations, production engineering, and an ability to exploit the experience curve. The key people are disciplined, cost and production-oriented, in production and control jobs, and risk avoiders. A centralized organization with tight controls provides an appropriate context.

Strategy	Drillers	Pumpers	Distributors
Structure	• Flat, loose • Amorphous	• Centralized • Tight control	• Decentralized • Loose control
Bottom-line Performance Incentives	• High	• None	• Low
People	• Product development	• Production control	• Marketing and distribution
Culture	• Stay loose • Move fast • Take risks	• Disciplined • Cost oriented • Avoid risks	• Promotion-oriented • Control risks
Key Success Factors	• Finding and keeping key people • Idea source • Get products to market quickly	• Exploit the experience curve • Operations • Production • Engineering	• Distribution channels • Inventory • Promotion • Positioning • Pricing

Figure 16.4   A Model of Hit Industries

The third type specializes in distribution. The distributors are the pipeline operators and retailers in the oil industry and the distributors and retailers in the film, DVD, and publishing industries. The key success factors in a distribution business usually include marketing, promotion, physical distribution, and access to or even control over distribution channels. The key people are in marketing and distribution. A decentralized structure with loose controls and some bottom-line incentives is often effective.

The hit-industry topology shows how the lack of fit between organizational components can develop. Typically, an organization starts as a drilling company. After establishing some products and experiencing rapid growth, the company finds that it desperately needs to control production costs, develop a secure, effective distribution channel, and professionalize the marketing effort. As a result, pumping and distribution people are brought in. The organization then takes the form of either a pumper or a distributor, depending on which function is most critical or which type of person becomes the CEO. In any case, the system, structure, and culture of the organization change, and the drillers who started the business become uncomfortable and leave, perhaps to start a competing business. When the existing wells dry up or are damaged by competition, no one in the organization is available to create new ones.

It is a challenge in any business to keep access to drillers. One approach is to keep the drillers satisfied by financial incentives and organizational mechanisms, such as ad hoc groups with extraordinary freedom and autonomy. However, these special incentives may create inequities and disincentives for others. If entrepreneurial engineers are becoming millionaires, whereas those charged with maintaining existing products are on a fixed salary, tensions are bound to mount. Furthermore, the entrepreneurial groups may need access to the facilities and expertise of the pumpers and distributors, and providing that access may compromise their separateness.

Another way to approach a fit problem is to restrict a business to one function and allow other organizations to perform the other functions. Venture capital firms restrict themselves to being drillers and do not become involved in the other functions. Publishers are largely distribution companies; their production is farmed out and the drillers are actually the authors, who are not part of the organization. A business without in-house drillers may have limited access to new ventures, however, because other firms may successfully contract with the best independent drillers. Also, the price for the proven drillers may become so high that profits are limited.

Problems can also arise when pumpers and distributors share an organization. If one of the two clearly dominates, the problem is minimized. If each is equally significant, however, there could easily be a fit problem.

ORGANIZING FOR INNOVATION

Although the achievement of high congruence among an organization's components and strategy leads to organizational effectiveness in the short to medium term, it can also inhibit desirable and even necessary change. An organization can become so integrated and the culture so strong that only compatible changes are tolerated. For example, when faced with a technological threat, firms often respond with even greater reliance on the obsolete familiar technology.

The challenge is to create an organization that can successfully operate a congruent strategy and still have the ability to detect the need for fundamental change. If a significant change in strategy is needed, a major organizational change undoubtedly will be required as well. Also, even in the context of a congruent strategy, there needs to be a capacity for ongoing innovation—the ability to create new or improved products or processes and enter new markets. Several approaches, including decentralization, task forces, skunk works, kaizen, and reengineering, are being used successfully to promote change and foster innovation.

Decentralization—Keeping Business Units Small

Michael Tushman and Charles O'Reilly have identified three firms that are good at both evolving and improving operations and generating revolutionary change: HP (Hewlett-Packard), Johnson & Johnson, and ABB (Asea Brown Boveri).[11] Each of these firms emphasizes autonomous groups. Johnson & Johnson has 165 separate operating companies, ABB has over 5,000 profit centers with an average staff of fifty each, and HP has over fifty divisions and a policy of splitting any division that gets larger than a thousand or so people. Small units are closer to customers and trends, can be agile and fast moving, and create motivated employees who feel an ownership of the operation. The result is a vital, innovative organization relatively unencumbered by a central bureaucracy.

Task Forces

Sometimes a firm will find that it must make a substantial change in operations because of a significant challenge, such as a deterioration in competitive position, or opportunity, such as a technological breakthrough. A cross-functional task force can look at the issues in depth and form a response that provides a meaningful change in direction.

Japanese companies infuse task forces with a sense of urgency to create significant change agents. The sense of urgency will usually involve a competitor-oriented goal, such as "beat Cat" in the case of Komatsu; specific objectives, such as reduction of costs by 20 percent; a tight time-table; and a process, such as total quality control or "just-in-time." The result is extreme pressure to work hard and perform and to break out of the mold and find creative new approaches.

Skunk Works

Major new business ventures may require separate entrepreneurial units because the slow decision-making process, the resource allocation biases against risky new businesses, and the overhead burden of the core organization are too great a handicap. Small, autonomous groups of people representing all the important functions join together to create a product or a business and nurse it through the early stages of life, often in an off-site garage operation called a skunk works. Used by 3M, IBM, Xerox, and many others, such a group is usually autonomous enough that it can bypass the usual decision process and resist pressures to conform to existing formal and informal constraints. A key to entrepreneurial units is to have a business champion committed to the concept. Texas Instruments reviewed fifty new product introductions and found that every failure lacked a voluntary product champion.[12]

Kaizen

Kaizen, which means ongoing improvement involving everyone from top management on down, has been the basis of an increase in productivity for many Japanese firms.[13] Particularly Japanese, it does not easily fit into the U.S. management style because it focuses on process rather than on results and because it depends on many small improvements rather than on a quick fix based on a dramatic new product or technology. The bottom line is never the motivation. Rather, the goal is continuous improvement throughout the organization.

Reengineering

Reengineering, the antithesis of kaizen, is the search for and implementation of radical change in business operations to achieve breakthrough results.[14] The basic idea is to start with a clean sheet of paper and ask, "If we were to start a new company, how would we operate?" Rather than attempting to refine and improve, the effort is to create a revolution from within. The key to reengineering is to break down the old functional units and approach the problem from an interdisciplinary view using cross-functional teams. The starting point is usually considering how customers would like to deal with the firm, rather than how the firm would like to deal with customers.

For example, GTE discovered that customers wanted a single phone number to call about any problem, rather than separate numbers for the repair, billing, and marketing departments. As a result it started a customer care center staffed by people who could field and deal with any inquiry. The goal was to have the people and systems in place so that 70 percent of all calls could be handled without being passed on to another department. This approach was indeed a radical departure, which ended up not only improving service, but also reducing costs.

Reengineering, both risky and expensive, is most appropriate when there is a strong threat from a changing environment or competitor and marginal improvements in the old operation simply will not get the job done. Without a major change in operations, the business will be in jeopardy.

Seeking Radical, Breakthrough Innovation

A truly paradigm-shifting, breakthrough innovation—as opposed to one that sustains the present course—can result in an enormous strategic payoff. Robert Stringer, a strategic consultant, suggests a variety of "breakthrough" strategies that successful companies can use (in addition to skunk works and decentralization) to reinvent themselves and their markets.[15]

- Make breakthrough innovations a strategic and culture priority, as General Mills has done in the cereal market.
- Hire more creative and innovative people. Citibank once hired packaged-goods marketers in order to vitalize its consumer business.
- Create "idea markets" where the best ideas in the organization compete for funding.
- Become an ambidextrous organization, meaning that the ability to commercialize radical innovation exists in the conventional organization (this solution is efficient, but difficult to implement).
- Use acquisitions, joint ventures, and alliances to bring in innovation. Cisco and Microsoft are case studies on how to do this.
- Participate in a corporate venture-capital fund or internal corporate venturing, whereby new businesses are managed apart from a company's existing business in order to provide entrepreneurs the level of autonomy that they value.

A RECAP OF STRATEGIC MARKET MANAGEMENT

Figure 16.5 provides a capstone summary of the issues raised in both strategic analysis and strategy development/refinement. It suggests a discussion agenda to help an organization ensure that the external and internal analysis has the necessary depth, breadth, and forward thinking and that the strategy creation and refinement process yields winning, sustainable strategies.

CUSTOMER ANALYSIS

- Who are the major segments?
- What are their motivations and unmet needs?

COMPETITOR ANALYSIS

- Who are the existing and potential competitors? What strategic groups can be identified?
- What are their sales, share, and profits? What are the growth trends?
- What are their strengths, weaknesses, and strategies?

MARKET ANALYSIS

- How attractive is the market or industry and its submarkets? What are the forces reducing profitability in the market, entry and exit barriers, growth projections, cost structures, and profitability prospects?
- What are the alternative distribution channels and their relative strengths?
- What industry trends are significant to strategy?
- What are the current and future key success factors?

ENVIRONMENTAL ANALYSIS

- What environmental threats, opportunities, and trends exist?
- What are the major strategic uncertainties and information-need areas?
- What scenarios can be conceived?

INTERNAL ANALYSIS

- What are our costs, strategy, performance, points of differentiation, strengths, weaknesses, strategic problems, and culture?
- What is our existing business portfolio? What has been our level of investment in our various product markets?

STRATEGY DEVELOPMENT

- What strategic options should be considered—quality, value, focus, innovation, global, product attributes, product design, product-line breadth, corporate social responsibility, brand familiarity, and customer intimacy.
- What assets and competences will provide the basis for a SCA? How can they be developed and maintained? How can they be leveraged?
- What value proposition will be the core of the offering?
- What are the alternative functional strategies?
- What strategies best fit our strengths, our objectives and our organization?
- What alternative growth directions should be considered? How should they be pursued? What investment level is most appropriate for each product-market—withdrawal, milking, maintaining, or growing?

Figure 16.5   Strategy Development: A Discussion Agenda

KEY LEARNINGS

- Four key organizational components are structure, systems, people, and culture. All must be in sync with each other and with the business strategy.

- The fit between components is illustrated by the hit-industry topology, which contrasts the functions of drillers (who develop products), pumpers (who focus on production), and distributors (who specialize in marketing and distribution).

- Organizational structure defines the lines of authority and communication and can vary in the degree of centralization and formality of communication channels.

- Management systems—including budgeting and accounting, information, measurement and reward, and planning—can all influence strategy implementation.

- People profiles and their motivation provide the bases of competencies needed to support SCAs.

- Because organizational culture—which involves shared values, norms of behavior, symbols, and symbolic activities—is difficult to change, the fit between culture and strategy is particularly important.

- A final challenge is to create an organization that can change rapidly through use of decentralization, task forces, skunk works, kaizen, and reengineering.

FOR DISCUSSION

1. The Korvette concept was started and run by one person and his group of friends. How could its failure have been avoided? Was the problem one of strategy (overexpansion), or was it organizational? Why?

2. What are the advantages of decentralization? Some people argue that more centralization in needed to develop and implement strategy in these dynamic times. Express your opinion, and illustrate it with examples. When would you recommend that the central team use a facilitative role, rather than impose its advice?

3. Evaluate Mintzberg's easy steps to destroying value. Which is the most common step?

4. GE's Jack Welch believes that people are the most important ingredient to success. What are the implications of that belief?

5. Assume that you are CEO of a company like Leapfrog, which sells entertaining, electronic-based learning devices for customers ranging from infants to high school students. Describe the culture you would like to develop and maintain. How would you do that?

6. Consider Power Bar, the strategy for which is summarized in the case on page 132. What implications for the culture, structure, systems and people would you suggest given the nature of the product and the company. Would this change when it was purchased by Nestlé?

7. Pick a bank or other service firm. Evaluate the organizational routes to innovation.

NOTES

1. Robert F. Hartley, *Marketing Mistakes*, 5th ed., New York: Wiley, 1992, Chapter 13.

2. Michael E. Raynor and Joseph L. Bower, "Lead from the Center," *Harvard Business Review*, May 2001, p. 97.

3. Henry Mintzberg, "Musings on Management," *Harvard Business Review*, July–August 1996, pp. 61–67

4. Henry Mintzberg, "The Fall and Rise of Strategic Planning," *Harvard Business Review*, January February 1994, pp. 107–114. Quotes are from p. 109.

5. "GE's Ten-Step Talent Plan," *Fortune*, April 17, 2000 p. 232.

6. Charles O'Reilly, "Corporations, Culture, and Commitment: Motivation and Social Control in Organizations," *California Management Review*, Summer 1989, pp. 9–25.

7. Ibid, p. 13.

8. Gordon Shaw, Robert Brown, and Philip Bromiley, "Strategic Stories: How 3M is Rewriting Business Planning," *Harvard Business Review*, May–June 1998, pp. 41 50.

9. This material draws on the article Gary L. Neilson, Bruce A. Pasternack, and Albert J. Viscio, "Up the e-Organization!" *Strategy & Business*, First Quarter 2000, pp. 52–61.

10. The hit-industry topology was developed in discussions with Dr. Norman Smothers.

11. Michael L. Tushman and Charles A. O'Reilly III, *Winning through Innovation: A Practical Guide to Leading Organizational Change and Renewal*, Boston: Harvard Business School Press, 1997.

12. Thomas J. Peters and Robert H. Waterman, *In Search of Excellence: Lessons from America's Best-Run Companies*, New York: Harper and Row, 1982, p. 203.

13. Masaaki Imai, *Kaizen*, New York: McGraw-Hill, 1984.

14. Thomas A. Stewart, "Re-engineering: The Hot New Managing Tool," *Fortune*, August 23, 1993, pp. 41–48.

15. Robert Stringer, "How to Manage Radical Innovation," *California Management Review*, Summer, 2000, pp. 70–88.

Charting a Risky Direction Without Internal Support

SAMSUNG ELECTRONICS

Samsung Electronics, which began in 1972 as a manufacturer of cheap black-and-white television sets, had sales of over $34 billion and a net profit of $5.9 billion in 2002—less than Microsoft's profits, but more than IBM and Nokia (who ranked third and fourth in industry profitability). In part due to its product leadership, Samsung achieved third place in worldwide mobile handset sales (after Nokia, and closing in on Motorola for second), became the second leading seller of semiconductors (after Intel), and was the largest manufacturer of television sets and computer monitors in the world.

The Samsung products delivered function and more. From plasma TV screens to robotic vacuum cleaners to refrigerator-freezers that tell you when you are low on milk to bracelet cell phones, they were cool and had a buzz about them. *Business Week* recognized Samsung as the top information technology company in the world, and its brand was valued by Interbrand at $8.3 billion (ranking thirty-fourth in the world). This performance was astounding, given that only five years earlier Samsung was financially crippled in the face of a Korean economic crisis and some bad strategic decisions.

In some respects, it was the worst of times in late 1996 when Yun Jong Yong became CEO of Samsung Electronics. He addressed the financial crisis in part by cutting some 24,000 employees, shutting factories, and selling business units. But in the face of this adversity, he set the stage for gaining global leadership by enunciating a bold strategy.

The strategy had several components. First, Samsung would change its market position in the United States and Europe from a price-oriented copycat manufacturer to a premium-priced product leader whose wares were sold in the most upscale retail outlets. (Almost no one on Yun's management team agreed with this direction, as it meant walking away from much of the firm's business and would be risky to implement.) Second, Samsung would continue its policy to be vertically integrated and turn its memory and component design and manufacturing into an asset by providing direct access to the latest technology. Nearly all other firms felt that strategic flexibility required moving away from vertical integration. Third, Samsung would be a leader in creating new products designed to be distinctive and cool; the organization would become much faster to market with these products. Fourth, it would build the brand, especially outside Korea, a step that would be crucial in becoming the leader in the near future.

The new course was somewhat aided by the new management initiative launched in 1993 by Lee Kun-Hee, the CEO of the Samsung Group (of which Samsung Electronics is a part). No less than a total change in the way that the group thought, worked, and served customers, the initiative included a focus on quality, listening to markets, creating distinctive advantages, being the best, anticipating the future, creating an organizational environment to foster innovation and growth, and contributing to a better global society. The initiative was relaunched in 1996 after it received little initial traction. As part of the relaunch, Lee in 1996 set up a training center for information-related infrastructure topics.

There were several key aspects to the implementation of Yun's strategy for Samsung Electronics. One was the hiring of Eric Kim to be the global marketing head in 1999. Kim, who left Korea at the age of thirteen, had an engineering and marketing background. He was determined to get the global silos to be on the same page. Toward that end he consolidated the disparate business operations and drove toward a single vision based on the new cool, upscale Samsung brand of technology leadership in digital convergence. He replaced the company's fifty-five advertising agencies with one global agency. In part to emphasize the global future of the firm, Kim made his first big presentation in Korea to four hundred top Samsung managers in English.

Another initiative was sponsorship and advertising. Yun believed that the new Samsung could best be communicated by sports sponsorship. The logic was that sports competition, which involved hard work by athletes striving to achieve their highest potential, suited the industry and the associations that Samsung wanted to nurture. Sports also provided a stage to demonstrate technology. Samsung sponsored several events, including the 1998 Bangkok Asian Games, but the crown jewel was the sponsorship of the Olympics, starting with the 1998 Winter Games in Nagano, Japan. In 1999, Samsung embarked on a $400 million advertising effort around the tag line "DIGITall." This slogan signaled that Samsung was a leader in the digital convergence world, which would apply to all people and all products.

Among the misadventures of Samsung that contributed to the financial crises of 1997 was its experience with AST, which in the early 1990s was among the top four manufacturers of personal computers in the United States. AST was struggling to keep up, however, and began losing money at an alarming rate—in part because its acquisition of the Tandy PC business in 1993 was not managed well, and also because its product development tended to be late (the firm missed a Christmas selling season one year). Meanwhile Samsung, which sold 30 percent of the computers purchased in Korea, tried and failed in its effort to crack the critical U.S. market, a failure attributed to a lack of marketing savvy and distribution clout. Its solution was to invest in AST in 1995, buying the entire company in 1997. A Korean CEO, inserted in 1996, instituted needed manufacturing efficiencies and some co-marketing efforts with Disney. When that did not stem the tide and an effort to focus on the business market failed, Samsung bailed out in December 1998, after having lost well over $1 billion.

FOR DISCUSSION

1. Yun lacked support for his new strategy. How important is organizational buy-in for a CEO's strategy? How valuable is it to have the buy-in be enthusiastic? How can the CEO gain support for a strategy?

2. What are the organizational implications of vertical integration and the new product program? With respect to vertical integration, how would you make sure that the component suppliers have incentives to become efficient even though their customer is captive?

3. How would you change the reward system to reflect the new strategy? In the past, all units were largely measured on sales and market share. How would you change that, if at all? How would you implement any changes?

4. Why didn't Lee's initiative gain traction in 1993? What is needed to make it happen?

5. How should Kim gain acceptance for himself and his ideas? Was it risky to speak in English? In creating a global strategy, would you use a top-down or bottom-up approach?

6. Do you agree with the logic of the Olympic sponsorship? How would you get organizational support for it? How would you decide what sports events to sponsor? Can you recommend a different strategy for communication instead of the sports connection?

7. What was the objective of the AST acquisition? Why did it fail?

Source: Samsung Electronics annual reports, 1997 to 2002; Cliff Edwards, Moon Ihlwan, and Pete Engardio, "The Samsung Way," *Business Week*, June 16, 2003, pp. 56–61.

Planning Forms

A set of standard forms can be helpful in presenting strategy recommendations and supporting analyses. They can encourage the useful consistency of the presentation over time and across businesses within an organization. They can also provide a checklist of areas to consider in strategy development and make communication easier. The following sample forms are intended to provide a point of departure in designing forms for a specific context. The external analysis in the example is drawn from the pet food industry. The forms are for illustration purposes only.

Planning forms need to be adapted to the context involved: the industry, the firm, and the planning context. They may well be different and shorter or longer given a particular context. Forms for use with other product types—an industrial product, for example—could be modified to include information such as current and potential applications or key existing or potential customers.

THE PET FOOD INDUSTRY

Section I. Customer Analysis

A. Segments

Segments	Market (Billions)	Comments
Dog—dry	5.3	*Largest segment, segmented nutritional offerings, growing*
Dog—canned	1.4	*Made from dairy products, etc.*
Cat—dry	2.4	*Second largest segment, nutritional offerings, accelerating growth*
Cat—canned	1.7	*Made from animal by-products, dairy products, etc.*
Dog treats	1.6	*Nabisco dominates with Milk-Bone*
Pet Specialty	3.1	*Large players—Science Diet and Iams, uses vets and pet stores, about 61% dog food, mostly dry, high growth (over 11%)*

B. Customer Motivations

Segment	Motivations
Dog—dry	*Nutrition, not messy, not smelly, healthy, easy to serve, teeth cleaning*
Dog—canned	*For finicky dogs, taste and nutrition variety*
Cat—dry	*Nutrition, healthy, easy to serve, complement to meal, teeth cleaning*
Cat—canned	*Taste and nutrition, cat will like, convenient sizes, easy to serve, finicky cats, variety*
Treats	*Complement to meal, reward, animal likes it, functional nutritional benefits*
Pet Specialty	*Health concern, scientific nutrition, perceived superior ingredients*

C. Unmet Needs

Information on pets
Further subneeds of segments (as defined by human nutrition, e.g., allergies)
Packaging/storing convenience

Section 2. Competitor Analysis

A. Competitor Identification

Most directly competitive: Nestlé Purina Petcare, Del Monte, Mars. Less directly competitive: Hill Petfood (Colgate Palmolive), Iams (P&G), Doane (supplier to Wal-Mart).

B. Strategic Groups

Strategic Group	Major Competitors	Share
(1) Mainstream brands from	Nestlé Purina Petcare	30%
large consumer firms	Mars	11%
	Del Monte	7%
(2) High-end specialty brands	Iams (P&G)	11%
	Hill's (Colgate-Palmolive)	12%
(3) Private-label brands	Wal-Mart	11%
	Other	15%

Strategic Group	Characteristics/ Strategies	Strengths	Weaknesses
(1) Mainstream brands from large consumer firms	*Mainstream products* • *Large portfolio of products* • *Heavy use of advertising* *Premium/niche products* • *Sell to multiple channels* • *Emphasis on quality improvement*	• *Production scale economies* • *Huge presence in supermarkets, where 35% of industry volume is sold* • *Deep global financial resources* • *Commitment to industry*	• *High-fixed cost commitment to capacity increases competitive pressure on all players to defend share through promotions, etc.* • *Perception as less nutritious than specialty brands* • *Supermarket channel is losing share to other channels* • *Private labeling at Wal-Mart and elsewhere is increasing*
(2) High-end specialty pet food brands	• *Narrowly focused, premium-priced product lines* • *High presence in non-supermarket channels, such as veterinary offices, pet breeders, and specialty stores*	• *Product line focus on health, natural ingredients, and nutrition, resulting in very strong consumer demand; high-margin business* • *First-in advantage to high-end specialty segment, resulting in a perceptual edge that supermarket brands find difficult to overcome* • *Sell through alternative channels, which are growing faster and are less competitive and offer limited access to other brands, a barrier to entry*	• *Higher ingredient and production costs* • *Recent introduction of Iams into grocery and mass merchandise channels narrow differentiation* • *All major national competitors are going after the fast-growing specialty channels*

Strategic Group	Characteristics/ Strategies	Strengths	Weaknesses
(3) Private-label pet foods	• Sell through multiple supermarkets and mass merchandisers under house brand designation	• High volume and low unit costs • Profit margins are attractive to retailers • Power of Wal-Mart as number one retailer (Wal-Mart's Ol' Roy has 10% of the market)	• Little brand differentiation • Low-margin business

C. Major Competitors

Competitor	Characteristics/ Strategies	Strengths	Weaknesses
Nestlé Purina Petcare	• Overall market leader, very broad product line • Increasing emphasis on niche product lines and upgrade of products to premium status • Proliferation of new products • Massive advertising and promotional spending to protect share • High commitment • Deep financial resources • Company takes long-term view on brand-building efforts; high level of commitment to brands • Global commitment to building brands	• Economies of scale, low costs • Supply-chain efficiencies	• No canned pet food business • Lack of true product innovation • Less developed in nonsupermarket channels • Weak presence in specialty segment

Competitor	Characteristics/ Strategies	Strengths	Weaknesses
Del Monte	• Emphasis on canned cat and dog treats, but competes in all segments of market • Low-cost producer strategy	• Economies of scale, low costs • Efficient distribution system	• Relatively weak in brand building • Milking strong brands, such as 9-Lives • Lack of product innovation
Mars	• Internationally dominant under same brand names as in the United States • Commitment to building brands • Upgrading supermarket brands for premium appeal	• Dog food expertise • Economies of scale, low costs • Deep financial resources • Private firm gives freedom from short-term pressures • Packaging renovation	• Lack of cat food expertise
Doane Products	• Largest private-label producer in the United States	• Economies of scale, low costs	• Low-margin business • Dependent on Wal-Mart
Hill's Petfood	• Leader in specialty and vet markets • Entry barriers in vet business for Science Diet brand	• Leading recipient of veterinary recommendation • Best niche-market product positioning in the industry	• No presence in supermarkets, where 42% of industry volume is sold
Iams (P&G)	• Traditionally a specialty market brand, with emphasis on specialty-store sales and referrals from pet breeders • Moved to grocery and mass merchandise channel which stimulated growth	• Deep financial recourses	• Strategic fit of pet food in portfolio

D. Competitor Strength Grid

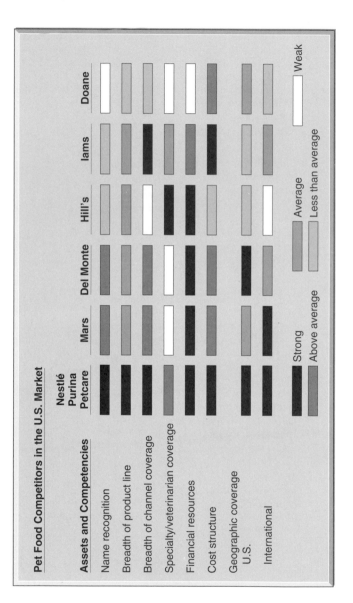

Section 3. Market Analysis

A. Market Identification: The U.S. Pet Food Market

B. Market Size

	1990	1995	2000	2003
U.S. industry sales ($ in billions)	7.7	9.1	11.1	12.6

Emerging Submarkets

- Special diet-based products
- Wal-Mart and other private-label products

Market Growth

- Supermarket—growing at 1 percent
- Specialty store—growing at 13 percent annually
- Mass merchandisers—growing at 14 percent

Factors Affecting Sales Levels

- Growth of pet population

Segments with High Unrealized Potential

- As U.S. households spend less for pet food on average ($60/year) than the rest of the world ($90), there may be potential for growth.

C. Market Profitability Analysis

Barriers to Entry

- Brand awareness, budget for marketing programs, access to distribution channels, large investment required for manufacturing.
- For pet specialty segment—loyalty to Iams and Hill's Science Diet.

Potential Entrants

- Other marketing giants, such as Unilever, might enter this industry if they feel it is attractive. However, the probability of new entrants is quite low, because pet food industry is already very competitive, with lots of incumbents, and barriers to entry are high.

Threats of Substitutes

- Human food leftovers
- Food cooked especially for pets

Bargaining Power of Suppliers

- Growing. Raw materials shared with human food markets. Consolidation of suppliers. Quality of raw ingredients requirements growing.

Bargaining Power of Customers

- Grocery stores, warehouse clubs have strong bargaining power over pet food suppliers.
- Specialty stores, veterinarians might have moderate bargaining power.
- Mass merchandisers (especially Wal-Mart, with around 30 percent of the volume in this category) have strong bargaining power.

D. Cost Structure

- Diversified firms have lower cost because of economies in advertising, manufacturing, promotion, and distribution.
- Specialized firms have higher costs.

E. Distribution System

Major Channels

- Supermarkets are dominant in terms of quantity they deal with (35 percent).
- Mass merchandisers handle about 17 percent of market and are increasing rapidly.
- Pet foods are effective traffic builders in supermarkets and mass merchandisers.
- Farm-supply stores are located in suburbs and local areas.
- Pet stores handle most premium brands and some national brands.
- Veterinarians handle only superpremium brands.

Observations/Major Trends

- Vets' sales are flat and have very high margins both for producers and for themselves.
- Specialty stores' sales have increased very rapidly.
- These two channels have captured high-involvement customers' needs to feed their pets healthier foods.
- Warehouses have gained footholds in market-leader brands.

F. Market Trends and Developments

- Premium and superpremium brands have grown, and most producers are introducing new products in this area.
- Large manufacturers are introducing new products continuously.

G. Key Success Factors

Present

- Brand recognition
- Product quality
- Access to major channels
- Gain market share in premium brands

- Introduction of new products
- Breadth of product line
- Marketing program
- Cost reduction
- Awareness or recommendation by specialists
- Packaging

Future

- Capture the trends of consumers
- Packaging
- Follow the trends of distributors

Section 4. Environmental Analysis

A. Trends and Potential Events

Source	Description	Strategic Implication	Time Frame	Importance
Technological	New product forms	Limited		Low
Regulatory	Impose standards of content	Limited		Low
Economic	Insensitive to economic changes	Very limited		Low
Cultural	Think of pets as members of families	Growth of superpremium brands	Since the mid-1980s	High
	Demand for new, healthy products	Introduction of healthy products		
	Users' needs have diversified	Multiple specialized segments		
Demographic	Household formation is slowing	Continued innovation of product and communications to keep brands relevant	Since the 1980s	Med–High
	The number of cats is increasing more than dogs			
	The baby boomer is aging			
Threats	Growth in the pet food industry depends on the popularity of pets	Potential decline in pet ownership will have a negative impact	Post-2010	Med–High
Opportunities	Growing market for premium brands	There is still room for growth in specialized segments	Since the mid-1980s	High
	Expanding market for private labels			

B. Scenario Analysis

Two most likely are:

1. Little growth in specialty-store and increase in superpremium segments.
2. High growth in both specialty-store and superpremium segments.

C. Key Strategic Uncertainties

- Will growth in demand for superpremium specialty products continue?
- Will specialty stores' share continue to grow at the expense of supermarkets?

Section 5. Internal Analysis

A. Performance Analysis

Objective Area	Objective	Status and Comment
1. Sales		
2. Profits		
3. Quality/service		
4. Cost		
5. New products		
6. Customer satisfaction		
7. People		
8. Other		

B. Summary of Past Strategy

C. Strategic Problems

Problem	Possible Action

D. Characteristics of Internal Organization

Component°	Description—Fit with Current/Proposed Strategy

° Structure, systems, culture, and people.

E. Portfolio Analysis

```
              High | SBUa              SBUb

   Business         
   Position              SBUe

              Low  | SBUc              SBUd
                   ------------------------------
                     High              Low
                     Market Attractiveness
```

Note: An SBU (strategic business unit) can be defined by product or by segment.

F. Analysis of Strengths and Weaknesses

Reference Strategic Group	Competencies/Competency Deficiencies, Assets/Liabilities, Strengths/Weaknesses with Respect to Strategic Groups

G. Financial Projections Based on Existing Strategy

	Past	Present	Projected
Operating Statement			
Market share			
Sales			
Cost of goods sold			
Gross margin			
R&D			
Selling/advertising			
Product G&A			
Div. & corp. G&A			
Operating profit			
Balance Sheet			
Cash/AR/inventory			
AP			
Net current assets			
Fixed assets at cost			
Accumulated depreciation			
Net fixed assets			
Total assets—book value			
Estimated market value of assets			
ROA (base—book value)			
ROA (base—market value)			
Uses of Funds			
Net current assets			
Fixed asset			
Operating profit			
Depreciation			
Other			
Resources Required			

Note: Resources required could be workers with particular skills or backgrounds, or certain physical facilities. A negative use of funds (i.e., profit) is a source of funds. Projected numbers could be for several relevant years.

Section 6. Summary of Proposed Strategy

A. *Statement of Vision*

B. *Strategy Description*

- Investment Objective   Product-Market

    Withdraw   ☐
    Milk   ☐
    Maintain   ☐
    Grow in market share   ☐
    Market expansion   ☐
    Product expansion   ☐
    Vertical integration   ☐

- Strategy Thrusts   Product-Market
    Quality   ☐
    Value   ☐
    Focus   ☐
    Innovation   ☐
    Global   ☐
    Other   ☐

C. *Assets and Competencies Providing SCAs*

D. *Strategic Position*

E. *Key Strategy Initiatives*

F. Financial Projections Based on Proposed Strategy

	Past	Present	Projected
Operating Statement			
Market share			
Sales			
Cost of goods sold			
Gross margin			
R&D			
Selling/advertising			
Product G&A			
Div. & corp. G&A			
Operating profit			
Balance Sheet			
Cash/AR/inventory			
AP			
Net current assets			
Fixed assets at cost			
Accumulated depreciation			
Net fixed assets			
Total assets—book value			
Estimated market value of assets			
ROA (base—book value)			
ROA (base—market value)			
Uses of Funds			
Net current assets			
Fixed assets			
Operating profit			
Depreciation			
Other			
Resources Required			
_____			
_____			
_____			
_____			

343